FROM SYMPOSIUM
TO EUCHARIST

FROM SYMPOSIUM TO EUCHARIST

THE BANQUET IN THE EARLY CHRISTIAN WORLD

DENNIS E. SMITH

FORTRESS PRESS
MINNEAPOLIS

Cover art: Banquet scenes from a Roman mosaic, Carthage, fifth century c.e. Musée National du Bardo, Tunis, Tunisia. Copyright © Gilles Mermet / Art Resource, New York. Used by permission.
Book design: Beth Wright

Interior illustrations (pp. 15, 16, and 17) are by Romney Oualline Nesbitt and are copyright © 2002 Romney Oualline Nesbitt and Dennis E. Smith.

Scripture quotations from the New Revised Standard Version Bible are copyright © 1989 by the Division of Christian Education of the National Council of the Churches of Christ in the USA and are used by permission.

The translation of the Passover Seder liturgy on pp. 147–49 is from Gordon J. Bahr, "The Seder of Passover and the Eucharistic Words," in *Novum Testamentum* 12 (1970): 181–202, and is used by permission of Brill Academic Publishers.

Library of Congress Cataloging-in-Publication Data

Smith, Dennis Edwin, date–
  From symposium to Eucharist : the banquet in the early Christian world
/ Dennis E. Smith.
    p. cm.
  Includes bibliographical references and index.
  ISBN 0-8006-3489-6 (pbk. : alk. paper)
  1. Lord's Supper—History. I. Title.
BV823.S62 2002
264'.36'09—dc21

                              2002152641

The paper used in this publication meets the minimum requirements of American National Standard for Information Sciences — Permanence of Paper for Printed Library Materials, ANSI Z329.48-1984.

Manufactured in the Canada
07   06   05   04   03   1   2   3   4   5   6   7   8   9   10

To Barbara, my wife,
and Adam, my son,
whose unfailing love and support
made it all possible
and worthwhile

CONTENTS

LIST OF ILLUSTRATIONS

PREFACE

I am pleased finally to publish this work in its complete form, having first addressed the subject in my Harvard dissertation, "Social Obligation in the Context of Communal Meals: A Study of the Christian Meal in 1 Corinthians in Comparison with Graeco-Roman Communal Meals" (1980). I have continued to enlarge and revise the original study. During that time there has also been a resurgence of interest in the subject, both in classical studies and in early Christian studies. My dissertation and my assorted articles on the subject have generated a bit of interest as well, and others have found them a resource on which to build their own research. Indeed, rather than fading over the years, the project has seemed to grow in importance. The perspectives I have developed in regard to the Greco-Roman banquet have proved to be illuminating for research in a number of areas of ancient study. Yet in my previous publications, I have been able to present only parts of the total picture, and I have often felt that no single part of the argument can be properly understood and evaluated without access to the complete argument.

Portions of this work appeared in preliminary form elsewhere. Parts of chapter 1 appeared in a preliminary form in *Many Tables: The Eucharist in the New Testament and Liturgy Today* (London: SCM and Philadelphia: Trinity Press International, 1990; Eugene, Ore.: Wipf and Stock, 2001 [reprint edition]), which I co-authored with Hal E. Taussig. The section on the Essene meal in chapter 6 is an adaptation and revision of my article "Meals" in *The Encyclopedia of the Dead Sea Scrolls*, edited by L. H. Schiffman and J. C. VanderKam (Oxford: Oxford University Press, 2000). The section on the messianic banquet in chapter 6 is an adaptation and revision of "The Messianic Banquet Reconsidered" in *The Future of Early Christianity: Essays in Honor of Helmut Koester*, edited by B. A. Pearson (Minneapolis: Fortress Press, 1991), 64–73. The section on the historical Jesus in chapter 8 is an adaptation and revision of "Table Fellowship and the Historical Jesus" in *Religious Propaganda and Missionary Competition in the New Testament World: Essays Honoring Dieter Georgi*, edited by L. Bormann, K. del Tredici, and A. Standhartinger

(Leiden: Brill, 1994), 135–62. The section on Luke in chapter 8 is adapted from "Table Fellowship as a Literary Motif in the Gospel of Luke," *Journal of Biblical Literature* 106 (1987): 613–38. Various parts of the overall thesis have been utilized in *Many Tables: The Eucharist in the New Testament and Liturgy Today* as well as in the following articles in *The Anchor Bible Dictionary*, 6 volumes, edited by D. N. Freedman (New York: Doubleday, 1992): "Meal Customs (Greco-Roman)," 4.650–53; "Meal Customs (Sacred Meals)," 4.653–55; "Messianic Banquet," 4.788–91; and "Table Fellowship," 6.302–4.

I must first thank my two major professors at Harvard, Helmut Koester, with whom I began the dissertation research, and Dieter Georgi, with whom I finished it and whose encouragement and guidance were especially helpful in bringing it to completion. In my research since then, as I have broadened the range of research and sharpened the arguments, I have been aided by a number of colleagues. The chapter on the sacrificial banquet was rewritten and revised during a National Endowment for the Humanities (NEH) seminar at Stanford University with Michael Jameson. My friend and colleague Stan Stowers also read that chapter and offered an extensive critique, for which I am deeply grateful, even though I decided not to go in the direction he recommended. The study of Ben Sira was first developed in an NEH seminar taught by Professor Louis Feldman at Yeshiva University, and it benefited from his wise guidance. An early draft of the chapter on the Jewish banquet was read by Alan Segal and Shaye Cohen, who offered many helpful critiques. The final form of that chapter was aided immensely by my good friend and colleague David Levenson, who saved me from many egregious errors and doubtless would have saved me from more if I had but listened.

Over the years, a number of friends and colleagues have offered support and encouragement to this project. Among that number are Ron Cameron, Burton Mack, and Robert Funk, who encouraged me early on to publish it; Michael White, who has followed my work closely over the years and has advanced and sharpened the arguments in his own work; and, above all, Hal Taussig, with whom I have worked in partnership on this issue for many years, from the time we co-authored another book on the subject until the present, and from whom I have learned much. I also thank my editors at Fortress Press, K. C. Hanson, who with congenial firmness shepherded this book to completion, and Beth Wright, whose close attention to detail and aesthetics brought this book to completion in much better shape and much more quickly than I would have ever thought possible.

I must also acknowledge the students, faculty, administration, and trustees of Phillips Theological Seminary, who together make up an amazing community for theological discourse and a supportive environment for creative research. I owe a special debt of gratitude to one of those students, Romney Nesbitt, who produced the drawings for the illustrations.

Finally, I thank my family—my wife, Barbara McBride-Smith, and my son, Adam McBride-Smith, to whom this book is dedicated—for it is they who had to live with it as an ongoing project and who often wondered if it would ever be completed but nonetheless never failed in their support.

CHAPTER 1

THE BANQUET AS SOCIAL INSTITUTION

"When you come together to eat . . ."
—Paul to the Corinthian Christians (1 Cor 11:33), ca. 50 C.E.

". . . It had been their custom to disperse and reassemble later to take food of an ordinary, harmless kind."
—Pliny the Younger, *Ep.* 10.96, describing the meetings of Christians in Bithynia, ca. 98 C.E.

"At the banquets which it was the custom of us young men to hold at Athens at the beginning of each week . . ."
—Gell., *NA* 15.2.3, on the regular meetings of his philosophical circle, ca. 160 C.E.

"I wish also to speak of their common assemblages and the cheerfulness of their convivial meals as contrasted with those of other people."
—Philo, *Contempl.* 40, referring to the communal meals of the Essenes, a Jewish sect, ca. 40 C.E.

"Calendar of dinners: March 8, birthday of Caesennius . . . his father; November 27, birthday of Antinous; August 13, birthday of Diana and of the society; August 20, birthday of Caesennius Silvanus, his brother . . . birthday of Cornelia Procula, his mother; December 14, birthday of Caesennius Rufus, patron of the municipality."
—From the statutes of the funerary society of Diana and Antinous, Lanuvium, Italy, 136 C.E. (*ILS* 7212.2.11–13).

"What sacrifice is acceptable to the gods without the participants in the feast?"
—Dio Chrysostom, *Orations* 3.97, ca. 104 C.E.

Whenever they met as a church, early Christians regularly ate a meal together. In this they were no different from other religious people in their world: for when any group of people in the ancient Mediterranean world met for social or religious purposes, their gatherings tended to be centered on a common meal or banquet. It did not matter whether it was a social or religious occasion; nor what the ethnic group might be, whether Jewish or Greek or some other ethnic group; nor what the social class might be. If it were a special occasion, whether religious, social, or political, more often than not a formalized meal functioned as a centerpiece of the gathering.

The meals at which they gathered also tended to follow the same basic form, customs, and rules regardless of the group, occasion, or setting. They followed the form of the banquet, the traditional evening meal, which had become the pattern for all formalized meals in the Mediterranean world in this period. In this sense, the banquet can be called a social institution in the Greco-Roman world.

This means that if we are to understand properly any individual instance of formalized meals in the Greco-Roman world, such as Greek philosophical banquets, or Jewish festival meals, or early Christian community meals, we must first understand the larger phenomenon of the banquet as a social institution. This perspective, that the banquet was one social institution that cut across ethnic, religious, and social lines, has not been given its due in scholarship. Instead, scholars have concentrated on comparing individual types of meals. This study seeks to define the banquet as a social institution in its own right in the ancient world and thereby provide a common model that can be utilized for the study of all data on formal meals from the Greco-Roman world.

DEFINITIONS AND QUALIFICATIONS

The Forms of Meals

Formal meals in the Mediterranean culture of the Hellenistic and Roman periods, the period encompassing the origin and early development of Christianity, took on a homogeneous form. Although there were many minor differences in the meal customs as practiced in different regions and social groups, the evidence suggests that meals took similar forms and shared similar meanings and interpretations across a broad range of the ancient world.[1]

This perspective is not a new one, but most studies of ancient meals do not give it the attention it deserves. For example, it is typical of studies of the Eucharist to assume that parallel types of meals from the ancient world should be analyzed as distinct entities.[2] Similarly, discussions of Greco-Roman meals often emphasize distinctions only, without reference to the larger similarities of meal customs in the culture.[3] This perspective is illustrated in the following diagram:

OLD MODEL:

MEALS IN THE ANCIENT WORLD (ALL SEEN AS DIFFERENT FORMS OF MEALS)

everyday meals · symposia · funerary banquets · sacrificial meals

mystery meals · everyday Jewish meals · Jewish festival meals · Christian Agapē · Christian Eucharist

Instead, I would propose a model something like this:

NEW PROPOSED MODEL:

COMMON BANQUET TRADITION
adapted to various settings

everyday meals · symposia · funerary banquets · sacrificial meals

mystery meals · everyday Jewish meals · Jewish festival meals · Christian Agapē · Christian Eucharist

Thus I propose that all special usages of meals draw from the same common tradition, the tradition of the banquet. The banquet was the evening meal, the meal to which the ancients gave the most symbolic significance. The banquet tradition is made up of a broad set of banquet customs and banquet ideology. I use the term *banquet customs* to refer to the standard ways in which ancient people planned, conducted, and behaved at their formal meals. In this category would be grouped a wide variety of social conventions ranging from the number and descriptions of courses to rules of etiquette. I use the term *banquet ideology* to refer to ways in which banquets communicated social values, including discussions of the ethical foundations for banquet customs found in various types of ancient literature. This category would also include the *social code* of the banquet, a term used in social science studies that refers to the more subtle, implicit ways in which values were communicated in banquet practices.

On the Origins of the Eucharist

Scholarship on early Christian meal traditions has tended to concentrate on the issue of the origins of the Eucharist and, furthermore, to define that issue in a deceptively narrow way. For example, two of the most significant studies of this subject in the last century are those by Joachim Jeremias and Hans Lietzmann.[4] They appear to develop radically different conclusions, but closer analysis reveals that they share similar perspectives.

Jeremias, for example, wished to identify the Passover meal as the original setting of Jesus' Last Supper and therefore as the source for the orthodox form and theology of the Lord's Supper. Recent studies, however, have seriously weakened if not effectively refuted his readings of both the Gospel text and Jewish tradition.[5] It is important, however, to note the perspective with which he began, namely, that there was *one* origin for the Christian Eucharist. This perspective has tended to dominate most studies of the Eucharist. It is a perspective that does not develop naturally out of the ancient evidence but rather represents a retrojection onto the ancient sources of the form taken by the Eucharist in the later "orthodox" church.

A similar perspective is adopted in a more self-conscious form by Hans Lietzmann. He specifically begins from the later period and works backward to search for origins. His disagreements with Jeremias are substantive and profound: he makes no connection with Passover traditions and does not presuppose a single origin for the Eucharist. Instead, he posits two basic forms of the Eucharistic liturgy. He then traces these two forms back to two separate origins in the tradition of the early church.[6]

Despite their differences, Lietzmann shares a basic presupposition with Jeremias. Like Jeremias, he constructs a model for analyzing the ancient data based on the form of the Eucharist in the later church. In neither case are the ancient data studied in its own right and on its own terms. The perspectives of Jeremias and Lietzmann can be diagrammed in this way:

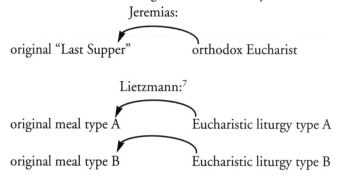

Jeremias:

original "Last Supper"   orthodox Eucharist

Lietzmann:[7]

original meal type A   Eucharistic liturgy type A

original meal type B   Eucharistic liturgy type B

In contrast I would propose the following model for early Christian meals:

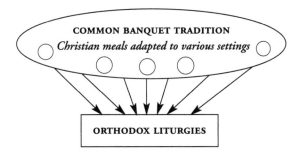

This model proposes a different theory for the development of the Eucharistic liturgies. The occurrence of meals in community settings and the symbolic value they carried were part of what I call the common banquet tradition. Early Christianity was made up of varied groups, however, who adapted the common banquet tradition to their own situations. This proposal fits the form of our data, which witnesses to a variety of ways in which early Christians practiced communal meals. The process eventually led to the collapsing of all these traditions into one orthodox form and liturgy. One would therefore expect to find a unified liturgy at the latter end of the process. In the early period, however, the liturgies of the church were just as diverse as were its other features.[8]

Sacred versus Secular

Many studies of early Christian meals attempt to compare them with forms of meals in their pagan environment. Invariably, however, what is compared is the assumed essence of the early Christian Eucharist, namely, its nature as a "sacramental" meal. This term refers to the special sense in which the Eucharist is seen to impart spiritual power. In most studies, it refers especially to the act of eating the flesh and blood of the deity.[9]

The larger category into which the "sacramental" meal is generally placed is that of the "sacred" meal. But the category of sacred meal also lacks clarity. When it is discussed, it tends to be treated as a form to itself. There is an assumption that it has little relation to the form of an ordinary banquet. Indeed, scholars in history of religions studies typically see *sacred* and *secular* as existing in two different realms. They then analyze the data based on this model. To be sure, they base this idea on foundational premises of the sociology of religion. Émile Durkheim, for example, defined the sacred and the profane as two separate realms of human existence.[10]

It is my contention, however, that the sacred versus secular model is not appropriate for ancient meals. Instead I consider meals to have an integrative function in ancient society in which they combine the sacred and the secular into one ritual event. Here I use the terms *sacred* and *secular* to refer to the degree to which meals might exhibit a religious purpose or might lack any religious emphasis at all. Most Greco-Roman meals would fall into a middle category in which they exhibit characteristics of both sacred and secular. Indeed, in ancient Mediterranean culture in general sacred and secular are interwoven and tend to be indistinct.[11]

To be sure, there are surely degrees of secularity or sacredness. On the one hand, in a normal formal meal, or banquet, it was customary to offer libations or prayers to the gods no matter how "secular" was the overall situation. This would be true even at such a manifestly secular meal as the banquet of Trimalchio, described by Petronius.[12] On the other hand, there were varying degrees in which a meal might have religious connotations, depending on whether it was connected with a sacrifice, a sanctuary, or a religious association. Nevertheless, what is common to all such examples is that the meal itself was of the same form, that of the ancient banquet.

QUESTIONS OF METHOD

Literary Analysis: Social Reality versus Narrative World

Since most of our data for banquets comes from literary sources or is influenced by literary traditions, it is necessary to posit a distinction between social reality and literary idealization.[13] Though we are purporting to study social forms, we do not in fact have access to "field reports" or other objectively gathered observations of social behavior at banquets.

To be sure, the descriptions of banquets that we do have clearly use patterns from the social world. That is to say, they represent accurately the values of the culture in regard to various social categories, such as class and stratification, for example. They thus provide us with sufficient evidence to reconstruct the social world and the function of banquets within it. What is more difficult, however, is determining to what extent a banquet reference in the data represents social reality or merely an idealized, imaginative reconstruction of it.

This problem, of course, is endemic to social science analysis in general. As soon as one extrapolates from a social event and begins to describe it in the technical terms of the discipline, one is clearly creating an imaginative world that cannot be completely equivalent to the real world.[14] This issue has also arisen in the study of narrative. That is to say, any human description of an event after the fact is always an extrapolated, imaginative reconstruction, a creation of a "narrative world," if you will, that must not be confused with the "real world."[15]

But in the study of historical data, this issue has a different dimension. Here all too often our only evidence is that of the narrative world. Furthermore, there is very little resistance in ancient culture to an extensive elaboration and creation of that narrative world. Indeed, the ancients would consider it more appropriate to embellish a description with a rich use of literary models and images than to give what today we might call a "factual" description. Lucian, for example, in his second century C.E. work *How to Write History*, compares the historian to a "Phidias," or sculptor, whose task is to reconstruct the historical events with sufficient artistic skill that they can be brought to life for the reader.[16]

Therefore, when we study the data before us, we must be conscious of the need to distinguish as much as possible between the narrative world of the text and any reconstruction of real events that we may wish to propose. In both cases, of course, we are receiving reliable information about the social world of which banquets are a part. And certainly we should not shrink from providing a description of the realities of banquets within that social world when the data allows us to do that. Indeed, if we determine that the narrative world is the most accessible to us, this would not devalue the data. After all, the narrative world provides a significant foundation for social patterns and constraints in the so-called real world.

Social Analysis

Recent studies in cultural anthropology have acknowledged the importance of meal customs and etiquette. Mary Douglas, who has analyzed meals in both ancient and modern cultures, is a leader in this research.[17]

Douglas's insights have provided correctives to the earlier observations of the leaders of the discipline, such as Claude Lévi-Strauss.[18] She criticizes Lévi-Strauss for his attempt to find universal meanings common to all humankind.[19] She suggests a method consistent with what Clifford Geertz calls "thick description."[20] That is, rather than proposing theories that explain all of human history, one should concentrate on intensive descriptions of individual examples, with an emphasis on their individuality. Only then might one tentatively propose explanations to explain the phenomena.

Some historians have begun to recognize the importance of these insights from the field of anthropology. For example, recent studies in Greek religion have referred to the need to relate it to its cultural context. Furthermore, Moses Finley, John Gould, and others point out that the nearest parallels to Greek religion may not be later western forms, dominated by Christianity, but rather may be such "primitive" forms as the religion of the Dinkas. Here they acknowledge their debt to the anthropological study of religion.[21]

Similarly, historians of Christianity have increasingly found social science approaches to offer valuable insights into the historical data. This is especially true among New Testament scholars, who have utilized a wide variety of social science approaches, sometimes combined with traditional historical perspectives and sometimes not.[22] The debate over the critical appropriation of models from the social sciences as opposed to or in combination with revised perspectives on traditional historical criticism continues.[23] On the one hand, the social science school argues for a strict application of social science models to the data. On the other hand, the social history school argues for a more eclectic approach, in which social science models are used where deemed appropriate, but rigorous historical critical analysis still dominates. I tend to follow the social history approach in this study. The goal will be to place the early Christian meal in its historical context, the culture of its day.

Yet if an aspect of culture is the subject of our study, what are the boundaries of that culture? Certainly early Christianity cannot be defined as a culture in itself. At most it is a movement within the culture that uses the rules of culture to define itself. Nor is the "biblical world" a culture in itself, as some studies have implied.[24] Rather, the boundaries of the culture we are considering are those of the Mediterranean world within the Greco-Roman period. Within that world there are individual ethnic groups, such as Greeks, Romans, Jews, Egyptians, Phrygians, and so on. Although each of these groups has its own traditions, all participate in the larger culture as well. In addition, it must be kept in mind that Christianity is not a distinct ethnic group. Consequently, the cultural context for the origins of Christianity is that of the ancient Mediterranean world circa 300 B.C.E. to circa 300 C.E.

CATEGORIES OF ANALYSIS

Idealized Model

In the literary data, descriptions and allusions to meals tend to presuppose an idealized model to which the meal in question is being compared. For example, the philosophical banquet, as presented in the tradition of symposium literature, becomes a dominant model to which later descriptions of banquets are consistently compared. Another type of idealized model that emerges from the study of the Near Eastern data is the messianic banquet, which can be termed the eternal banquet of the gods. Thus it is appropriate in analyzing our data to ascertain whether the author is presupposing an idealized model of the banquet as the point of reference.

Another way to view the idealization of the banquet is in terms of the "social code" it represents. As pointed out above, among cultural anthropologists Mary Douglas has devoted the most attention in recent years to the study of meals as an aspect of culture. In one of her earlier studies, she notes: "If food is treated as a code, the messages it encodes will be found in the pattern of social relations being expressed. The message is about different degrees of hierarchy, inclusion and exclusion, boundaries and transactions across the boundaries. Like sex, the taking of food has a social component, as well as a biological one."[25]

Douglas's observations apply quite well to the ancient data. Indeed, she presents these comments in an article in which she analyzes dietary laws in the Old Testament. Here she proposes that the dietary laws be understood as a form of social code in which they express social realities as understood within the culture. Thus the dietary laws of the Hebrews are found to correlate with various other religious laws in which they draw boundaries between themselves and their neighbors.[26] Similar observations can be made about the Greco-Roman data. The categories discussed below are representative of the social code of ancient banquets.

Social Boundaries
As Mary Douglas notes, the defining of boundaries is primary to the social code of banquets. That is to say, whom one dines with defines one's placement in a larger set of social networks. Because of the clear boundary-defining symbolism of table fellowship in the ancient world, banquets became a significant feature of various identifiable social groups. The social code of the banquet represents a confirmation and ritualization of the boundaries that exist in a social situation.

Social Bonding
The act of dining together is considered to create a bond between the diners. In the ancient world this symbolism was carried by various elements of the

banquet, such as the sharing of common food or sharing from a common table or dish. But above all it simply derived from the fact that the diners shared the event together. To be sure, the diners were normally already bonded into some sort of social network that existed before they gathered for dining. Thus the most common banquets were those of a family, a host and his close friends (less common a hostess and her friends), or the members of a formally organized club or religious group. The banquet could also create ties that did not previously exist. One example is the Greek tradition of *xenia,* or the extending of hospitality to a stranger or foreigner, which usually meant inviting the stranger to one's table. Even in this case, however, there was an assumed social network to which one was usually responding in offering such hospitality; that is to say, one would tend only to extend it or expect it in a situation of social connection or social parity.

Social Obligation
As a corollary of social bonding, sharing a meal also created a sense of ethical obligation of the diners toward one another. Today we might refer to this as the rules of meal etiquette. But for the Greeks, what we moderns refer to as etiquette was part of the larger category of social ethics. While we tend to view meal etiquette as a convention of culture without significant connection to morality or ethics, the Greeks addressed banquet rules in the context of serious ethical discussions. They presented philosophical dialogues on "symposium laws" and catalogued meal behavior under ethical categories such as friendship, joy, or pleasure. Such categories formed the basis for debates about various aspects of social ethics. These philosophical discussions provide evidence for us of the importance the culture placed on a banquet occasion as a form of serious social interchange. But even more important, they provided for the ancients a set of rhetorical categories utilized in banquet discussions in a variety of contexts throughout the Greco-Roman period. Consequently, the concept of social obligation at the banquet as defined in the philosophical tradition provides categories and terms that came to be utilized in all levels of our data.

Social Stratification
Another significant feature of ancient banquets was the always-prominent idea of social ranking. The banquet provided a significant means for one's status in society to be formally recognized and acknowledged. Two aspects of the banquet especially carried this symbolism: the custom of reclining and the custom of ranking places at table.

The act of reclining in itself was a mark of one's rank in society: only free citizens were allowed to recline. Notably excluded were women, children, and slaves. If they were present at the banquet, they would sit.[27]

Those who reclined were further ranked by the places assigned to them at the table. Though the positions might vary based upon local custom or table arrangement, there was almost always an honored place at any table. Others were ranked according to their position relative to the honored place.

Social stratification was deeply embedded in ancient society. The patron-client system was one form in which it was manifested.[28] The banquet provided a means to honor and maintain that system. Even if the system that prevailed in society was to be overruled at the table, it was usually replaced by another system mirroring the one it replaced. Thus ancient clubs and associations were organized in such a way that individuals from a low status in society could achieve a higher-status designation at the club banquets based on their rank within the club.[29]

Social Equality

Those who dined together were to be treated equally. This was a standard feature of ancient dining protocol. It functioned as an elaboration of the concept of social bonding at the meal and was a strong feature of banquet ideology at all levels of the data. The idea was that a meal that was shared in common and that created a sense of community among the participants should be one in which all could share equally and with full participation. In essence, then, a meal conceived in this way had the potential to break down social barriers and allow for a sense of social ordering internal to the group.

Normally, however, this concept tended to operate in tandem with the category of social stratification. That is to say, some individuals might be considered more "equal" than others. For example, the concept of "equal feasts" is a standard feature of the heroic banquets in Homer. Yet as Gregory Nagy points out, these should be understood as giving everyone their due on an equal basis *according to their relative status*.[30] Equality would not be understood as it is today, but rather would operate along with concepts of social status.

The tension between social stratification and social equality at banquets has also been noted in a study of Eurasian societies by Jack Goody:

> In looking at the cuisines of the Eurasian societies, we noted a set of specific characteristics: 1. The link between cuisine and "class," with social groups being characterized by different styles of life. 2. The contradictions, tensions and conflicts connected with this differentiation.

> The various forms include the contradiction between ideologies of equality . . . and ideologies of hierarchy . . . as well as the conflict, at the individual as well as the group level, between fasting acknowledged as "good" and feasting as "pleasurable."[31]

The same inherent tensions will be noted in ancient banquets. One feature may dominate at one time and another feature at another time, yet they always remain in an uneasy tension. This is part of the richness of banquet ideology and helps to promote many of the debates and discussions we will find in our data.

Festive Joy

A banquet was an occasion of "good cheer" or "pleasure," viewed here as values that governed the proper meal. Another term for the good cheer of the banquet was *festive joy (euphrosynē),* which was seen as an essential component of the "proper" banquet. As such, it was spoken of as the gift of the god(s), and often associated with the wine. Festive joy was viewed not as an individual experience but as a social experience inherent to the overall communal function of the banquet. Indeed, a proper banquet could be judged by how well it promoted festive joy. Consequently, festive joy could also function as a category governing social obligation at the banquet.

Banquet Entertainment

The ancient banquet presupposed entertainment as part of the event. This could vary from party games to dramatic presentations to music to philosophical conversation. It developed elaborate and specific variations according to the different settings and circumstances in which the banquet would be held. But no banquet would be complete as a social event without some form of entertainment.

The perspectives and categories of analysis outlined above have emerged from my study of ancient banquets. What follows is a collection of data presented as evidence for these conclusions. The collection is not comprehensive but rather intended to be representative. The types of banquets analyzed, however, *are* considered to be as comprehensive in scope as I can determine. Together they constitute evidence that the banquet was a single social institution that pervaded the culture as a whole.[32]

CHAPTER 2

THE GRECO-ROMAN BANQUET

"The Romans . . . are fond of quoting a witty and sociable person who said, after a solitary meal, 'I have eaten, but not dined today,' implying that a dinner always requires friendly sociability for seasoning."
—Plutarch, *Table Talk*

"After all, one of man's greatest achievements was the invention of food, not just fodder. All animals eat fodder. Man invented food. Food is not merely something that you put in your stomach and digest. Food is an occasion for a social act. It's an occasion for meeting. It's an occasion for conversation. Food is something that stirs the senses."
—Lewis Mumford, *The Ecological Conscience*

As Plutarch and Mumford attest, both ancients and moderns recognize the difference between eating to satisfy hunger alone and eating as a social event. To be sure, even the hastily consumed snack at the fast food outlet has its social components. But it is the formal meal with which we are here concerned, the meal at which one "dines" rather than "eats," as that unnamed Roman put it. These distinctions make sense even to us today. *To dine* suggests a certain formality in terms of dress, table setting, order of the meal, types of foods offered, and expected behavior or etiquette. All of these expectations can be distinguished in our minds, and usually are, from those connected with other types of eating occasions: a cocktail party, a buffet, a pizza with friends after a sports event, or a snack taken alone.

For the ancients, such distinctions were present to an even greater degree than in our society. Indeed, the formal meal, or banquet, was a richly textured social institution of the first order. In their world both "entertainment" and "hospitality" were of exceptional social importance and were experienced primarily on the occasion of a banquet. The banquet provided an opportunity for social intercourse in a large variety of settings and contexts. Indeed, to dine with one's friends was one of the most significant social occasions to be experienced in the ancient world. But it was more than a mere social event. At various times, it could serve as the setting for a variety of important cultural functions, from initiation of youth into adult male society to communion with the gods. Oswyn Murray's remark about the Greek Archaic period could be applied to the Hellenistic and Roman periods as well: "It is from the symposiast's couch that Greek culture of the Archaic age makes most sense."[1]

Of course, dining customs as a form of social code can be said to be present in all structured societies in all historical periods, as the many studies of Mary Douglas have so eloquently brought to our attention.[2] But nevertheless a meal speaks a symbolic language that can be considered unique to a particular society. For example, the idea that sharing a meal together creates a sense of social bonding appears to be a universal symbol. Yet the nuances of how this is communicated and to what degree will vary from culture to culture.

In applying these observations to the ancient world, two points need to be stressed. The first is obvious but must be re-emphasized: the ancients are different from us, so also their meal customs and rules of etiquette are different. The second point is less obvious and will require an extended argument. The peoples of the Mediterranean world of the period circa 300 B.C.E. to circa 300 C.E. tended to share the same dining customs. That is, the banquet as a social institution is practiced in similar ways and with similar symbols or codes by Greeks, Romans, Jews, Egyptians, and so on. The similarities did not nullify the existence of variations here and there. Those variations, however, drew from a common set of banquet customs, symbols, and codes that were the same throughout the Mediterranean world.

THE CUSTOM OF RECLINING

One indicator of common table customs for the ancients was the universal practice of reclining at table. It is remarkable to note that Greeks, Romans, and Jews shared not only the custom in this period but also a similar tradition as to its history. In each case, the tradition was that their people once sat when they ate, but in more recent history they began to recline.[3] Furthermore, reclining is spoken of in these traditions in a positive way, for, after all, it had become an accepted custom. The change is seen not as "degeneracy" but as "progress."

When we try to account for the history of this custom in more scientific terms, we can develop a general theory of its origin and diffusion. The first examples of the use of this custom are found in the Near East. Although the origins are obscure, it is reasonable to postulate an origin among nomadic tribes.

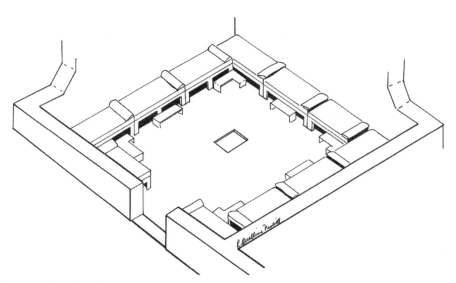

Figure 1: A Typical Greek Dining Room
A reconstruction of a dining room from the Asclepius Sanctuary at Corinth. The sanctuary contained three such rooms of the same size arranged side by side. Because the rooms were furnished with stone couches, of which several survived (see figure 2, below), we are able to reconstruct the arrangement of furniture as shown in this diagram. Markings in the floor indicated the location of removable tables. The stone block in the middle of the floor is conjectured to have held a brazier of some kind for cooking or warming food. The dining rooms date from the fourth century b.c.e. and were in continuous use until the Roman period in Corinth. They were built as part of the sanctuary accessory buildings, with the temple proper being located on an upper level just to the east of the dining rooms. (See Roebuck, *Corinth XIV,* 51–57, esp. 52 fig. 13, plan C.)

The arrangement of couches shown here was typical of Greek dining rooms, whether in private houses, public buildings, or temples. It was common that a room designed to contain dining couches would have an off-center doorway and an uneven number of couches, as shown here, to allow for an arrangement of couches so that all of the diners would recline on the left elbow. This room held eleven couches; the other most common styles held either seven or nine couches.

Figure 2: A Stone Couch from the Dining Room of the Asclepius Sanctuary at Corinth
Originally the couch would have been covered with cushions and pillows.

Figure 3: Reconstruction of a Greek Symposium The Corinth dining room pictured on the previous page is shown here as it might have looked during a symposium. The couches have been numbered according to their most likely ranking, since the ranking order proceeds from left to right.

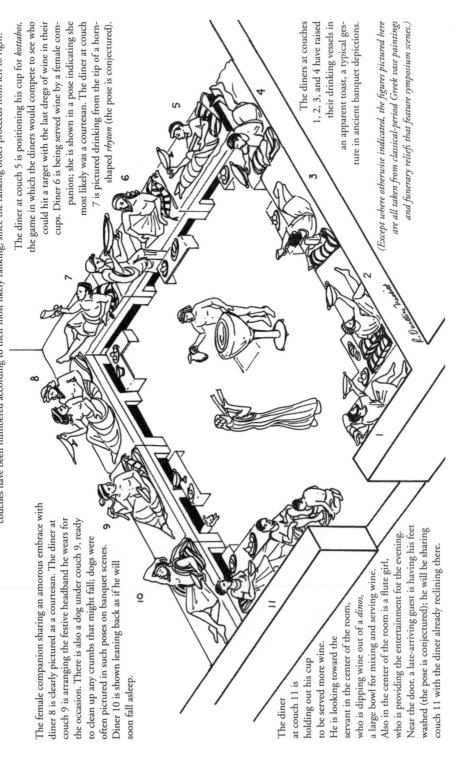

The diner at couch 5 is positioning his cup for *kottabos*, the game in which the diners would compete to see who could hit a target with the last dregs of wine in their cups. Diner 6 is being served wine by a female companion; she is shown in a pose indicating she most likely was a courtesan. The diner at couch 7 is pictured drinking from the tip of a horn-shaped *rhyton* (the pose is conjectured).

The female companion sharing an amorous embrace with diner 8 is clearly pictured as a courtesan. The diner at couch 9 is arranging the festive headband he wears for the occasion. There is also a dog under couch 9, ready to clean up any crumbs that might fall; dogs were often pictured in such poses on banquet scenes. Diner 10 is shown leaning back as if he will soon fall asleep.

The diners at couches 1, 2, 3, and 4 have raised their drinking vessels in an apparent toast, a typical gesture in ancient banquet depictions.

(Except where otherwise indicated, the figures pictured here are all taken from classical-period Greek vase paintings and funerary reliefs that feature symposium scenes.)

The diner at couch 11 is holding out his cup to be served more wine. He is looking toward the servant in the center of the room, who is dipping wine out of a *dinos*, a large bowl for mixing and serving wine. Also in the center of the room is a flute girl, who is providing the entertainment for the evening. Near the door, a late-arriving guest is having his feet washed (the pose is conjectured); he will be sharing couch 11 with the diner already reclining there.

Figure 4: Reconstruction of a Roman Banquet in a Triclinium

The scene pictured here is arranged on a mosaic floor from a Roman-period dining room (the mosaic is now on display at the Pergamon Museum in Berlin). The design of the mosaic marked the area along the walls where the couches were to be arranged in the typical Pi shape of a Roman triclinium or three-couch room. The couches in this style of dining room were able to accommodate at least three diners each. The room would therefore normally hold nine diners, as pictured here. The couch on the right was designated *locus summus*, meaning "highest position"; the middle couch was called *locus medius*, or "middle position"; and the couch on the left was *locus imus*, or "lowest position." These designations indicated general ranking around the table, with some exceptions. As customs evolved, the highest-ranking became position 3 at *locus medius*, located where it joins *locus imus*; this position was designated *locus consularis*, "the consul's position" (Plut., *Quaest. Conv.* 1.3). The host could be placed at position 1 on *locus summus*, as in Petronius's depiction of the banquet of Trimalchio (*Sat.* 31.8; Smith, *Cena Trimalchionis*, 66–67), or, more commonly, at position 1 on *locus imus*, located where this couch joins *locus medius*, and thus in close proximity to *locus consularis*. In our reconstruction, the three diners on *locus imus* are all women. They have been placed here in imitation of a reference in Lucian's *Symposium* in which the women present at a wedding banquet were all arranged on the same couch (Luc. *Symp.* 8). The musicians providing the entertainment and the style of the tables in front of the couches have been copied from the fifth-century–c.e. Roman banquet scene shown on the front cover of this book.

Since such tribes would live in tents with very little furniture, reclining would be a suitable posture for eating.

By the time we can clearly find the custom, however, it is present not among a nomadic people but among a settled people. Furthermore, it is connected not with poverty or simplicity, but with luxury, wealth, and power. This is seen in the iconography of the ancient Near East reliefs where the custom is portrayed. Furthermore, the earliest evidence of the Greeks' adoption of this custom is also iconographical, in which numerous funerary reliefs show the deceased reclining at banquet.

These materials have been analyzed in detail in a series of studies by Jean-Marie Dentzer.[4] Dentzer shows how the iconography used by the Greeks exhibits similarities to that seen in Assyrian reliefs. Thus he postulates that the custom originated in Greece at about the time that the reliefs began to appear, namely, in the sixth century B.C.E., and that it was borrowed from the Assyrian culture.[5] About 1,000 years later, in the late fourth century C.E., we begin to find evidence of a shift to the sitting posture for formal banquets,[6] signaling a cultural change that eventually became the new universal norm for dining.

When the Greeks adopted the custom, they also adopted the trappings, or customs and "social code," that went with it. This is seen in the iconography. In the Assyrian reliefs, it is the king who reclines, surrounded by various symbols of luxury, wealth, and power. Similarly, in the Greek reliefs, the deceased is shown in an idealized pose, and if other representations are present, besides the deceased and the couch, they tend to enhance the imagery of luxury, wealth, and power.[7]

Dentzer's study has brought to our attention that the custom of reclining is a symbol of a much larger phenomenon. That is, it was adopted not just as a change of posture, but as a change of "social code." Furthermore, it included with it other customs that tended to correlate with that social code. For example, along with reclining, the Greeks adopted a different meal as the major meal of the day; it was no longer the noon meal but the evening meal that was the "banquet." Other customs became a fixed part of the banquet as well, such as the order and courses of the meal and various aspects of etiquette. When the Romans and the Jews adopted the custom of reclining, they too were not just changing posture, but adopting a fully developed social institution, namely, the Greco-Roman banquet.

DEFINING THE DATA FIELD

The term *Greco-Roman* is being used here to refer to the combined culture of the Mediterranean world of circa 300 B.C.E. (Alexander the Great) to circa

300 C.E. (Constantine). The major cultural influences of this time and place were those of the Greeks and then later the Romans, whose culture was largely adapted from that of the Greeks.

When discussing a topic as elusive as table customs, one must draw from disparate data and develop a composite picture. Much of the basic data, as will be seen, derives from the classical periods and literatures of the Greeks (sixth to fifth centuries B.C.E.) and the Romans (second century B.C.E. to second century C.E.). Greek customs are most easily reconstructed in the Greek cities proper during this period, while Roman customs are primarily documented in the city of Rome itself during the late republic and early imperial periods.

Nevertheless, such data as is available for the rest of the Mediterranean culture tends to reflect the same basic table customs and ideology as found in the classical literature. Thus the evidence supports the hypothesis that basic customs tended to be the same throughout the Mediterranean world during this period.

Of course, there were variations here and there. In fact, ancient writers such as Plutarch and Athenaeus paid a great deal of attention to variations in table customs in different regions and ethnic divisions of the Roman Empire. Athenaeus, for example, noted that the Cretans continued to sit at table long after the Greeks had adopted the practice of reclining (4.143e). Yet those variations that did appear tended to be minor compared to the larger aspects of customs held in common.

Since this is a study of an aspect of culture, however, we must delineate as much as possible the distinct groups with which we are dealing. In terms of ethnic identity, we will be defining meal customs among Greek-speaking individuals of various extractions, from a pure Greek background to those from other ethnic traditions who have adopted the Greek way of life. Romans are identified as generally Latin-speaking or having Latin-derived names, although they may communicate in Greek if they are located in the eastern sections of the empire (e.g., Greece and eastwards).

Judaism during this period was highly hellenized, not only among those Jewish groups that spoke and wrote in Greek, but also in pockets of Hebrew and Aramaic conservatism. Indeed, even when scholars argue that rabbis from the backwaters of Palestine were not affected by Greek ideas in any significant way, they nevertheless acknowledge that other aspects of culture did infiltrate. Consequently, whenever we find Jews practicing the same basic table customs as the Greeks and Romans, we assume that it reflects the hellenizing of that aspect of Jewish culture.

On the other hand, early Christianity is not a culture to itself. Thus whenever we wish to define the cultural identity of a particular Christian group, we must do so on the basis of other aspects of their cultural or ethnic heritage, generally either Greco-Roman or Jewish.

Besides ethnic differentiation, we must also deal with differentiation of social class. By and large our evidence will reflect the values and customs of the upper, cultured classes. We cannot easily account for differentiations of customs and values in the lower classes, since we have very little evidence to go on. However, since we are dealing with a specific social institution, namely, the banquet, rather than meal customs in general, we can expect some uniformity of customs and values to be connected with it in whatever level of society it might be found.

FEATURES OF THE ANCIENT BANQUET

Where the Banquet Fit in a Normal Day's Activities

Greek meal customs became crystallized in their basic forms in the classical period.[8] Although much was retained from the Homeric period, there were significant changes as well.[9] For example, as has already been mentioned, there was a change in the meal posture from the Homeric practice of sitting at table to the oriental practice of reclining.[10] This was accompanied by a change in the time of day when the major meal would be eaten. In the Homeric period, the major meal, known as the *deipnon,* was most often eaten at midday. There were customarily two other meals, the *ariston,* or "morning meal," and the *dorpos,* or "evening meal."

Although these are the names normally applied to these meals, it should be noted that labels for meals were not strictly adhered to in Homer. Indeed, other terms for meals also occur. Furthermore, the term *deipnon,* although normally used for the midday meal, is also occasionally used for the morning meal (*Od.* 9.311, 15.76, 19.321). By and large, however, it tends to be the term used to designate the most important meal of the day.[11]

By the time of the classical period, namely, in the sixth and fifth centuries B.C.E., the *deipnon* had moved to the evening. The midday meal was then called *ariston* and breakfast went by the name of *akratisma.* The *akratisma,* as the name implies, consisted of little more than bread dipped in unmixed wine *(akratos)* and was normally taken at sunup. The midday meal was also a rather light meal.[12]

But by far the most important meal of the day was the *deipnon,* now translated "dinner" or "supper," which, when it was extended into a significant social event to which guests would be invited, became what we call a "banquet." For with the change to the evening hour and the adoption of reclining with all its accoutrements, the *deipnon* took on the character of a more leisurely meal, one appropriate to the posture of reclining. It became not only the one formal meal of the day but also potentially the social highlight of the day as well. As a banquet, it would thus function not only to allay the appetite but also to provide an entire evening's entertainment.

Similar customs had developed among the Romans, largely adopted and adapted from the Greeks.[13] The Romans also had a tradition of three meals to the day—the *ientaculum,* or breakfast, the *prandium,* or midday meal, and the *cena,* or evening meal. The *cena* became equivalent to the Greek *deipnon* as the most important meal of the day and the meal to which one would invite guests for an evening's entertainment.

The *ientaculum* was usually taken at sunup or at the third or fourth hour of the day, that is, 6:58 to 9:29 in summer and 9:02 to 10:31 in winter.[14] It was a light meal, but evidently not as light as the Greek *akratisma.* The elder Pliny described his breakfast as "light and simple in the old fashioned way" (Pliny *Ep.* 3.5.10). A typical menu might include bread with salt and one or two of the following: dried fruit, olives, cheese, or eggs.[15] The drink could be milk or mulsum, a drink made of wine mixed with honey.[16]

The *prandium* was eaten at midday or about the sixth hour; that is, 10:44 to 12:00 in summer and 11:15 to 12:00 in winter.[17] Since the *cena* could follow this meal as little as three hours later, the *prandium* tended to be a light meal. It often consisted of *reliquiae* or leftovers from the day before.[18] Seneca's meal is probably more sober than most, but is illustrative of the nature of the *prandium:* "Dry bread, no need of a table, no need to wash my hands afterwards" (*Ep.* 83.6).[19] A more typical menu might include a portion of meat or fish with fruit and wine.[20] Indeed, there are even some examples of inviting guests to one's midday meal, which evidently would call for the meal to be more elaborate.[21]

The *cena* was the evening meal and the major meal of the day. It usually began at the ninth hour and ended at dark, which meant that a normal meal might last anywhere from two and a half to three and three-quarters hours, although many lasted much longer. In the summer, the ninth hour began at about 2:31 to 3:46 and sundown did not come until about 7:30. In the winter, the ninth hour came at about 1:20 to 2:13, but since darkness could come as early as 4:30, a meal might be more likely to last until after dark.[22] Among the Greeks, on the other hand, the *deipnon* generally took place shortly before sundown or sometimes even after sundown, and it could extend until late in the evening well after dark. For both Greeks and Romans, when the evening meal was a formal banquet, it was expected to be an extended event of three hours or more, since it was more than just an occasion for eating but included a long period of relaxed drinking with entertainment.

Prior to the evening meal the upper classes among the Greeks and, later, the Romans, preferred to spend the afternoon in exercise followed by a bath. This regimen was recommended as conducive to health and as an excellent preparation for the heavy meal that was anticipated.[23] If one were attending a banquet for the evening, special attention would be given to grooming the body with perfumes and oil, and special dining clothes would be worn for the occasion.[24]

The placement of the banquet in the typical Roman day is illustrated in this quotation from Martial: "The first and the second hour wearies clients at the levee, the third hour sets hoarse advocates to work; till the end of the fifth Rome extends her various tastes; on the sixth gives rest to the tired [the *prandium* and/or siesta]; the seventh will be the end. The eighth to the ninth suffices for the oiled wrestlers [the bath]; the ninth bids us crush the piled couches [the *cena*]" (*Epig.* 4.8).

Invitations to a Banquet

Invitations were assumed to be a normal part of the formal banquet. To send invitations out a few days in advance so as to fill the quota of guests would, of course, be a practical consideration. Whether invitations were communicated verbally or written evidently could vary, and we have examples of both kinds.

In Xenophon's *Symposium,* Callias issues invitations to his banquet on the afternoon before the meal when he chances upon Socrates and a few companions (3–4). In Plato's *Symposium,* on the other hand, Agathon issues his invitations the day before the meal (174A). He then tells Aristodemus, whom Socrates has invited, "only yesterday I went round to invite [*kalein*] you, but failed to see you" (174E). Though Socrates takes the liberty to invite Aristodemus without consulting the host, Aristodemus is careful to insist that he has not come uninvited (*aklētos,* 174C) but has been invited by Socrates (174E). This illustrates the significance given to the propriety of an invitation.

This example also sets up the phenomenon of the uninvited guest, a phenomenon that becomes a stock motif in the literary genre of the symposium (to be described further below). In Plato's version, it is Alcibiades who arrives late and uninvited. He disrupts the meal with good-humored ribaldry, having come from his revelries at another party that evening, and asks if he may join the group (212D–213A). He does so only when Agathon, the host, extends to him an invitation on the spot ("and Agathon invited [*kalein*] him," 213A). Later, another group of less disciplined uninvited "revelers" *(kōmastai)* arrive, having secured an entrance when the door is opened for a departing guest. They are allowed to take over the symposium and impose their own drinking rules, leading to the gradual dissolution of the entire occasion (223B). The uninvited guest became a standard literary figure, but how common this practice was at actual meals is less clear.

Examples of written invitations have been preserved from the Hellenistic period in Egypt. Here they are found among other everyday documents written on papyrus that have survived in the dry sands of Egypt, documents that include private letters, bills of account, and other records of everyday affairs. These are actual written invitations, not literary idealizations, and, as such, represent significant primary data.

These invitations clearly exhibit a standard literary form. In his 1975 study of the form of papyrus invitations, Chan Hie Kim identified thirty letters of invitation of which twenty-five share a common structure.[25] A subsequent publication of two more invitations from the collection at Columbia University brings the total of papyrus invitations known to me to thirty-two.[26]

A common form of the papyrus invitation is seen in the following: "Chaeremon requests you to dine at the banquet of the Lord Sarapis in the Sarapeion tomorrow, the 15th, at the 9th hour."[27] Kim has outlined the basic structure of the invitations as follows: (1) There is an invitation verb, which in this case is *erotan* but in other cases is *kalein*. Apparently the two words are interchangeable as terms for "invite." The invitation verb is followed by (2) the reference to the invited guest, always given as the second person pronoun. Since those invited are never named, Kim surmises that the same invitation could be used by a messenger who would read it to the various individuals whom the host would designate.[28] Next is (3) the naming of the host. Item (4) is the purpose of the invitation, which is consistently expressed with the verb *deipnein* ("to dine"). The next items are (5) the occasion, (6) the place, (7) the date, and (8) the time.

It is the occasion and place that raise the most intriguing questions. In the example text, we have a reference, also found in eleven other papyrus texts, to the *klinē* of Sarapis, a highly popular Hellenistic-Egyptian deity. The term *klinē*, which is translated above as "banquet," literally means "couch." It is used here in a technical sense to refer to a specific type of meal, perhaps a type of sacrificial meal; this concept will be discussed further in chapter 4. Note that the *klinē* could be held in a temple, as in the model text above, or in a private home, as is found in three other extant texts.[29]

Twelve of the texts in Kim's list offer invitations to wedding feasts, of which the following is an example: "Dioscoros invites you to dine at the wedding of her son on the 14th of Mesore in the temple of Sabazius from the ninth hour, farewell."[30] Here the wedding feast is to take place at a temple. In other cases, it took place at the home of the parents of the bride or groom: "Herais requests your company at dinner in celebration of the marriage of her children at her house tomorrow, the 5th, at 9 o'clock."[31] Four other invitations list the occasion as a birthday feast, of which the following is an example: "Diogenes invites you to dinner for the first birthday of his daughter in the Serapeion tomorrow which is Pachon 26 from the eighth hour onwards."[32] Apparently the location of the feast could vary from a temple to a private home regardless of the occasion for the meal.

How many guests to invite is an interesting question. One factor, of course, would be the size of the facilities, but since these tended to follow standard patterns, there were obviously other factors defining the proper number to include in such an occasion. Varro is quoted to the effect that the smallest number should be three and the largest number nine, "for it is disagreeable to have a great number, since a crowd is generally disorderly, and at Rome it stands, at Athens it sits, but nowhere does it recline."[33]

Here he sees the problem as an ethical one as well as a practical one, since there is not room for everyone in a large crowd to be accommodated comfortably. Plutarch argues similarly in his discourse "On those who invite large numbers to dinner."[34] On the one hand, he says, if the crowd is too great for the available space, then it is no longer a proper party and is an insult to the guests: "For the size of a party also is right so long as it easily remains one party. If it gets too large, so that the guests can no longer talk to each other or enjoy the hospitality together or even know one another, then it ceases to be a party at all."[35] On the other hand, even if space is available, the gathering should be kept small:

> if both space and the provisions are ample, we must still avoid great numbers, because they in themselves interfere with sociability and conversation. It is worse to take away the pleasure of conversation at table than to run out of wine. . . . People who bring together too many guests to one place do prevent general conversation; they allow only a few to enjoy each other's society, for the guests separate into groups of two or

three in order to meet and converse, completely unconscious of those whose place on the couches is remote and not looking their way because they are separated from them by practically the length of a race course. . . . So it is a mistake for the wealthy to build showy dining rooms that hold thirty couches or more. Such magnificence makes for unsociable and unfriendly banquets where the manager of a fair is needed more than a toastmaster.[36]

The solution he suggests is to entertain frequently so that the guest list can be kept small and manageable: "The rest of us can protect ourselves against the risk of gathering too large a crowd by entertaining frequently in small groups . . . three or four guests at a time."[37] Like Varro, then, Plutarch favors a small banquet. But whereas Varro allows for a range of three to nine banqueters, Plutarch seems to prefer a maximum of about five (the host plus four guests).

Dining Rooms

Archaeological discoveries have provided us with plans for typical dining rooms in the Greek and Roman world. Although Greeks and Romans developed different patterns for dining-room design, they both followed similar conventions.[38] Dining rooms were designed so that couches could be arranged around a central axis and diners could share tables and communicate easily with one another. The same form was used for domestic, public, and religious settings, supporting the argument that the same meal customs were followed for banquets regardless of the setting or context. Consistent with the preference in the literary evidence for small banquets, dining rooms tended to be constructed to allow for five, seven, nine, or eleven couches in an intimate arrangement. Although larger banquet rooms have been found, they tend to be designed in such a way that dining couches could be arranged in clusters of small groups, as evidenced, for example, at Troizen, or at the Asklepieion at Corinth.[39]

The dining room in the Greek house is commonly referred to as the *andron,* which translates to mean "men's room."[40] This is where male guests were to be entertained by the paterfamilias. Except for this room, the designation of men's quarters and women's quarters in the typical house does not seem to have been standardized, since no clear pattern can be defined in the archaeological remains.[41]

Excavations at Olynthus have given us our most definitive evidence for the form of the Greek house. Here it was typical for dining rooms to be designed with a pebble mosaic decoration on the floor and a short raised platform along the wall where the (wooden) couches would be placed. In some cases, there was an entry room as well. It was also common to place the dining room within easy access of the front door so that guests could be accommodated without disturbing the rest of the house.[42]

The Olynthus dining rooms were designed so that couches would be arranged along the wall end to end, allowing the diners to recline on their left elbows and eat with their right hands. This was a typical arrangement for a Greek dining room. When a room was designed especially for couches in this form, it meant that only an odd number of couches could be set up, since a space had to be left for entrance into the dining room. It also meant that dining rooms often had off-center doorways to allow for the couches to be placed so that the head of each couch would abut the foot of the other.[43]

Couches were normally made of wood and have not tended to survive in situ. Dining rooms are therefore identified not so much by the furnishings as by the decorations in the room, especially when space has been marked out for the couches, and, in some cases, simply by the aspect of the room, such as the use of off-center doorways.[44] In a few cases, notably in certain Greek sanctuaries, permanent stone or masonry couches were used and so have survived in situ. A well-known example of such stone couches is found at the Corinth Asklepieion.[45]

Whether permanent or portable, couches were covered with pillows to make them comfortable for reclining. Tables were placed in front to hold the food, and often they would be arranged in such a way that the diners would share from the same table. The Greek term for the dining couch, *klinē*, was the same term also used for a couch for sleeping and for the couch on which a body was laid out in funeral ceremonies, and there was often very little difference between the sleeping couch, the funerary couch, and the dining couch.[46]

The Roman triclinium, or "three-couch" room, followed a different format.[47] Here the standard couch was intended to hold three diners, so that a triclinium was expected to accommodate nine diners in all. Based on numerous examples of masonry couches found at Pompeii, a standard format for the triclinium can be traced. The masonry couches are more like wide platforms on which pillows would be placed. Once more the diners would be arranged on their left elbows so that they could eat with their right hands. The couches would be arranged in a "Pi" shape, with the common table to be placed in front of them.[48]

A later development in dining room design was the *stibadium*. Here the couches were arranged in a semicircular format or Sigma shape. There were

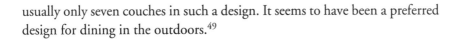

usually only seven couches in such a design. It seems to have been a preferred design for dining in the outdoors.[49]

The Order of the Meal

The Greeks customarily had two well-defined courses in their banquet. The first course was the *deipnon* proper, during which the meal of the evening would be eaten. The second course was the symposium *(symposion)* or "drinking party," which would be an extended period of relaxed drinking during which the entertainment of the evening would be presented.

The Romans had the same two basic courses, to which they added a course of appetizers at the beginning of the meal, called the *gustatio* or *promulsis*. During the Roman period, the Greeks added an appetizer course as well, known as the *propoma*.[50] Following the appetizer course was the meal proper, which the Romans referred to as the *fercula* or "courses." It was divided into the *prima cena,* the *altera cena,* and the *tertia cena.* The *altera cena* was also sometimes known as the *caput cenae,* designating it as the chief dish.[51]

The name the Romans gave to the last course was *comissatio* or *convivium,* both of which are usually translated "drinking party." This course was also called "second tables" *(mensae secundae).*[52] It tended to be more of a dessert course than in the Greek tradition, with nuts, fruits, and sweet cakes *(bellaria)* being served.[53] It was especially, however, a time for serious drinking and entertainment. In some cases drinking and entertainment would take place during the meal as well. Quite often in such cases the *convivium* might be reserved especially for conversation.[54]

Martial describes a three-course meal provided by a host whom he castigates for serving gourds for every course: "Gourds you will eat at once even among the hors-d'oeuvre, gourds he will bring you in the first or second course, these in the third course he will set again before you, out of these he will furnish later on your dessert."[55] Here he refers to the *gustus,* the *prima, altera,* and *tertia cena,* and the *epidipnis,* a term for the dessert course derived from the Greek term *epideipnis* referring to the course following the *deipnon.*

At a Greek meal, when the guests arrived, certain rituals normally took place before the meal began. A servant would meet the guest at the door and lead him to the dining room. There other servants would remove his shoes and wash his feet, after which he would be ready to take his place on a couch. The standard formula is described in Plato's *Symposium:* "So the attendant washed him and made him ready for reclining."[56]

After the guests had reclined, the slaves brought them water for washing their hands, as in Athenaeus: "Water over the hand, tables brought in."[57]

Since utensils were not used, except for the occasional use of a spoon, they ate with their hands.[58] Bits of bread functioned as napkins on which the hands were wiped during the meal. These were then thrown on the floor, along with bones and other scraps, which were then eaten by the dogs that were often present for this purpose.[59]

The food was brought in by the slaves on the tables, if they were the normal portable kind, or on trays if the tables were permanent. Athenaeus, quoting Philoxenus of Leucas (date unknown), describes the scene: "And slaves twain brought unto us a table with well-oiled face, another for others, while other henchmen bore a third, until they filled the chamber."[60] The tables were arranged one to a couch or group of couches, so that in many cases diners might share from the same table. Athenaeus refers to the custom of eating from the same table in Arcadia, which carried with it a symbolic sense of equality at the table: "The Arcadians entertain at their celebrations masters and slaves, setting one table before them all; they freely serve food for all to share, and mix the same bowl for all."[61] Lucian refers to the same motif, but with a typical satirical point of view, when he has two diners who share from the same table fight over the larger portion of the serving.[62]

To conclude the main course (the *deipnon*) and mark the transition to the second course (the *symposium*), an elaborate formal ritual took place. First the tables were removed and the floor swept. Then water was passed around for washing the hands. Next a libation of unmixed wine was offered "to the good daemon" or "Good Deity" (*agathou daimonos*), and a "paean" was sung (*paianizein*). In addition, garlands and perfumes might be passed around for the guests.

These rituals are enumerated in various sources as follows:

> Now, at last, the floor is swept, and clean are the hands of all the guests, and their cups as well; one slave puts plaited wreaths on their heads, another offers sweet-smelling perfume in a saucer; the mixing-bowl stands full of good cheer [*euphrosynē*]; and another wine is ready, which promises never to give out. . . .[63]
>
> After this, it seems, when Socrates had taken his place [or "reclined" (*kataklinento*)] and had dined [*deipnēsanto*] with the rest, they made libation and sang a chant to the god [*asanta ton theon*] and so forth, as custom bids [*ta nomizomena*], till they betook them to drinking.[64]
>
> When the tables had been removed and the guests had poured a libation and sung a hymn [*epaianisan*], there entered a man from Syracuse, to give them an evening's merriment.[65]

As is clear from these quotations, the order and specific number of pre-symposium rituals varies. But it is clear that, at the least, a ritual libation and removal of the tables commonly marked the transition from the eating to the drinking part of the meal. Then the wine would be brought in for the mixing, and the "second tables" of food for the "dessert" or drinking course would be provided.

The wine ceremonies varied somewhat from place to place, but the description provided by Diodorus Siculus is considered representative: "It is the custom, they say, when unmixed wine is served during a meal to greet it with the words, 'To the Good Deity! [*agathou daimonos*]' but when the cup is passed around after the meal diluted with water, to cry out 'To Zeus Savior! [*Dios Sōtēros*]'" (4.3). Other sources agree that the first libation was given with unmixed wine and was dedicated to the "Good Deity,"[66] but in some cases this libation was given immediately after the meal rather than during it. The second ceremony connected with Zeus Savior refers to the wine mixing that took place just prior to the drinking party proper. The first cup from the bowl of mixed wine was dedicated to Zeus Savior.

The reference to the "Good Deity" was generally understood as a reference to Dionysus, but there was disagreement as to the meaning of the dedication to Zeus Savior. These interpretations are enumerated by Athenaeus:

> When the unmixed wine is poured during the dinner [*deipnon*], the Greeks call upon the name of the "Good Deity," giving honor to the deity who discovered the wine; he was Dionysus. But with the first cup of mixed wine given after the dinner they call upon Zeus the Savior, because they assume that he, as the originator of rainstorms, was the author of the painless mixture derived from the mingling of wind and rain.[67]
>
> He [Amphictyon, King of Athens] also instituted the custom of taking just a sip of unmixed wine after meat as a proof of the power of the "Good Deity," but after that they might drink mixed wine, as much as each man chose. They were also to repeat over this cup the name of Zeus the Savior as a warning and reminder to drinkers that only when they drank in this fashion would they surely be safe.[68]

These explanations of the dedication to Zeus Savior are obviously moralizing attempts to explain an already-existing custom. It is probable, however, that these libations originated in reference to household deities.[69]

Another common custom called for three bowls to be mixed at one time. The first cup from each of these bowls would then be dedicated to different deities: the first to the Olympians, the second to the Heroes, and the third to Zeus Savior. This custom is referred to in the following reference: "They mix the first krater to Zeus Olympios, the second to the Heroes, and the third to Zeus Savior."[70]

The method for offering a libation at a meal has been explained in this way. Whenever the wine was ladled into the cup, the name of the deity was pronounced over it in the genitive case, "to the Good Deity" *(agathou daimonus)* or "to Zeus Savior" *(Dios sōtēros)*. The host or symposiarch would then pronounce the name of the deity again and pour out a portion into the fire or onto the floor. He would then take a sip and pass the cup around for each guest to sip, saying the name of the deity in the genitive as they did so.[71]

Also in connection with the pre-symposium ritual a "paean" was often sung. This was probably a solemn song or chant, although in other contexts a paean would be a victory or triumphal song. The specific content of such a hymn at the close of a meal is not clear, but it does appear to have had religious significance. Thus in Plato's *Symposium* the guests are said to have "sung a hymn to the god."[72]

Following these ceremonies, the final course of the meal would be served, that is, the "second tables" or the "dessert" course *(tragēmata)*. Here the food served included various fruits and nuts, with copious portions of salt included, the purpose being to provoke the thirst for greater enjoyment of the drinking.[73]

Athenaeus remarks on the nature of the dessert course as follows:

> Aristotle in his treatise *On Drunkenness* uses the term "second tables" much as we do in this passage, thus: "In general, dessert [*tragēma*] must be distinguished from the meal in that the one consists of eating, the other of munching [*trōgalios*]. This last is the traditional word among the Greeks, since they serve the things to be eaten in the form of things to chew [*tragēma*]. Hence the first man to term this a 'second table' was probably right; for as a matter of fact the eating of the 'munchies' course [*tragēmatismos*] makes a kind of subsequent meal, and the 'munchies' themselves [*tragēmata*] are served as a second dinner."[74]

Athenaeus continues in subsequent sections of book 14 to describe various dishes of the dessert course. He summarizes the proper ingredients of the dessert course in 14.642a (quoted from Amphis, a Middle Comedy poet from the fourth century B.C.E.): "Cakes of fine meal, good wine, eggs, sesame-seeds, perfume, a wreath, a flute-girl."

This part of the meal was also called the *symposion* or *potos,* the "drinking party," for it was this part of the banquet that was set aside for serious drinking. In the Roman period, wine was often drunk during the meal as well as during the symposium. The division between courses nevertheless continued, as illustrated by Plutarch's reference to the "philosophical talk at the drinking party" *(philosophein para poton),* which took place "after dinner" *(meta deipnon).*[75]

Could there be a symposium without a *deipnon?* In some cases guests were invited for the symposium alone, indicating that it could be conducted separately from the meal. Furthermore, in symposium literature, the symposium itself, where the drinking and conversation took place, is given the greatest attention, as, for example, in the *Symposia* of Plato and Xenophon. It should also be noted that the transitional ritual described above implies a clear break between the two courses, with the symposium beginning with its own libations. Indeed, the symposium became identified virtually as an institution in its own right, so that in much of the literature, it is the only part of the meal that is remarked upon.

Could there be a *deipnon* without a symposium? Certainly it would be difficult to imagine a formal meal where there was no drinking of wine. Since the Greeks preferred to drink their wine mixed, and since the mixing ceremony did not take place until the main course was completed, it would seem quite unusual for a formal meal not to conclude with some drinking and conversation or entertainment, that is, with the basic ingredients of a symposium. The drinking party, therefore, must be seen as the ordinary conclusion to a formal meal, or banquet. As Robert Flacelière states, "Every formal dinner . . . consisted of two successive stages: first came the satisfaction of one's hunger by the banquet proper, and secondly . . . there was the business of drinking . . . a process accompanied by all sorts of incidental entertainment."[76]

The Menu

Since the banquet was an occasion for entertaining guests, the menu would tend to represent the finest one could offer. The normal diet would doubtless be much simpler.[77]

A typical menu at the Greek banquet might consist of bread and various vegetables, with fish or meat if the meal was especially extravagant. There were many grades and varieties of breads since it was the staple of the diet.[78] Vegetables might include lettuce, beans, onions, leeks, herbs, and olives. Fish was especially prized and was available in many varieties.[79] The Roman diet was characterized by a lavish use of a fermented fish sauce known as *garum*, which was used to flavor meats and other foods. Meat, however, was scarce, and was generally available to the populace only on festive occasions whenever sacrifices were made. In fact, most meat for the Greek table (other than game) seems to have originated as sacrificial meat; thus the term *hiereion* ("sacrificial meat") came to signify meat in general.[80] The usual types of meats were beef, lamb, pork, and goat. Sausages made from these were also available. Game was rarely a staple in the urban diet but was more widely available in rural areas. A cookbook from the Roman period, written by Apicius, gives a sense for some of the flavors of Roman foods, although some of the ingredients and amounts are obscure to us.[81]

Wine was always drunk mixed; the Greeks considered it boorish to drink one's wine unmixed *(akratos)*.[82] The drinking of mixed wine *(kekramenos)* was so prevalent that the regular term for wine *(oinos)*, if otherwise undefined, usually meant mixed wine. Thus Plutarch states "we call a mixture 'wine' [*oinos*] although the larger of the component parts is water."[83]

Common proportions were five parts water to two of wine or three of water to one of wine. Athenaeus refers to "an oft-repeated proverb" on the subject of traditional mixtures as follows: "'Drink either five or three or at the least not four.' For they say one should drink two parts wine to five of water, or one part wine to three of water."[84] Plutarch alludes to the same tradition when he records a symposiac discussion on the topic, "On 'Drink five or three, not four.'"[85]

Drinking the wine mixed, of course, meant that much more wine could be consumed before an unsociable state of drunkenness would be reached. What was the percentage of alcohol in a typical mixture? Oswyn Murray has speculated that it would be somewhat equivalent to a modern glass of beer.[86] This would allow the drinking to continue over an extended period as described in the literature. Wines from certain regions had come to be recognized for their quality early on, so that an ancient form of wine snobbery is often found in both Greek and Latin literature.[87]

Drunkenness and extravagant behavior are common features in the literary descriptions of banquets, but these occur along with standard depictions in which the banquet is seen as a noble and cultured affair. What must be noted is that the literature simply does not provide us with a straightforward description of a normal Roman meal. Rather, what we have are literary presentations that vary between extravagant exaggeration and brief glimpses.[88] A famous example is the presentation of the banquet of Trimalchio in Petronius's *Satyricon*. Here the theme of the boorishness of the new rich is enhanced by a wildly extravagant description of elaborate dishes. Too often Petronius is read as the norm for Roman banquets rather than what his work is, a literary exaggeration. Nevertheless, it contains valuable data about the ideological function of the banquet in the ancient social world.[89]

Organization and Leadership at a Banquet

Arranging the Guests. The guests were placed on the couches according to their relative social rank, since each position at the table had an imputed ranking attached to it. Social rank generally followed certain well-known rules and was considered an appropriate recognition at the banquet as at other social occasions. One's rank could vary depending on that of the other diners. For example, a foreign dignitary would tend to outrank all other guests and so would displace those who might otherwise have a proper claim to the first rank at the table.

Ranking of the guests was a given and always had to be dealt with. Choosing the proper position for one's guests was the mark of a good host, and called for the most careful forethought so as to avoid insult and embarrassment. The location of the first rank and the other relative rankings around the table might vary depending on the local tradition and the arrangement of the couches. But it was a feature that was always present at a banquet.

The Host. The host would generally be the one in charge of the guest list, the menu, and the provision of a place for the banquet. In addition, the host would designate the positions that the guests would occupy at the table and, if other differentiations among the guests were to be applied, the host would be in charge of those as well.

The Symposiarch. A symposium often began with the selection of a presiding officer or "symposiarch" from the number of the participants. The symposiarch then set the rules for the drinking party to follow.

In Plato's *Symposium* Agathon's guests decided to proceed without a symposiarch and let each individual regulate his intake of wine on an individual basis. They then agreed on a subject for discussion and on an order of speakers.[90] But when Alcibiades arrived later, he appointed himself symposiarch ("ruler of the drinking party" [*archōn tēs poseōs*]) in order to dictate that the others drink more.[91] What this incident illustrates is the presupposition that there were duties normally attended to by the symposiarch, so that if there was no one filling that role, these matters had to be attended to in some other way.

The position of symposiarch, or its equivalent, is found to be present in the organization of clubs, as will be explored in chapter 5, as well as in other banquet settings. In the Roman period, however, whenever Plutarch was chosen to be symposiarch at one of the banquets he attended, the custom was called an "ancient" one that was in danger of being abandoned.[92] This suggests that it had become a less common practice, but that it was still well known as a traditional form of banquet organization.

When a symposiarch had been chosen, his first duty was to decide the proportions of the mixture of water to wine in the *krater,* or wine bowl, which had been brought in by the servants for this purpose.[93] He also decided what would be the sizes of the portions of wine to be served to the guests. A popular custom was to begin with small cups and conclude with larger ones.[94] Another custom was to take turns toasting one's neighbor or drinking to his health. The Romans called this "drinking in the Greek way."[95] In Plato's *Symposium* the procedure includes an encomium in praise of the neighbor to one's right: "it behooves me to praise my neighbor on the right."[96] In the context, this seems to represent a drinking rule added by Alcibiades in his role as self-appointed symposiarch. The passing of the cup would then serve as a sign of surrendering the speaking responsibility to the next in line.[97]

The Guest of Honor. The person occupying the highest position at table would be the guest of honor, and the other diners would be arranged according to rank to his right. The Romans designated the highest position to be that of the "consul," indicating in political terms its significance as a position of honor and authority. If an actual consul was not present, the person occupying that position would presumably inherit at least in a metaphorical sense the status implied by the title.

The Symposium and Entertainment at the Banquet

Various activities commonly took place at symposia, such as party games, dramatic entertainment, and philosophical conversation. A popular game was *kottabos,* whereby the last drops in the wine cup would be flung at a target in the middle of the room, with various prizes won or good-luck omens indicated for the one who successfully hit the target.[98] Indeed, it was so popular a sport that Theraphrastus complained that Greeks wasted most of their wine playing *kottabos* rather than drinking it.[99] Part of its appeal doubtless lay in its erotic overtones, since often the prize for a successful toss would be sexual favors.[100] Other games included riddles and various similar intellectual exercises to stimulate the conversation.[101] What is notable about all these games is the element of competition, a theme that inheres in the symposium for much of its history.[102]

The standard entertainment was provided by the flute girl, who was introduced to the gathering during or after the opening ceremonies of the symposium. A flute girl seems to be the most consistent feature of entertainment at a symposium, being included in virtually every pictorial representation of a symposium and mentioned in nearly every description.[103] Since flute girls and other entertainers were traditionally the only women allowed at a Greek symposium in the classical period, they tended to be considered as little more than harlots, and it is likely that many of them were.

However, Lucian's satirical treatment of the flute girl at a banquet is instructive. In his *Symposium,* in which he lampoons every literary convention of the symposium tradition, one of the revelers attempts to ravish the flute girl.[104] It is interesting that the activity is presented as another example of boorish manners. Indeed, the flute girl is presented as more victim than instigator. Nevertheless, the assumption in the satire appears to be that such activities were not uncommon. Certainly it was a literary and artistic convention to classify flute girls with harlots, and such stereotyping doubtless took place in real social situations as well.[105]

Although flute girls were often held in low esteem, we cannot conclude that all of them were harlots. Indeed, flute girls were also essential fixtures at any Greek sacrificial ceremony and thus played an important role in Greek religion as well. On this basis Plutarch argues that they were essential to the banquet: "The flute we could not drive away from the table if we wanted to; it is as essential to our libations as the garland, and it helps impart a religious tone to the singing of the paean."[106] He goes on to add, however, that while the flute can calm the soul, it can also rouse it if played with too much emotion.[107] Yet it is clear that the flute girl served an important role in society, even though her reputation had been sullied by innuendo and stereotyping.

Other entertainers at the symposium included dancers, acrobats, and various types of musicians. Also prominent in symposium tradition is the presentation of literary works, especially poetry. Indeed, L. E. Rossi has observed: "I have been persuaded for some time that all Archaic poetry composed for solo delivery, that is to say monodic poetry, was in origin intended for the *symposion.*"[108] The symposium thus provided the setting for the development of a significant form of Greek literature.

In Plato's *Symposium* the only entertainer was the flute girl, who was dismissed so that they might turn to conversation as their entertainment.[109] In

Xenophon's *Symposium* there were dancers and acrobats in addition to the flute girl. The closing entertainment was a mimic dance in which Dionysus and Ariadne were portrayed in a romantic interlude that aroused such intense desires in the banqueters that "those who were unwedded swore that they would take to themselves wives, and those who were already married mounted horse and rode off to their wives that they might enjoy them."[110]

The themes of drunkenness and prurient entertainment became stock features in various portrayals of symposia. Symposia in fact became infamous for extravagant and even bizarre behavior by entertainers and by the banqueters themselves. Various promiscuous and lewd activities became stock subjects for vase painters and were widely represented.[111] The images range from showing the diners being sexually teased to their actually sharing sexual favors. Their paramours are both female prostitutes (often the flute girls) and young boys. Clearly the erotic themes were well established in the symposium tradition, so that the vase paintings can be interpreted to represent both an idealization and an aspiration for the dinner party.[112] These themes were also taken up by various moralists and critics of society such as the satirists who exaggerated the decadent activities at symposia for effect.

What the vase paintings show is not the common practice at banquets in general but an idealization of the banquet as an aristocratic, elite institution in Greek imagination. Certainly some would aspire to emulate what the vase paintings picture, if they had the means. But much more common would be the use of the banquet for a variety of social interactions. Michael Jameson, for example, imagines the use of the dining room in the private house for such purposes as "farm and business deals, marriage negotiations, politics on the local level and relating to the numerous cult organizations to which Greek men belonged."[113]

Since a great emphasis was placed on drinking, drunkenness was naturally a common occurrence and was a convenient excuse for any otherwise abnormal behavior. Once more the archetypical example in the literary tradition is found in Plato's *Symposium*. Here Alcibiades plays the role of the drunken table companion, who arrives already drunk and exhibits bizarre behavior throughout the meal. Much later, in the Roman period, Plutarch refers to this incident as a standard example of drinking habits at the symposium, thus indicating how Plato's picture of Alcibiades had assumed status as an archetype.[114] Similarly, it is noteworthy that Plato's *Symposium* ends with the guests all drinking themselves into a stupor.[115] And in Lucian's satirical version of the philosophical symposium, which he represents as a gathering of eminent philosophers from every school, the festivities end in a drunken brawl.[116]

The Roman upper classes became especially infamous for their excesses at table.[117] The more austere among them, such as the elder Pliny, railed at the increasing decadence of the age.[118] Indeed, the drunkenness and gluttony connected with extravagant banquets had become such an issue in Roman society that sumptuary laws were passed specifying a limit to the amount of money that could be spent on individual banquets.[119] Nevertheless, complaints like Pliny's continued, especially from the satirists.

That excesses and prurient activities did take place frequently cannot be denied. But these should not be considered inherent to the meaning of the symposium. In fact, the ideal type of the symposium could also be stated in another form, for which once more the *Symposium* of Plato is a supreme example: "'Since it has been resolved, then,' said Eryximachus, 'that we are to drink only so much as each desires, with no constraint on any, I next propose that the flute girl who came in just now be dismissed: let her pipe to herself or, if she likes, to the women-folk within, but let us seek our entertainment today in conversation.'"[120] Here the ideal is an emphasis on light drinking, only a little light entertainment, and most of the time to be devoted to philosophical conversation.

Plutarch devoted one of his symposiac discussions to this passage from Plato. He interpreted this reference in Plato to be normative for philosophical banquets in general, for it emphasizes the unique combination of the serious and pleasurable that one is found in the ideal symposium setting.[121] Thus Plutarch defined the symposium in this way: "A dinner party is a sharing of earnest and jest, of words and deeds."[122]

Plutarch's definition implies an idealization of the institution of the symposium. A similar perception is alluded to by Athenaeus, when he describes the dinner parties of philosophical sects who came together "not that they should indulge in intemperance when they came together, but that they might carry out with decency and refinement the practices which accord with the idea of the symposium [*ta kata ton tou symposiou logon*]."[123] The "idea of the symposium" to which he refers is obviously an idealization that he interprets as being inherent in its definition. The tradition of the philosophical banquet, with its emphasis on conversation at table, is central to this definition.

Similarly, the infamous Roman *cena/convivium* is perhaps too often associated exclusively with the exaggerated extravagance pictured in the lengthy burlesque description of the banquet of Trimalchio in Petronius's *Satyricon*. There is also another tradition in Roman society, one in which the banquet was no less a social occasion but which was not marked by excessive extravagance. Even the elder Pliny continued his austere meals for two to three hours, thus evidently including pleasant conversation or other entertainment appropriate to his disposition and preference.[124]

Cicero provides a further example of this tradition in the Roman world:

> I have always had my club companions. . . . I used to dine with these
> companions—in an altogether moderate way, yet with a certain ardour
> appropriate to my age, which, as time goes on, daily mitigates my zest
> for every pleasure. Nor, indeed, did I measure my delight in these social
> gatherings more by the physical pleasure than by the pleasure of meet-
> ing and conversing with my friends. For our fathers did well in calling
> the reclining of friends [*epularem amicorum*] at feasts a *convivium,*
> because it implies a communion of life. . . . And every day I join my
> neighbors in a social meal which we protract as late as we can into the
> night with talk on varying themes.[125]

To be sure, Cicero is here contrasting the moderate feasts of his old age with the "immoderate banquets" *(immoderata epulae)*[126] that must have been more common. Yet he can nevertheless give the term *convivium* a noble meaning, suggesting that the term did not have for him the necessary connotation of "debauch" but could be used in an idealized sense. That idealization included the type of entertainment found at his *convivia*. That is, as was consistent with the tradition of the philosophical banquet, his *convivia* included elevated conversation at table that extended well into the night.

SPECIAL MEAL OCCASIONS

Much like what we do today, ancients tended to mark special events and rites of passage with banquets. For example, friends might be invited to celebrate a victory at an athletic or musical competition. Various festivals on the religious calendar would be marked not only with public feasts but also with private celebrations. Examples of celebratory banquets can be gleaned from Plutarch: "When Sarapion won the prize with the chorus he directed for the *phyle* Leontis, he entertained at a victory celebration at which I was present." "We were celebrating the victory of Sosicles of Corone, who had won the prize over all the poets at the Pythis." "On the occasion of a banquet during the festival of the Elaphebolia . . . we were entertained at dinner by Philo the physician."[127] Birthdays, weddings, and funerals were also occasions for festive meals.

The Birthday Banquet

Birthday celebrations included a set of religious rituals as well as a banquet. Individuals would celebrate not only their own birthdays, but also those of their dead relatives and patrons. In fact, in the Roman world the birthday commemoration was a regular part of the patronage system.[128] To celebrate a patron's birthday was a recognized means for the client to bestow honor on the patron. Horace even referred to the birthday of his patron as being "a solemn day for me and almost holier than my own birthday."[129]

The Wedding Banquet

The wedding banquet was a widely practiced nuptial celebration among Greeks and Romans.[130] Plutarch describes such an event in this way:

> Of all the occasions for a banquet, none is more conspicuous or talked about than a wedding. When we offer sacrifice to the gods, or honor a friend on the eve of a journey, or entertain guests from abroad, it is possible to do so unnoticed by many of our intimates and relatives; but a wedding-feast betrays us by the loud marriage cry, the torch, and the shrill pipe, things which according to Homer even the women stand at their doors to watch and admire. Consequently, since no one is unaware that we are receiving guests and must have invited them, we include all our relatives, acquaintances, and connections of any degree, because we are afraid to leave anyone out.[131]

The occasion for these observations is, in fact, Plutarch's celebration at the wedding of his son Autobulus.[132]

Among the Greeks, the wedding banquet could be given by the family of either the bride or the groom, or the two families could give the feast together.[133] It was expected to be an event that would showcase the family's status. In fact, the social pressures put on the celebrants sound strangely modern: "At their marriage men invite a crowd to the banquet so that there may be many witnesses to testify that the hosts themselves are of good family and that their brides come from good families."[134] So luxurious had these banquets become that by the end of the fourth century, Athens passed laws to limit to thirty the number of guests that could attend a wedding banquet.[135]

The menu could also get quite elaborate, but one item in particular seemed to be necessary at a wedding banquet: sesame cakes. This traditional food was thought to impart fertility to the couple, though all in attendance would also eat it.[136] The banquet was normally held at the home of the host, but such celebrations could also be held at sanctuaries.[137]

The wedding banquet was apparently like any other symposium with one major exception: the women of the family were expected to be present. They tended to be grouped together at their own tables apart from the men.[138] In Lucian's *Symposium,* for example, which is actually a wedding feast, the women occupy a couch to themselves.[139]

The wedding banquet came to be a stock motif in myth and literature. A favorite story among the Greeks was the myth of the wedding banquet of the Lapiths. This legendary tribe of humans had invited their distant relatives, the centaurs, who were half-horse and half-man. Befitting their status as part animal, the centaurs became drunk and began to force themselves on the Lapith womenfolk. A great battle ensued in which many centaurs were slaughtered. The Greeks loved this story so much that they often illustrated it on temple pediments, such as at the temple of Zeus at Olympia and the temple of Hephaestus at Athens.

Interestingly, this theme of strife at the wedding banquet recurred in many forms. Lucian's satyrical symposium, for example, which ended in a drunken brawl, was a wedding banquet. This may have become a popular literary motif because of the inherent sexual tension that was present at a banquet at which respectable women were present.

The Funerary Banquet

The Greek funeral consisted of three parts, the *prothesis,* or laying out of the body, the *ekphora,* or conveying of the body to the place of interment, and the deposition of the body, which could be by either inhumation or cremation.[140] After the *ekphora* came the *perideipnon,* or funerary banquet, which in the classical period took place in the home of the deceased. It was an occasion comparable to any other banquet, only in this case it was held in honor of the deceased. This is clear in a fragment from a Greek drama, in which a cook refers to his skills in making the funerary banquet a joyous occasion: "Whenever I turn my talents to the *perideipnon,* as soon as they come back from the *ekphora,* all in black, I take the lid off the pot and make the mourners smile; such a tickle runs through their tums—it's just like being at a wedding."[141]

A popular motif in funerary art in fourth-century Athens showed the deceased reclining at a banquet. This image is subject to three possible interpretations: (1) the deceased is shown enjoying table fellowship with the living at the funerary banquet, (2) the deceased is shown in a joyous afterlife characterized by a luxurious banquet, or (3) the deceased is idealized in a representation of the status he enjoyed in his lifetime. The most likely explanation is the last, that the deceased is being idealized as he wished to be remembered. Since these images show the deceased surrounded by the trappings of luxury and reclining on a couch in a position that fit his privileged station in life, a theme intensified by the fact that accompanying figures often included a wife who sat and servant who stood at the ready nearby, this explanation makes the most sense of the data. Furthermore, the Greeks did not have a sufficient sense for a sentient afterlife to suggest that they would have imagined a banquet in the hereafter.[142]

Rites at the tomb suggested that the dead were being invited to share in table fellowship with the living or, at least, were being fed. Here, the evidence is mixed. On the one hand, the food and drink offerings seem to have been intended for them to enjoy, as seen by the fact that some graves, both inhumation and cremation types, had pipes inserted so that the offering would reach the remains. These pipes have been referred to by scholars as "feeding tubes."[143]

On the other hand, the basic Greek belief was that the dead could no longer enjoy the pleasures of the living. Thus a fragment from a choral lament, perhaps meant for the symposium at a *perideipnon,* expresses the view that what distinguishes the dead from the living is especially the fact that they can no longer enjoy the pleasures of the table:

> Then he will lie in the deep-rooted earth
> and share no more in the symposion, the lyre,
> and the sweet cry of flutes.[144]

The same sentiment is expressed in a text from Theognis: "Nobody, when the earth once covers him and he descends to the darkness, the abode of Persephone, can rejoice in hearing either the lyre or the flute player, or be gladdened by the gifts of Dionysus. Knowing this, I follow my heart's desire while my limbs are yet nimble and I bear my head unshaken."[145] The funerary banquet *(perideipnon),* therefore, was an occasion in which the deceased was honored, but he was not considered to be present at the meal. As Murray concludes: "There existed in the Greek world a polarity, a more or less absolute distinction between the world of the *symposion* and the world of the dead."[146]

The same was not true for the Romans, where the evidence is much stronger that the dead were considered capable of receiving sustenance from the living. Roman burials more commonly contained the "feeding tubes" described above. And some elaborate tombs have been found in which kitchens were provided for the use of the celebrators who came to the tomb to enjoy a feast in memory of the deceased.[147]

Roman funerary ritual specified a series of feasts to be held in honor of the deceased: (1) The *silicernium* was eaten at the tomb on the day of the funeral. (2) The *cene novendialis* was a celebration to mark the end of the nine day period of mourning. (3) The *Parentalia* was a festival on the religious calendar in which families would visit the graves of dead relatives and have a feast there. (4) The *Lemuria* was another religious festival in which banquets in honor of the dead would be celebrated. (5) The *dies natalis,* or birthday of the deceased, was also celebrated yearly by friends and relatives with a banquet.[148]

The funerary societies of the Greeks and Romans existed for the purpose of providing proper burials and funerary banquets for their dues-paying membership. They will be studied more extensively in chapter 5.

SOCIAL CLASS AND STATUS AT THE BANQUET

The meal customs most commonly represented in our literature tend to be those of the aristocratic class. For example, as has already been noted, the custom of reclining was adopted from a context in which it was associated primarily with the posture of a ruler at table. It continued to carry this symbolism when applied to the Greek context, so that those who reclined tended to be associated with the ruling class. Thus the reclining posture was traditionally reserved for free citizens; women, children, and slaves were to sit when they ate.[149]

These customs are related to the fact that the symposium of the classical Greek period tended to be a celebration of aristocratic male culture. Consequently, respectable women were not a part of the gathering. If women were present, they would be either flute girls or *hetairai* (female companions or prostitutes). That is to say, they would have a subservient role, primarily one in which they were treated as sexual objects.[150] Indeed, one of the institutional features of the symposium tradition was the motif of violence against women.[151]

Yet there were variations on this theme, instances in which women are found at banquets in roles other than those of sexual subservience. Joan

Burton has traced a pattern of inroads in Greek culture through the centuries.[152] She points out the existence of female members of the Pythagorean societies, the Pythagorikai, in the Archaic period in Greece.[153] In the fifth century, we have instances of Athenian women attending banquets with their husbands. There is also the case of Aspasia, a woman who began as a *hetaira,* or courtesan, but progressed to the point that she became famous in the literature as a female who could spar intellectually with men at symposia.[154] Thus by the Hellenistic period, though we have few records to go on, there is a likelihood that respectable women could be found more and more at symposia, especially since this was a period in which women were receiving greater rights and public visibility in Hellenistic culture.[155]

These developments are reflected in late republican Rome as well. By the first century c.e. there is evidence that respectable women of the Roman aristocratic class were increasingly to be found at banquets and would often recline.[156] This represented a change from the well-known earlier custom, identical to that of the Greeks, in which women did not normally appear at the banquet, and when they did, they sat. This is noted as a change in customary behavior in the first century b.c.e. by Cornelius Nepos:

> On the other hand, many actions are seemly according to our code which the Greeks look upon as shameful. For instance, what Roman would hesitate to take his wife to a dinner party? What matron does not frequent the front rooms of her dwelling and show herself in public? But it is very different in Greece; for there a woman is not admitted to a dinner party, unless relatives only are present, and she keeps to the more retired part of the house called "the woman's apartment."[157]

By the second century c.e., however, the inclusion of women at dinner parties appears to have become more acceptable in the Greek world as well. At Lucian's *Symposium,* which was a wedding feast, and thus an occasion when women would be expected to be present, the women "occupied" their own couch: "On the right as you enter, the women occupied the whole couch, as there were a good many of them, with the bride among them, very scrupulously veiled and hedged in by the women. Toward the back door came the rest of the company according to the esteem in which each was held. Opposite the women, the first was Eucritus. . . ."[158] Whether these women were reclining or sitting is not clear, but since they occupied a couch, it is likely that they were reclining. Reclining would also be appropriate since it was considered especially accommodating for a large number who share a couch.

On the other hand, whenever an uninvited guest arrives late to Lucian's banquet, since all the couches are taken, he is offered a place to sit. He is insulted and refuses on the grounds that such a posture is "womanish and weak" *(gynaikeion kai malthakon)*.[159] Rather, he elects to recline on the floor. Here, sitting versus reclining at a meal is clearly interpreted as indicative of social rank, and the ancient designation of women as representative of those at the bottom of the social ladder is invoked. Whether Lucian intended to picture the women at this particular banquet as reclining or sitting is not entirely clear, however.

This allusion to the traditional subservient position of women at the banquet, at a time when customs had apparently begun to change, points out how practice and tradition may sometimes be at odds. Whether women had a position of equality at the table, therefore, is an issue in which the difference between literary idealization and historical reconstruction must be carefully weighed. In addition, the idea that a woman who attends banquets can by definition be considered a prostitute is found throughout the Greco-Roman period. This means that a "respectable" woman might attend a banquet, but in certain contexts she could still be in danger of being condemned for her actions.[160]

Because reclining was a posture that required that one be served, it tended to be associated with a class that owned servants. Consequently, servants were, in a sense, as much a part of the "furniture" of a reclining banquet as were the couches or mattresses for reclining. Usually the host provided all of the servants for the meal,[161] but there are examples of situations where individuals brought their own servants who then stood behind them and administered to their needs.[162]

Those who reclined at a banquet, therefore, indicated thereby their status in society-at-large. Yet there were still distinctions of status among the recliners themselves, indicated especially by the ranking order of the guests, since different values were assigned to the positions around the table. The locations of these rankings appear to have differed among Greeks and Romans,[163] but their existence was a given at any formal meal. Thus the issue of status was a problem that had to be resolved at every meal, either by assigning positions according to some standard of ranking within society, thus inviting possible jealousies and hard feelings at what should be a pleasurable event,[164] or by attempting to do away with rankings altogether. The latter option would not automatically solve the problem, since some would be insulted if they did not receive their due recognition.[165] Consequently, the question of status and ranking among the guests appears to lie behind many of the disputes at meals and called for rules and regulations to create a more orderly environment.

Differing status could be designated at meals in other ways. In some cases, a larger portion was designated to an honored member of a meal community. For example, a worshipper might be honored with a special portion at a sacrificial meal as a reward or honor.[166] But sometimes status among guests would be indicated by the host, who would serve a lower quality of food or wine to those whom he considered to be of a lower rank. Although this appears to have been a widespread practice in the Roman period, it was roundly condemned by various moralists of the time.

For example, Martial frequently complains about being served a lesser fare as one who is at the table as a client of his patron, the host:

> Since I am asked to dinner, no longer, as before, a purchased guest [i.e., client], why is not the same dinner served to me as to you? You take oysters fattened in the Lucrine lake, I suck a mussel through a hole in the shell; you get mushrooms, I take hog funguses; you tackle turbot, but I brill. Golden with fat, a turtledove gorges you with its bloated rump; there is set before me a magpie that has died in its cage. Why do I dine without you, although, Ponticus, I am dining with you? The dole has gone: let us have the benefit of that; let us eat the same fare.[167]

Here it should be noted that although Martial relates an experience that must have been all too common in the Roman world, he can nevertheless present a moral argument in opposition to this custom that also is derived from meal tradition.

Similarly, Pliny describes a meal at which the host provided food to his guests according to their status, with those of a higher status receiving the best.[168] He notes that it is better to share the same fare so that the guests may be true dining companions *(convictores)*[169] not divided according to rank but sharing an equal table.[170] His companion points out that he often shares in the same fare as his lower-class guests for the sake of economy. Pliny, however, rebukes the economic argument and counsels sharing of the finer fare: "Believe me, if you restrain your greedy instincts, it is no strain on your finances to share with several others the fare you have yourself." He warns against "being taken in by this extravagance under guise of economy which is to be found at the table in certain homes."[171]

Both Martial and Pliny, therefore, can be seen to be reflecting aspects of common meal etiquette even as they argue against prevailing customs.

These traditions of banquet ethics and etiquette will be discussed further in chapter 3.

Finally, the question naturally arises whether the banquet customs outlined here could only have applied to the upper classes in the Greco-Roman world. Certainly many aspects of these customs were more appropriate to the upper classes, such as the necessity of servants or even the leisure time to devote to a long evening meal. Yet I would still argue that the banquet served as the model for any social class that wished to participate in a ceremonial or celebrative meal of some kind.[172] Thus such features as the division of the meal into courses, the connection of entertainment with the symposium course, the question of status, and the custom of reclining itself—all were particulars of the institution of the banquet that tended to accompany it at whatever level of society it was found. Plutarch refers to the ubiquity of banquet customs when he notes: "After dinner even common, unliterary people allow their thoughts to wander to other pleasures, as far away as possible from the concerns of the body. They take up conundrums and riddles, or the Names and Numbers game."[173]

CONCLUSION

This chapter has outlined the basic meal customs of the Greco-Roman world as defined in Greek and Roman literature, art, and archaeology. These customs form the basis for the practice of the Greco-Roman banquet throughout the culture. Some items, such as the menu, will obviously change, but the basic model will remain the same. In the next chapter we will see how the banquet was given ideological underpinnings in the philosophical banquet tradition.

THE PHILOSOPHICAL
BANQUET

"To consign to utter oblivion all that occurs at a drinking-party is not only opposed to what we call the friend-making character of the dining table, but also has the most famous of the philosophers to bear witness against it—Plato, Xenophon, Aristotle, Speusippus, Epicurus, Prytanis, Hieronymous, and Dio of the Academy, who all considered the recording of conversations held at table a task worth some effort."
—Plutarch, *Quaest. conv.* 612D–E.

"At the entertainments which it was the custom of us young men to hold at Athens at the beginning of each week, as soon as we had finished eating and an instructive and pleasant conversation had begun . . ."
—Gell., *NA* 7.13.12.

When analyzing the data for ancient meals, it is always appropriate to ask, "Is it real or is it fictional?" The above quotation from Plutarch is found in a context in which he is purportedly presenting conversations at actual meals in which he participated. Yet when he reports such events, he does so in conscious imitation of the literary genre of the symposium, as he tells us here in so many words. Consequently, while there may be some real data here, it is clearly couched in the form of an idealization.

This is found to be true in most of our data. As in Plutarch, even if real meals are being reported, there is a tendency to idealize them according to the literary traditions of the symposium. Furthermore, there is no need for a real meal to stand behind a literary symposium. For example, Plutarch himself wrote a first-person account of a banquet of the seven sages (*Convivium septem sapientium*). Since the seven sages were largely legendary figures and Plutarch dates this meal three hundred years prior to his own time, he is clearly utilizing the literary genre of the symposium in a fictional mode.[1] A similar device is used in his *Quaestiones convivales* (or "Table Talk"), where he also writes from the perspective of a participant at the meals, but here he describes them as having taken place in his own time and place with his friends and family in attendance. Certainly it is fair to say that many of these discussions may have taken place in one form or another at actual meals.[2] But the form in which he recorded them is clearly an idealization of himself and his friends that he wrote according to the conventions of the genre as he understood it. In fact, he wrote these dialogues to serve as examples of "proper" meal conversation.[3] That is, they were to serve as models for conducting actual symposia. Similar qualifications would apply to meal descriptions in other genres. For example, the symposium form is used by satirists, but this by no means implies that actual meals lie behind the satirized descriptions.

We therefore have two interrelated phenomena that go by the name "symposium." On the one hand, there is the symposium as social institution, in which actual meals were conducted according to a social pattern of codes and customs. On the other hand, there is the symposium as literary form, in which meals, particularly those of the famous philosophers, were idealized according to established literary patterns and topoi. Distinguishing where one begins and the other leaves off calls for exercising extreme care and subtlety in reading the data.

Furthermore, the interrelation of these phenomena is quite complex. As has already been mentioned, the reporting of meals tended to assume the literary form of the symposium as a matter of course—that was simply the way one talked about meals in written form. Thus we cannot expect to find any descriptions of ancient meals that do not partake of this idealization. In addition, oral and written data of genres other than the symposium can be found to have been influenced by that form when discussing meals. For example, even such varied sets of data as rules of conduct at club banquets and the order of the liturgy at the Jewish Passover exhibit the influence of the symposium form.

It must also be acknowledged that the symposium as literary form is itself a reflection of the form and associated values of the symposium as social institution. Thus even the idealized record of a meal can be used to reconstruct actual meal practices. One must be careful, of course, not to read a literary idealization as if it is an anthropological description. But one can nevertheless trust that a commonplace idealization of a meal does reflect accepted views as to what is "proper" for one to practice at one's own meals. Furthermore, it is also apparent that the literary form tended to have a reverse effect and be read as a kind of "model" for how an ideal meal should be conducted.

In order to sort out this complex data, I will first summarize the basic motifs and topoi of the symposium genre. Then I will discuss the philosophical banquet as a social institution. Finally, I will note the importance of the philosophical banquet and philosophical discussions of meal etiquette in defining the basic patterns of the social code of meals in the ancient world.

THE SYMPOSIUM AS A LITERARY GENRE

The symposium genre was highly popular and influential far beyond philosophical circles. It enjoyed a long period of popularity extending from at least the sixth century B.C.E. to the medieval period and beyond. It was adapted for use in satire, in Jewish writings imitative of the genre, and even in the earliest form of the liturgy for the Jewish Passover. Aspects of the genre lie behind meal descriptions and allusions in all of ancient literature, including especially Jewish and Christian writings of the period of this study.

The most influential single pieces representative of the genre are the symposia of Plato and Xenophon, both of which present a meal as the setting for a dialogue of Socrates. When allusions are made to specific works of the genre, invariably one or both of these are mentioned. In many cases, however, there are not explicit references to the genre. Rather, one finds allusions and various literary forms derived from the genre that testify to its pervasive influence on any literary efforts to speak of meals, real or imagined.

In a classic study of the symposium genre, Josef Martin identified stock characters and stock motifs that can be traced throughout symposium literature.[4] The stock characters included the host, the jester, the uninvited guest, the physician, the late-arriving guest, the whiner, the insulted guest, the heavy drinker, and the pair of lovers. Among the stock motifs was the use of a quarrel or contest as a topos on which to build the narrative. Martin's study reminds us that the genre tended to occur in a narrative format. The motifs of the genre, however, could occur in a variety of forms. That is to say, the symposium narrative became embedded in the culture and profoundly influenced meal practices as well as literary descriptions throughout the period of this study.

THE SYMPOSIUM AS A SOCIAL INSTITUTION

The term *symposium* was simply another name for the banquet, although it tended to emphasize the latter part of the banquet, the drinking party during which the entertainment of the evening would be presented. The term therefore came to represent the event as a whole in its aspect as social entertainment. Indeed, if it is the banquet that carries the primary symbolism of meals, it is the symposium that carries the primary symbolism of the banquet. Here were found those activities for which the Greco-Roman banquet became famous.

The philosophical symposium was the best-known subcategory of the institution. Though it partook of all of the normal characteristics, it also added its own features and motifs. Indeed, it was the tradition of the philosophical symposium that refined this institution and made of it a significant bearer of Greek culture.

As has already been mentioned, the literary genre of the symposium is largely connected with the philosophical tradition and, in fact, functions to idealize the social gatherings of philosophers. Nevertheless, it appears that the symposium was also an actual social institution utilized as a normal feature of the philosophical schools. As such, it especially emphasized the utilization of the symposium as a time for philosophical discourse.

PHILOSOPHICAL DISCOURSE AT THE SYMPOSIUM

When philosophers and those of their circles gathered for banquets, they sought for their entertainment not the usual party games and prurient activities, but rather chose to be entertained by uplifting conversation on an appropriate subject in which everyone could participate. At least, that is the way they preferred to think of their meals. Indeed, the philosophical discourse at the symposium is the predominate motif in the symposium genre. The archetype for this pattern is often taken to be the symposium of Socrates himself as described by Plato:

> "Since it has been resolved then," said Eryximachus, "that we are to drink only so much as each desires, with no constraint on any, I next propose that the flute-girl who came in just now be dismissed: let her pipe to herself or, if she likes, to the women-folk within, but let us seek our entertainment today in conversation."[5]

This pattern prevails throughout the history of the symposium genre. Furthermore, there is abundant evidence that it also served as a model for the conducting of actual meals.

Athenaeus provides us with a useful description of the phenomenon and its perceived justification:

There are in the city [Athens] meetings of many philosophic sects— . Diogenists, Antipatrists, so-called, and Panaetiasts. Theophrastus even bequeathed money for a meeting of this character, not—Heaven forbid!—that they should indulge in intemperance when they came together, but that they might carry out with decency and refinement the practices which accord with the idea of the symposium.[6]

Here he not only describes this as a general practice of philosophical groups, but also defines succinctly the values and social patterns and customs they associated with these meals. The phrase "the idea of the symposium" *(ta kata ton tou symposiou logon)* is especially important here. It expresses the sense that there was a clearly defined ideal type of the proper symposium that was utilized as a pattern for philosophical banquets. Furthermore, the values connected with that ideal type are defined as "decency and refinement" as opposed to the uncontrolled behavior that might be characteristic of banquets elsewhere.

The "idea of the symposium," which defined proper behavior at a banquet, was elaborated in much detail in philosophical discussions about etiquette and ethics at the meal. Among the subjects discussed was that of proper conversation at the banquet.

THE ETHICS OF SYMPOSIUM CONVERSATION

Choosing a Topic

Plutarch defined proper symposium conversation in two ways. First, the topics selected must be appropriate to the occasion. Second, the conversations themselves must be conducted in the proper manner. The overall standard in both cases was the definition of the meal itself; that is, the communal function of the meal served as the basis for defining proper conversation.

He labeled those topics considered suitable for symposium discussions *symposiaka* or "symposiac topics." Within that category were those topics that were specifically concerned with the "proper business of drinking parties"[7] or the details of the symposium setting itself. He labeled these *sympotika* or "sympotic topics." Under this category were listed topics concerned with meal etiquette, such as "whether philosophy is a fitting topic for conversation at a drinking-party" (1.1) or "whether the host should arrange the placing of his guests or leave it to the guests themselves" (1.2).

Symposiac topics, on the other hand, would include such issues as "whether the hen or the egg came first" (2.3), "what is the reason why alpha stands first in the alphabet" (9.2), or "whether it is more plausible that the total number of stars is even than that it is odd" (9.12). These types of questions are described as "possess[ing] an attractive theme more suitable to the moment than pipe and lyre." They are of the category of pleasurable diversions and are suitable for the banquet to the extent that they contribute to the general "pleasure" *(hēdonē)* of the occasion.

As Plutarch goes on to say, "some dinner and symposium preparations . . . rank as necessities. . . . Others are diversions introduced for pleasure's sake, and no essential function attaches to them."[8] Examples of necessities are wine, food, couches, and tables, while examples of pleasures are music, spectacles, and jesters, such as Philip the buffoon in Xenophon's *Symposium.* As the argument proceeds, certain philosophical topics concerned with meal etiquette are equated with the category of necessities, but even the pleasurable topics are deemed acceptable.

A similar perception of suitable topics for a meal discussion was presented by Aulus Gellius. At the table of Taurus the philosopher, the topics chosen for discussion were often concerned with the affairs of the meal. On one occasion Plato's view of drunkenness was discussed in reference to the issue of how much drinking is advised for the banqueters.[9] Another topic of discussion that arose from the setting was "why oil congeals often and readily, wine seldom, vinegar hardly ever."[10]

But other more general topics were also chosen for their appropriateness to the occasion. The conversation was to be "instructive and pleasant."[11] Thus: "The questions, however, were neither weighty nor serious, but certain neat but trifling problems, which would pique a mind enlivened with wine."[12] He gives as examples of such "playful subtlety" *(subtilitatis ludicrae)* these questions: "When did a dying man die—when he was already in the grasp of death or while he still lived? And when did a rising man rise—when he was already standing or while he was still seated? And when did one who was learning an art become an artist—when he already was one, or when he was still learning?"[13] Although these questions were viewed by many of the banqueters as "pointless and idle sophisms," Taurus reminded them that they in fact had been seriously debated by philosophers such as Plato himself.[14]

Thus a careful balance was proposed between the instructive and the pleasant. Topics were to be of a light and entertaining character such as was appropriate for those who were drinking, but they were nevertheless to be sufficiently serious that philosophical minds could still be properly exercised. Taurus referred to such conversation as the *tragēmatia* or the very "dessert" course itself.[15] Plutarch had made a similar statement a generation earlier: "At parties men of wit and taste hurry at once after dinner to ideas as if to dessert, finding their entertainment in conversation."[16]

Conducting a Discussion Correctly

Plutarch emphasized maintaining a balance between entertainment and serious discussion. When discussing the topic "whether philosophy is a fitting topic for conversation at a drinking-party,"[17] the objection was raised that it was not fitting on the grounds that "philosophy is not a suitable thing to make sport with and . . . we are not on these occasions inclined to seriousness."[18] In the ensuing dialogue, both Crato and Plutarch speak in opposition to this view, but both concede at the outset the special nature of the symposium setting.

Crato argues that philosophy is the "art of life" and is therefore properly present at all "amusement and pleasure" since it contributes even here "the qualities of proportion and fitness." Indeed, since the wine is known to make one more talkative, it is ridiculous to exclude "the best conversations."[19]

Plutarch argues that a good philosopher can adapt his discussion to the setting "so long as it does not transgress propriety," for "the height of sagacity is to talk philosophy without seeming to do so, and in jesting to accomplish all that those in earnest could."[20] He then defines other types of *sympotika* or drinking-party topics:

> Some are supplied by history; others it is possible to take from current events; some contain many lessons [*paradeigmata*] bearing on philosophy, many on piety; some induce an emulous enthusiasm for courageous and great-hearted deeds. If one makes unobtrusive use of them to entertain and instruct his companions as they drink [*diapaidagōgein tous pinontas*], not the least of the evils of intemperance will be taken away.[21]

Thus, in the setting of a symposium, the philosopher is to make his comments in an entertaining fashion, using interesting examples from events of the past or present. But his goal is not only to entertain but also to instruct; for Plutarch this always means to provide lessons in moral philosophy. Thus the end result should be to "induce an emulous enthusiasm for courageous and great-hearted deeds and . . . charitable and humane deeds."[22]

Plutarch enlarges on his definition of proper philosophical conversation in another section of his *Quaestiones convivales*. Here he emphasizes that it should be "orderly and profitable" *(tetagmenōs kai ōphelimōs)* as opposed to "conversation that drifts about randomly and foolishly at a party." The latter is "vinous babbling," that is, "engaging in empty and frivolous conversation." Thus, "The outcome of undisciplined chatter and frivolity, when it reaches the extreme of intemperance, is violence and drunken behavior—an outcome wholly inconsistent with culture and refinement."[23]

Orderly conversation for Plutarch, then, has purpose, accomplishes something, and is organized around a suitable topic such as those he suggests. It models itself on the philosophical dialogue. In addition, it is "profitable"; that is, it has "something speculative [and] some instruction in it."[24]

THE THEORETICAL BASIS OF MEAL ETHICS

Koinōnia

One of the central concepts defining the theoretical basis for meal ethics is *koinōnia* or "sharing," which refers in a larger sense to the communal nature of the meal situation itself. For example, Plutarch uses this concept in discussing proper conversation at the meal. Here he argues that the topics chosen should be simple enough that all can take part in their discussion, even the less intellectual of the guests.[25] In this argument, he refers to "the fellowship of the drinking party" *(hē sympotikē koinōnia)*[26] as basic to the definition of a symposium and to the ethics of the meal. By this term he means the sharing of food, drink, and entertainment that is at the heart of the meal occasion.

Plutarch argues from the general to the particular using external examples of sharing; the values demonstrated in the examples are the same that should define conversation: "For just as the bodies of men who are drinking are accustomed to sway in time with pantomimic and choral dancing . . . just so their spirits are harmoniously and profitably stirred by subjects of inquiry that are easy to handle."[27] Another analogy is the common sharing from the wine bowl: "Indeed, just as the wine must be common to all, so too the conversation must be one in which all will share" *(hōs ton oinon koinon . . . kai ton logon)*.[28] If the conversation is not shared in by all, but everyone discusses his own individual interests, "gone then is the aim and end of the good fellowship *(koinōnias)* of the party, and Dionysus is outraged."[29] In other words, the essence of commensality, of the meaning of sharing wine together, is violated if the conversation is not shared as well. And such "good fellowship" is seen as inherent in the gift of wine as intended by its giver, the god of wine, Dionysus.

Elsewhere the operative symbol is the sharing from a common food platter, so that whenever this symbol is not present, that is, whenever individual portions are served to each diner, then "companionship perishes" *(apollytai to koinon)*.[30] According to the logic of this argument, to divide the food into individual portions is to "create many dinners and many diners." Thus no one is a "fellow-diner" *(syndeipnos)* with anyone.[31]

Friendship
The communal nature of the meal was also affirmed by reference to the idea of friendship, a category that was basic to ancient philosophical discussions of social ethics. A variety of terms were used in meal texts to refer to this category, compound words formed from *philos,* "friend," such as *philia, philophrosynē,* and other related terms. Plutarch, for example, refers often to what he calls "the friend-making character of the table" *(to philopoion tēs trapezēs)*.[32] For him, a communal meal is more than just the satisfying of hunger—it is a time for making friends: "A guest comes to share not only meat, wine, and dessert, but conversation, fun, and the amiability that leads to friendship *(philophrosynē)*." One who shares only the food has been a "fellow-diner only with the stomach, not with the mind."[33]

Here again the metaphor of the sharing of food and drink defines the relationships. But also operative in the definition is the notion that the essence of a proper formal meal is the bond of friendship that it creates. Here, as elsewhere in Greek philosophy, friendship functions as an ethical term.[34] Indeed, the definition of meal ethics according to the principle of friendship is found as early as Plato, who states that the goal of the so-called symposium laws is to make the participants in a banquet friends rather than enemies.[35] In the context of the meal, then, friendship defines the nature of the participants' social obligation toward one another.

Pleasure
Another category for defining relationships at the meal is the concept of "pleasure" *(hēdonē)*. The meal provides pleasure for everyone present, and thus activities and behavior should be conducted in such a way that pleasure is shared by all. Here pleasure would function to define ethical behavior at the meal.

AN ETHICAL ARGUMENT OBSERVED

An example from Plutarch illustrates the discussion of meal etiquette on the basis of standard ethical principles. The topic for the discourse is "whether the host should arrange the placing of his guests or leave it to the guests themselves."[36]

The setting is a meal given by Plutarch's brother Timon, to which a full quota of guests had been invited. Although the guests represent a variety of levels of status in society, Timon invites them to recline where they wish. When a foreigner arrives and sees the guests so arranged, he immediately leaves because he sees no place remaining worthy of his honor. This event provides the topic for the discussion during the symposium, that is, "after the dinner had come to an end."[37] Here there is an incidental nature to the selection of the topic for discussion, since it arises out of an issue presented by the situation of the meal itself. This method of selecting topics was a regular motif in symposium literature and a particular favorite of Plutarch's.[38]

Plutarch's father, Autobulus, introduces the topic of the evening by defending the old custom of "assigning to each person his suitable position."[39] This custom belonged to a meal characterized by "good order" *(hē eutaxia),* and good order was a necessity for "the most pleasurable of dinner parties" *(to symposion hēdiston).*[40] Here good order is the primary virtue based on the ethical principle of pleasure.

Timon counters with his own definition of what makes a meal friendly and pleasurable. In the first place, for the host to assign the positions at table makes him a "judge over his friends," which serves to "annoy" rather than "entertain" the guests. He is no longer a host, but a judge, and his friends find themselves treated as if they are in a contest rather than at a dinner party. "[This is] he who, instead of playing the host, makes himself a juryman and a judge over people who do not call upon him to decide an issue and are not on trial as to who is better than who, or worse; for they have not entered a contest, but have come for dinner."[41]

In addition, Timon continues, to judge among the guests only encourages their vanity. This too is contrary to the concept of meal fellowship, since the host "refurbishes a vanity which I think much more fitting for men to have washed from their soul than the mud from their feet, if they are to meet and drink with each other easily and without affectation."[42] In place of vanity and rivalry, he proposes equality at the meal: "If in other matters we are to preserve equality [*hē isotēs*] among men, why not begin with this first and accustom them to take their places with each other without vanity and ostentation, because they understand as soon as they enter the door that the dinner is a democratic affair and has no outstanding place like an acropolis where the rich man is to recline and lord it over meaner folk?"[43] In Timon's argument, then, the principle of friendship calls for equality at the meal.

The third argument Plutarch states is his own, in which he plays the role of mediator.[44] Whenever one is entertaining "young men, fellow citizens, and intimates," one should let them choose their places. But when one is "engaged in learned talk" with "foreigners or magistrates or older men," one should yield to "custom and usage" *(synētheia kai nomos)*.[45] His authority for "custom and usage" turns out to be a selection of quotations from the *Iliad* and the *Odyssey* in which a meal includes an assigned place at table and in which the gods take specified positions at table. Thus he uses literary stereotypes to define "custom."

The final argument is by Lamprias, Plutarch's other brother.[46] He argues that the placing of guests should be determined not by prestige but by "pleasure" *(to hēdy)*. Accordingly, guests should be placed together who have something in common or who will be agreeable to one another, and guests should be separated if they are contentious. In his words: "For it is not prestige, but pleasure which must determine the placing of guests; it is not the rank of each which must be considered, but the affinity and suitability of each to each, as is done when other things are associated for a common purpose."[47]

This discussion about the meal setting presupposes that positions at table always carry a connotation of relative ranking. Custom dictates that these rankings be determined especially by civic status. "For the man of quality does not have his honor and his station in the world, yet fails to receive recognition in the place he occupies at dinner."[48] Such a ranking at the meal belonged to an individual as his right; it was his "customary honor."[49]

Individuals were to be judged as to their relative status according to their "age," "political office," or "some other similar distinction."[50] In addition, "foreigners"[51] were given special distinction, "relatives" could be honored, and "fame" was singled out.[52] Such distinctions and honors were considered essential to the makeup of cultured society, and the banquet normally functioned within society to buttress its view of status.[53]

What Timon proposed in opposition was that the meal gathering should be considered separate from other institutions of society. For whenever one assigns positions by civic status, one "transfers empty fame from market place and theater to the dinner party."[54] Rather, the meal community should function according to its own rules and not those of society-at-large. Accordingly, one should symbolically enter a new community when one crosses the threshold of the dining room ("immediately upon entering the door").[55] Likewise one should symbolically wash away the values of society with the ceremony of washing the feet at the beginning of the meal ("it is more fitting to wash vanity from the soul than mud from the feet").[56] The principle by which this community is to be governed in its social relationships is the same that Plutarch himself invoked, that is, "friendship."[57] However, in this case friendship is interpreted to signify equality in social relationships, that is, where the rich do not lord it over the poor.[58]

MEAL ETHICS AND EPICUREAN PHILOSOPHY

The image of a community existing separately from society, forming itself according to the ethical principles of friendship and pleasure, and realizing this communal identity especially in a banquet setting is strongly reminiscent of Epicureanism. The followers of Epicurus formed themselves into communities separate from society. In these Epicurean "cells" participation in politics was discouraged, as was any seeking after civic status or wealth, and membership was open to various levels of society, notably women and slaves.[59] The founding principle of these communities was "friendship" *(philia)*, which was defined as the basis of a social ethic among like-minded individuals. The joys of this friendship were especially celebrated at communal banquets, which were customarily held once a month as designated in the will of Epicurus himself. It would appear, therefore, that Epicureanism may have been quite influential in the discussion of meal ethics in popular philosophy of the first and second centuries C.E. and should be examined more closely.

The "will" of Epicurus is found in Diogenes Laertius. The section providing for a memorial banquet states: "And from the revenues . . . let them . . . make separate provision . . . for the customary celebration of my birthday on the tenth day of Gamelion in each year, and for the meeting of all my School held every month on the twentieth day to commemorate Metrodorus and myself according to the rules now in force."[60] These monthly banquet meetings continued to be practiced in the first century C.E.[61]

The ethical thought of Epicurus was especially developed from the concepts of "friendship" *(philia)* and "pleasure" *(hēdonē)*. Epicurus was well known in the Greek world for his view of pleasure as the end of life and as the highest good. That view is stated succinctly as follows: "We say that pleasure is the beginning and end of the blessed life, for this we know is the first and kindred good."[62] This idea was often vilified and ridiculed, and Epicurus contributed to this attitude by often stating his philosophy in harsh terms. For example: "The beginning and root of all good is the pleasure of the belly; even wisdom and culture must be referred to this."[63] Here he is evidently talking about pleasure primarily in its negative sense, as in *ataraxia* or "lack of anxiety."[64] He saw this as basic to human nature, since one's first impulses are toward satisfaction of hunger and thirst.[65] And, since there can be no pleasure until these basic needs are gratified, then "the pleasure of the belly" is indeed the root of all pleasure. The issue here is not freedom from pain per se but rather "a right attitude to bodily feelings."[66]

Epicurus also spoke of other forms of pleasure as only "variations" on the basic pleasure: "Pleasure in the flesh admits no increase when once the pain of want has been removed; after that it only admits of variation."[67] In other words, there are not higher forms or more perfect pleasures; basic pleasure cannot be improved upon. But basic pleasure in this context is probably to be understood in negative terms, and its variations are the positive expressions of pleasure. These are the terms he uses when he speaks of "static" and "active" pleasure: "Peace of mind and freedom from pain are pleasures which imply a state of rest; joy and delight are seen to consist in motion and activity."[68] Here he defines static pleasure in negative terms, as it applies both to the body ("freedom from pain") and to the mind ("peace of mind"). Active pleasure is defined in positive terms, *joy (chara)* and *delight* or *festive joy (euphrosynē)*. These latter terms appear to refer specifically to the mind, but Epicurus's system is such that they surely must refer to the body as well.[69]

These categories of pleasure are defined further when they are subsumed under a discussion of "desires":

> Of our desires some are natural and necessary; others are natural, but not necessary; others, again, are neither natural nor necessary, but are due to illusory opinion. ([The scholiast[70] adds:] Epicurus regards as natural and necessary desires which bring relief from pain, as, e.g., drink when we are thirsty; while by natural and not necessary he means those which merely diversify the pleasure without removing the pain, as, e.g., costly viands; by the neither natural nor necessary he means desires for crowns and the erection of statues in one's honor.)[71]

It is notable that in this interpretation of Epicurus, meal experiences are utilized as examples for acceptable desires, whereas unacceptable desire is that for public acclaim.

In many ways the Epicurean banquet offered a unique microcosm of all that was basic to the philosophical system of Epicurus, for here one experienced "static" pleasure, or the satisfaction of basic needs, as well as the variations of pleasure, "joy" *(chara)* and "festive joy" *(euphrosynē)*. These aspects of pleasure at the banquet were not meant to imply that the concept of pleasure as the highest good was to be defined as "unbroken succession of drinking-bouts and of revelry," but rather it was to be defined as "sober reasoning."[72]

Consequently, the Epicurean gatherings were called both "joyous feasting" and "philosophizing together" in this revealing description of an Epicurean banquet from the first century B.C.E.:[73]

> Nor to those who toil in anxiety[74] but those who keep in mind the ideal forms of the perfect and perfectly blessed beings must be invited to enjoy the feast and laugh like the others, indeed all those who are part of the household, and not at all omitting any of the outsiders who are well-disposed to the teachings of Himself [Epicurus] and his friends. For our doing this is not for the purpose of winning an empty and unnatural popular leadership, but, acting in accordance with the basic laws of nature, we hereby bring to remembrance all those who are well-disposed to us so that they might celebrate together with us those rites which are proper for those who philosophize together so as to attain blessedness.

Here "enjoy the feast and laugh" functions as a description of the banquet. The term *to laugh* is used elsewhere in Epicurus as one of many synonyms for "pleasure." For example, there is a famous saying of Epicurus as follows: "it is necessary to laugh and to do philosophy together."[75] The idea is that for Epicurus, if the goal of philosophical speculation is pleasure, then the process of doing philosophy is itself a pleasure. Conversely, when the community "celebrate[s] those rites which are proper for those who philosophize together," it does so in the same spirit, by placing the philosophical discourse in the setting of a festive meal.

Here is also to be found a sense of community exclusivity vis-à-vis the outside world. Those who are invited to the meal are "those of the household" as opposed to "the outsiders," although the latter are allowed to participate if they are sympathetic to the teachings of Epicurus. In addition, participation in the community is explicitly contrasted with participation in the political order of the day ("not for the purpose of winning an empty and unnatural popular leadership").[76] Indeed, Epicurus advised against participation in politics and society precisely because it could not guarantee the "security" it seemed to assure.

The reason for seeking public acclaim or wealth could be explained as a search for "security from fellow men" as in this example from Epicurus's *Basic Doctrines:*

> Some men have sought to become famous and renowned, thinking that thus they would make themselves secure against their fellow-men. If,

then, the life of such persons really was secure, they attained natural good; if, however, it was insecure, they have not attained the end which by nature's own prompting they originally sought.[77]

Clearly, such strivings do not always produce security. On the other hand, the function of the Epicurean community was to provide just that security, that is, "the security of a quiet private life withdrawn from the multitude" for the wise individual was to "live a secret life" in contrast to the life of public service.[78] Epicurean "security," therefore, could only be found in a closed society of friends organized according to the ethic of friendship.

Friendship was an ethical term to which all the philosophers had devoted a great deal of discussion.[79] But Epicurus's view differed from those of Plato and Aristotle, and therefore from the prevailing Greek tradition, precisely in his placing friendship outside of public life and defining it as realizable only in a closed community.[80] He saw friendship as essential to happiness and security, but these ideas, of course, had to be understood in his terms: "Friendship is prompted by our needs . . . but it is maintained by a partnership in the enjoyment of life's pleasures."[81] Thus friendship can only be properly realized in an association of like-minded individuals who seek pleasure according to the correct principles. But conversely, the implication is that pleasure is especially, or perhaps only, available in a community of friends.[82]

Indeed, the Epicurean community tended to view itself as a haven from the vicissitudes of life or "fortune." As opposed to the insecurity of the competitive political life, they created an environment based on the principle of secure friendship. According to Epicurus, these two ideas went hand in hand: "[The wise man] will be armed against fortune and will never give up a friend."[83] On the one hand, this perspective promoted a sense of security realized in opposition to the outside world. On the other hand, it was based on a genuine feeling of regard for one's friends. The latter sentiment was apparent in Epicurus's own character, which was often championed as the real test of his philosophy by his later followers. It became the most appealing and most readily identifiable feature of his philosophy in later generations.[84]

A few statements by Epicurus on social ethics have been preserved, most notably the statement that the wise man "will on occasion die for a friend."[85] But by and large the ethical implications of his doctrine were left for later generations to work out, and this was not always easy to do. Indeed, one reason why appeal was so often made to the character of Epicurus as the proper interpretation of the ethical implications of his system is that the system in itself did not so easily yield practical results. Indeed, in some cases, there were logical inconsistencies that caused a splintering of his school into different branches.[86]

This lack of a firm sense of orthodoxy on ethical questions as well as the general syncretistic nature of philosophical ethics in the first century B.C.E. to second century C.E. means that Epicurean ideas in this period would not necessarily be found only among those who called themselves Epicureans. Plutarch, for example, although he denounced Epicureanism in several dialogues, nevertheless exhibited Epicurean influence in his ethical theory.[87] Thus, as Philip Merlan reminds us, "The *communis opinio* that Epicureanism is not included in late Greek syncretism needs some qualification."[88] It appears even more likely that whenever social obligation at communal meals was discussed on the basis of pleasure and friendship the ideas would derive in some way from the system of Epicurus or in dialogue with it.

POPULAR MORALITY AND SATIRE

The term often used to define the ideas on morality held in common throughout an ancient culture is *popular morality*, a term popularized by K. J. Dover in his study of the classical period in Greece.[89] Dover identified popular morality as the unsystematic, folk tradition of Greece and proposed that it is especially preserved in non-philosophical writings in the form of unstated ethical presuppositions.[90]

This same perspective can be applied to the Greco-Roman period. However, in this period, philosophy became concerned almost entirely with issues of morality, so that even philosophical writings, such as those of Plutarch, for example, have a popular quality to them.[91] We therefore find that the same ideas that are stated in explicit terms in the philosophical writings are presumed and stated in other terms in non-philosophical literature. That they exist elsewhere is not to be attributed primarily to the influence of a particular philosopher, though on more specific issues this may be true, but rather to the fact that the same moralistic premises and cultural presuppositions are shared in the culture at large. That is to say, it is popular morality that is thereby exhibited.

Satire provides an excellent example of popular morality in ancient literature.[92] As a style of literature, satire operates out of a specific moralistic perspective as the basis for its ridicule of the foibles of society. It does not offer a systematic presentation of its moral principles; rather, it assumes them. Consequently, satire offers an example of moralistic writing presented in a non-philosophical form.[93]

Satire is also especially useful for our discussion because of its extensive use of the motif of the banquet.[94] The banquet theme was commonly employed as the setting for comments on gluttony or ostentatiousness, societal evils particularly associated with the wealthy or pretended wealthy. This commonplace theme may go back to the earliest origins of the genre of satire. It is a reliable theme already for Plautus, whose comedies provide a critique of society similar to that of satire.[95] Lucilius (ca. 180–102 B.C.E.) and Varro (116–27 B.C.E.) both chose banquet settings for a number of satires. Lucilius especially, in his description of the banquet of Troginus the soldier, in which he mocked the whole idea of the formal meal, anticipated many of the later themes connected with the banquet.[96] The best example of this type is Horace's description of the banquet of Nasidienus. His basic theme in this satire is a critique of the excesses and bad taste of the newly rich as exhibited in the menu and other trappings of the banquet.[97] A similar theme is taken up by Petronius in the *Cena Trimalchionis* ("Banquet of Trimalchio") portion of his *Satyricon*. The object of his critique is the freedman Trimalchio, who reaches a new low in vulgarity and boorishness.[98]

With Petronius especially we move well beyond satire as a genre, which is properly a Latin verse form, to satire as a literary style. Indeed, Petronius's work has been identified as a form of the romance genre.[99] But the perspective is that of the satirical tradition. And while he uses a different genre, he consciously adapts for his purposes one of the stock motifs of satire, that of the banquet.

Another writer of this period, Lucian of Samosata, also wrote from the point of view of the satirist and even imitated elements of Menippean satire in some of his works.[100] He wrote in several genres, in fact, but consistently with a satirical style. In his *Symposium* he took up a particular aspect of the banquet motif in satire in which symposium literature and the philosophical banquet were ridiculed. His use of the motif may be closely related to Menippus's non-extant *Symposium,* as has often been suggested, but it is clear also that he makes reference to the classics of the genre, particularly the *Symposium* of Xenophon, to which he appends the mythical narrative motif of the wedding feast that ends in strife.[101]

In Lucian's *Symposium* each of the philosophical schools is represented among the guests by individuals whose bearing and personalities exhibit them as caricatures of their respective schools. The Cynic is rude and boorish, for example, while the Platonist is stiff and aloof. When the Epicurean enters, the two Stoics turn their backs on him. Rather than the elevated conversation that should have taken place with such distinguished guests, the symposium is characterized by petty disagreements that eventually disintegrate into a brawl,[102] with the Stoics and the Cynic taking sides against the Epicurean and the Peripatetic, while the Platonist referees. The narrator, Lycinus (Lucian), notes with irony the fact that the unlettered guests were dining with decorum, while the educated guests were brawling. He concludes, "it is not safe for a man of peace to dine with men so learned."[103]

THE BANQUET AS CULTURAL SYMBOL

In satire, the banquet was seen as a symbol for the excesses of luxurious living, or, in Lucian specifically, as a symbol for the pretensions of cultured living. The banquet worked as a symbol because it was perceived as the preeminent social event for the exhibition of refined living. And as a symbol, it was widely utilized in ethical discussions, for it indicated what the cultured life should not be, in the case of satire, or what the cultured life should be, in the case of philosophical ethics. Thus the banquet as cultural symbol transcended genre and literary context. It carried such a symbolic force in itself that it could function as a paradigm for comments on social ethics in a variety of contexts.

The banquet as a social institution took on a certain outward form and order that from the beginning was connected with the cultured life. Indeed, the aspect of reclining at a meal in a setting of luxury was an early iconographic symbol for the aristocratic life. Consequently, the various meal customs were capable of differing interpretations according to the context in which the meal occurred. For example, the philosophical schools traditionally defined the entertainment portion of the symposium as a time for elevated conversation. Meal etiquette was likewise given an interpretation in philosophical discussion under the heading of social ethics. Here the social relationships and social obligation of participants at a meal were defined according to the ethical principles of friendship, pleasure, and joy, which were considered inherent in the meal institution itself.

Certain themes were consistently connected with meal ethics. One of the most persistent of these themes was the question of status, which recurred in various forms. Plutarch's discussion of ranking at a meal is an excellent example. The question arises because of the custom of assigning places according to rank; thus the question seems to be inherent to the meal institution itself. The discussion then raises a fundamental question: whether the meal is going to be defined as a reflection of society or as an institution separate from society with its own rules. In either case, the ethical principles of friendship, pleasure, and joy would function but in different ways. In a sense, the banquet motif in satire fits into the same discussion, for it presents the meal as a reflection of society, but by ridiculing the society there represented, it implicitly refers to an ideal type of the proper meal that places in relief the foibles of society.

The symposium tradition as defined in this chapter provided a rich philosophical underpinning for the development of the ideology of the banquet. It added philosophical elaboration to what were, in effect, the cultural values of the banquet. Consequently, as the banquet was adapted to fit other contexts, it continued to manifest the principal motifs identified in chapter 1, utilizing the form outlined in chapter 2, and drawing on the rich philosophical elaboration discussed in this chapter.

At this point in our study, the primary features of the ancient banquet are in place. The examples to be explored in subsequent chapters will draw on these same features and adapt them to fit their contexts. Sometimes these adaptations will produce new emphases. But the basic model, the model of the Greco-Roman banquet, will remain the same.

CHAPTER 4

THE SACRIFICIAL BANQUET

"What sacrifice is acceptable to the gods without the participants in the feast?"
—Dio Chrysostom, *Or.* 3.97, ca. 104 C.E.

With these words Dio Chrysostom clearly defines the banquet as an inherent part of sacrificial ritual. Since sacrifice is the primary religious ritual of all people in the Greco-Roman world, this puts the sacrificial banquet at the heart of the religious life of the ancients. It is the basic type of meal indicated by the widely used categories "sacred meal" or "cultic meal." The question remains, however, whether the sacrificial banquet should be considered a religious meal or whether it was a secular appendage to the religious occasion that was the sacrifice.

As I stated in chapter 1, it is my hypothesis that the banquet as a social institution was an occasion in which secular and sacred were combined together. In the case of the sacrificial banquet, the religious meaning inherent in the meal would simply be enhanced by its association with the sacrifice. The sacrificial banquet provides a key test case for this hypothesis because it had a specifically religious connection yet was not clearly a separate kind of meal. Many have concluded that it was simply the secular or profane aspect of the sacrificial ritual. In the study that follows, I will be arguing that the banquet was, in fact, inherent to the sacrificial ritual. The sacrificial meal, then, is a prime example of the merging of sacred and secular.

HOW MEAL RELATES TO SACRIFICE[1]

The first issue that arises in scholarly debate is whether the meal is to be considered a part of the sacrificial ritual itself or whether it is a separate activity. The ritual of sacrifice included the slaughter, butchering, and burning of a portion of the animal at the altar. The meat that was to be eaten, however, was taken from the altar to be prepared and eaten elsewhere. This separation of the eating of the meat from the ceremony at the altar suggests to many interpreters that the meal belongs to the secular rather than the sacred sphere. This would mean that the banquet could be designated as simply the human celebration that followed the religious ritual itself.

How might we determine the sense that these ceremonies carried in the Greek mind? To answer this question, we must look at how sacrifices are talked about in Greek literature. The fullest descriptions of sacrifice are found in Homer. Though these descriptions derive from a very early period in Greek history, they nevertheless were understood by later Greek readers as representing their own sense of sacrifice as well. The following text from the *Iliad* is a typical description of a sacrificial banquet in Homer: "But when the thigh-pieces were wholly burned and they had tasted of the inner parts, they cut up the rest and spitted it, and roasted it carefully, and drew all off the spits. Then, when they had ceased from their labor and had made ready the meal, they feasted, nor did their hearts lack aught of the equal feast."[2] Here we find that the sacrifice concluded with a meal, which is invariably the case in Homer. One could conclude, then, that the sense of sacrifice represented here is much like that stated by Dio Chrysostom in the quotation at the beginning of this chapter, that is, that a sacrifice properly conducted would include a festive meal.

A study of the vocabulary of sacrifice provides another window into the understanding of this ritual in the minds of the Greeks.[3] Here we find that there are two basic terms for two basic types of blood sacrifice. The term used for the most common form of sacrifice, in which a portion of the animal is burned at the altar and the rest is eaten, is *thysia*. The other type of sacrifice is termed a *sphagion*. This term denotes a sacrifice by slaughter without burning; in this case the entire animal was offered.[4] Consequently, since the entire animal was given to the deity, a *sphagion* was a sacrifice without a feast.

The term *thysia* is used quite consistently with explicit or implicit reference to the feast accompanying it.[5] It would appear, then, that they were often conceived of as part of the same ritual. For example, Plato seems to connect them as part of the same ritual in this phrase: "when offering a sacrifice and feasting."[6] In another case he notes that "sacrifices and feasts . . . give honor to the gods,"[7] thus including the feast with the religious aspect of the overall ritual.

Similarly, Xenophon describes a sacrificial ritual in this way: "we share with you in the most august sacred rites and in the most splendid sacrifices and feasts."[8] Here the locations of the two adjectives effectively divide this ceremony into two aspects, the "sacred rites" *(hiera)* and the "sacrifices and feasts" *(thysia kai heortē)*. Jean Casabona interprets this to mean that a distinction is made between the divine and human sides of the ritual.[9] If that is the case, it is notable that "sacrifice" is included on the human side and includes the feast.

Numerous other examples provide evidence that for the Greeks, "banquet and sacrifice are two aspects of the same event."[10] Indeed, the two were so closely connected that a sacrifice *without* a feast had to be specifically defined as a "banquetless sacrifice" *(thysiai adaitoi)*.[11] Consequently, if the religious event that was the sacrifice tended always to include a feast, then the feast must relate in some sense to the overall religious meaning. Defining the banquet as the secular part of the total event does not do justice to its importance. Rather, the feast should be seen as an event partaking of both sacred and secular meanings.

A DESCRIPTION OF A SECOND-CENTURY *THYSIA*

Plutarch describes a second-century sacrifice in this way:

> There is a traditional rite of sacrifice *(thysia)*, which the archon performs at the public hearth but everyone else at home, called the driving out of *bulimy.* . . . When I was archon, a larger number than usual participated in the public rite. After we had completed the ritual acts and returned to our places at table, we discussed first the term [i.e., *bulimy*].[12]

Here the entire rite in which all participate is included under the term *sacrifice (thysia)*. It consists of two parts, the *prescribed ritual (ta nenomismena)* and the banquet ("we reclined" [*kateklinēmen*]). What is meant by the term *prescribed ritual* would normally be the ritual acts that take place at the altar. In this case, however, it refers to a special ritual connected with the festival of *bulimy*. Plutarch describes this ritual as consisting of driving a servant out with wands while saying the words, "Out with *bulimy,* in with wealth and health."[13]

Since the "prescribed ritual" was performed *during* the meal (indicated by the phrase following the ceremony, "we reclined *again*" [*palin*]), and for many was a ritual that could be performed at home, it is not clear whether this ritual of sacrifice included a ceremony at the altar or merely the ceremony of *bulimy* described by Plutarch. But by all means it included a banquet. That is to say, the ceremony indicated by the term *sacrifice (thysia)* seems to have included both the "ritual acts" and the banquet.

WHERE THE SACRIFICIAL BANQUET TOOK PLACE

The ritual described above by Plutarch gives rise to another question about sacrificial banquets. For as Plutarch describes the ceremony, they recline at table in the same area where the public rite takes place, here specifically at the "public hearth." It is a rite in which a large number of people had taken part ("many") yet obviously only a few share in the banquet Plutarch describes. Indeed, he specifically states that the same *thysia* was continued "at home" by everyone but the archon and his guests.

In this case, then, the ritual could take place at the public altar or at home; the location did not seem to be important. Indeed, this corresponds to the data on sacrifices in general. That is, there were no regular rules. The meal connected with the sacrifice could take place in a variety of places.

Civic Ritual at the Prytaneion

The location of the "public hearth" for the *bulimy* ceremony described by Plutarch above would be at the Greek structure known as the "prytaneion." This was a characteristic civic structure in Greek cities. A study of the architectural form of the prytaneion has shown that these structures always contained, in addition to the hearth, a dining room that served various civic functions.[14] These dining rooms were of a traditional form, with couches arranged along the walls for reclining, and tended to be modest in size. Thus their form corresponds to Plutarch's description of a public ceremony with a smaller select group dining at the public hearth itself.

Sacred Laws: Eating in Sacred Precincts

The social environment in which the sacrificial meal was to take place was often determined by the sacred laws of the individual cults. For example, Pausanias referred to a law in existence in the second century C.E. at the sanctuary of Asclepius at Epidaurus that forbade carrying sacrificial meat from the site: "All the offerings [at the sanctuary of Asclepius at Epidaurus], whether the offerer be one of the Epidaurans themselves or a stranger, are entirely consumed within the bounds. At Titane too, I know, there is the same rule."[15]

The type of rule to which Pausanias referred occurs in sacred laws of the various Greek cults. Such rules are rather common in the classical period but not so common in the Roman period, although, as Pausanias notes above, they are still to be found here and there.[16]

Such a law is often stated with the technical phrase "do not carry away" *(ou phora)*, which is applied to an individual sacrifice in the official list of prescribed sacrifices, as seen in these examples: "Those who sacrifice to Hestia are not to carry out [*ouden exepheron*] any of the sacrificial meat."[17] "None of the meat is to be carried out [*me einai ekphorēn*] of the *temenos*."[18] Other examples make the same point with different terminology: "The sacrificial meat is to be consumed at the site [where it is sacrificed]."[19] "It [the sacrificial meat] must be eaten at the site."[20] The underlying idea in these cases was that all of the sacrificial meat of a specified sacrifice had to be eaten within the bounds of the *temenos* (temple area). None could be carried away to be eaten later as was the practice otherwise.

As a sacred law, such a rule would appear to derive from some notion of cultic piety, whereby certain sacrifices were of an especially sacred nature.[21] Another interpretation has been proposed, however, suggesting that the law appears to serve a social rather than specifically religious function. This theory was proposed by Sterling Dow in a study of the sacred calendar of Erkhia (fourth century B.C.E.).[22] This inscription provides a detailed list of the various festival sacrifices in the ritual year. There are fifty-six different sacrifices enumerated in the preserved inscription; of these, twenty-two are marked "do not carry away" *(ou phora)*. Those that are so marked have no obvious traits in common. Thus, whether or not a sacrifice was so designated does not appear to relate to particular deities, nor to particular festivals, nor to particular types of animals sacrificed, nor even to earlier ancestral regulations, since three such prohibitions were added to the inscription at a later date.[23]

Dow suggests that such an evident lack of precision in the use of the restriction speaks against its referring to ancient cultic laws. Rather, he interprets its function to be an attempt to bring about a more equal distribution of meat on specified occasions. Without this restriction, the officials and other special groups, who always got first choice anyway, would evidently get the majority of the meat to carry away to their households, leaving none for the worshippers. On days when the restriction was in effect, one would get only as much as he or she could eat at the time. Since these were public sacrifices, it would mean that more members of the Deme could be fed whenever the restrictions were in effect. Thus to Dow, the imposition of the restriction "do not carry away" in this situation was "purely a secular matter."[24]

Dow's interpretation has been critiqued as not applicable to sacred laws in general, though it may be appropriate in this one instance.[25] It clearly correlates with the emphasis in the social code of the banquet on social equality. Furthermore, Dow's judgment that it was "purely a secular matter" seems overdrawn. In fact, as will be seen later in this chapter, the ideal of social equality was often related especially to "religious" meals.

Dining at Greek Temples

The Design of the Greek Temple Precinct. When evaluating the sacred laws relating to Greek sacrifice, it is helpful to keep in mind the physical space presupposed in these regulations. The Greek *temenos*, or temple precinct, was generally marked off with boundary markers. Within that boundary one was subject to the jurisdiction of the temple and its sacred laws. The boundaries, therefore, designated the area of the "sacred" as opposed to the area of the "profane" or secular.[26] For this reason it has been traditional to regard meals specified to take place in the *temenos* area as somehow having a greater religious significance. In order to examine this point more closely, we must give attention to the design of the *temenos*.

An analysis of the Greek *temenos* from the archaic period reveals that a standard pattern was operative and seemed to relate to religious sensibilities. In the traditional design, one can differentiate between "essential" and "nonessential" structures, to use the terms of Birgitta Bergquist.[27] The essential elements are those invariably found and always given central significance in the design, that is, the temple and altar, along with the accompanying boundary wall and entrance.

Other structures may be present but are evidently not necessary. They provide for various other functions of the temple: priests' quarters, treasuries, and banquet houses. These nonessential structures tend to be located in secondary areas; that is, they were situated in a separate space from that of the temple-altar complex, preferably on the periphery along the boundary walls.

Bergquist concludes that this arrangement of space relates to the secondary function these structures had—the "more profane . . . activities of the worshippers within the temenos." Thus this separation between the temple-altar area and the secondary area "expresses the two different aspects of the sacrificial festival: the contact of the worshippers with the divinity and their contact with each other, i.e., the social function."[28] It must be pointed out, however, that all of these functions still take place within the *temenos* walls.

By the Hellenistic period, however, the design of the *temenos* had changed. No longer were the temple-altar complex and the secondary structures clearly differentiated in the design. Rather, they were arranged in an axial alignment in which the temple facade blended in with the *stoai* surrounding the entire *temenos* and to which the other structures were attached. Thus the secondary structures were no longer formally set apart but rather "accepted together with the essential elements and the ritual activities in the one, large, undifferentiated area of the temenos."[29] The same description applies to non-Greek structures in the Greek world of the Hellenistic and Roman periods, particularly sanctuaries of Roman religion and of the Oriental cults.[30] Consequently, the division between sacred and profane activities in the temple complex seems to be less well defined in the Greco-Roman period than it was in the archaic period as interpreted by Bergquist.

Dining Rooms at Greek Temples. Dining rooms were commonly located at Greek temples; thus provisions were provided for eating meals at the site. It must be noted, however, that the meals eaten at temple dining rooms may not necessarily be sacrificial meals. After all, "full service" sanctuaries were also expected to provide hospitality facilities for pilgrims. Furthermore, temple dining rooms tended to have the same structural characteristics as dining rooms in public secular buildings and private homes. This indicates that the meals held in them were not formally different from normal "secular" meals.

The preferred design for temple dining rooms was to provide several small rooms in standard sizes, either seven-, nine-, or eleven-couch rooms. This corresponds to the stated preference for small banquets in the philosophical literature. Some temples, however, provided space where large groups could dine together, somewhat in the style of a large cafeteria, although even in these cases the space is often divided into smaller sections around a central cooking area.[31]

The sanctuaries that provided stone couches in their dining rooms give us the clearest indication of the arrangement of furnishings (see figure 1, p. 15). Here we find that the couches were arranged along the walls with the tables placed in front of them. The diners all reclined in the same direction around the room. The size of these couches suggests that there was only one diner per couch.

One must assume a similar arrangement in sanctuary accessory buildings where couches were not preserved, because they were made of wood, but where other structural features suggest that the buildings were designed for dining. Even where permanent dining rooms were not provided, dining at the site obviously took place. There is clear evidence that temporary structures were often provided and even outdoor dining was not uncommon.[32] Of course, one would expect that such temporary dining facilities would also be present at those sanctuaries where permanent facilities existed so as to take care of the occasional overflow crowds at festival time.

Just as the design of the *temenos* changed in the Hellenistic and Roman period, so also did the design of many of the temple dining rooms. For example, cultic dining is said to have taken place within Roman temples, not just in accessory buildings.[33] The same is true of the temples of some of the Oriental cults in this period. Whether these examples refer to meals within the temple *cella,* where the statue of the deity is located, or in some other part of the temple complex is unclear.

It is clear from all of the evidence, however, that meals commonly took place at temples and that facilities were regularly provided for them. Furthermore, it is also clear that the facilities provided are identical in design to dining facilities in public and private secular architecture. There is no evidence to suggest that the form of dining that took place in sanctuaries was any different from the form of dining practiced elsewhere. Of course, many of these meals undoubtedly represented hospitality provided to pilgrims. However, in most cases there would also have been a religious component to the meals, as indicated by the location and the relation to the ritual of sacrifice. What that religious component was needs now to be investigated.

WHAT MADE THE SACRIFICIAL MEAL "RELIGIOUS"?

Was It the Occasion?

A sacrificial meal was obviously connected with the occasion of the sacrificial ritual. Yet what was that connection? Since the sacrifice took place at the altar, and the meal did not, this has led to the conclusion that the meal was a peripheral event, associated with but not inherent to the sacred character of the sacrificial ritual itself. This is the conclusion of Michael Jameson in his study of Greek ritual: "Associated with the rites [of sacrifice], but not themselves ritual acts, are the feasting that often follows animal sacrifice (which may be the scene of further ritual), and the athletic, musical, and dramatic competitions. . . . The meal that follows in many Homeric descriptions of sacrifice . . . was enjoyable and socially important but not an essential part of the sacrifice."[34]

This interpretation is supported by the rather inconsistent ways in which the sacrificial meat was handled: it could be eaten on the spot, either by personal choice or by edict of the sacred laws; it could be taken home and eaten later; or it could be sold to vendors to resell at the marketplace. Indeed, since virtually all meat that would appear on the table would presumably have come from a sacrifice, it is probable that all meat meals could be considered "sacrificial meals." These factors would seem to generalize the concept of "sacrificial meal" to the point that a specific religious significance could no longer be attached.

Yet what then is meant by this statement of Dio Chrysostom? "What sacrifice is acceptable to the gods without the participants in the feast?" Does this not suggest that the meal was somehow conceived of as part of the central meaning of the ritual? At the least, Dio's statement implies that the ancients conceived of sacrificial meal as an inherent part of the sacrifice.

One way in which the occasion of sacrifice would be enhanced would be at festival time. At such a time, general sacrifices would be made on behalf of the larger body of worshippers, and all would share in the bounty of the feast. Presumably, then, all of the celebratory banquets, wherever they were held, would be considered part of the overall ritual. This would be a case where the occasion would clearly define the meal as "sacrificial" and therefore "religious."

One can imagine other occasions in which the meal would be closely tied to the sacrificial ritual proper. Indeed, Dio seems to presuppose that this was the norm. Consequently, whatever may be determined to be the specific religious content of the sacrificial meal, the occasion of sacrifice with which it was connected was one factor that could contribute to that content.

Was It the Food?

The victim in a *thysia* sacrifice was called a *hiereion,* a term designating its "sacred" nature and separation from the secular realm. Thus one would presume that the meat would thereby have gained a sacred character, separating it in substantive terms from meat that had not come from the altar. Yet there is no evidence that meat from a sacrifice was handled differently from other food. In terms of ritual, there appears to have been no ceremony moving the meat from the sacred realm, presumably associated with the altar, to the secular realm.[35] Yet sacrificial meat certainly entered the secular realm; for example, it could end up being sold at the meat market. The apostle Paul refers to this in 1 Cor 10:25 and 28 and suggests that the purchaser would not know whether meat had come from a sacrifice or not. According to Paul, then, sacrificial meat that ended up at the market was intended to be treated like any other meat; it was not reserved for a special use.

In other cases, apparently, a shopper *could* identify meat that came from a sacrifice. Aesop refers to his having "purchased tongues from sacrificial pigs when he arrived at the marketplace."[36] However, the sense of the passage appears to be that such meat would be so identified because it was of a higher quality.[37] There is no indication that the designation as sacrificial meat gave it a sacred quality.

The closest one comes to the idea that the meat from the altar had a special numinous quality is with the *ou phora* ("do not take away") rules. Yet here, as we have noted, there appears to have been no clear consistency as to which sacrifice had to be consumed within the confines of the sanctuary and which could be carried away. The ritual at the altar, presumably, was the same. The primary difference had to do with the place and setting where it was to be eaten and the feast's inherent connection to the ritual at the altar.

Was It the Location?

If a meal was held within the *temenos* area of the temple grounds, or, in some cases, in the temple itself, would it have a greater religious significance than meals held in non-sacred areas? As we have noted above, certain sacred laws, notably the *ou phora* rules, designated that the meat had to be eaten on the temple grounds. But these laws do not provide clear indication of special religious significance. They are not consistently applied and certainly are not the rule for meals following a sacrifice.

Dining rooms were commonly provided at sanctuary sites. They indicate that meals were a necessary and significant part of the activities connected with the sanctuary. Indeed, the evidence we have suggests that they were often given elaborate architectural treatment, indicating that the provision of elegant dining facilities was often an important matter to a sanctuary.

The question is what kinds of meals were eaten in temple dining rooms. We might first note that they do not differ in form from secular dining rooms. Thus the form of the meals for which they were designed would be that of the normal banquet. There is no evidence that meals of a significantly different form took place at sanctuary sites.

How meals at temples were understood by the ancients is especially indicated by references found in the collection of invitations to the *klinē* of Sarapis. These invitations are part of a larger corpus of papyrus fragments from Egypt, all of which date from the first to the fourth centuries C.E.[38]

Some of the meals indicated in these invitations are secular in nature yet take place in a sanctuary. For example, a marriage feast takes place "in the temple of Sabazios" and a birthday feast takes place "in the Sarapeion [sanctuary of Sarapis]."[39] On the other hand, eleven of the extant invitations define the meal as a religious one, particularly as the "banquet" (*klinē*, literally "couch") of Sarapis. Of these, three place the banquet in a Sarapeion, as in the following example: "Chaeremon requests you to dine at the banquet of the Lord Sarapis in the Sarapeion tomorrow, the 15th, at the 9th hour."[40]

There are eleven invitations to the banquet of Sarapis, and each uses this basic form. Two others locate the meal in the Sarapeion, like this one,[41] and two locate it in an accessory building of the Sarapeion ("in the 'house' [*oikos*] of the Sarapeion").[42] One of these is of special interest since the invitation is extended by a woman, Herais. As the hostess, she would obviously be a full partner in the banquet. J. R. Gilliam has noted occurrences of women reclining at meals in pictorial depictions of banquets of Isis and Osiris.[43]

Three other invitations locate the *kline* in other sacred buildings that were probably associated with Sarapis: one "in the birth-house" *(en tō lochiō)*[44] and two "in the temple of Thoeris" *(en tō thoēpiō)*.[45] But three of the invitations to the "banquet of Sarapis" locate it in private homes: "in the house of Claudius Sarapion," "in his own home," and "in his ancestral home."[46]

That the "banquet of Sarapis" was a sacrificial meal has been established by Herbert C. Youtie. He refers especially to a papyrus letter of a banquet host to his father that speaks of his preparations for a *klinē* of Sarapis. The preparations include the provision for a rather large amount of wood: "For there is need of five loads. If you need me, send me word, and I will come down, with two friends as well, in order that you may not tire yourself. For a man cannot refuse our lord Sarapis. It is another two months until the banquet. If you are able to bring up the wood with your donkey, bring it up, and you will get the money to cover your expense." Youtie interprets this to mean that the banquet occasion included a sacrifice.[47]

What is striking in the collection of invitations, however, is that the sacrificial meal, the *klinē*, could be held in a variety of locations, both "sacred" and "secular," and still have the same meaning. This correlates with the earlier discussion, in which it was pointed out that the form of facilities and thus the form of the meal at temples was the same as that found in the secular world. Indeed, one of the controversies related to the interpretation of the Sarapis meals has been over whether these were sacrificial (thus Youtie)[48] or purely secular (thus Milne)[49]. I would suggest instead that the line between sacrificial and secular is not that strict.

Thus the religious nature of the meal is not defined by its location, for a sacrificial meal can take place in either a temple or a private home, and a secular celebration can take place in a temple. What is involved is a "normal" banquet that can be held anywhere, but in this case has been redefined to fit the special meanings attached to the sacrificial meal.

Was It the Special Presence of the Deity?

The Deity as Guest. It appears that there were many variations on how a deity could be related to the sacrificial meal. In a basic sense, the presentation of the animal at the altar represented a gift to the god, and the burning of a portion on the altar represented the god consuming his portion of the food. Thus a classic critique of Greek ritual decries the fact that the Greeks give to the gods only what they do not find edible themselves. It is also true that the high fat content of the portion placed on the altar would make it burn well.

But would the god be present in some sense at the banquet? One specific type of sacrificial meal specifies the presence of the deity as guest. This is the *theoxenia,* a term that literally means "hosting the gods." Here the deity's presence is normally signified by providing him or her a place at table and/or a portion of food.[50] There is no doubt that such a meal had special religious overtones. Yet even here the form of the meal appears to be "normal"; the gods are merely being entertained. Furthermore, it appears to be a special case. Whether it is a unique form of sacrificial meal or reflects explicitly what sacrificial meals tended to include implicitly is difficult to say. Jameson, for example, refers to the *theoxenia* as a "distinctive kind of ritual" that is unrelated to a normal sacrificial meal.[51]

The Deity as Host. In a more general sense, the meal could be conceived of as provided by, and therefore hosted by, the god.[52] This is the sense of the description in Xenophon's *Anabasis:* "The goddess provided for the worshippers barley meal, bread, wine and dried fruit, and a portion of the sacrificial victims from the sacred land and a portion of the animals captured in the hunt."[53] Here it should be noticed, however, that temple funds were used to pay for the meal. This is then the primary way in which the goddess is seen as host. It is unclear whether a sacrificial meal in which the worshipper provides the animal from his own funds could also be conceived as a meal hosted by the deity.

The Deity as Miraculously Present in the Food. A classic anthropological argument proposes that the sacramental meal was one in which the deity was considered equivalent in some sense to the food that was consumed. Consequently, when one consumed the food, one was "eating" the deity. To be sure, this argument is not connected with the sacrificial meal per se but has come to be used as a standard definition of the sacred meal in whatever context it might be found.

This phenomenon is most clearly seen, of course, in the Christian Eucharist of late antiquity. Scholars then argue back from that phenomenon to seek for precedents in pagan ritual. That there were such precedents is a valid assumption. However, the classic arguments for a pagan archetypical sacramental meal have been severely weakened in recent research.

The most widely accepted identification of a pagan archetype of the sacramental meal is the "theophagy" that has been identified in Dionysiac tradition.[54] This idea has been refuted in several more recent studies.[55]

Perhaps the most radical revision of the older scholarship on the Dionysiac theophagy is that of Albert Henrichs. He concludes: ". . . The startling idea that the ritual practice of the eucharist constitutes a symbolic theophagy . . . is unparalleled outside Christianity."[56] Henrichs points out that the very few references we have in Greek religion for such a phenomenon occur in fictional narratives rather than in references to actual rituals. The argument may, of course, be overstated; if the idea of theophagy is present in the literature, it could contribute to later interpretation of ritual.[57]

THE SACRED BANQUET

Earlier in this study, in chapters 2 and 3, we found that all banquets could be assumed to have a religious component. This can be seen by the many references to libations and hymns that accompanied the various parts of the meal. Here we have found that the form of the sacrificial banquet was the same as the form used for a banquet in other settings and circumstances. Consequently, the religious component of the sacrificial banquet is best understood as an enhancement of the religious potential of symbols already present in the standard form of the banquet. That is to say, certain segments of the meal ritual would be given special emphasis or interpretation due to the connection with the designated sacrifice. That this was the case is illustrated by the example of the sacrificial meal described by Plutarch that was discussed earlier in this chapter.

This means that we need not seek an "orthodox" form of sacrificial meal. Rather, the sacrificial component could have been emphasized in a variety of ways. Furthermore, since the "sacred" is inherent in the banquet as social institution, it would not require manipulation of the form of the meal to provide an enhancement of the religious component.

In the past, scholars have often decried the lack of piety at sacrificial meals, as characterized by their nature as "carousal." Perhaps such interpretations reflect a misunderstanding of the sacred in Greek society. Indeed, the very form of a festival suggests that sacred events are not to be defined exclusively as solemn rather than boisterous. Furthermore, the concept of celebration can be seen to be inherent in the social code of the banquet. Thus I would suggest that the occasion itself, with its sense of celebration and revelry, is the essence of the sacred that the meal communicates rather than being the secular component.

An indication of the way in which such a meal was viewed by a worshipper may be derived from a description of an Isis cult meal. In Apuleius's *Metamorphoses,* Lucius describes the final stage of his initiation into the mysteries of Isis in this way: "Then I celebrated the most festive birthday of the sacred rites (or: the festal day of initiation as if it were a birthday) and there were delightful feasts and elegant banquets *(suaves epulae et faceta convivia).*" Here he enjoys festive banquets as the conclusion of his initiation rite, banquets that are especially characterized by "good cheer." Indeed, the banquets are defined as birthday celebrations. This is clearly an interpretation of the culmination of the initiation rite: now he has been reborn. But the use of this image also gives a context for the celebration itself, for it is defined as equivalent to the celebration at a birthday feast but with a religious content. Consequently, the "good cheer" experienced at the banquet, which was a normal part of a festive meal, has been given a religious content.

THE FESTIVE BANQUET

Religious banquets in the ancient world are regularly characterized as occasions for joy and celebration. I would propose that it is that factor itself, the festive joy that is so inherent to the "sacred" banquet, that represented its primary "religious" content.

Good Cheer and Banquet Ideology

The normal connection of "good cheer" with a banquet is often indicated in Greek by such terms as *festive joy (euphrosynē)* and *celebration (euōchia).* For example, festive joy was especially associated with the good cheer brought about by the wine. Thus a sixth-century-B.C.E. poet refers to "a cup full of good cheer" *(kratēr mestos euphrosynēs).*[58] So also an epitaph from Memphis celebrates the *euphrosynē* and *aglaia* of a young man who was buried by his "companions"; the sense is: "he was always a cheerful drinking companion."[59] Such "festive joy" was seen as such a basic feature of the banquet that it came to be used as a term meaning "banquet" in itself.[60] This usage suggests that this is a feature that can be idealized as so basic to the banquet experience that it can be a rule by which to judge the "proper" banquet.

This term comes to be a primary feature of the sacrificial banquet as well, as seen, for example, in the phrase *"thuete Pani euphrainesthe,"* which can be freely translated: "Enjoy the joyful feast at the sacrifice to Pan."[61] Here also it functions as a typification of the banquet that comes to stand for the banquet as a whole. A sixth-century-C.E. Christian text uses the same terminology to describe a Christian meal: "celebrating the joyous feast [*euphranthentes*], they glorified God."[62]

As indicated by the Christian text, "good cheer" experienced at a drinking party, though it was connected especially with the wine, was not understood to be a reference to drunkenness per se. Rather, it referred to the sense of pleasure and joy central to the social institution of the banquet. As such, it could also be interpreted as an aspect of social morality. For example, Dio Chrysostom relates it to the virtue of friendship.[63] Friendship, he says, is a necessary ingredient of a banquet. In his argument, *festive joy (euphrosynē)* is used as a parallel term to *symposium,* and both are used in reference to a banquet setting where "good will among the participants" is necessary for the event to be "pleasurable." The implication is that festive joy is a social experience deriving from, as well as contributing to, the "friendship" that is also fundamental to the banquet. Dio goes on to extend the illustration to another type of banquet, that held at the "sacrifice" *(thysia),* which is validated ("acceptable to the gods") by the "communal festive meal" *(suneuōcheisthai).* Here, then, the sacrificial meal, like the concept of "festive joy" and the symposium itself, derives its significance from its communal nature. Consequently, "festive joy" is not to be understood as an individual experience but rather as a social experience based on the form and function of the banquet of which it is an inherent part.

The Festive Meals at Panamara

A more direct connection of festive joy with religious experience at a sacrificial banquet is provided by a series of official invitations to the cult banquets of Zeus of Panamara in the region of Caria in Asia Minor.[64] In about the second century C.E. a number of these invitations were inscribed on stone and set up at the cult site at Panamara.[65] In them the god invites various cities of the region to attend his festive celebrations.

A standard form is as follows: "The god invites you to the sacred feast . . . in order that you may partake of the festivity which he provides."[66] Characteristically, the "sacred feast" *(hēhiera hestiasis)* is defined here as a banquet at which the god provides "festive joy" *(euphrosynē).*

In the festival invitations provided for various cities, it is regularly specified that the festival will be an occasion for festive joy as provided by the god.

Here one might note that the god is pictured as host of the banquet. His banquet is one that compares favorably with banquets held anywhere in the Greco-Roman world, for the god will see that festive joy flows freely. Thus the term *festive joy* shifts from being purely a secular term to a term that is hereby given a religious value. These references are reminiscent of the "joyous banquet" in Hebrew tradition. It is the joy and celebration itself that is the religious component in the meal. Of course, it could be said that the Zeus Panamaros data represents a unique rather than common interpretation of the sacrificial meal. However, since the term and the concept it refers to are traditional in Greek society, I would argue that here we have articulated what is probably present but unstated in common Greek festival piety.

An invitation extended to the Rhodians highlights other aspects of the Panamara festival meal: "Since the god invites all people to the feast and provides a table shared in common and offering equal privilege to those who come from whatever place they may come . . . I [the priest] invite you [the Rhodians] to the (house of the) god . . . to share in the festivity which he [the god] provides."[67] In this invitation the political motivation of the sanctuary officials is clear. The god has singled out the Rhodians not only because of their "excellent reputation" but also "because there exists between our cities a kinship to one another and a commonality of sacred rites *(tōn hiepōn koinōnia).*"[68] Thus it functions to define the political ties the sanctuary claims to have with one of the powerful cities in the area.[69]

The ties of the outlying cities with this local deity are especially defined by the banquet, as seen in the invitation just quoted. Note the striking universalism in the claims: the god invites "all people" to his banquet.[70] But he offers "a table shared in common and offering equal privileges" *(koinē kai isotimos trapeza).* In other words, the communal ties appealed to by the god especially come to focus in the meal. The common table symbolizes the common "kinship" *(syngenia)* and "sacred rites" *(hiera).*

The god's table is also characterized as one of "equality" *(isotimos).*[71] In other meal contexts, such a concept refers to the breaking down of the social barriers often reinforced by meal customs. In this case, in addition to social class, such barriers might derive also from the fact that worshippers would be coming from different cities that might impart to them different degrees of prestige. To overcome this potential difficulty and ensure that a true spirit of commonality and festive joy can be experienced at the meal, all worshippers are to be treated equally at the meal. How this is to be done is not indicated, but one might suggest that such common means of exhibiting social rank as assigning positions at the table or providing different quality or quantity of food would not be practiced. The idea of equality at the meal, a concept also found in popular morality of the time, is here defined as an aspect of a religious meal imparted to the meal by the god.

These ideas are connected in another writing from the same period in which the Roman festival of the *Saturnalia* is given a moralistic interpretation. The *Saturnalia* was a one-day slave's holiday in which the slaves were allowed to take the prerogatives of the upper classes at the festival banquet. Lucian uses this institution to satirize class structure in the context of meal customs. Using the motifs of a symposium conversation and an epistolary correspondence of a priest with *Kronos* (i.e., *Saturnus*) he has the god advise, "Let every man be treated equal, slave and freeman, poor and rich."[72]

The god then provides the following "symposium laws":

> Each man shall take the couch where he happens to be. Rank, family, or wealth shall have little influence on privilege. All shall drink the same wine, and neither stomach trouble nor headache shall give the rich man an excuse for being the only one to drink the better quality. All shall have their meat on equal terms. . . . Neither are large portions to be placed before one and tiny ones before another, not a ham for one and a pig's jaw for another—all must be treated equally.[73]

Here a traditional festival is interpreted as a paradigm for a critique of society. Lucian's satire is not to be taken as a religious text, nor is it to be read as a revolutionary tract,[74] but it does illustrate specific ways in which a moralist of this period might interpret the concept of "equality" at a festival meal.

The rites at Panamara are also called a "mystery": "Our ancestral god is feasting all men. It is fitting above all that the priest invite your city to his mystery [*to autou mystērion*]."[75] Here "mystery" clearly refers to the sacred banquet. Indeed, at this period the banquet appears to have become the essential aspect of the mystery celebrated at Panamara.[76] Yet all we can determine about the banquet itself suggests that it is quite ordinary in form. This is especially indicated by the fact that it is characterized by "festive joy" (*euphrosynē*) and even advertised on that basis.

The use of this term to describe the banquet has suggested to earlier interpreters that its nature is that of a "carousal," an orgiastic banquet with no apparent religious meaning. Seemingly in support of this view is this description of sacred banquets provided at Panamara by a group of benefactors: "They entertained at the tables of the god for the whole year at every appointment to a position and at every birthday of the inhabitants. With great generosity and class they provided on these occasions sumptuous banquets, unexcelled in their splendor and lavishness, for the city and the region and the representatives of all humanity."[77] Such a description of a banquet that is otherwise dubbed a "mystery" has led to considerable consternation among many scholars. Typical is the response of G. Cousin and G. Deschamps. They see here a "complaisant interpretation" of the ancient rite that has brought about a "distortion of the sacred oblation," thus transforming the "solemn occasion" into an "immense festivity." The priests appear to be blatantly advertising their cult with offerings of food and drink; in effect they offer a "divine tavern."[78]

Rather, as P. Roussel has suggested in response, one can determine by the very gravity of the language employed in the invitations that they are intended to express actual piety. The banquet is the "table of the god," at which the priest acts as the "host" in place of the god. All indications suggest that it is a sacrificial banquet that, for this cult at least, has become the essential mystery rite. And the festive joy that is a proper part of any banquet is here seen as the gift of the god.[79]

The Meaning of *Festive Joy*

Since festive joy, then, is associated with a mystery rite, is it to be interpreted with a special, mystic sense?[80] This does not appear likely since it is such a common term in a banquet context. If the basic meaning of the term is therefore operative here, these banquets are to be characterized by normal banquet conviviality, such as is aspired to at every "proper" banquet. As we have already noted, however, the term has been given an elevated connotation in this context since it is designated as a gift of the god.

This idealized use of the concept of festive joy is quite similar to the usage of Dio Chrysostom discussed above. As in the Panamara invitations, there was a sense in which the term could be seen to transcend the purely secular and mundane. The interpretation of banquet conviviality as a gift of the god thus would give a more profound significance to the convivial experience. In this way the connotative sense of the term would move from "carousal" to "religious festive joy" primarily because of the change in the context and interpretation of what might essentially be the same banquet experience.

This reinterpretation of festive joy corresponds to a great extent to the use of "pleasure" in philosophical discussions of meal ethics. In both cases, the basic social function of the meal, that of giving pleasure, has been idealized and made into a principle by which to define the proper meal. Indeed, such a relationship between philosophical ethics and religious piety is characteristic of this period.[81] Thus Plutarch described a sacrificial meal as one of his paradigms for proper philosophical discussion at a banquet.[82] Yet the subject discussed on that occasion was the sacrificial ritual itself, so that the dialogue functioned not only as a philosophical discourse but also in a quasi-liturgical sense.

CONCLUSION

Any banquet in the Greco-Roman period could have been connected with a sacrifice in some way; in fact, among Greeks and Romans, they almost always were. Whether or not that was the case, however, did not change the form of the banquet. Nor did it change the ideology of the banquet. Instead, as we have seen, the sacrificial meal was indistinguishable from other manifestations of the Greco-Roman banquet. And it utilized the common meal symbols of celebration, community, and equality as constituent parts of its religious definition and developed rules of social obligation based on that idealization of the meal. Consequently, the sacrificial banquet, seen here as the archetype of the "sacred" or "cultic" banquet, can be understood as a subtype of the Greco-Roman banquet.

CHAPTER 5

THE CLUB BANQUET

Some associations appear to be formed for the sake of pleasure, for example religious guilds and dining-clubs, which are unions for sacrifice and social intercourse.
—Aristotle, *Eth. Nic.* 8.9.5 (1160A)[1]

The old lawgivers, providing for the modern dinners, ordained both the tribe and the deme dinners, and over and above these the dinners of the sacred bands, the brotherhood dinners, and again those which are called "orgeonic."
—Athenaeus 186a

There were a variety of clubs and associations in the Greek and Roman world.[2] These clubs existed from classical times to late antiquity and were formed for various purposes: for example, as funerary societies, trade guilds, religious societies, or political associations.[3] But in virtually every case where we have documented records of club activities, we find that the banquet emerges as one of their primary reasons for gathering.

Greek clubs were voluntary associations that seem to have originated primarily as religious organizations whose purpose was to provide a means for individuals to share the expense for a sacrifice, particularly if the deity being honored was not normally included in state sacrifices and festivals.[4] The communal sacrifice would also include a communal meal, of course, and by sharing the expenses here as well they could provide for themselves a regular schedule of festive celebrations.

Greek clubs existed as far back as Solon (594 B.C.E.) and before. Solonian law states concerning clubs: "If a *demos,* or *phratries,* or *orgeones* of heroes, or *gennetai,* or messmates [*syssitoi*], or funerary associates, or *thiasotai,* or *pirates,* or traders make arrangements among themselves, these shall be binding unless forbidden by public writings."[5] Thus we find the basic terminology of Greek clubs testifying to a significant variety of forms and purposes already in existence as early as Solon.

The quotation from Aristotle at the opening of this chapter provides a summary of basic data about clubs in ancient Greek society. Here we find references to what appear to be two types of clubs, *religious guild (thiasos)* and *dining club (eranos)*, both included under the category of "association" *(koinon)*. In actuality, these terms tend to be used interchangeably and merely refer to the different dimensions of the clubs. As religious organizations, these clubs provide communal sacrifices. Their sacrifices also include an emphasis on the sacrificial banquet; thus they provide "social intercourse" *(synousia)*. Indeed, the banquet became so important to their self-identity that they could be said to exist "for the sake of pleasure" *(hedonē)*.

As we have already seen, the term *pleasure* when applied to meals was not a derogatory term but had significant moral and ethical content in both philosophy and religion. The same sense of the term is present here. Thus when clubs are said to exist for the sake of "pleasure," this should be understood to be a reference not to an antireligious characteristic but to the specific type of religious activity in which they specialized. Indeed, pleasure was something they took seriously. Furthermore, it was defined in terms of the communal nature of the occasion, as indicated by the other term that refers to their self-identity, that of "social intercourse." Pleasure and social intercourse therefore defined the highest ideals to which clubs aspired at their meetings. Thus the rules of behavior at club banquets tended to emphasize ways in which the pleasure inherent in the occasion could be shared in by all.

In the Hellenistic and Roman periods, clubs became even more ubiquitous as society became more cosmopolitan and the Greek city-state declined in importance. In this new social world, clubs offered a means of social identity to individuals who lacked the strong social moorings of their ancestors. Clubs came to be organized for a variety of reasons, as "trade guilds," burial societies, religious societies, ethnic organizations, and so on. But their primary purpose was to provide social intercourse and cohesion for their members, and the central activity for meeting those goals was the banquet.

Most of our evidence for clubs is contained in their various statutes and dedications that survive as inscriptions. These inscriptions were normally posted at their meeting places. They provide an inside look at the form and activities of the clubs. They include such things as the requirements for membership, the amount of the dues to be paid by each member, the names and duties of officers, the specified meeting times, and the rules of conduct expected of members at meetings. In addition, they usually specify the official name of the group and the deity or deities to whom the club is dedicated.

The clubs of the Greco-Roman world provide for us a model of the ideals of the banquet in an institutionalized form. For the ancients they also provided a model for how a group should organize itself. Thus any group that sought to maintain its group identity tended to model itself on the clubs. Consequently, both Christian and Jewish groups were often taken to be equivalent to religious clubs by the ancients, and, indeed, there is some truth to this. In order to fully appreciate this fact, we must first understand the nature and organization of the clubs.

This analysis will be divided into three parts, roughly corresponding to three different periods and/or types of social organization. We will first look at the form of clubs in the classical Greek period. Then we will examine specifically Roman types of clubs. Finally, we will look at typical features of clubs in the Greek world of the Roman period. In each case, we will summarize general features of the evidence and then provide a test case analysis of a typical club of that type.

GREEK CLUBS

Names and Types

Clubs were designated by "generic" names and names that were specific to a particular group or type of club. Generic names refer to their identity as an officially organized body calling itself by one of the common terms that we translate as "club." Specific names represent to a great extent what a club thought to be central to its self-identity. There were a variety of ways in which a club could so identify itself, such as by common ethnic or family background, by common occupation, by shared religious convictions or preference, or by contractual agreement to provide for the funerals of its members from a common purse, what is commonly referred to as a funerary or burial society.

Poland identifies the three most common "generic" names of Greek clubs in the classical period as follows: *eranos, thiasos,* and *orgeones.*[6] They all are technical terms that are translated "club," "association," or "guild" or are simply transliterated. The term *eranos* is used in Homer to refer to a meal paid for by the common contributions of the participants.[7] When used as a term for a club, it tends to emphasize its social aspects. A *thiasos* was originally a religious association, but the term tended to take on a more general sense and refer to the banquets themselves or, in the plural, to the banqueters.[8] To Athenaeus these two terms were synonymous: "The same [dinner gathering] may be called either *eranos* or *thiasos,* and the members who come together *eranistai* or *thiasotai*."[9] The third term in general use in this period, *orgeones,* referred to a special class of Attic religious club. The term may be roughly translated "sacrificing associates."

Most Greek clubs also had individualized names that reflected a great deal about their nature and self-identity. Some names emphasized the religious worship that united the membership and gave it its identity, such as: "Sacrificers" *(thusiastai),* "Worshippers" *(therapeutai),* "Mystagogues" or "Initiates" *(mystai),* "Sacrificing Priests" *(hierourgoi),* and "Temple Attendants" or "Deacons" *(diakonoi).* Others indicated that the social relationships were primary: "Companions" *(symbiōtai),* "Intimates" *(synēthei),* "Clansmen" *(phratores),* "Friends" *(philoi),* "Comrades" *(hetairoi),* "Brothers" *(adelphoi),* and "Funerary Fellows" *(homotaphoi).* Some clubs were named after their patron deity such as the "Asklepiasts," or devotees of the god Asclepius, the "Dionysiasts" or devotees of the god Dionysus, and the "Sarapiasts," or devotees of the god Sarapis. Other clubs might simply refer to themselves by a general collective term: "Tribe" *(phylē),* "Sect" *(hairesis),* "Assembly" or "Synagogue" *(synagōgē),* "Congress" or "Sanhedrin" *(synedrion),* "Guild" or "Synod" *(synodos),* or "Association" *(koinon).*[10]

Often names of clubs and officials make specific reference to the centrality of the banquet. For example, a society of Sarapiasts in Thasos named themselves "the Order of the Drinking Cup" *(kōthōnes).*[11] In other cases meetings were designated as "symposia" or "drinking parties."[12] The officials of a club were often named for their roles in the meal, thus indicating its central importance to the meetings of the club. Some of the functional titles are: "presider at the table" *(klinarchos),* "chief presider at the table" *(prōtoklinarchos),* "head of the feast" *(archieranistēs),* "presider at the drinking party" or "symposiarch" *(symposiarchos),* "officer of the table" *(kleinokosmos),* and especially "host" *(hestiatōr).* One suspects that other functionaries, such as the "servants" *(hypēretai* or *diakonoi),* the "choral singers" *(hymnōdoi),* and the "theologians" *(theologoi),* may have performed their duties in the setting of a meal or its accompanying entertainment. In other cases, the expenditures of clubs often indicate provisions for meals, especially the wine, and often these constitute the major or sole specified budget items. Other expenditures often listed include dining furnishing for the clubhouse such as "tables" *(trapezai)* and "couches" *(klinai).*[13]

The Association of *Orgeones*

Inscriptions that preserve the statutes of Greek clubs give us an inside view of these clubs. One of the best examples is an inscription of *orgeones* from

Athens. The inscription dates from the third century B.C.E., but it quotes an earlier statute that may date from as early as the fifth century B.C.E. We thus get a view here of the ongoing history of a club over a period of 150 to 200 years. Special attention is given in these statutes to the proprieties to be observed at the banquets held by the association.[14]

> Lysias of Plotheia, son of Periandros, said 'May it be well: / Resolved by the *Orgeones:* In order that the community of / sacrifices might be observed for all time by the corporation / of Kalliphanes and of the Hero / (5) Echelos, after those who owe something to the / community record (what they owe) on a stone *stele,* it shall be set up alongside the altar / in the temple, (recording) both the sum total and the interest which / each has accumulated. The ancient decrees shall also be recorded / on the *stele* / (10) The inscribing and the erection of the stele shall be commissioned, and / whatever is spent for these things shall be charged to the corporation. /
>
> Decreed by the *Orgeones:* The host shall offer the sacrifice / on the 17th and 18th of *Hekatombaion.* / On the first day he shall sacrifice a suckling pig to the Heroines and / (15) a full-grown victim to the Hero; and he shall set up a table and on the / second day, a full-grown victim to the Hero. He shall reckon up his / expenses and spend no more than the revenue. / (He shall distribute) the flesh as follows: to the *Orgeones* present [a portion], / to sons a portion not exceeding a half, and to the wives of the *Orgeones* / (20) who are present with them a portion equal to that of the independent women [members], to daughters / a portion not exceeding a half, and to one female attendant (for each matron) a portion not exceeding a half. / (He shall deliver) the portion of the woman to the man. / / Decreed by the *Orgeones:* The host (with reference to) the interest . . .

This group of *orgeones* identify themselves as worshippers of the hero Echelos and "the heroines," a group whose specific identity is unknown. They define themselves as "the community of sacrifices" (*hē koinōnia tōn thusiōn,* lines 2–3),[15] a designation that effectively defines the origin and central function of the *orgeones* associations. They seem to have originated as sacrificial clubs, thus the rough translation "sacrificing associates."[16] Many such organizations worshipped heroes and/or heroines like this one. Others, however, worshipped higher deities, although *orgeones* of that type tended to be associated with foreign deities.[17]

The *orgeones* in this inscription mention only one official, the "host of the feast" (*hestiatōr,* line 12). He is charged with various duties: sacrificing the various animals, keeping the expenses within the budget, and distributing the meat according to the specifications laid down in the decree (lines 14–18). He also sets up the cult table (line 15) and evidently presides at the table. As presider, he is therefore in charge of distributing the meat according to the specified formulas. Furthermore, he would evidently carry out this task at a community banquet because, since absent members do not receive a portion (line 18), we may conclude that the meat must have been consumed on the spot. It is notable that though his duties include activities that might be termed those of a priest and a treasurer, it is his presiding at the table that gives him his title. This was evidently the most important aspect of his function.

The same is true with other *orgeones*. When we can identify their primary official he is referred to as the "host." Thus, for example, a decree of the *orgeones* of Amysos, Asklepios, and Dexion, dated 313/312 B.C.E., honors two "hosts" for their service to the club. Here it is further specified what their duties were: ". . . The hosts . . . managed well and honorably the club's affairs and the sacrifices."[18] The term *sacrifices* is interpreted to refer to the sacrificial rite in its entirety, a ritual that includes a sacrificial banquet.[19] Consequently, Ferguson concludes: "The importance of the Host attests the importance of the *hestiaseis* or *deipna* [banquet] . . . in the activity of the old Attic *orgeones*."[20]

The text refers to two days of sacrifice (lines 14–16), so the feasting probably also took two days. The *orgeones* feast as a family, with wives, sons, daughters, and even maidservants included in the distribution (lines 18–22). The size of the portion distributed to each classification of diners would serve to indicate their relative status. Thus the members, referred to as the *orgeones,* and the "women," who are evidently their wives, receive a full portion, whereas children and maidservants receive no more than a half portion. That there are maidservants indicates that the *orgeones* are made up of rather well-to-do citizens. Since it must be specified that only one maidservant can receive a portion, presumably some members had more than one and had to be restrained from taking too much meat for their households.[21]

Are there women members? The question centers on the interpretation of lines 19–23, with the reconstruction of line 20 being especially important. W. S. Ferguson says unequivocally that there were only adult male members. His reconstruction of line 20, "if an ox were sacrificed," means that if the victim were smaller women would get no portion and thus would not participate in the meal. He interprets the term in line 20, *eleuthepai,* as "respectable women" in general, that is, wives, widows, spinsters—all female family members who are not daughters or servants.[22]

Benjamin D. Meritt interprets two classes of women who receive equal portions with members (or at least the second of these does), "wives" (gynaikes) and "independent women" (eleutherai), that is, women who are members in their own right.[23] Franciszek Sokolowski rejects the reconstructions of both Meritt and Ferguson. He reads lines 19–20 as referring to wives who are respectable and of noble birth. These are allowed to share in the meal but evidently are not members.[24]

Choosing one from the three proposed reconstructions is difficult, leaving the exact reading of the text in doubt. Nevertheless the possibility of female membership must remain an open question. Indeed, the fact that the "independent women" shared equal portions with male members speaks strongly for the interpretation that they are members. It must also be noted, however, that they are not included under the term orgeones. Further, the "women" (gynaikes), a term that refers to wives and perhaps "independent women" as well, must receive their portions from the men (lines 22–23). Thus while these women do receive a portion of the meat equal to that of the men, their position in the community is seen to be subordinate to that of the men.

Where Greek Clubs Met

These orgeones have their own hieron or temple (line 7), at least by the third century B.C.E. This temple has an altar (line 6 reconstructed) and a sacred table (line 15). The form of many such tables is known from archaeological finds of marble tables that were part of a sanctuary's furniture.[25] The type that has been so identified usually had three sections, one or more of which was carved in the form of a type of tray used in carving meat. Thus it is conjectured that it was used both for depositions for the god and as the surface for carving the meat into portions to be distributed to the worshippers. This is probably the type of table usually referred to by such phrases as "table of God" (trapeza tou theou) and "sacred table" (hiera trapeza). Since one of the table fragments of this type was inscribed with a decree from a group of orgeones, it is likely that it is the type referred to by the term table (trapeza) in our inscription.

One of the cult tables that has been discovered contains an unusual inscription: en tō thiasō. This expression is not common to orgeonic inscriptions on cult tables but seems to define a common perception about the significance of the table. Usually such inscriptions define how the inscription is to be displayed. Since the term *thiasos* does not normally refer to the structure or hall where an association met, the phrase is probably best translated "in the midst of the association."[26] This inscription, then, serves to emphasize the symbolic nature of the table as the central focus of the community consciousness of the association.

But where did these *orgeones* dine? Their clubhouse includes a "temple" *(hieron)*, but other facilities that may have been included are not noted. Another inscription from a group of *orgeones,* those of the Hero Egretes, provides a more detailed description of a clubhouse: "Whenever the *orgeones* sacrifice to the Hero in the month of *Boedromion* [September], Diognetus is to place the house at their disposal, which includes the *cella* which is to be opened and an accessory room and the kitchen and couches and tables for two table settings *(triclinia)*."[27]

This inscription, dated 307/306 B.C.E., describes the terms of a lease of the clubhouse to an individual for his private use. The agreement specifies that the lessee must allow the *orgeones* to use the facilities for their normal activities during the year and especially allow free use of facilities needed during the annual sacrifices. The facilities needed on this special occasion are listed, all located in connection with the "clubhouse" *(oikia)*. Besides a "temple," which is perhaps just a temple *cella,* there is an "accessory room," which was a temporary wooden shed or shelter used by those who assisted in the ceremonies,[28] a "kitchen," "dining couches" *(klinai),* and "tables for two triclinia." Clearly, we have here a prototype for a clubhouse where the club members can hold sacrifices as well as banquets.

The phrase "tables for two triclinia" suggests that this clubhouse had two dining rooms, both of which allowed for a triclinium arrangement of couches. The dining furnishings must be portable, since it is specified that they are to be available for the *orgeones* on demand. Since they are used for dining rather than for the distribution of meat, these tables must be of a different type than the sacred tables discussed above.

The term *triclinium* normally refers to a standard dining-room arrangement of couches along three walls of the room. Whether that is its meaning in this period is not clear, however, since the archaeological evidence for dining rooms from this period does not match such a description.[29] Thus it is difficult to determine whether the three-couch arrangement refers to couches arranged on three walls, three couches arranged on three walls, or simply to a normal rectangular dining arrangement (as opposed to other, less common types). Nor do we know how many each couch would hold. Vase paintings, however, illustrate couches of a size to hold two, three, four, and even five on a couch.[30]

Various changes took place in the organization and nature of Greek clubs in the Hellenistic and Roman periods. For example, the *orgeones* type of organization appears to have disappeared in the Roman period.[31] Another change often noted is the increasing significance given to the banquet as the primary activity of a club. The scholars who mention this development often conclude that it represents a decline in the original religious ideals of the association.[32] Such judgments, however, represent an incorrect understanding of the function of the banquet in the Greco-Roman world. This point will be elaborated further as we look at other examples of private clubs in the Greco-Roman world.

ROMAN *COLLEGIA*[33]

Names and Types

Roman clubs served a variety of functions, took a range of forms, and were found in all classes of society. But they all shared a few basic characteristics, chief among them being some kind of religious character and an emphasis on their social function. They were called by a variety of names—*collegium, corpus, sodalitas, sodalitium,* and so forth—but the usual general term under which they may be grouped is *collegia*.[34]

In Roman society there were official, public *collegia* as well as private ones. The official priestly colleges administered to the official state cults. Examples of public colleges include the four great colleges of public priests, the *pontifices,* as well as the priestly colleges of various official cults, such as the *collegium Capitolinorum,* which administered to the cult of Jupiter Capitolinus. Private religious colleges were usually concerned with nonofficial cults, especially those of foreign gods, such as Bacchus, Cybele, Isis, and Mithras. Among the most common private colleges were the *collegia Isidis,* which were found throughout the empire. Many foreign cults that began in Rome as private cults were later adopted as public cults, as was the case at different times with the cults of Isis, Cybele, and Mithra. Private religious colleges often had another function besides the practice of a private cult. That is, they were usually a professional or funerary club as well. For example, the *collegium Aesculapi et Hygiae* and the *cultores Dianae et Antinoi,* discussed below, were private religious colleges as well as burial clubs.[35]

Professional corporations, probably the most common of Roman clubs, were organizations of individuals who had in common the practice of the same trade, craft, or occupation. They often functioned with political interests, but not in the sense of today's trade unions. Their goal was not economic advantage but status or honor, which was prized more than wealth in Roman society.[36] Such trade guilds seem to have originated in Roman society and spread from there to the rest of the Hellenistic world. By the first and second centuries C.E., they had spread throughout the provinces of the Roman Empire, including the Greek East.[37]

The other major type of Roman club was the burial society. These were organized for the purpose of providing decent burials for their members from a common fund based on the regular collection of dues. They were especially found in the lower orders of society, among slaves and freedmen who could not otherwise be assured of being provided with a decent burial. These clubs often owned their own common burial plot or *columbarium*. Their meetings for collecting dues, which were usually once a month, tended to be banquets with a professed religious or funerary aim.[38]

Whatever the professed reasons for banding together, however, most Roman clubs, like their Greek counterparts, functioned especially as social organizations. That is, they provided an opportunity for one to belong to a society that provided, within itself, the surrogate benefits of an enlarged family[39] as well as those of a miniature *polis*.[40] In effect, they provided a form of "social security," that is, a community to which one could belong, as well as what can be termed "burial insurance" for each of their members.[41]

The most visible and widespread social activity of clubs was the banquet. Here the non-wealthy could pool their funds and provide for themselves banquets that often rivaled in luxury those of the upper classes. Such banquets became one of the most common features of the clubs, so that some suggested by their names that they had no other reason for assembling together, such as the Pompeiian "Late-night Drinkers" *(seribibi)*.[42] Other names of clubs that give central significance to the banquet include: "Society of Diners" *(collegium comestorum),* "Table-companions of Concord" *(convictor Concordiae),* "Table-companions who customarily [gather] to eat a meal" *(convictores qui una epula vesci solent),* "Comrades of the Symposium" *(sodales ex symposia),* and "Banqueters of Elvenia" *(triclinium Elvenianum).*[43] Thus Jean-Pierre Waltzing observes: "One is tempted to believe that religion and the cult of the dead were only pretexts. When a college accepted a bequest on the condition to honor a god, the emperor, or its patron, or to maintain the tomb of a foreigner, I imagine that they saw in this the occasion for a festive banquet and the means to pass a day in cordial intimacy."[44]

To many of the Roman moralists, the clubs were nothing more than groups of disorderlies and drunks.[45] And, to be sure, clubs had become such a problem in society that they were at various times banned by imperial edict and thus deemed *collegia illicita*. The riot at the gladiatorial games at Pompeii in 59 c.e. is a well-known example of political agitation that produced restrictions on local *collegia*. It resulted in laws limiting any Pompeiian assemblies for ten years and disbanding any illegal associations.[46] An example of the legal approach taken to Roman clubs is found in a law summarized by Marcianus and recorded in Justinian's sixth-century-c.e. *Digesta* as follows: "In sum, then, unless an association or any such body assembles under the authorization of a decree of the senate or of the emperor, it meets contrary to the decree of the senate and imperial mandates and enactments."[47]

Although disorderliness may have been all too common, nevertheless the clubs took steps to address such problems and provided in their by-laws ideal models for the forms club banquets and other meetings should take. One of the best-preserved examples of typical by-laws of Roman *collegia* is that of the Society of Diana and Antinous.

The Society of Diana and Antinous

The Society of Diana and Antinous was a burial society dedicated to the goddess Diana and the deified Antinous. The lengthy inscription of its by-laws was found in Lanuvium, Italy, and is dated in the year 136 c.e. This inscription (see pages 126–28) is one of the most elaborate of its type ever found, and it has had an influential role in the interpretation of *collegia,* especially of their organization, expenditures, banquets, and rules of conduct.[48]

The club provided a defense of its legality by quoting an excerpt from the current law defining the legal standards for *collegia*. The excerpt reads: "Clause from the Decree of the Senate of the Roman People: These are permitted to assemble, convene, and maintain a society: those who desire to make monthly contributions for funerals may assemble in such a society, but they may not assemble in the name of such society except once a month for the sake of making contributions to provide burial for the dead" (lines 1.10–13). Since this was a burial society that met only once a month to collect dues, it was a legal organization. However, the club met for two banquets in August, on August 13, the "birthday of Diana and of the society," and on August 20, the birthday of the patron's brother (line 2.12). Waltzing suggests that this was allowed under the provision of the law concerning *collegia* that allowed meetings for religious purposes, which stated: "But they are not forbidden to assemble for religious purposes, provided however that nothing is thereby done contrary to the senate's decree by which illegal associations are enjoined."[49] Thus a *conventus* or "business meeting" would not apply, but a banquet could be defined as a religious meeting.[50]

The law concerning *collegia* also refers to the connection of the funerary societies with the lower classes: "The lower classes are, however, permitted to make monthly contributions [to a society], provided, however, they meet only once a month, so that no illegal association may assemble under a pretext of this kind."[51] Note that the College of Diana and Antinous included slaves in its membership (lines 2.3,7). The laws also provide for this eventuality: "Slaves may be admitted into societies of the lower classes with the consent of their masters."[52] Thus the College of Diana and Antinous, like most other burial clubs, was evidently a *collegium tenuiorum* or a "society of the lower classes."

This club was founded on January 1 in the year 133 C.E. (line 1.14), but the inscription dates from the year 136 C.E. Its self-identity as a burial club is seen not only in the legal definition it provided for itself, as quoted above, but also in the exhortation members of the club evidently addressed to one another: "May we have made proper and careful arrangements for providing decent obsequies at the departure of the dead!" (lines 1.15–16). Thus a significant portion of the by-laws is concerned with specifications for the funeral arrangements to be provided for the membership (lines 1.14—2.6).

Like the majority of Roman clubs, it operated with the support of a wealthy patron. The function of the patron was to donate *sportulae* to the club, that is, gifts of food or money. The *sportula* was basically a dole given by the wealthy to their clients. A *cena recta,* or formal banquet, was often given instead of money and was considered more honorable than merely a gift of food.[53] To be a patron brought considerable status to an individual, which was considered a higher good than simply the possession of money. As Plutarch stated: "Most people think that to be deprived of the chance to display their wealth is to be deprived of wealth itself."[54]

Here the specified gift of the patron is money: "Lucius Caesennius Rufus, patron of the municipality . . . promised that he would give them . . . out of his generosity the interest on 15,000 sesterces, to wit 400 sesterces, on the birthday of Diana, August 13, and 400 sesterces on the birthday of Antinous, November 27" (lines 1.1–6).

In return for the beneficence of the patron, a guild would honor him with titles and dedications.[55] These honors added to the status of the patron, therefore giving him a return for his investment. And the members, who by and large were from the lower orders of society, benefited from the patron's munificence.

This society honors its patron in a special way, by means of a feast on the respective birthdays of the patron, each of his parents, and his brother. These feasts are listed in the section labeled "calendar of dinners" (lines 2.11–13). Such "birthday" feasts would have originally been domestic celebrations; the reference here is to the family ideal on which the club models itself.[56] In this case, the individuals being honored would have probably made donations to pay for their honorary feasts.[57] Other feasts take place on the "birthdays" of the patron deities, Diana and Antinous. Indeed, the "birthday" of Diana is also celebrated as the "birthday" of the society itself. Thus the founding date of the society, which is given as January 1, 133, was evidently celebrated on the date when the statue of Diana was dedicated, which was then termed the "birthday of Diana and of the society."[58]

These specified banquets were thus celebrated on the "festive days" (*dies solemnes,* line 2.24) significant to the society. They furthermore served to solidify the bonds between client and patron, whether the patron be human or divine. Not incidentally, they also served as a means for maintaining that relationship for the implicit purpose of securing further favors.

There were evidently other club meetings besides the banquet meetings. At a non-banquet meeting *(conventus)* the official business of the club was carried out (line 2.23). But five of the monthly meetings per year were banquets, and no business was to take place at these meetings "so that we may banquet in peace and good cheer on festive days" (lines 2.23–24).

Indeed, the banquet tended to dominate the life of the club as pictured by this inscription. As already mentioned, the banquet was the principal means of honoring the patron, his family, and the patron deities. It is also at the banquet that the only worship activities are specifically mentioned (lines 2.29–30). In addition, part of the fees paid by the members, besides money, was "an amphora of good wine" (lines 1.21, 2.7–8, 2.15), evidently to be consumed at the meetings.

One of the most important offices in the club was that of *quinquennalis.* His primary function was to perform the central ritual at the banquet (lines 2.29–31). He in turn was rewarded by the bestowal of a sign of status: he received an extra portion at the banquet, either of food or of the distributions of money. If he had done an especially good job, he continued to receive extra portions even after his term of office had expired "as a mark of honor" (lines 2.21–22). His "honorarium" was designated as a double share while in office and a share and a half after serving if he served well. Among the other officers, the "secretary" (scriba) and the "summoner" (viator) also received a share and a half during their terms of office (lines 2.17–22).[59]

The quinquennalis was also accorded the honor of being treated with the utmost respect at the banquet, evidently taking the place of honor in the seating arrangements. Thus an especially heavy fine was imposed on any members who failed to acknowledge his status: "Any member who uses any abusive or insolent language to a quinquennalis at a banquet shall be fined 20 sesterces" (lines 2.27–28).

Another of the principal officers of the club was the magister cenarum ("master of the feast"), whose duty was to arrange for the banquet (lines 2.14–16).[60] There were four magistri chosen at a time, indicating that at least four separate banquet groupings were being arranged. Each member was to serve in this office whenever his name came up on the membership list. They served a term of one year (lines 2.7–10).

Apparently the role of the magister cenarum corresponded to that of a host at a standard formal banquet. The duties of this officer were specified as follows: "Masters of the dinners . . . shall be required to provide an amphora of good wine each, and for as many members as the society has, a bread costing 2 asses, sardines to the number of four, a setting, and warm water with service" (lines 2.14–16). The basic menu, then, consisted of bread, fish, and wine, which were to be apportioned equally among the members. Besides the food, the magister cenarum was to provide the stratio or table service; that is, he was to see that the dining room was provided with all necessary furnishings. This would probably include furnishing pillows and other couch coverings, dishes, napkins, and so forth. He was also to prepare the bath facilities for the members so that when they bathed before the banquet, they would have warm water and servants to provide a rubdown. On the birthday feasts of the deities, the quinquennalis provided perfumed oil for the rubdown (lines 2.30–31). Clearly the banquet was intended to be a proper one, with all the elements a luxury banquet should have.

The quinquennalis also performed a special religious ceremony at designated banquets. Dressed in a special white garment, he would perform a ritual ceremony with incense and wine: ". . . On the festive days of his term of office each quinquennalis is to conduct worship with incense and wine and is to perform his other functions clothed in white . . ." (lines 2.29–30). The nature of the ceremony is not entirely clear, but it evidently included a libation in honor of the individual whose birthday was being commemorated. But it was no ordinary libation such as might be a part of any formal banquet—the specifications of incense and a white garment suggest it is a special ceremony of some significance to the club.

Clearly, the banquets of the Society of Diana and Antinous were not simply drunken parties. Rather, they are described as festive occasions, and rules are specified so that the banquet may be characterized by "peace and quiet" as well as by "good cheer": ". . . If any member desires to make any complaint or bring up any business, he is to bring it up at a business meeting, so that we may banquet in peace and good cheer on festive days" (lines 2.23–24). Here, as in the sacrificial banquet and the philosophical banquet, where *euphrosynē* was the determinative characteristic, "good cheer" had a positive sense.[61] It was an idealized sense of festivity, one that required certain restrictions on the conduct of the participants.

These restrictions are specifically defined in the rules of conduct listed next. These rules would appear to apply primarily to the banquet meeting. They could apply as well to business meetings, of course, but it is significant that they are listed immediately after the atmosphere of the banquet is properly defined and just before its chief ritual is described.

The rules of conduct are as follows: "It was voted further that any member who moves from one place to another so as to cause a disturbance shall be fined 4 sesterces. Any member, moreover, who speaks abusively of another or causes an uproar shall be fined 12 sesterces. Any member who uses any abusive or insolent language to a *quinquennalis* at a banquet shall be fined 20 sesterces" (lines 2.25–28). The last rule explicitly refers to the banquet setting. The *quinquennalis* received an honorary portion at the banquet and presided at its central religious ritual. His function was therefore parallel to that of a host or symposiarch at a formal banquet. As such, he would sit in the position of honor and would preside over the order of the banquet. Thus it is quite likely that insolence toward the *quinquennalis* was such a serious offense (it incurs the largest fine) because it was essential for an orderly banquet that his directions be respected.

The rule against taking another's place so as to cause a disturbance suggests that a value was placed on one's assigned position at the meeting. This, of course, makes sense in the context of a banquet meeting, where each position at table had a value assigned to it. To take another's position would therefore be a personal insult and a seditious act toward the community. So also abusive and argumentative behavior was all too common at drinking parties. This was contrary to the atmosphere of "peace and good cheer" (line 2.24) that was to characterize the festive banquets of this society. The reference to causing "an uproar" is rather general; it refers to any disturbance of the community at large. The phrase "any member who speaks abusively of another," however, is more specific in that interpersonal relations between individual members are referred to and made a problem for the entire community. One wonders if such disputes between members would produce the complaints that were to await the business meeting. If so, then perhaps the rule at line 23 is a parallel to the forensic function that the business meetings served in other associations, such as in the Society of the *Iobakchoi,* to be discussed below, and perhaps in the Guild of Zeus Hypsistos. This interpretation is certainly consistent with the general tenor of all the rules of conduct, which have as their purpose the well-being of the community as a whole.

This well-being is thus identified with a properly conducted formal banquet, that is, a banquet characterized by "peace and good cheer." These terms, of course, function to define the social relationships of the members as experienced at the banquet. They have this function not just in a descriptive sense but in a prescriptive sense as well. By means of the ideal type of banquet that is thus characterized, an idealization that was clearly understood as the "proper" form of a ritual meal, the banquet functioned to define community relationships.

Where Roman *Collegia* Met

The meeting place of the Society of Diana and Antinous was in the temple of Antinous (1.1). There are other examples of *collegia* meeting in temples, and in some cases it is mentioned that they banqueted there as well. For example, a "Society of Rag Dealers" *(collegium centonariorum)* "sacrificed and banqueted in the temple as was their custom."[62] The "Worshippers of Hercules" *(cultores Herculis)* met at the temple of Hercules for an annual sacrifice and banquet. The "Table-companions of Concord" *(convictores concordiae)* are assumed to have taken their banquets in the temple of Concord.[63]

Usually, however, the meeting house was called by the general name "clubhouse" *(schola),* and it was there that facilities for dining were located. For example, it is in the "*schola* under the portico consecrated to Silvanus and the College of his Sodality" (lines 7–8) that this club sacrificed and banqueted (lines 11–12).[64] Other *scholae* are said to contain such facilities as "preparation rooms" *(apparatoria)*, probably for preparing meals, a "kitchen" *(culina)*, "tables" *(mensae)*, a "cistern" *(cisterna)*, and "banquet rooms" *(triclinia)*.[65]

Indeed, functions ascribed to *scholae* and to *templa* are so similar that they can be deemed synonymous terms in many contexts where they refer to meeting houses of *collegia*.[66] That is, the structures referred to by these terms may be different, but they all provide the same facilities. A chapel may be part of a *schola* just as a triclinium may be part of a *templum*. Thus the Society of Diana and Antinous probably ate their banquet in the temple of Antinous in rooms provided especially for this purpose.

Examples of meeting houses of various trade guilds have been found in the excavations at Ostia. Here there are several types of structures that can tentatively be associated with trade guilds. One such structure is merely a large undivided hall. Another type is what is called a courtyard temple, of which four examples have been suggested as the temples of trade guilds. These have a typical form in which a courtyard is located in front of a temple. Thus the courtyard could have functioned for the social activities of the guild. In other cases, temples with adjoining halls may have belonged to guilds. In none of these examples, however, is it clear what sort of social activities may have taken place within them.[67]

The best example of an all-purpose meeting hall at Ostia, and the best attested as a guild hall, is that of the College of the Carpenters (Builders in Wood). The ground plan is similar to that of a large private house, in that the major rooms are located around a central courtyard. But it is actually not a *domus* but the bottom floor of an *insula* or apartment house such as is common in Ostia. Thus it is estimated that there were originally five to six floors with a capacity to house from 120 to 196 people.[68]

The structure was originally constructed in 119–120 C.E.[69] By 198 it was in use as the Carpenters' Guild meeting hall, as evidenced by an inscription listing the membership role of the college found in the ruins on the base of a statue of Septimius Severus.[70] Prior to its use by the college, it seems to have functioned as a normal apartment structure, or perhaps as an inn.[71] But the interior room arrangements in their latest phase would reflect the adaptation of the structure to the needs of the college.

Four of the rooms around the courtyard are designed as triclinia, with permanent concrete *podia* built along their walls to serve as dining couches.[72] These *podia* are of a different style than the stone couch structures found in classical Greek dining-room structures. Their greater height (0.70 meter) and depth (ca. 0.50 meter) give them a significantly different aspect, and their form is such that there is no attempt to give them the appearance of a conventional "couch," although the pillows and other coverings would apparently have served to do this. Indeed, their height is such that it was necessary to build steps into them on both sides next to the doors in order to make it easier to mount them.

Because of the form of these couches, the arrangement of diners would correspond to that found in the common Roman triclinium or Pi-shaped dining hall.[73] The usual number of diners would be three to a couch or nine to a triclinium, if more than three diners shared a couch, as was commonly done. The clubhouse of the College of the Carpenters therefore contains space for thirty-six to dine in comfort at one time, although more than that could be accommodated. It should be noted that the membership list for the club included at least 350 names.[74]

The meeting house of the College of the Carpenters was located adjacent to the forum in Ostia. Such a location was evidently preferred by trade guilds in general in the Roman world; thus there are many examples of such guilds located near fora in such cities as Beneventum, Falerium, Praeneste, Pompeii, and Rome.[75] The evidence suggests that these types of clubs had some connection with the political leaders of the city.[76]

Other types of clubs were often located in areas appropriate to their central purpose.[77] Thus many religious guilds were located in temples, as was the college of Diana and Antinous mentioned above. Burial clubs were often located outside the city near the burial grounds. Thus the "College of Aesculapius and Hygieia" met and banqueted at its clubhouse located between the first and second milestones of the Appian Way: "Salvia Gaia daughter of Marcellina . . . gave as a gift to the College of Aesculapius and Hygiaea a place for a chapel with a vine trellis and a marble statue of Aesculapius and a roofed terrace adjoining it in which the members of the college whose names are recorded above may dine. It is located on the Appian Way between the first and second milestones."[78] The entire complex of chapel and covered terrace is called a *schola* later in the same inscription (lines 11 and 13). Thus this *schola* has two chambers, one a religious shrine and the other a dining area, both of which are located in a cemetery area. This arrangement illustrates the combination of religious, funerary, and social functions in a *schola*.

Obviously, the locations of *scholae* were not standardized and would depend on several external factors: availability of land or space, preferences of the patron, financial capabilities of the club, and so on. Indeed, the meeting place was often given to the club by the patron, as was the case with the

College of Aesculapius and Hygiaea in the inscription quoted above, and many clubs met in the homes of their patrons. On the other hand, quite often meeting locations would correspond to the predominant aim or identity of the club—thus a funerary club met at a cemetery site, a religious club at a temple, a professional club at the forum.

GRECO-ROMAN CLUBS

Names and Types

In the Eastern Mediterranean world of the Roman period, there was an increase in the proliferation of clubs. It was a time when the city-state had declined and the individual was seeking new social structures on which to build a sense of belonging and stability. To fill this need, new forms of clubs took shape, influenced not only by Greek tradition but also by Roman forms of clubs. In addition, the banquet took on an increased role in the life of the clubs.

For examples of the varieties of clubs during this period, we can look to Delos, an important Hellenistic city from which we have extensive remains.[79] Like Ostia, Delos was a major port city and trading center that had attracted a wide variety of merchants and tradesmen from all over the Mediterranean world. Many of these merchants banded together into ethnic communities organized as trade and religious associations.

The Delos association known as the Poseidoniasts of Beirut provides an example of the complex nature of a typical Greco-Roman club. This was a guild of Syrian merchants who organized themselves under the patronage of Poseidon. They named themselves "the association of the Poseidoniasts of Beirut: merchants, ship owners, and agents." They built a sumptuous clubhouse in which were found four *cellas,* one of which was dedicated to the goddess Roma.[80] It is thought that they may have formed a major part of the constituency of the elaborate sanctuary of the Syrian gods on the island. Indeed, they may have used one of the several dining rooms provided in this sanctuary, although there is no specific evidence to this effect.[81]

In Syria, the dining facilities of various religious associations have been found. A number of these associations are connected with the Romanized form of the worship of the Syrian gods just as we find at Delos. Inscriptional evidence also attests to various *thiasoi* in the regions adjacent to Syria.[82] In Palestine, for example, the Qumran sect had organizational aspects similar to those of Greco-Roman clubs.[83] The same can be said of the organization of early Christianity as it spread over the eastern Mediterranean.[84] Indeed, early Christian groups tended to be categorized as religious associations by local authorities.[85]

In Egypt there were various forms of religious and secular associations, some conforming to classical Greek models and some reflecting indigenous religious elements. Philo refers to "religious clubs" *(thiasoi),* "synods" *(synodoi),* and "dining clubs" *(klinai),* all of which he characterizes as groups that, in his opinion, exist primarily for the purpose of holding drinking parties.[86] Strabo spoke of a "synod" *(synodos),* of "men of learning" *(philologoi andres)* in Alexandria who took their meals at a "common mess hall" *(syssition)* at the Museum.[87] There was, in fact, a wide variety of Egyptian clubs sharing several indigenous characteristics.[88]

The Guild of Zeus Hypsistos

The Guild of Zeus Hypsistos was an Egyptian association that shared characteristics of both Greek and Egyptian religious associations.[89] Its statutes are preserved in a papyrus copy that dates from the latter Ptolemaic period, or circa 69 to 58 B.C.E. It was probably located in Philadelphia.[90] The statutes are translated as follows:[91]

> Horion son of Haryotes, . . . /
> thirty-two, total 32, /
> May it be well. / The law which those of the association of Zeus the highest made in common, that it should be authoritative. / (5) Acting in accordance with its provisions, they first chose as their / president Petesouchos the son of Teephbennis, a man of parts, worthy of the place and of the company, / for a year from the month and day aforesaid, / that he should make for all the contributors one banquet a month in the sanctuary of Zeus, / at which they should in a common room pouring libations, pray, and perform the other customary rites / (10) on behalf of the god and lord, the king. All are to obey the president / and his servant in matters pertaining to the corporation, and they shall be present at / all command occasions to be prescribed for them and at meetings and assemblies and outings. / It shall not be permissible for any one of them to . . . or to make factions / or to leave the brotherhood of the president for another, / (15) or for men to enter into one another's pedigrees at the banquet or / to abuse one another at the banquet or to chatter or / to indict or accuse another or to resign / for the course of the year or again to bring the drinkings to nought or / . . . to hinder the / (20) [leader?] . . . contributions and other [____?] / levies and shall each pay . . . / If any of them becomes a father, (he shall contribute? . . .).

The community describes itself in general terms as "the association (synod) of Zeus Hypsistos" (line 4). The deity after which the association is named, Zeus Hypsistos, is an aspect of Zeus that is not unknown on Greek soil, but since Hypsistos is a rather vague epithet it is not clear what the origin of the Egyptian cult might be.[92] The term *synod (synodos)* is especially common in Egypt as a generic term for religious and other types of associations. Like many other terms used to describe associations, it has a variety of connotations. For example, it is sometimes associated with the banquet meeting itself, as seen in Philo, who refers to dining clubs in Alexandria that "the local people call 'synods' [*synodoi*] and 'banquets' ['couches'] [*klinai*]."[93] Other associations that go by the name "synod" share with this one several distinct characteristics not common to Greek associations. For example, they tend to meet in a public temple rather than a private shrine or private structure of some kind, just as this guild meets in "the sanctuary of Zeus" (lines 8–9).[94]

In addition, several Egyptian guilds like this one incorporate themselves for only a year at a time (see line 7), whereas Greek associations tended to incorporate themselves on a permanent basis. Finally, this guild has only two officials, and the second of these, the "attendant," is to be obeyed just like the "president" (lines 6 and 11). Most Greek associations, however, had a multiplicity of officials, and when they had an "attendant," he had a strictly subordinate role. A. D. Nock attributes these characteristics to indigenous Egyptian influences on what is otherwise a Greek form of club.[95]

It is the communal banquet that this club especially shares in common with other Greek and Roman clubs. It is called a "drinking party" (*posis,* line 8) and a "symposium" (lines 15, 16, 18). Both of these terms emphasize the second course or the drinking party proper, but they often function as general terms for a banquet as well.[96]

Other terms used here for the meetings of this club are *meetings (synlogoi), assemblies (synagōgai),* and *outings (apodēmiai,* line 12). *Meetings* and *assemblies* appear to refer to the same thing without specific reference to different purposes of the meetings.[97] It should be noted, however, that both terms occur in reference to banquet meetings. For example, Philodemus (first century B.C.E.) refers to "symposia and other meetings" *(symposia kai alloi syllogoi).*[98] Athenaeus relates how his predecessors "used the verb 'assemble' [*synagein*] of drinking one with another and 'assembly' [*synagōgion*] of the symposium."[99] The evidence does not suggest, however, that the word "assembly" was used exclusively for banquet rather than business meetings.[100]

"Outings," on the other hand, has the sense of "traveling abroad." For the club it would mean meeting elsewhere than in the usual meeting place. In the papyri, there are other examples of clubs meeting outside their primary place of origin for religious or honorific rites that called for such a pilgrimage. Among these examples, incidentally, are cases in which the term also refers to an outdoor meal or "picnic."[101]

There is also a reference to "command occasions" (line 12) for meetings. These would be the meetings called by the president on other than regular meeting days, but again their purpose is not defined. Thus there is no clear indication in these references that they ever gathered for any other purpose than banqueting together. Indeed, the only descriptions of events at the meetings refer to the banquet, including the rules of conduct that are preserved. Therefore Nock compares this club not to the normal Greek religious association but to the type of club known as a "dining club" *(eranos)*.[102] Nock's distinctions may not be appropriate to the data, however, since this group had a decidedly religious aspect to their banquets.

The meal is accompanied by religious rites that are described in this way: "a banquet *(posis)* . . . at which they should . . . pouring libations [*spendein*], pray [*euchesthai*], and perform the other customary rites [*talla ta nomizomena*] on behalf of the god and lord, the king" (lines 8–10). The phrase has an interesting parallel in Plato's *Symposion:* "They made libations [*spondas poiēsasthai*], hymned the god [*asantas ton theon*], and performed the other customary rites [*talla ta nomizomena*], then turned to the drinking [*trepesthai pros ton poton*]."[103]

Thus we are concerned here with terminology that referred not only to sacrificial rites but also to the normal religious aspect of a formal symposium. The form is the same; what has changed is the content of the rites. Here they specifically refer to the civic cult, the worship of the Ptolemies. In addition, the libation was possibly directed to the patron deity, Zeus Hypsistos, although this is not specifically stated.[104] The rites, therefore, are given a content that especially conforms to the political realities and religious piety of this Egyptian association. The symposium thereby is made to serve a communal function that has a particular reference to the self-identity of this group.

The monthly banquet is to be provided by the president as his major duty (lines 6–8). But since the participants are called "fellow-contributors" (*syneisphoroi,* line 8), it would appear that the president does not really finance the meal but only organizes it, unlike the *magister* of the Society of Diana and Antinous but like the "host" *(hestiatōr)* of the *orgeones.* Also like the *orgeones'* host, the president of this club fulfills the function of a symposiarch by presiding at the meal and seeing that the rules are obeyed. This is inferred from the statement: "All are to obey the president and his servant in matters pertaining to the corporation" (lines 10–11). Note that the only rules listed here that presumably constitute that which is to be obeyed are rules concerned with the banquet, so that the setting for obedience is the banquet.

The first set of rules concern loyalty to the club. Members are to contribute to the common fund (lines 7–8), be present at all specified meetings (line 12), and obey the president and his servant in all matters pertaining to the club (lines 10–11).

The designation of the members as fellow-contributors also calls attention to the social bonds created by the shared financial responsibilities that are required of each member. Their organization is described further as the "brotherhood of the president" (line 14), which is rather unique as a term of identity for a club.[105] It occurs in the context of a strong appeal for loyalty to this particular body: "It shall not be permissible . . . to leave the brotherhood of the president for another" (lines 13–14). Somehow the president is seen as the focus for the sense of unity of the group. This image would be enhanced by his serving as host for the communal meal.

Indeed, the meal becomes synonymous with community identity to such an extent that to hinder its communal purpose in any way is to violate the community itself. Thus members are required to be present (lines 11–12), are specifically prohibited from joining another such group (line 14), are required to participate for the full year that the statutes cover (lines 17–18), and, above all, are not to cause "schisms" (*schismata,* line 13) within the group.[106] Indeed, they are not to do anything that would work against the convivial spirit of the occasion: "They are not to bring about the dissolution of the convivial occasion" (line 18). What is at stake here is the commonplace assurance that everyone at a properly run banquet will have a good time, but here that idea has been elevated to serve as the very glue that holds this community together.

Thus when specific aspects of behavior are mentioned, they all refer to typical kinds of disruptive conduct to be found at drinking parties. Though symposia were traditionally occasions for dialogue and discussion, members were to keep their discussions civil and were not to argue: "[Members are] not to abuse [or 'speak abusively,' *kakologein*] one another at the banquet" (lines 15–16). Furthermore, they were not to engage in class disputes or arguments over relative status: "[Members are] not to enter into one another's pedigrees at the banquet" (line 15).[107] Such arguments were all too common in a setting where one's status was indicated by the place one occupied at table. Thus one may compare the rule to take the place of another in the Society of Diana and Antinous (line 2.25) and in the Society of the *Iobakchoi* (line 74) or the topos in oral tradition and literature whereby a distinguished guest will be insulted and leave if he finds that a place worthy of his position has not been reserved for him.[108]

The restriction against "speaking out" or "chattering" (*lalein,* line 16) is unclear. Conversation was an expected part of a symposium. This could therefore be a reference to undisciplined speaking, as in the case when one spoke out of turn or without permission from the symposiarch. Such an instance is referred to in the rules of conduct of the Society of the *Iobakchoi* (lines 107–110) and in the rules of conduct at Christian worship services in Corinth (1 Cor 14:26-33a). A similar idea may be contained in the reference to "quiet" (line 2.23) that should govern the meetings of the Society of Diana and Antinous and "good order" (line 65) that should govern the meetings of the Society of *Iobakchoi.* However, one should not rule out the possibility that such references refer not only to disorderly speaking but also to a sense of ritual solemnity appropriate to the religious nature of such meetings. Here, however, the emphasis must be on orderly speaking at the meal, since other rules presume that the meal was not conducted in silence.

The other rules, "not to indict or accuse another" (line 17), refer to the method by which disputes among the members were to be settled. These are forensic terms and refer to formal accusations made before a court. The members of this guild are thus prohibited from taking disputes within their community to the public courts. The implication is that such disputes are to be settled within the community. This is the same type of rule found among the *Iobakchoi* (lines 84–94) and the Corinthian Christians (1 Cor 6:1-8).

Where Greco-Roman Clubs Met

The meal of the Guild of Zeus Hypsistos is held in a "common room" (*andrōn koinos,* line 9) at the sanctuary. The term for *common,* however, can also mean "belonging to the club."[109] The term for *room (andrōn)* is often used to signify a dining room and so surely means that here.[110] Thus the phrase "common room" could also be translated "club dining room." This would signify that while the club met at a public temple, it used its own dining room, which it either owned or rented.

Greek temples often had adjacent structures set aside for the social activities of the cult. Such structures were even more common in Egyptian and Syrian sanctuaries. These accessory structures were often called simply "houses" *(oikoi),* but specific descriptive terms could also be used, such as "dining hall" *(histiatorion),* "dinner hall" *(deipnētērion),* and so on.[111]

This leads to the suggestion that the term *room (andrōn)* in the Zeus Hypsistos statutes might refer to a building within the *temenos* rather than a single room. Indeed, there is even an indication that the building may have contained two dining rooms rather than one, since the president and his assistant both appear to function as symposiarchs. This would be sufficient to accommodate the entire club, whose membership is estimated by Skeat and Roberts to be about forty.[112]

There are other instances in which clubs name themselves after their meeting house. In one such case from this same period, the meeting house that the club adopts as its name is identified as a dining hall. This is suggested in a study by Louis Robert of two inscriptions from Athens that are dated 112–110 B.C.E.[113] These inscriptions are both from the same association, which identifies itself as "The House" *(oikos)* in the first and "The House [*oikos*] of the Great Gods [the Samothracian Gods]" in the second. A reference in the second inscription notes the central club activities: "He sacrificed the sacrifices on behalf of the banqueters" (lines 9–10).

Robert cites several examples where the name "house" is used not only for the clubhouse but also as the name of the club itself.[114] One such example, in fragmentary form, refers to an association of Piraeus identified as "the fellow diners in the house of [name obscured]." In other examples in which the term is mentioned, it is often associated with a meal. Robert concludes that in the case of the Athenian association, the name "the House of the Great Gods" clearly identifies it as a religious association. But "the essential aspect, giving its name to the association, was the banquet hall."[115]

THE SOCIETY OF *IOBAKCHOI*

This Athenian society of the second century C.E. provides such extensive and significant information about Greco-Roman clubs that it merits a section to itself. The inscription recording the "minutes" of this club provides us with an inside look at the religious activities and rules and regulations of this organization. What we find here can be considered to be representative of religious societies of this period and type.

This association of worshippers of Dionysus or Bakchos called themselves *Iobakchoi,* possibly deriving their name from the Athenian festival of Dionysus, the *Iobakcheia.*[116] The 163-line inscription recording the renewal of the statutes of the club provides us with exceptional information about them.

The inscription itself (see pages 129–31) dates from sometime in the late second or early third century C.E.[117] However, since the statutes were already in existence when the events described in the inscription took place, having been drawn up by the previous priests Chrysippos and Dionysios (see lines 10–11),[118] the club is thought to date from at least the mid-second century c.e. Indeed, the priest who is recorded as relinquishing his post to "the most excellent Claudius Herodes" (line 9) had already served as vice-priest and priest for a total of forty years, twenty-three of those as priest (lines 5–7). The inscription records this transfer of office (lines 1–9), the vote to renew the statutes (lines 10–31), and the statutes themselves (lines 32–163).

The Called Meetings of the *Iobakchoi*

Occasions for Meetings. In order to determine the occasions for meetings and the types of meetings, one must engage in some minor textual criticism, for references to the meetings of the *Iobakchoi* do not always correspond. The first reference, at lines 42–44, lists the following meetings: "The *Iobakchoi* shall meet on the ninth of each month and at the yearly festivals, at the *Bakcheia,* and on any extraordinary feast of the god." Here we have two types of meetings referred to: regular monthly meetings and meetings held in conjunction with festivals of Dionysus. Of the latter there are apparently three categories: regular yearly festivals, special festivals, and the *Bakcheia,* a reference to an otherwise unknown festival. Either this was a special festival held in honor of Dionysus,[119] or the term may be used here in a collective sense to refer to the special festivals of this association.[120] In the latter case, there would presumably be more than one such meeting per year.

Two additional meetings are referred to later, however. The members were to meet on "the tenth day of the month *Elaphebolion*" (lines 120–21), which was the date for the state festival of Dionysus at Athens, also known as the "Great Dionysia."[121] And there were meetings especially called to celebrate honors to individual members: "those days when legacies or honors or appointments are celebrated" (lines 153–55; also see lines 127–36).

Other references either referred to different meeting dates from those listed at 42–44 or were the same meetings but called by different names. For example, at lines 151–55, in addition to the monthly and yearly festival meetings, reference is made to the special kind of Dionysiac meeting called the *stibas* and to "the customary days of the god." Both of these references, of course, could refer to meeting days already mentioned. Nevertheless, such a variety of references to meeting dates is problematic.

One proposed explanation is that more than one set of statutes have been combined here.[122] This would mean that some parts of the statutes date from an earlier period in the club's history and derive from a different authorship.

This is, of course, the form taken by the *orgeones* inscription. In that case, however, it is clearly stated that the "ancient decrees" are being restated. Here it is not so apparent that earlier material is being included, but there are several problems with the text that are cleared up if that is the case.

For example, many of the technical terms pertaining to the club and its activities are not always used consistently, a point that will be discussed in more detail later. Consistent with this is the fact that the present form of the statutes is somewhat confused. Subjects are taken up in what appears to be a random manner, with some rules repeated but in a different form. For example, entrance requirements are discussed at lines 32–41 and again at 53–62; in each case different details are discussed. Similarly, the references to penalties at 48–53 and 67–72 are basically the same in content, yet stated differently. Thus the theory that this document represents a conflation of data from different periods in the history of the club has much to commend it and provides a logical explanation for the textual phenomena observed.

Business Meetings. When all of this is taken into account, we can reconstruct the following picture of the meetings of the *Iobakchoi*. There appear to be two basic types of meetings. The first of these is the "assembly" or *agora*. This can be termed a business meeting, since it is the occasion for voting on business pertaining to the club. For example, the meeting on which the statutes were voted, on the eighth day of *Elaphebolion,* is termed an *agora* (line 3). This is also the name given to a meeting called especially for the purpose of judging a disciplinary matter at which the members would vote on the issue (lines 86–87) and that they were required to attend (lines 96–99). To this one may compare the business meeting or *conventus* of the Society of Diana and Antinous (lines 23–24).

Banquet Meetings: The Stibas. The second type of meeting is the banquet meeting. This seems to be the form of all nonbusiness gatherings of the club. Certainly the festival meetings would all include banquets, as would any special "feast of the god" (line 44). However, all meetings of this type appear to be included under the technical term *stibas*.

Stibas is actually not used consistently in this document. For example, in lines 112 and 152 it is used with the term *yearly festival,* as if it, too, is a separate festival meeting. Indeed, L. Deubner interprets it as such. He sees the *stibas* as the most important festival of the club, next to the yearly festival, because of the rituals connected with it in this inscription.[123] Elsewhere in the inscription, however, the term seems to be used in a different sense. For example, at lines 46–49 failure to pay the monthly contribution for wine incurs the penalty of exclusion from the *stibas*. To be penalized only at a yearly festival meeting would scarcely be sufficient to encourage monthly payment of dues. In this case, then, the term seems to refer to banquet meetings in general. Again, one can explain these discrepancies by proposing that this is a conflated document. Thus at one point the term may have referred to a yearly festival meeting, perhaps at a time when the club met for such activities less frequently. Later, however, it apparently came to refer to all banquet meetings.

The term *stibas* in its basic sense refers to a couch or bed of straw placed on the ground. It was used by soldiers in the field for sleeping as well as for reclining at meals.[124] It was a form of dining couch associated with rustic, even primitive, settings and was not always associated with straw, such as in the phrase "*stibas* of wood."[125] The term *stibas* was particularly associated with Dionysiac piety and seemed to have had a special meaning in that setting, as did the related term *stibadeion* or *stibadium* in Latin. This latter term came to refer to a particular kind of Roman dining-couch arrangement, also called a *sigma,* which was semicircular in shape rather than the normal rectangular shape.[126] Thus it is thought that the term *stibas* had also come to be used as a technical term in Dionysiac associations, such as this one, for a dining couch or perhaps a straw mat that was decorated in a special way.[127] For example, Herodes Atticus is said to have reclined on an "ivy-covered *stibas*" at a Dionysiac banquet.[128]

When the *Iobakchoi* used this term, it may have signified, among other things, that they dined on decorated couches, or, if the term is to be taken in a more specialized sense, that they utilized the more rustic dining arrangement in which straw mats were spread on the floor. Therefore, the term *stibas* and the special nature of the decorations it implies may have functioned to call to mind an earlier time of Dionysiac revels in a rustic setting, perhaps connected with the Dionysiac grotto.[129]

The primary significance of the term for the *Iobakchoi,* however, is the symbolic value given to it as a technical term. Not only was it used to refer to a dining couch, but also it had come to stand for the banquet meetings in general. Note, for example, that the term *feast (hestiasis)* is used with a meaning parallel to that of the term *stibas* in lines 48–49 and 104–5. Also, at lines 111–15, the term *stibas* is used in a context in which it is seen to refer to the meeting in general. Here the "customary rituals" and the "libation" are designated to take place "at the *stibas.*"[130] In such a usage, *stibas* may have indicated that a special setting was used for the meal. But it especially carried the sense of a meeting with a special atmosphere, most notably a solemn one. For at the *stibas* loud and unruly behavior was proscribed, and "good order and quietness" (lines 63–65) were upheld.

The *stibas* called for such an atmosphere because of the various rituals that took place at it, notably the dramatic ritual (lines 65–66) and the "customary rituals" (lines 111–15). The interpretation of these rituals will be discussed in more detail below. What is important to notice at this point, however, is that in effect what is known about the religious life of the *Iobakchoi* took place at the *stibas*. Only the yearly sacrifice is not specifically connected with the *stibas* (lines 117–21), but it can be related to it by implication, since sacrificial portions were distributed according to roles taken in the dramatic ritual, a ritual that of course took place at the *stibas*.

The *stibas* served not only as the primary setting for the religious activities of the *Iobakchoi* but also as the focus for community solidarity. It was from the *stibas* that one was excluded as a punishment for failure to pay the dues or fees and to which one was admitted when proper payment was made or when the priests had judged one otherwise worthy of admittance (lines 46–53, 67–72). Thus admittance to or exclusion from the *stibas* represented, in effect, admittance to or exclusion from the community itself. The term *stibas* came to symbolize the community activity par excellence and thereby the community itself.

What Took Place at *Iobakchoi* Meetings

A Drinking Party. The primary and indispensable ingredient for the meetings of the *Iobakchoi* was wine. Each member was required to pay a fixed amount each month for the wine (lines 46–47). In addition, various occasions required the payment of a libation. It was part of the entrance fee (line 38). It was a required gift to the community by a member who had received any civic honor (lines 127–36, 153–55). It was provided by the club as a special honor on behalf of the treasurer, thus known as "the treasurer's libation" (lines 157–58). Clearly the term refers to a ceremony in which the community would share in the wine being offered. Thus an individual who provided a libation evidently was to provide enough wine for a drinking ceremony, or perhaps for an entire drinking party.[131] The term does not appear to refer to a fixed amount, but rather to the ceremony per se. The amount might depend on the means and generosity of the donor. But whenever the club honored a deceased member, a single jar of wine was specified as the amount to be shared by those who attended the funeral.[132]

A Sacrificial Meal. On festival occasions one would expect that the club would have sacrificial meat for their meal. But only one sacrifice is specifically mentioned in the inscription. This is on the occasion of the state festival of Dionysus on the tenth day of the month *Elaphebolion*.[133] The sacrifice was performed by the *archibakchos* (lines 117–21), an official otherwise unknown except in this inscription.[134] His duties here correspond to what we might normally ascribe to a priest.

Distributions of Meat. The portions of meat were to be distributed in the following manner: "And when portions are distributed, let them be taken by the priest, vice-priest, *archibakchos,* treasurer, cowherd, Dionysus, Kore, Palaimon, Aphrodite, and Proteurythmos; and let these names be apportioned by lot among all the members."[135] The first five names appear to refer to officers of the club.[136] The latter five are names of deities that must represent roles taken by various members at the ritual drama (see lines 45, 65–66).[137] Nothing is said about the rest of the membership receiving anything, but one might suppose that they would divide whatever was left after the honored members received their portions. Similar designations of special portions to be distributed to honored members are frequent in statutes of clubs; see, for example, the *orgeones* inscription discussed above.

Customary Rituals. At the banquet meetings, a major role was played by the religious rituals. Among these were the "customary rituals" (lines 111–12) performed by the priest. Most probably what is signified here is their own version of the libation customary at any formal meal. This text can be compared to similar terminology from Plato's *Symposium* and from the by-laws of the Guild of Zeus Hypsistos, which refer to the "customary rites," especially the libation, with which the drinking party traditionally began.

The Yearly Festival. A special *stibas* was held for "the yearly festival," which included the offering of a special libation for "the Festival of Arrival" (line 113) and a "theological discourse" or "sermon" (line 115). Also there may have been a "speech" (line 107) given by one or another of the members at the direction of the priest (lines 107–10). The festival referred to here was evidently the *Anthesteria* festival held yearly in connection with the arrival of the new wine in the month *Anthesterion.* During this celebration of the season's new wine, the jars were opened and a libation poured out to Dionysus before any was drunk.

The Festival of Arrival. The ceremony associated with the *Anthesteria* is attested elsewhere, notably in various cities of Asia Minor (Smyrna, Ephesus, Miletus, and Priene).[138] It evidently included a processional celebrating the "arrival" or "bringing home" of Dionysus, in which Dionysus was carried on a ship that rode on a cart, a motif pictured on several vase paintings.[139] There is some question as to the form taken by the "arrival" festival in the Roman period, since Plutarch says that it was no longer practiced in its traditional form in his day.[140]

The "sermon," however, is a traditional part of the *Anthesteria* festival that is attested in the Roman period. Philostratus mentions it in this reference: "And he is said to have rebuked the Athenians for their conduct of the festival of Dionysos, which they hold at the season of the month *Anthesterion . . .* when he heard them dancing lascivious jigs . . . in the midst of the solemn and sacred epic of Orpheus."[141] The connection with Orpheus correlates with the sense of the term *theologian* in Asia Minor, where the "hymnists" *(hymnōdoi)* of the imperial cult often also had the title of "theologians" *(theologoi)*. Their function was to sing hymns in honor of the emperor.[142] Thus the "sermon" here has been conjectured to be some form of "prosaic hymn" in praise of Dionysus.[143] Consequently, during the annual *Anthesteria* festival in Athens, the *Iobakchoi* celebrated with their own special version of the traditional "arrival" festival in a ceremony that included a special libation, a traditional "sermon," and, of course, a drinking party.

A Ritual Drama. An even more elaborate ritual is described as follows: "No one is allowed to sing, cheer, or applaud at the *stibas,* but with all good order and quietness they shall speak and act their allotted parts under the direction of the priest or the *archibakchos*" (lines 63–67). The phrase "speak and act their allotted parts" is interpreted as a reference to a ritual drama performed by the *Iobakchoi.* Some scholars interpret it as equivalent to "the things said and the things done" that are characteristic of mystery rites.[144] Certainly the reverential atmosphere in which the ceremony is to take place is consistent with such an interpretation.

Participation in these rites was required of each member (lines 45–46), and, if they performed their roles well, they received special honor. Roles were assigned by lot from the membership (lines 125–27), and, whenever one's turn came to play such a role, he received a special portion from the sacrificial distribution as a symbol of the rank and status connected with these roles. The assigned roles that are known to us are those of five officers and five deities as named in the sacrificial distribution list quoted above. Probably only the names of the deities represented roles, with the actual officers taking their own parts in the ceremony.[145] However, the plot of the mythic drama in which these characters played their roles is unknown to us.

Dramatic presentations were, of course, not uncommon as a part of symposia entertainment. A particularly apt parallel is the pantomime presented in Xenophon's *Symposium.* Here two dancers portray Dionysus and Ariadne as lovers.[146] Although the presentation is intended as entertainment, it functions well in the setting, in which "love" *(erōs)* had been a topic of conversation and in which Dionysus would always be considered present symbolically as god of the vine. Xenophon's story ended with a practical if not moralistic application: "At last, the banqueters, seeing them in each other's embrace and obviously leaving for the bridal couch, those who were unwedded swore that they would take to themselves wives, and those who were already married mounted horse and rode off to their wives that they might enjoy them."

The *Iobakchoi* ritual could have functioned in a similar way, that is, as the entertainment segment of the symposium. Of course, the plot must have been different from the presentation in Xenophon. Indeed, the presence of officials of the club in the cast along with mythical figures suggests that the plot had special significance to the communal identity as well as the religious piety of the club. One might conjecture that it was concerned with a mythological version of the founding of the club. It also had a more direct communal function than normal symposium entertainment of this sort in that the members themselves played the roles in the drama. Finally, its religious nature is given emphasis by the injunctions that it be conducted with the proper spirit.

Dances are known to have occurred regularly in Dionysiac ritual, and a frequent role to be played in them was that of the "cowherd," who is listed among the *Iobakchoi* characters as well.[147] Pantomimic dance was especially widespread and popular. In his discourse on dance, *De saltatione*, Lucian notes that Dionysiac and Bacchic ritual is almost entirely dance. He catalogues various subjects that were acted out in pantomimic dance and notes an especially well-known Bacchic dance: "And certainly the Bacchic dance that is especially cultivated in Ionia and in Pontus . . . has so enthralled the people of those countries that when the appointed time comes round they each and all forget everything else and sit . . . looking at titans, corylantes, satyrs, and rustics. Indeed, these parts in the dance are performed by the men of the best birth and first rank in every one of their cities." Martin P. Nilsson concludes: "The office of the *boukoloi* in Pergamon, perhaps elsewhere too, was to dance at the biennial festivals of the god, just as the Maenads did."[148]

Accordingly, the ritual drama of the *Iobakchoi* may best be seen as a pantomimic dance along the lines of Dionysiac ritual known from elsewhere. Whether it also functioned as a mystery rite cannot be decisively determined. Certainly it appears to be intended to be a solemn religious event since the rules are especially strict about maintaining good order and quietness during the ceremony. Yet nothing in the text requires that it be interpreted as a mystery rite, so it is perhaps best to consider it as simply a form of traditional

Dionysiac ritual that has been especially adapted to fit the needs of this group.

On the other hand, one should also avoid the overinterpretation of André Festugière and Nilsson, both of whom appropriately deny that mystery rituals are involved here, yet also devalue the banquet itself. They note that the changes the Dionysiac associations underwent in the Hellenistic period included an increased emphasis on the banquet at the expense of traditional "religious" rites. Nilsson, in fact, emphasizes that Hellenistic mystery associations in general used the cultic tradition merely as a pretext to meet for feasting and enjoyment.[149] On the other hand, he also acknowledges that the *Iobakchoi* represent a special case, since they can be deemed to be "closely connected with the Dionysiac mysteries both by [their] hierarchy and by certain ritual performances."[150] Nilsson, then, wants to see a contrast between feasting and religious ritual. Rather, as we have seen, feasting and enjoyment can be seen as inherent to religious ritual.

Rules and Regulations

Dues. Community identity of the *Iobakchoi* was especially defined by the payment of dues, fees, and penalties, for if one failed to pay these he was excluded from the community (lines 48–53, 60–61, 67–72, 99–107). Indeed, payment of dues was fulfilling an obligation not only to the society but to the gods as well (line 56). Being a member could be quite expensive. One had to pay "entrance fees" upon entering the organization (lines 37, 61, 103), a "fixed monthly contribution for wine" (lines 46–47), monthly and yearly festival fees (lines 68–70), and fines if one misbehaved at the banquet (lines 79–83, 90–102, 109–10, 144–45). To become a member, one made application to the priest and was voted on by the assembly as to worthiness and suitability (line 36);[151] part of that judgment would surely be based on one's ability to pay the dues and fees (see also line 49).

Rules of Conduct. To be a member of the *Iobakchoi* obligated one to obey the prescribed rules of conduct at meetings. They saw in the statutes the assurance of "stability" and "good order" (lines 15–16). Indeed, "good order" or *eukosmia* was the byword of social obligation to the community. The "disorderly" were termed *akosmoi* (lines 73, 137–38). The "orderly officer," or sergeant at arms, was named the *eukosmos* (lines 94, 136). It was he who carried the *thyrsos,* the traditional staff of Dionysus.[152] The disorderly person was designated as such by the placing of the staff next to him (lines 136–41). The use of the *thyrsos* as the agency of discipline had an especially significant symbolic meaning. The *thyrsos* symbolized the god Dionysus and the festive spirit he brought to a banquet; the presence and will of Dionysus was invoked symbolically when the *thyrsos* was used.

Those who failed to leave quietly when asked to do so by the orderly officer were forcedly ejected by his assistants (lines 141–44). These assistants were termed *horses* (*hippoi,* line 144). Their colorful name suggests an association with the mythic horse-like *sileni* in the Dionysiac cycle.[153] But according to their function, they may appropriately be termed "bouncers."[154]

Examples of unruly behavior are summed up in the various rules of conduct. Most of these rules clearly apply to conduct at a banquet. Indeed, the meeting from which the unruly and loud were to be ejected is said to be taking place in a "banqueting-hall" (*histiatoreion,* lines 136–41). Especially condemned is fighting or coming to blows, as well as any insulting or abusive language or activities toward another. Thus punishments are prescribed for the following abuses: "If anyone starts a fight or is found being disorderly or occupying the couch of another member or using insulting or abusive language to anyone . . ." (lines 72–75). Note that "occupying the [banquet] couch of another member" is considered abusive behavior. This is understandable when one takes into account the importance of ranking at table at ancient banquets. An individual's place indicated his relative rank in the community, and to violate it was a personal insult and a threat to the stability of the community.

On the other hand, to proscribe fighting or coming to blows appears especially surprising. It seems to suggest that such activity at banquets was not uncommon, a conclusion one can also draw from Lucian's satirical view of a banquet that ends in a brawl, which began with arguments over positions at the table and over different-sized portions of food.[155] One could interpret this to mean that boorish behavior was the rule and that such rules only point out how uncontrolled the behavior was at such banquets. On the other hand, it can also be emphasized that the existence of such rules in the statutes of the *Iobakchoi* showed that they valued orderliness and enforced it strictly. Furthermore, they did so by means of a rich ethical tradition that defined proper behavior at the banquet on the basis of the ideal of the banquet.

Settling Disputes. The *Iobakchoi* not only instituted rules to govern behavior but also required that any community disputes be settled within the community. Whenever a member had been wronged, a formal judicial process was provided for that individual to receive satisfaction (see lines 72–102). If the abuse was primarily verbal, as in the phrase "one who has been insulted or abused" (lines 75–76), then the one who had been insulted was to provide two members as sworn witnesses in his behalf (lines 76–77). The guilty party was then to pay a fine. The same process was followed if a quarrel or fight ensued. In that case the party responsible for starting the fight was fined (lines 80–81).

If one were accusing another of striking him, however, as in the phrase "the one who was struck" (line 85), the charge was considered more serious. In this case, a written complaint was filed with the priest or vice-priest, who then called a business meeting *(agora)* at which the entire membership would decide the question. In effect, the entire community would act as a jury. An individual judged guilty by this process faced a stiff penalty: not only was he fined, but he was also excluded from community gatherings for a period to be determined by the community (lines 88–90).

Failure to attend a business meeting was considered a punishable offense, for which one would be fined (lines 96–99). Even more serious an offense, however, indeed as serious as fighting, was adjudged to the one who took his complaint to a public court rather than to the community: "And the same penalty [that is, the same as for the one judged guilty of striking another] shall be imposed also on the one who was struck if he does not seek redress with the priest or the *archibakchos* but makes a public accusation" (lines 90–94). The implication is that if one who was wronged took his complaint to an outside court ("makes a public accusation") he committed an offense to the community just as grave as if he had struck another member.[156]

Rules and Ritual. Social obligation also applied to ritual functions. The rituals at the *stibas* were to be conducted with the proper reverence, that is, "with all good order and quietness" *(eukosmia kai hēsychia,* lines 64–65). "Good order" therefore indicated social obligation not only in the sense of proper behavior toward others in the community but also, by implication, in the sense of proper behavior in the presence of the god. Thus each member was not only required to take part in the ceremonies (lines 45–46) but to do so in the proper spirit. Indeed, the penalties for unruly and loud behavior (lines 136–41) may apply to these restrictions governing the rituals, but this is not clear. In one case, however, delivering a speech without permission of the priest was punishable by a fine (lines 107–10).

Dramatic presentations and serious discourse were not at all out of order in a meal setting, of course. But in the case of the *Iobakchoi* these activities had been given special meaning by the club. The entertainment had become a ritual drama. The conversation had become a discourse on a topic related to the cult (*theologia,* line 115). Whenever anyone else spoke, it was at the direction of the priest, suggesting that the conversation was expected to be not only orderly but appropriate to the occasion and to the community. Perhaps, analogous to the *theologia,* it was expected that any discourse at the banquet relate to communal concerns of a religious or festive nature.

Thus social obligation to the community for the sake of "good order" involved a profound concept of community solidarity. One had a responsibility for proper behavior toward one's fellow members on an individual basis; thus there was a simplified code of social ethics (pertaining to insults, fighting, and so on) with a judicial system to back it up. One also had a responsibility to the community at large, so that a disturbance of a community function, such as loud or boisterous behavior, was proscribed and punished. One was obligated to the community to pay one's dues, not only money but also wine. One was required to participate in meetings as well, and to do so in the proper spirit. Community responsibility extended to the requirement to participate in judicial measures against a fellow member and to settle all disputes within the community. By means of the latter requirement, social obligation to the community was made to override one's personal view of justice. On the other hand, the implied obligation of the community to the individual was such that fair and prompt attention to individual complaints was doubtless expected.

Where the *Iobakchoi* Held Their Meetings

The *Iobakchoi* apparently called their meeting house a *Bakcheion,* as is suggested in line 101: "The treasurer shall have power to forbid him entry into the *Bakcheion* until he pay." They also refer to the meeting house itself, or a part of it, as a "banquet hall" *(histiatopeion):* "And anyone beside whom the *thyrsos* is laid, if the priest or *archibakchos* so decide, shall depart from the banquet hall" (lines 139–41).

The term *Bakcheion* is especially common as a designation for the meeting house of a Dionysiac association and is often found with this meaning in other Dionysiac inscriptions.[157] However, this term has other meanings as well. It is a favorite generic term for a Dionysiac association,[158] and it is so used here (lines 8, 16, 37, 56, 148). Thus, in the communal cry of the *Iobakchoi* they boast, "Now we are the first of all the *Bakcheia*" (lines 26–27). A related term in the feminine form *Bakcheia* is used as a reference to a Dionysiac festival that was celebrated by this association (line 43).[159] Here I will adopt the term *Bakcheion* as the preferred term for the meeting house.

The *Bakcheion* of the *Iobakchoi* has been excavated.[160] It has been identified as such by the fact that the column containing the inscription of the club statutes was found within its ruins. It is located on the southwest slope of the Areopagus in Athens and is dated to about the mid-second century C.E.

The *Bakcheion* of the *Iobakchoi* was a large rectangular building with three rooms.[161] The main room is a long hall 18.8 meters long by 11.25 meters wide. This hall is divided into a large central aisle and two small side aisles by two rows of four columns each. At the center of the east wall is a rectangular apse. There is also a small *cella* to the north of the apse and entered only through it. The main entrance into the structure itself has not been preserved, but the layout of the building suggests that it would probably have been in the center of the west wall opposite the apse. The overall form of the main hall and apse is, of course, quite similar to the basilica form later adopted by the Christians for use as an assembly hall. Several Roman *scholae* also have similar forms.[162]

Since most meetings of the club were banquet meetings, and since the meeting house also included a "banquet hall," it is surprising that this structure does not have a more conventional dining-room form. Rather, its form suggests an emphasis on the assembly, with special focus on the activities in and in front of the apse. The hall would certainly accommodate business meetings as well as speeches and sermons. In addition, there is clearly ample space for dramatic presentations, although if the structure had been designed especially for them, one would have expected a small theater or *odeion* rather than an assembly hall.

The form and arrangement of dining furnishings for the numerous banquets of the club is not known since none of these furnishings have survived. However, the fact that the main furnishings were called *stibades,* or "straw mats," rather than "couches" suggests that the banquet setting was of a specific form. How the room was adapted to serve the needs of a "banquet hall" is not clear, however.

CONCLUSION

Nilsson speaks for many other scholars when he describes the "very numerous associations of the Hellenistic and following age, which, under the pretext of honouring some god after whom the association was named, assembled in order to enjoy themselves and to feast."[163] For example, one may compare the more recent comment of Ramsay MacMullen in regard to funerary societies: "Their objects were simple, summed up in the phrase 'social security': to have a refuge from loneliness in a very big world, to meet once a month for dinner, to draw pride and strength from numbers, and at the end of life (if one's dues were paid up) to be remembered in a really respectable funeral."[164] However, as we have seen, an increasing emphasis on the banquet is neither a negative feature per se nor inconsistent with the earlier history of associations.

The banquet was often the central activity of clubs regardless of their purported reason for organizing together.[165] Its function was primarily social, marked by "good cheer." Yet the nature of the "good cheer" to be experienced at the meal was defined by the rules governing it. In this sense, "good cheer" in one club is roughly equivalent to "good order" in another.

The meal was a symposium, a typical formal meal and drinking party, in which an emphasis was placed on luxurious dining and copious drinking. Yet symposia had their own rules as well. Thus the conversation accompanying them was to be proper and orderly, conducted at the direction of the symposiarch, and perhaps even directed to topics appropriate to community life and self-identity. The symposium included a libation at the beginning; the club banquet adapted the libation to fit its own religious piety. The symposium traditionally included entertainment, such as poetic readings or pantomimic dances. The *Iobakchoi* in particular adapted this custom to their own purposes, with an encomium of praise to the god and a ritual drama that may have been in the form of a pantomimic dance.

The custom of assigning positions by rank at the table was a standard accompaniment of the banquet. It served a useful function in the clubs by identifying the individuals who were especially honored by the club. Yet it also was a continual source of friction among members, so that laws had to be passed to keep members from trying to usurp the position of another. If this were allowed, not only would chaos result, but also one of the methods by which the club awarded status to its members would be overthrown. To provide honors to its members was an important social function of the clubs and one of their reasons for existing. Another way in which the meal and its customs contributed to this aspect of community life was by the awarding of different sizes of portions to members on the basis of their rank in the community.

Unruly and abusive behavior was also to be expected at any drinking party, but many clubs formulated a way to handle such indiscretions, so that community solidarity could be preserved. They formulated rules to control such behavior during meals and other rules to keep side effects afterwards to a minimum. In this respect, they appeared to be heeding the saying quoted by Plutarch, "I dislike a drinking companion with a good memory." What Plutarch had in mind was consistent with the goal of the clubs: ". . . that one should remember either none of the improprieties committed over cups or only those which call for an altogether light and playful reproof."[166]

So also the clubs forbade taking community disputes to public courts, but the *Iobakchoi* in particular provided an opportunity to air grievances before the community itself. Other clubs with similar references to inter-community disputes probably had similar systems for handling them. By such a system as this the meal fellowship was made to extend beyond the actual meal gathering itself. Thus the social obligation toward the community fostered by the communal meal continued to define relationships toward meal companions and toward the community even after the meal was over.

The banquet meeting was usually separated from business meetings of the club. This indicates that only certain kinds of activities and discussions were considered appropriate for a meal setting. Just as the "problems for symposiac discourse" of Plutarch were considered appropriate topics for a philosophical meal,[167] so also the behavior, topics of discussion, and ritual of a club were defined according to their appropriateness to the meal setting and to the community. The bases for such considerations were "peace and quiet" or "good order and quietness." These terms were connected with religious and ritual values within the respective communities. As applied to otherwise normal rules of social etiquette and ethics, they gave a religious value to the concept of social obligation at community banquets.

EXCURSUSES

Statutes of the College of Diana and Antinous (Lanuvium, Italy, 136 c.e.)

[This translation is from Naphtali Lewis and Meyer Reinhold, *Roman Civilization*, 2 vols. (New York: Harper, 1966), 2.273–75.]

In the consulship of Lucius Ceionius Commodus and Sextus Vettulenus Civica Pompeianus, May 28.

[Column 1]

(1) At Lanuvium in the temple of Antinous, in which Lucius Caesennius Rufus, / patron of the municipality had directed that a meeting be called through Lucius Pompeius / . . . us, *quinquennalis* of the worshippers of Diana and Antinous, he promised that he would give them . . . / out of his generosity the interest on 15,000 *sesterces*, to wit 400 *sesterces*, on the / (5) birthday of Diana, August 13, and 400 *sesterces* on the birthday of Antinous, November 27; / and he instructed the by-laws established by them to be inscribed / on the inner side below the tetrastyle [of the temple] of Antinous as recorded below. /

In the consulship of Marcus Antonius Hiberus and Publius Mummius Sisenna, January 1, the Benevolent Society of Diana / . . . and Antinous was founded, Lucius Caesennius Rufus son of Lucius, of the Quirine Tribe, being for the third time sole magistrate and likewise patron. /

(10) Clause from the Decree of the Senate of the Roman People /

These are permitted to assemble, convene, and maintain a society: those who desire to make monthly contributions / for funerals may assemble in such a society, but they may not assemble in the name of such society except once a month / for the sake of making contributions to provide burial for the dead. /

May this be propitious, happy, and salutary to the Emperor Caesar Trajanus Hadrian Augustus and to the entire / (15) imperial house, to us, ours, and to our society, and may we have made proper and careful arrangements for / providing decent obsequies at the departure of the dead! Therefore we must all agree to contribute faithfully, / so that our society may be able to continue in existence a long time. You, who desire to enter this society as a new member, / first read the by-laws carefully before entering, so as not to find cause for complaint later or / bequeath a lawsuit to your heir.

By-laws of the Society /

(20) It was voted unanimously that whoever desires to enter this society shall pay an initiation fee / of 100 *sesterces* and an amphora of good wine, and shall pay monthly dues of 5 *asses*. It was voted further that if anyone / has not paid his dues for six consecutive months and the common lot of mankind befalls him, his claim to burial shall not be considered, / even if he has provided for it in his will. It was voted further that / upon the decease of a paid-up member of our body there will be due him from the treasury 300 *sesterces*, from which sum will be deducted a funeral fee / (25)

of 50 *sesterces* to be distributed at the pyre [among those attending]; the obsequies, furthermore, will be performed on foot. /

It was voted further that if a member dies farther than twenty miles from town and the society is notified, / three men chosen from our body will be required to go there to arrange for his funeral; they will be required to render an accounting / in good faith to the membership, and if they are found guilty of any fraud they shall pay a quadruple fine; they / will be given money for the funeral expenses, and in addition a round-trip travel allowance of 20 *sesterces* each. But if a member dies farther than / (30) twenty miles from town and notification is impossible, then his funeral expenses, / less emoluments and funeral fee, may be claimed from this society, in accordance with the by-laws of the society, by the man who buries him, if he so attests by an affidavit signed with the seals of seven Roman citizens, and / the matter is approved, and he gives security against anyone's claiming any further sum. Let no malice aforethought attend! And let no patron or patroness, master /

[Column 2]
or mistress, or creditor have any right of claim against this society unless / he has been named heir in a will. If a member dies intestate, the details of his burial will be decided by the *quinquennalis* and the membership. /

It was voted further that if a slave member of this society dies, and his master or mistress / unreasonably refuses to relinquish his body for burial, and he has not left written instructions, a token funeral ceremony will be held. /
(5) It was voted further that if any member takes his own life for any reason, whatever, / his claim to burial [by the society] shall not be considered. /

It was voted further that if any slave member of this society becomes free, he is required to donate / an amphora of good wine.

It was voted further that if any master, in the year when it is his turn in the membership list / to provide dinner, fails to comply and provide a dinner, he shall pay 30 *sesterces* into the treasury; / (10) the man following him on the list shall be required to give the dinner, and he [the delinquent] shall be required to reciprocate when it is the latter's turn. /

Calendar of dinners: March 8, birthday of Caesennius . . . his father; November 27, birthday of Antinous; / August 13, birthday of Diana and of the society; August 20, birthday of Caesennius Silvanus, his brother; . . . / birthday of Cornelia Procula, his mother; December 14, birthday of Caesennius Rufus, patron of the municipality. /

Masters of the dinners in the order of the membership list, appointed four at a time in turn, shall be required to provide / (15) an amphora of good wine each, and for as many members as the society has a bread costing 2 *asses*, sardines to the number of / four, a setting, and warm water with service. /

It was voted further that any member who becomes *quinquennalis* in this society shall be exempt from such obligations[?] / for the term when he is *quinquennalis*, and that he shall receive a double share in all distributions. / It was voted further that the secretary and the messenger shall be exempt from such obligations[?] and shall receive a share and a half / (20) in every distribution.

It was voted further that any member who has administered the office of *quinquennalis* honestly shall [thereafter] receive a share and a half / of everything as a mark of honor, so that other *quinquennales* will also hope for the same by properly discharging their duties. /

It was voted further that if any member desires to make any complaint or bring up any business, he is to bring it up at a business meeting, so that we may banquet in peace and / good cheer on festive days. /

(25) It was voted further that any member who moves from one place to another so as to cause a disturbance shall be fined / 4 *sesterces*. Any member, moreover, who speaks abusively to another or causes / an uproar shall be fined 12 *sesterces*. Any member who uses / any abusive or insolent language to a *quinquennalis* at a banquet shall be fined 20 *sesterces*. /

It was voted further that on the festive days of his term of office each *quinquennalis* is to conduct worship with incense / (30) and wine and is to perform his other functions clothed in white, and that on the birthdays / of Diana and Antinous he is to provide oil for the society in the public bath before they banquet.

Statutes of the *Iobakchoi* (Athens, second to third century C.E.)
[The translation is adapted by the author from M. N. Tod, *Sidelights on Greek History* (repr., Chicago: Ares, 1974), 86–91; and Thomas L. Robinson, "Dionysos in Athens" (unpublished seminar paper, Harvard Divinity School, December 11, 1972); Greek text in *LSG,* 95–100, no. 51.]

To Good Fortune. /
In the archonship of Arrios Epaphrodeitos, on the eighth day of the month / Elaphebolion, a meeting / was convened for the first time by the priest appointed / (5) by Aurelios Neikomachos, who had been / vice-priest for seventeen years and priest / for twenty-three years, and had in his lifetime resigned his position / for the honor and glory of the Bakcheion / in favor of the most excellent Claudios Herodes. / (10) Since he had been appointed by Herodes as vice-priest, he [Neikomachos] read aloud the statutes / of the former priests Chrysippos and Dionysios. / And when the priest / and the archibakchos and the patron had given their approval, all cried out: / "Let us adopt these statutes forever." "Well spoken, priest." "Restore / (15) the statutes: you ought to." "Stability / and good order to the Bakcheion." "A stele for the statues." / "Call the question." The priest said: "Since / I and my fellow-priests and / all of you agree, we will call the question as you have / (20) requested." And the presiding officer, / Rufus son of Aphrodeisios, put it to a vote: "All those in favor / of having the statutes which were read / inscribed on a stele, raise / your hands." Everyone raised his hand. They cried out: "Long / (25) live the most excellent priest Herodes." / "Now you are fortunate; now we are first of all / the Bakcheia." "Well spoken, vice-priest." "Let the stele / be set up." The vice-priest said: "The stele shall rest / on a pillar and the statutes shall be inscribed, / (30) for the officers will have power / that none of them be repealed." /

No one may be a Iobakchos unless / he first register with the priest / the customary declaration and / (35) be approved by a vote of the Iobakchoi / on whether he appears worthy and suitable / for the Bakcheion. The entrance fee / for one whose father is not a member shall be 50 *denarii* and a libation. / Likewise let those whose fathers are members register / (40) for 25 *denarii,* paying half-subscription / until they attain puberty. /

The Iobakchoi shall meet on the ninth of each month, / and at the yearly festivals, at the Bakcheia, / and on any extraordinary feast of the god; / (45) and each one is to speak or act or try to distinguish himself, / and pay a fixed monthly / contribution for the wine. / If anyone does not fulfill his obligation, he shall be excluded from the *stibas.* / Those who are enrolled by vote must be able to fulfill the obligation / (50) except on occasions when they are traveling / or bereaved or sick or in case the person / who is to be admitted into the *stibas* should be utterly indispensable, / which must be decided by the priests. If / the brother of a Iobakchos enters, after approval by vote, / (55) he shall pay 50 *denarii.* If a consecrated child who has been appointed as a non-member / has paid what is due to the gods and to the Bakcheion, / he shall be a Iobakchos with his father on the payment of one / libation by his father. / The priest shall give a letter to the one who has made his declaration and has been elected, / (60) stating that he is a Iobakchos, provided that he first / pay to the priest the entrance fee, / the specific amounts going into this sum being registered in the letter. /

No one is allowed to sing, / cheer, or applaud at the *stibas,* but with / (65) all good order and quietness / they shall speak and act their allotted parts under the direction of / the priest or the archibakchos. None / of the Iobakchoi who has not contributed / for the ninth-day feasts and the yearly festivals / (70) shall enter the *stibas* until / it is determined for him by the priest / that he either pay the dues or enter. /

If anyone starts a fight or is found being disorderly / or occupying the couch of another member or using insulting / (75) or abusive language to anyone, the one who has been abused / or insulted shall present two / Iobakchoi testifying under oath that they heard / him being insulted or abused, / and he who was guilty of the insult or abuse shall pay / (80) to the society 25 light *drachmas,* or he who is the cause / of a fight shall pay / the same amount of 25 drachmas, or they will not be allowed to attend the / meetings of the Iobakchoi until they pay. /

If anyone comes to blows, he who was struck shall register the fact in writing / (85) with the priest or the vice-priest, / who will then be required to convene an assembly, and / the Iobakchoi shall decide the matter by vote, under the leadership / of the priest. And he shall be assessed the penalty of exclusion / for a period to be determined / (90) and the payment of up to 25 denarii of silver. / And the same penalty shall be imposed also on the one who was struck / if he did not seek redress with the priest or / archibakchos but made a public accusation. / And the same penalty shall be imposed on the orderly officer / (95) if he failed to eject those who were fighting. / If any of the Iobakchoi who knows / that an assembly must be convened for this matter is not / present, he shall pay to the society / 50 light *drachmas.* But if, when he is asked to pay, he refuses compliance, / (100) the treasurer shall have power to forbid him / entry into the Bakcheion / until he pay. If any of those who / enter fail to pay the entrance fee / to the priest or vice-priest / (105) he shall be excluded from the banquet until he pays, / and payment shall be exacted in whatever manner / the priest may command.

No one shall deliver a speech / unless the priest or vice-priest has given permission; / otherwise he shall be liable to a fine / (110) of 30 light *drachmas* to the society. /

The priest shall perform the customary / rituals at the *stibas* and at the yearly festival, / in a worthy manner, and shall offer / for the *stibas* one libation at the Festival of Arrival [*Katagogia*] / (115) and a sermon [*theologia*], which / Neikomachos began to make / during his priesthood in order to distinguish himself. /

The archibakchos shall offer the sacrifice / to the god and set forth the libation / (120) on the tenth day of the month Elaphebolion. / And when portions are distributed, / let them be taken by the priest, vice-priest, / archibakchos, treasurer, *boukolikos,* / Dionysos, Kore, Palaimon, / (125) Aphrodite, and Proteurythmos; and / let these names be apportioned by lot / among all the members.

Whoever of the Iobakchoi obtains / a legacy or honor or appointment shall set before the / Iobakchoi a libation worthy of the appointment, / (130) marriage feast, birth, *Choes* [pitcher feast], *ephebia* [coming of age], / citizen-status, the office of wand-bearer, membership in the council, / presidency of the games, councillorship in the Panhellenic league, membership in the senate, / position as legislator, or any position of authority at all, / delegate to a sacrifice, police magistrate, winner in the games, / (135) or any other honor attained by a Iobakchos. /

The orderly officer shall be chosen by lot or / appointed by the priest. And he shall bear / the *thyrsos* of the god to whomever is disorderly or creates a disturbance. / And anyone beside whom the *thyrsos* is laid, / (140) if the priest or archibakchos so decide, / shall depart from the banquet hall. If / he refuses to go, he shall be ejected outside the vestibule / by those appointed by the / priests, namely the *hippoi* ["bouncers," literally "horses"], and he shall be liable to the fines / (145) imposed on those who fight. /

The Iobakchoi shall elect a treasurer / by ballot for a two-year term; and he shall receive / for the financial records everything that belongs to the Bakcheion, / and he shall deliver this in turn to / (150) the next treasurer after him. / At his own expense he shall provide lamp oil / for the ninth-day feast, the yearly festival, the *stibas,* / and all the days customarily devoted to the god / as well as those days when legacies or honors or appointments / (155) are celebrated. He shall choose a secretary, / if he so desire, at his own risk. / And he shall be granted / the libation for the treasurer, and shall be free from the payment of fees / for his two-year term.

Whenever any / (160) Iobakchos dies, a wreath up to 5 *denarii* in value shall be provided / for him, and a single jug of wine shall be set before / those present at the funeral, / but anyone who was not present shall not partake of the wine.

CHAPTER 6

THE JEWISH BANQUET

The Lord spoke to Moses, saying: Speak to the people of Israel and say
to them: These are the appointed festivals of the Lord that you shall
proclaim as holy convocations, my appointed festivals.
—Lev 23:1

If they make you master of the feast, do not exalt yourself;
be among them as one of their number.
Take care of them first and then sit down;
when you have fulfilled all your duties, take your place,
so that you may be merry along with them
and receive a wreath for your excellent leadership.
—Sir 32:1-2

So, to prevent our being perverted by contact with others or by mixing
with bad influences, he [God] hedged us in on all sides with strict obser-
vances connected with meat and drink and touch and hearing and sight,
after the manner of the Law.
—*Letter of Aristeas* 142

Rabbi Yochanan and Rabbi Eleazar used to say, "So long as the Temple
stood, the altar made atonement for Israel. Now a man's table makes
atonement for him."
—*b. Ber.* 55a[1]

Meals held a special place in the social world of Second Temple Judaism. The
religious calendar was marked by numerous feasts whose origins were traced
to the very beginnings of Jewish tradition. The law or Torah included a number of dietary restrictions that marked off observant Jews from the rest of
ancient society. Various Jewish groups who organized as separate sects within
Judaism tended to celebrate their separateness and cohesiveness by holding
special meals together.

In the Greco-Roman period, meals functioned within Judaism in ways
quite similar to what we have found in Greco-Roman society at large. That is

to say, when they gathered for a banquet, Jews, like their Greek and Roman counterparts, reclined at a meal that was characterized by rules of etiquette and ethical values and was organized into courses in exactly the same form as banquets in the rest of the Greco-Roman world. Thus in the above quotation from Ben Sira, one finds a description of the "symposiarch" that fits quite well with general Greco-Roman customs.

That Jews in this period shared Greco-Roman meal customs has been stated often in various studies. It is supported by both literary and nonliterary data. The origins of these customs in Judaism is not easy to trace, but they are known to Jews as early as the eighth century B.C.E. as evidenced in Amos 6:4-7 in a woe addressed to Israelite leaders:

> Alas for those who lie on beds of ivory,
> and lounge on their couches,
> and eat lambs from the flock,
> and calves from the stall;
> who sing idle songs to the sound of the harp,
> and like David improvise on instruments of music;
> who drink wine from bowls,
> and anoint themselves with the finest oils,
> but are not grieved over the ruin of Joseph!
> Therefore they shall now be the first to go into exile,
> and the revelry of the loungers shall pass away.

Here we have references to various motifs with parallels in the Greek symposium tradition: reclining, banqueting in luxury, wine mixed in bowls, anointing with oil, music as table entertainment, and the use of banquet imagery to critique social stratification (rich versus poor). Thus even in this early period developments in meal customs in the Jewish world paralleled the customs developing in the Greek world.[2]

Evidence for the Greco-Roman form of Jewish meals is also found in the rabbinic literature, as we will see below. Consequently, over a wide period of Jewish history, beginning in the Second Temple period and extending into the early rabbinic period, meal traditions were highly influenced by the Greco-Roman banquet tradition. I will now sketch a few examples to illustrate this point.

THE BANQUET TRADITION IN BEN SIRA

A good starting point for our study is Ben Sira, which is dated prior to the Maccabean revolt, or about 200 to 180 B.C.E., and is thought to have been written in Jerusalem. Here we find the testimony of a scholar in Judaism from the wisdom tradition who is engaged in training the well-to-do young men of his society in the rules for ethical living. This document holds a special place in all of wisdom literature because of its specific references to the primary place of the law and the cult in a context in which the wisdom tradition is being passed on. It is thus part of a society fully embedded in Jewish tradition, both because of its explicit statements of support for Torah and temple and because of the role that is being played by this teacher and his followers in providing schooling for aristocratic members of Palestinian Jewish society.

In this regard, it is notable that a significant part of the instruction concerns meal etiquette. And these rules of etiquette attest to meal customs and ethical perspectives directly parallel to those of the Greco-Roman world.[3] Thus when our author speaks of his having received part of his education by traveling in foreign lands,[4] we must take him for his word and assume that he dined at many a Greco-Roman table as a foreign dignitary. Interestingly, at no point in his discussion does he refer to any dietary restrictions that might limit his participation or that of his students in Greco-Roman banquets. His own experience and the experience he envisions for his charges is markedly cosmopolitan.

The Form of the Meal

Invitations. Meal customs in Ben Sira included the use of invitations, as seen in 13:9: "When an influential person invites you, be reserved, and he will invite you more insistently." This text suggests little as to the form of the invitations, but we know of both formal (or written) and informal invitations in the Greek world. In Plato's *Symposium* the invitations appear to be delivered orally by the host as he meets his friends in the marketplace.[5] On the other hand, we also know of written invitations from a later period in Roman Egypt.[6] Note that here in Ben Sira, the invitation is given by an "influential person," namely, one who outranked the person receiving the invitation. Consequently, the invitation, the suggested response, and the meal that was to follow were embedded in the ancient patronage system.

A Luxurious Setting. The meal itself was a formal occasion with a luxurious setting and much food and wine. Sometimes such a setting was viewed positively, as an opportunity to enjoy the good things in life, as in 31:12—32:13. For example, wine is praised as having been "created to make people happy" (31:27), and music at the meal is praised as "a ruby seal in a setting of gold" (32:5). In other texts, luxury at the table is viewed as a sign of excess; thus at

18:32-33, the sage counsels: "Do not revel in great luxury, or you may become impoverished by its expense. Do not become a beggar by feasting with borrowed money, when you have nothing in your purse."[7] In any case it is clear that a formal banquet is understood to offer a bounteous table in luxurious surroundings. This is a long-standing Near Eastern tradition, as is evidenced by the eighth-century reference in Amos 6:3-6 to the table of luxury.[8] Here Amos is negative toward the luxurious banquet as symbolic of excess. In other Jewish literature on this topic, only Eccl 3:13 and Ben Sira present a clearly positive view toward luxurious secular dining.[9] Their view is consistent with the Greek tradition, in which the banquet is connected with the ideals of civilized living.[10]

Ranking of Guests. Individuals appear to have been arranged at the table according to rank as suggested by 12:12: "Do not put [your enemy] next to you, or he may overthrow you and take your place. Do not let him sit at your right hand, or else he may try to take your own seat." The text refers to a situation in which one has invited an enemy into one's home (as in 11:29 and 11:34). The advice is not to place him at one's right lest he try to take one's seat of honor. The host in this case would occupy the place of honor, and the next highest rank would be located to his right. Since such hospitality would most commonly take place at a meal, this text most likely refers to a meal setting. The advice here is reminiscent of meal customs in the Greek world, where ranking was always assigned to certain positions at the table. The host would normally take the first position with his honored guest located to his right. Other rankings would also continue to the right.[11]

The Symposiarch. In 32:1-2, quoted at the beginning of this chapter, Ben Sira gives advice on how one should preside at the meal. Note how the presider had the special responsibility to act on behalf of the others ("be among them as one of their number. Take care of them first," 32:1). What these duties consisted of we are not told, but one must assume that they involved regulating the various activities at the meal that are described in this context (31:12—32:13), that is, regulating the provisions of food and wine and overseeing the entertainment. The individual who served well was rewarded with a "wreath."[12] Most scholars recognize here the Greek custom of electing one of their number to be the symposiarch.[13] This individual normally had the responsibility to decide the proportion to be followed in the mixing of the wine with water. In addition, he might oversee the entertainment, particularly if it took the form of an organized discussion of some kind.[14]

Music. The normal entertainment appears to have been music. At 32:3-6, various options for entertainment are discussed. Here it is advised that one may speak words of wisdom, but "do not interrupt the music" (v. 3), imply-ing that musical entertainment was to be expected. Indeed, music at the ban-quet is given the highest praise in a remarkable encomium at verses 5-6: "A ruby seal in a setting of gold is a concert of music at a banquet of wine. A seal of emerald in a rich setting of gold is the melody of music with good wine."

The type of music provided is evidently referred to at 40:20-21, where the music that accompanies wine is that of "flute and harp." In the ancient Near East the luxurious banquet appears to have regularly included music, as attested by Amos 6:4-6 and by various artistic representations of banquet scenes.[15]

Music was also a normal part of the Greek banquet, and the flute girl is a regular feature in Greek representations of banquet scenes.[16] It is notable that Ben Sira has such a high regard for music, in contrast to Amos, for whom music is to be associated with the other excesses of the banquet, and in con-trast to Plato's *Symposium,* where the flute girl is dismissed so that the ban-queters can entertain themselves instead with enlightened conversation.[17] To be sure, the reference in Plato is not meant to be a negative comment about music, but it does suggest that philosophical conversation is to be given a higher place.[18] On the other hand, the overwhelming opinion in the Greek world was that music was an essential part of the banquet. With this point of view, Ben Sira is in firm agreement. Thus at 32:36, Ben Sira represents the opinion that the meal and its entertainment have an intrinsic value in them-selves, whether or not wise conversation is included.

Posture at the Meal. The evidence is unclear as to whether the diners were sitting or reclining.[19] Both types of descriptions occur, as in 32:1-2, in which the master of the feast first sits and then reclines. At this period in the Mediterranean world, virtually everyone reclined at their formal meals.[20] For the most part, our data indicates that Jews in the Hellenistic period did also.[21]

Thus the texts in Ben Sira that clearly refer to reclining are consistent with the general customs of the day. But the readings that refer to sitting are problematic. Rudolf Smend has proposed a solution as follows: he suggests that they sat at the first course of the meal, during the time in which they ate, and then they reclined during the second course of the meal (the sym-posium), during which time they drank and enjoyed the entertainment of the evening.[22] This suggestion makes sense of the confused data in the text and represents the form of Jewish meal evidenced in the Mishnah, as dis-cussed later in this chapter. It also can be seen to correlate with 32:1-2, where the master of the feast first sits and then reclines. However, it may be anachronistic to apply the text from the Mishnah to the time of Ben Sira, since they are separated by several centuries of social and religious history. Indeed, the Mishnah may simply be preserving, anachronistically, the older custom of reclining in an age when customs were changing to sitting at the table. In the final analysis, the issue of posture at the table in Ben Sira and its checkered textual history remain obscure.

Entertainment and Table Talk. When music was not present, conversation could serve as an alternative form of entertainment at the meal, as evidenced in the following text from 32:3-4: "Speak, you who are older, for it is your right, but with accurate knowledge, and do not interrupt the music. Where there is entertainment, do not pour out talk; do not display your cleverness at the wrong time." It should also be noted that the entertainment accompanied the wine ("a concert of music at a banquet of wine," 32:5; "the melody of music with good wine," 32:6). This suggests that the order of the meal that Ben Sira describes may be considered equivalent to the traditional order of the Greco-Roman banquet: a *deipnon,* in which the actual eating took place, followed by the second course, the *symposion,* in which there was an extended period of drinking accompanied by entertainment. The idea that elevated conversation could substitute as the entertainment of the evening at a formal banquet is consistent with Greek tradition.[23]

It is at this point that we can see clear correlation between the primary activity of the sage, that is, engaging in wise discourse, and the banquet as a setting for serious discourse. At 32:3–6, as already noted, the instruction on proper conversation at the meal includes the ruling that by no means is the conversation to override or interrupt the primary entertainment of the evening. Thus Ben Sira envisions a "proper" meal that may not include wise conversation; both wine and music, for example, have an intrinsic value in themselves, as indicated in 31:27-28 and 32:5-6.

Whenever conversation does take place, Ben Sira has advice as to how it is to proceed. His advice is divided among age groups. The older man speaks freely and fittingly, but even he is advised to speak at the proper time and on a proper subject. The young man is only to speak if asked and then is to speak as little as possible, concentrating on moderation in speech (32:7-9).

These instructions are to be related to others in Ben Sira on the subject of wise conversation, such as at 33:4-6; 34:9-12; and 37:16-26. The type of instruction is generally the same whether or not the setting is specifically stated to be a meal. Thus the wise man speaks with understanding generally (34:9) and at a meal (32:3). He is to be prudent and careful in his speech when in the company of "outsiders," particularly if at the table of a powerful man (13:8-13, 21-23).

Wise conversation is especially concerned with the law (39:8). So also the wise man is to seek out righteous men as his table companions so that the conversation may be centered on "the law of the Most High": "Let your conversation be with intelligent people, and let all your discussion be about the law of the Most High. Let the righteous be your dinner companions, and let your glory be in the fear of the Lord" (9:15-16).[24] This text is especially revealing, for it makes specific what had been implied before, that activities of the greatest importance are to take place at the formal banquets that the sage attends. Thus it is clear that the banquet is a pre-existing institution of which the sage approves and that he has adapted to serve as the setting for the exercise of wisdom in the most mundane sense (by exhibiting "good manners") and in the most profound sense (by discoursing on the law).

Rules of Etiquette and Ethics

The sage is concerned to instruct the student about proper behavior at meals. Here we find some typical, and some not-so-typical, rules of etiquette:

a) When giving a banquet, be "generous" rather than "stingy with food" (31:23-24).
b) Do not invite a stranger (12:29-34).
c) Be moderate in regard to food: do not be greedy in reaching for food nor in chewing food; do not overeat (31:12-18).
d) Drink wine, but in moderation (19:1-3; 31:25-30).
e) Avoid the overly luxurious banquet (18:37; 29:21-23; 31:19-22; 37:27-31).
f) Consider the needs of the tablemate (31:15-17; 41:19).
g) Preside with the needs of others in mind (32:1-2).
h) Eat with "the righteous" so that the conversation will be on the law (9:15-16).
i) Speak carefully and at the appropriate time (13:8-13; 32:3-9).
j) Do not attempt to rise above one's position (13:11; 32:1).
k) Do not linger overlong at the table (32:11).

These table rules correlate well with the "symposium laws" and the banquet rules of clubs and associations as outlined above in chapters three and five.

Social Aspects of the Data

It appears that actual meals of the sage and his circle are being referred to. This is suggested by the way in which specific situations are mentioned ("When an influential person invites you . . ." [13:9]; "If they make you master of the feast . . ." [32:1]) and by the fact that rather practical advice is being given ("Do not reach out your hand for everything you see . . ." [31:14]; "Eat what is set before you like a well brought-up person . . ." [31:16]). Thus it would seem likely that formal meals were a regular part of the life of the sage and his circle.

Two types of meals can be delineated. One type would be meals at the home of someone outside the circle of the sage. Such individuals are usually referred to as wealthy or powerful (13:9; 31:12). When the sage is invited to the home of such a one, it is seen as an opportunity to exhibit the life of wisdom, which the individual does by practicing "good manners" (31:12-18). In this case, the text has the tone of an Emily Post guide for the young man from an aristocratic family.

On the other hand, other texts suggest a greater distance between the circle of the sage and "high society." Thus at 13:8-13, in a context in which association with the upper class is viewed in an extremely negative light, the meal at the table of the rich man is viewed as a kind of "enemy camp," where the sage is tested and must be very careful of what he says. Perhaps connected with this negative evaluation of the "rich man's table" is a group of texts that decry overly luxurious banquets and refer to them as examples of the life of excess that the sage and his circle are to avoid (18:32-33; 19:2; 23:6; 29:22-28; 40:29).

Other references suggest a social context in which formal meals are eaten at the home of someone within the circle of the sage. Thus at 9:14–16, the sage advises to seek out wise men as one's dinner companions so that the conversation will be centered on "the law of the Most High." This certainly gives a great deal of importance to the dinner conversation and appears to contrast with the meal "at the table of the great" (31:12), where one is only to speak when it does not interrupt the music (32:3-6).

Also referring to the meals held within the circle of the sage may be the collection of texts that warn against fair-weather friends at table (6:10-12; 37:1,5). Here the sage warns against those who are friends only in a time of prosperity, whenever they can enjoy the delights of one's table. Since these are individuals who call themselves "friends" and whom one entertains at one's own table, then the setting suggested is that at the home of one of the sage's listeners.

In evaluating these references, I would tend to agree with George Nickelsburg that the references to meal customs we have noted here suggest that the sage and his circle tended to be from the aristocratic class.[25] This position is contrary to that of Victor Tcherikover and others who argue that the strong references to the incompatibility of the rich and poor are indicative of Ben Sira's identification with the poor.[26] Supporting the latter view are the various texts already mentioned that are opposed to the excesses of the luxurious table. On the other hand, since Ben Sira assumed the regular presence of his listeners at such meals and since he was so concerned with the proprieties of behavior at them, he clearly was quite comfortable attending them and was apparently a welcome guest.

Indeed, Ben Sira championed the aristocratic life in his encomium to the life of leisure as a necessity for the proper cultivation of wisdom (38:24—39:11). In the context, he has just praised various persons for their particular contributions to society: wives (36:21-26), friends (37:1-6), counselors (37:7-18), teachers (37:19-26), physicians (38:1-15), the dead (38:16-23), craftsmen (38:24-34), and finally the ideal wise man (39:1-11).[27] Note especially the direct contrast with those who work with their hands: the farmer cannot become wise (38:25), nor can the craftsman (38:27), the smith (38:28), or the potter (38:29). These all have their proper place in society, but only "the one who devotes himself to the study of the law of the Most High [i.e. as his occupation]" will be "sought out for the council of the people," will "attain eminence in the public assembly," will "sit in the judge's seat," and so forth (38:31—39:1). Thus Ben Sira sees himself as a "professional" sage. He has applied himself to the study of the traditions (39:1-3) and has traveled in foreign lands serving "the great" and "rulers" in his search for wisdom (34:9-12; 39:4). He clearly identifies himself as separate from the common working people; he belongs with the rulers of the people.

On the other hand, he does not totally identify with the aristocratic class. Thus there is tension at the table of a powerful man (13:8-13). Indeed, Ben Sira expresses a doctrine in which the poor and rich are seen as of two different orders of existence who do not really belong together: "What does a wolf have in common with a lamb? No more has a sinner with the devout. What peace is there between a hyena and a dog? And what peace between the rich and the poor?" (13:17-18).[28] In light of the analysis I have given above, in which it appears clear that Ben Sira sees himself as at least equal to aristocrats, I would conclude that these "poor versus rich" texts are to be interpreted rhetorically. That is, whenever Ben Sira contrasts poor and rich, wise and fool, humble and proud, he is applying stereotypical images from the wisdom tradition to his own social situation.

These texts certainly reflect an "us versus them" mentality. It would appear, however, that the primary point of reference is not "rich versus poor" but "wise versus fool," as at 10:23, for example: "It is not right to despise one who is intelligent but poor." That is, the outsiders are the aristocrats of Palestinian society whose ways and ideas Ben Sira criticizes.[29] The "insiders" of the circle of the sage are those in his "school." These individuals are free to mingle with the aristocrats, and so are at home with upper-class society, but because of their identification with the school of the sage, they see themselves as of a separate order.

Literary Aspects of the Data

Relation to Wisdom Literature. Ben Sira writes with a self-conscious relationship to the wisdom tradition and uses motifs from Wisdom literature, particularly Proverbs. At several points, he reflects a direct adaptation of portions of Proverbs; for example, his personification of Wisdom in chapter 24 is an adaptation of Proverbs 8. Similarly, like Proverbs, he refers to the meal as a symbol for the study of wisdom; compare Sir 24:21 with Prov 9:5-6. None of the extant Jewish Wisdom literature that is prior to Ben Sira, however, shows any concern for meal etiquette to the extent that Ben Sira does.

On the other hand, many have pointed out similarities between Ben Sira and Egyptian Wisdom literature on meal etiquette. For example, in 2450 B.C.E., *The Instruction of Ptah-hotep* gives the following advice:

> If thou art one of those sitting at the table of one greater than thyself, take what he may give, when it is set before thy nose. Thou shouldst gaze at what is before thee. Do not pierce him with many stares, [for such] an aggression against him is an abomination to the *ka*. Let thy face be cast down until he addresses thee, and thou shouldst speak [only] when he addresses thee. . . . As for the great man when he is at meals, his purposes conform to the dictates of his *ka*. He will give to the one whom he favors.[30]

Clearly, there is a remarkable similarity to Sir 13:8-10: "Take care not to be led astray and humiliated when you are enjoying yourself [i.e., in feasting]. When an influential person invites you, be reserved, and he will invite you more insistently. Do not be forward, or you may be rebuffed; do not stand aloof, or you will be forgotten." Ben Sira therefore draws on a rich tradition in Wisdom literature in developing his meal ethics.

Relation to the Greek Symposium Tradition. Ben Sira seems also to have been well read in Greek symposium literature. The extended collection of meal sayings at 31:12—32:13 is quite similar to material in the symposium literary tradition. This is a literary tradition that not only includes the *Symposia* of

Plato, Xenophon, and others, especially sources preserved in Athenaeus's collection of symposiac miscellanea, but it also includes those works of literature that make use of the banquet motif, such as works of satire. Among the works in this tradition is the Jewish *Letter of Aristeas,* which may be roughly contemporary with Ben Sira, although it is evidently from Alexandria rather than Palestine.[31]

Literary parallels to symposium literature are especially concentrated in 31:12—32:13, which may be outlined as follows: general etiquette at the table (31:12-18), gluttony (31:19-22), liberality when hosting a meal (31:23-24), wine (31:25-30), arguments at the table (31:31), presiding at the table (32:1-2), entertainment: speaking (32:3-9) and music (32:5-6), and prudent departure from the meal (32:10-13). Especially reminiscent of the symposium tradition is the encomium to wine (31:27-28), the encomium to music (32:5-6), instructions on how to preside at a meal (32:1-2), and the discourse on gluttony versus moderation (31:19-22). These examples are similar not only in subject but also in form and secular tone to material in the symposium tradition.[32]

Relation to the Greek Philosophical Tradition. As I argued in chapter 3, the banquet became a fixture in philosophical schools, just as the symposium form of literature became a stock motif in philosophical writings. The banquet is said to have served an educational purpose in philosophical schools and was evidently so used by many such schools.[33] These banquets were defined as occasions for a certain type of philosophical discussion at table, as typified by Plato's *Symposium.* Thus the literature helped to define the social institution of the philosophical banquet.

The relation of Ben Sira to an actual school setting in Palestine has been much debated.[34] Certainly there is much evidence in the text that such a school may have existed. For example, Ben Sira refers to a "house of instruction" (*oikos paideias,* 51:23), which in one Hebrew recension is in the form *Bet ha Midrash,* a term that came to be used for the school of the rabbis.[35] He is quite self-conscious about his role as a "professional" sage who has studied the traditions, written as well as oral, and who gives instruction to the learner (24:30-34; 33:16-18). Consequently, whenever he gives such significance to the meal as a place of instruction, he appears to be describing its function in his "school" in the same terms as the banquet would be described in the philosophical schools. Furthermore, his possible use of literary motifs from the symposium tradition further supports the argument that his school is at least partially modeled after the Greek philosophical schools.

The type of argument Ben Sira used as the basis for meal etiquette appears to be derived from Greek philosophical tradition as well. In the philosophical schools meal etiquette tended to be discussed under the topic of the ethic of friendship.[36] Thus one's behavior at the banquet was to be such that it contributed to the enjoyment of all the guests as a whole. This may be compared to the idea in Ben Sira that such rules as "do not reach" or "do not be insatiable" are placed under the rather lofty category of actions that do not "give offense," are "thoughtful," and derive from "judg[ing] your neighbor's feelings by your own" (31:14-17).

Even more significant, however, may be the use of the term *paideia* (Hebrew: *musar*) as the ethical term on which "good manners" at the table are based (31:17,19). The term is, of course, highly significant in the context of Greek education, connoting the instruction that imparted to the student the fullness of Greek civilization. The Hebrew term *musar* is the term that the LXX generally translates as *paideia* and is most likely the term so translated here in Ben Sira. *Musar* had a similar connotation to *paideia* as a term for instruction, although in the Hebrew context, instruction included a strong emphasis on discipline and chastisement. This is the primary term for describing the instructional activity of the sage in the wisdom tradition.[37] In this context in Ben Sira, however, in which meal etiquette is part of the instruction of the sage, the concept has taken on a meaning closer to the Greek idea of *paideia*.

In conclusion, we have found that the meal references in Ben Sira exhibit a relation to Greco-Roman meal traditions in terms of (1) the form of the meal, (2) the types of etiquette discussed, (3) the philosophical basis for etiquette, (4) the similarities to the symposium literary tradition, and (5) the function of the meal in the life and teaching of the sages (as compared to philosophical banquets). The sage in Ben Sira is therefore quite at home in the practice and ideology of the Greco-Roman banquet.

THE BANQUET TRADITION IN RABBINIC LITERATURE

At the other end of the chronological spectrum for our study is the rabbinic literature. Although the rabbinic literature is often used to define the basic forms of Judaism in the earlier periods, particularly the late Hellenistic and early Roman periods, scholars still debate the extent to which this literature can be applied to earlier periods. For our purposes, however, we can use this data as a bookend for the latest period of our study, thus suggesting a con-

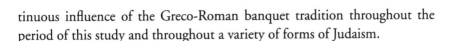

tinuous influence of the Greco-Roman banquet tradition throughout the period of this study and throughout a variety of forms of Judaism.

The Form of the Banquet

The form or liturgy of the Jewish "festal meal" or banquet is given in several texts from Tannaitic literature. These texts all date from the third to seventh centuries, but are thought to contain traditions that date from as early as the first century C.E. Together these texts provide a "liturgical order" for Jewish meals and describe a form of meal that we can recognize as that of a Greco-Roman banquet in its basic features. The following is a representative text from the Tosephta:

> What is the order of the meal? The guests enter [the house] and sit on benches, and on chairs until all have entered. They all enter and they [servants] give them water for their hands. Each one washes one hand. They [servants] mix for them the cup; each one says the benediction for himself. They [servants] bring them the appetizers; each one says the benediction for himself. They [guests] go up [to the dining room] and they recline, and they [servants] give them [water] for their hands; although they have [already] washed one hand, they [now] wash both hands. They [servants] mix for them the cup; although they have said a benediction over the first [cup] they say a benediction [also] over the second. They [servants] bring them the dessert; although they said a benediction over the first one, they [now] say a benediction over the second, and one says the benediction for all of them. He who comes after the third course has no right to enter.[38]

The form of the meal as indicated by this text may be reconstructed as follows. There were three courses: the appetizer course, the main course, and the dessert course. These are marked off in the text by the movement of the guests from vestibule to dining room, the change of posture to accompany the change of setting,[39] and the cups of wine and accompanying rituals.

The guests first gathered in an anteroom, which was provided with benches for sitting. Servants brought them water to wash one hand, presumably the only hand to be used in eating the appetizers. They were then served the wine, which was apparently mixed in the cup rather than in a common bowl,[40] and each said his own benediction over the wine. The appetizers were then served.

After the appetizer course, the guests then gathered in the dining room proper, where they reclined for the main course. Here they were again provided with water, and this time they washed both hands. The second cup of wine was mixed, and another wine benediction was spoken. Note that immediately after the second cup the dessert course is served. Thus, the serving of the second cup probably represents the beginning of the third course, the dessert or symposium. This is suggested by a text from the Mishnah: "If he said the Benediction over the wine before the meal he need not say it over the wine after the meal."[41] This does not preclude wine being served during the meal, however, since a later verse provides for this eventuality.[42]

In the Tosephta text an interesting distinction is drawn in the benedictions said over the wine. While sitting in the anteroom, each was to say the benediction for himself. But after reclining in the dining room, if another benediction was spoken, it was to be said on behalf of all. This same point is made in a Mishnah text: "If men sit [apart] to eat, each should say the Benediction for himself; if they reclined [around the table together] one should say the Benediction for all. If wine is brought to them during the meal each should say the Benediction for himself; but if after the meal, one should say the Benediction for all."[43] This text appears to be giving a legal definition to a social convention. The social convention is that a group reclining around a table together becomes a table community. The text indicates that the symbolism of table fellowship is especially carried by the setting in which they recline together rather than sit.[44] The second reference, distinguishing between wine served during the meal and wine served at the end of the meal, appears to represent the function of the wine in these two situations. Served during the meal, wine is evidently considered only an accompaniment. But the cup that is mixed at the end of the meal, and thus at the beginning of the symposium, is traditionally a ceremonial cup. The same wine serving is spoken of by Plutarch as the symbol for the unity of the table community.[45] So also here, the ceremonial cup carries the symbolism of a unified table community; thus the benediction over the cup should be said on behalf of all.

The traditional wine benediction was as follows: "Blessed art Thou, O Lord, our God, King of the universe, Creator of the fruit of the vine."[46] To this may be compared the traditional wine benedictions that are found in the Greco-Roman tradition. In that tradition the prayer would be to Dionysus, the god of wine and, in the Greek view, the "creator of the fruit of the vine."

The form of the meal represented here clearly corresponds to that of the Greco-Roman banquet.[47] Such features as reclining, three courses, washing the hands, mixing the wine with water, and saying a blessing over the wine are some of the more obvious elements. This form of meal would evidently be the one utilized on any occasion in which a formal, ceremonial meal was called for. This is consistent with the function of the banquet in the Greco-Roman world in general.

The Passover Meal

The Passover feast is one of the major festivals in the Jewish year. It was primarily a sacrificial meal prior to the destruction of the Temple in 70 C.E. and thus required a pilgrimage to Jerusalem where the sacrifice was held. The Passover sacrificial ritual differed from other sacrifices in that the layperson performed his own sacrifice, although presumably the priest would have to officiate in parts of it, most especially in the ritual activities concerning the sacred blood of the animal.[48]

The most elaborate description of a Passover meal is found in the *seder* (or "order") in the Mishnah. However, "no fixed Seder liturgy was in existence before the second third of the second century C.E."[49] This is the earliest date one can propose for the completion of the basic seder given here, although clearly it was adapted and augmented for many centuries afterward.[50] Nevertheless, it is not unlikely that this form had already begun to develop some of its basic features earlier in the Greco-Roman period.

The Mishnah version of the Passover Seder is as follows:

> 1) On the eve of Passover, close to *minhah,* one does not eat until it gets dark. And even a poor man in Israel does not eat until he reclines. And they do not give him less than four cups of wine, and even [if it must come] from the charity plate.
>
> 2) They mix for him the first cup. The School of Shammai say, one recites the benediction over the day, and after that, one recites the benediction over the wine. But the School of Hillel say, one recites the benediction over the wine, and after that, one recites the benediction over the day.
>
> 3) They bring before him. He dips with the lettuce until he reaches the course of bread. They bring before him unleavened bread, lettuce, fruit puree, and two cooked dishes, even though the fruit puree is not a commandment. Rabbi Eleazar bar Zadok says, "It is a commandment." And in [the days of the] Temple, they used to bring before him the carcass of the paschal lamb.
>
> 4) They mix for him the second cup. And here the son questions his father. But if the son has not [enough] knowledge, his father instructs him. "Why is this night different from all [other] nights? For on all

[other] nights we eat [either] leavened or unleavened bread; tonight, only unleavened. For on all [other] nights we eat various kinds of herbs; tonight, bitter herbs. For on all [other] nights we eat flesh roasted, stewed, or boiled; tonight, only roasted. For on all [other] nights we dip once; tonight, twice." And according to the understanding of the son, his father instructs him, beginning with disgrace and concluding with praise. And he expounds from "A wandering Aramaean was my father" [Deut 26:5] until he finishes the entire section.

5) Rabban Gamliel used to say, "Anyone who has not said these three things on Passover has not fulfilled his obligation. And these are: paschal lamb, unleavened bread, bitter herbs." "Passover" because the Place passed over the houses of our fathers in Egypt. "Unleavened bread" because our fathers were redeemed from Egypt. "Bitter herbs" because the Egyptians made bitter the lives of our fathers in Egypt. In each and every generation one is obligated to see himself as if he went out of Egypt, as it is said, "And you shall tell your son on that day saying, 'Because of what the Lord did for me in my exodus from Egypt'" [Exod 13:8]. Therefore we are obligated to thank, to praise, to laud, to glorify, to exalt, to honor, to bless, to extol, and to adore him who has done for our fathers and for us all these signs, bringing us from slavery to freedom, from sorrow to rejoicing, from mourning to a feast day, from darkness to great light, from servitude to redemption. And [therefore] let us say before him, Praise ye the Lord!

6) How far does one recite? The School of Shammai say, "Up to, '. . . the joyous mother of children'" [Ps 113:9]. But the School of Hillel say, "Up to '. . . flint into a spring of water'" [Ps 114:8]. And one concludes with Redemption. Rabbi Tarphon says, ". . .who redeemed us and redeemed our fathers from Egypt." But he did not add a conclusion. Rabbi Akiba says, "Therefore, may the Lord, our God and the God of our fathers, bring us in peace to the other feasts and pilgrim festivals which are coming to meet us, while we rejoice in the building of your city and are glad in your service [worship]. And may we eat there from the sacrifices and from the paschal lamb etc. . . . ." until "Blessed are you, O Lord, redeemer of Israel."

7) They mix for him the third cup. He says a benediction over his meal. [They mix for him] the fourth [cup]. He completes the Hallel over it and also says the benediction for the song over it. Between these cups, if one wishes to drink, let him drink. Between the third and the fourth he must not drink.

8) They may not conclude after the paschal lamb with dessert. If some of them fell asleep, they may [continue to] eat. If all [fall asleep], they may not [continue to] eat. Rabbi Jose says, "If they take a nap, they may

[continue to] eat. If they fall into a deep sleep, they may not [continue to] eat."

9) The paschal lamb makes the hands unclean after midnight. The *piggul* and the Remnant make the hands unclean. "If one recites the benediction for the paschal lamb, it exempts [him from] the one for the festal offering. If one recites the one for the festal offering, it does not exempt [him from] the one for the paschal lamb." These are the words of Rabbi Ishmael. Rabbi Akiba says, "That one does not exempt this one, and this one does not exempt that one."[51]

The form of the meal as indicated by these texts is virtually the same as that of the festal meal outlined above, except that it is more elaborate, includes more ceremonial cups of wine, and specifically rules out the dessert course. The four ceremonial cups of wine instead of two are evidently specific to the Passover tradition. The specification that there be no dessert on this occasion only points out the fact that a normal festal meal would include a dessert. For the Passover, however, there was a tradition that the paschal lamb be the last food served, thus the rule that there be no dessert course.[52]

The meal would not take place until dark (v. 1), marking the beginning of Passover evening and also marking this as a *deipnon* or evening meal. The serving of "lettuce" with the first cup of wine and up to the course of bread evidently corresponds to the appetizer course.[53] There is some confusion in the text as to the beginning of the main course, but it appears to begin before the second cup.[54] Here the traditional items of the Passover menu are served: unleavened bread, "bitter herbs" or lettuce, *haroseth* or "fruit puree," and "two cooked dishes," which evidently are meant to take the place of the paschal lamb. The text mentions that the paschal lamb was the main course prior to the destruction of the Temple, indicating a sense that this liturgy maintains a continuity with that earlier period.

After the second cup, thus apparently during the "symposium," the "table talk" takes place. This is consistent, of course, with the symposium tradition. Thus the fact that the meal took this form, in which specific subjects were designated for discussion over wine, corresponds to the form followed especially in the philosophical schools and adapted into the general ideology of the Greco-Roman banquet.

The third and fourth cups would represent additional ceremonial cups that had been added to the liturgy over the years. They obviously do not represent courses. And since the second, third, and fourth cups are all mentioned after the main course but during the "table talk," they would evidently be a part of the symposium following the meal proper. The text nevertheless exhibits some confusing elements that are evidently to be attributed to the growth and development of this tradition over the years. Thus the benediction over the meal mentioned after the third cup is evidently out of place and represents a later development during a time when the order of the liturgy and the customary order of festal meals in general no longer matched.

Not only is the meal form that of the Greco-Roman banquet, but also the literary form of the haggadah itself is related to the literary form of the symposium.[55] This correlates with the point made earlier in this study that the symposium literary tradition tended to dominate virtually all reports of meals in this period.

Here it is exhibited first of all in the aspects of meal form already noted: the specification that they recline, the division of the meal into two (or three) courses, and the benediction over the wine that begins the symposium proper.[56] But it is especially the "table talk" section (4–6), with its emphasis on appropriate subjects for discourse at table, that parallels the "proper" way a meal should be recorded according to the symposium tradition.[57] Even the use of a question-and-answer format and the motif of instruction are part of the symposium tradition, as is the motif of composing etymological word games on the food.[58]

Other features can also be seen to relate to the symposium form. For example, the fact that prayers are mentioned, as well as their form and placement (a blessing over the wine), are paralleled in symposium literature.[59] Furthermore, the reference to the accommodation of the poor at the table (v. 1) relates to the general ideology of the Greco-Roman banquet in which issues of social status are consistently addressed. Symposium literature is rich with such references.[60]

BANQUET TRADITIONS AND JEWISH SECTARIAN GROUPS

The Judaism of the Hellenistic and Roman periods, that is, the time between Ben Sira and the Mishnah, was especially characterized by the existence of a variety of sectarian groups.[61] In many cases, these groups found meals to be an effective means for defining boundaries and group identity. They therefore exemplify the continuing influence of Greco-Roman meal traditions in this period.

Pharisees

The pre-70 c.e. Pharisees have been characterized as a table fellowship sect because of the preponderance of evidence that purity of the table was a prime concern of theirs.[62] Indeed, it was their adherence to their own special traditions in regard to the purity laws, and especially the dietary laws, that necessitated their separation from the rest of Judaism. This made the meals of the Pharisees take place separate from those of their compatriots. Jacob Neusner has persistently argued, however, that this in itself would not mean that they would celebrate communal meals together as a result of being Pharisees.[63] But it does mean that their meals, wherever they were celebrated, would be taken under the aura of purity.

In this sense, the table of the Pharisees was always sacred. This idea became fully established after the Temple's destruction, as expressed in a third-century rabbinic source: "As long as the Temple stood, the altar atoned for Israel, but now a man's table atones for him."[64] Neusner provides a helpful description of the Pharisaic perspective:

> [According to the Pharisees] the table of every man possessed the same order of sanctity as the table of the cult. . . . Eating unconsecrated food as if one were a Temple priest at the Lord's table thus was one of the two indications that a Jew was a Pharisee, a sectarian. The other was meticulous tithing. Both the agricultural laws and purity rules in the end affected table fellowship: How and what one may eat. That is, they were "dietary laws."[65]

It is the Pharisees who are the primary innovators in the interpretation of the purity laws. They reinterpreted the cultic traditions connected with the temple to apply to private life, in effect relocating the place of purity from the temple to the community itself.[66] Again, it is Neusner who clarifies this point:

> They [the Pharisees] therefore held one must eat his secular food, that is, ordinary, everyday meals, in a state of purity *as if one were a Temple priest.* The Pharisees thus arrogated to themselves—and to all Jews equally— the status of the Temple priests and did the things which priests must do on account of that status. The table of every Jew in his home was seen to be like the table of the Lord in the Jerusalem Temple.[67]

Neusner's position, however, has been challenged, most notably by E. P. Sanders. Sanders argues that the concern about the purity of food among the Pharisees concerned priestly food (second tithe, sacrifices, and heave offering) rather than ordinary food.[68] Hannah K. Harrington has recently argued in favor of Neusner's position, concluding: "In no way do the Pharisees think of themselves as priests, but they do strive for a holiness above and beyond what the Torah prescribed for the lay Israelite."[69] In light of the debate between Jesus and the Pharisees on handwashing before meals (Mark 7:1-15), which means that the Pharisees would be applying the laws of ritual purity to the table, Harrington's argument in support of Neusner makes sense.

Understood in this way, the meals of the Pharisees can be seen to have functioned to mark the boundaries between them and others. As such, their meals functioned just like other meals in various other groups in the Greco-Roman world.

Ḥaverim

Related to the Pharisees is a group identified in the Mishnah as *ḥaverim* or "companions." This group defined itself over against the larger body of Jews known as the *'ammei ha-'arets* or "people of the land." They are characterized by their punctilious observance of purity laws as opposed to the lax observance of the *'ammei ha-'arets*.[70] Most scholars therefore interpret the term to be either a synonym for Pharisee, perhaps the name by which they knew themselves as opposed to the term *Pharisee* (or "separatist"), which was given to them by others,[71] or a group formed within the Pharisaic movement.[72]

In the Mishnah, a distinction is drawn between the *ḥaverim* and the "rest of the people" *('ammei ha-'arets)*. These Mishnaic texts are uniformly concerned with observance of purity laws and tithes, and consistently define the *ḥaver* as one who upholds these as opposed to the *'ammei ha-'arets*.[73] Since the purity laws and tithes also affected dietary laws and would then define who eats what and with whom, the identity of the *ḥaver* would especially be associated with the table. Aharon Oppenheimer therefore concludes, "It is very probable that the *ḥavurah* ['fellowship'] held communal meals."[74]

This correlates well with the meaning of the term *ḥaverim,* a term that refers to a social grouping with an emphasis on the bonds of friendship, not unlike other terms used by Greco-Roman dining clubs to define themselves.[75] To organize on the model of a Greco-Roman club would be a common option taken in the ancient world by various groups who sought to define themselves as distinct social entities within their social world.[76]

Essenes[77]

Both Philo and Josephus describe the Essenes as a sect within Judaism. Their descriptions coordinate well with what we read in the Dead Sea Scrolls about the community of Qumran. Consequently, the Qumran community is thought by most scholars to be an Essene community.[78]

The Essenes disputed the authority of the ruling priestly families in Jerusalem and so had withdrawn from the rest of Judaism to set up a separate community defined by the temple purity laws. Purity was so closely associated with the boundaries of the community that purification rituals were required for entrance into membership. Once one was a member, one was expected to observe all of the laws of purity in one's daily life and to live from day to day in a state of cultic purity even more demanding than that found in the Temple cult in Jerusalem.[79] An important focus of community life was the common meal, which came to be one of the strongest symbols of membership in the community.

The importance of the communal meal at Qumran is indicated in this summary statement from the Rule of the Community regarding community life: "They shall eat in common and bless in common and deliberate in common" (1QS 6:2–3). Although the scrolls do not indicate how often the communal meals were held, Josephus notes that the Essene meals took place twice a day: once in the late morning, when they took a break from their morning labors, and once in the late afternoon, when they finished their labors for the day.[80] Before each meal, Josephus notes, they would purify themselves with a bath and put on special garments. The scrolls also connect purificatory ablutions with entrance to the "pure meal" of the community (1QS 5:13–14).

The Rule of the Community describes the common meal as follows: "Wherever there are ten men of the Council of the Community there shall not lack a Priest among them. And they shall all sit before him according to their rank and shall be asked their counsel in all things in that order. And when the table has been prepared for eating, and the new wine for drinking, the Priest shall be the first to stretch out his hand to bless the first-fruits of the bread and new wine" (1QS 6:3–6).

Like other gatherings of the community, the meal required at least "ten men" and the presence of a priest. No mention is made of women participating in the meal, a point also made by Josephus.[81] When they arrived in the dining room, the men were to sit "according to rank," which corresponds to Josephus's note that they were served "in order."[82] The meal began with a benediction by the priest, also emphasized by Josephus, who adds: "none may partake until after the prayer."[83] Josephus also mentions a prayer by the priest at the end of the meal, a practice not referred to in the scrolls.

Apparently, at the same gathering, there was to be the study of the law: "And where the ten are, there shall never lack a man among them who shall study the Law continually, day and night, concerning the right conduct of a man with his companion. And the Congregation shall watch in community for a third of every night of the year, to read the Book and to study Law and to pray together" (1QS 6:6–8). It is notable that the study of the law is here connected with the assembly for the meal, corresponding to similar references in Ben Sira and the Mishnah, and in Philo's description of the meals of the *Therapeutae* (discussed below). This can be related to the philosophical tradition whereby elevated conversation was to be the symposium entertainment. Notice also that the specific focus for the study of the law concerns social ethics ("concerning the right conduct of a man with his companion"), a subject that is also related to the philosophic symposium tradition.[84]

The Rule of the Community specifies prayers over both the bread and the "new wine." This does not mean that only bread was eaten; rather, the prayer over the bread would be intended to cover all the food. According to Josephus, the menu included bread and an unspecified common dish served to each participant.[85] The reference to "new wine" is unusual, since it is not the normal term for wine but rather refers either to lightly fermented new wine or simply to grape juice. It would appear to correlate with the sobriety of the community that their wine had limited alcoholic content.

One aspect of their cuisine appears to have been meat. At various locations at Qumran, burials of animal bones encased in pottery vessels have been found.[86] The bones appear clearly to be remains from meals since they derive from edible animals (goats, sheep, oxen) and have been separated and cleaned of flesh. Why the remains of meals were buried so carefully remains a mystery. It has been suggested that they were remains of sacrificial meals, but no signs of sacrifice have been found at the site and burial of sacrificial remains in this manner is unprecedented, so this interpretation is problematic.[87]

Two separate rooms among the archaeological remains at Qumran have been proposed as dining halls. The original excavator, Roland de Vaux, proposed that a large rectangular room, 22 meters long and 4.5 meters wide, was the community dining hall. His identification was based on the fact that an adjacent room contained a storage cache of some one thousand serving vessels. He also noted that the room was designed so that it could be washed and drained with water, consistent with its proposed use for dining. There is no indication as to what the furnishings for dining might have been.[88]

A reexamination of the excavation data by Pauline Donceel-Voûte has resulted in a new theory that the second floor of locus 30, previously identified as the scriptorium, was instead used as a dining room.[89] The plastered furnishings found in the debris from the room, originally identified by de Vaux as a "bench" and "writing table,"[90] would in this reconstruction be identified as a low platform placed along the wall on which the "couches" (formerly identified as "writing tables") would rest. Donceel-Voûte argues that this reconstruction better fits the form of the remains and, furthermore, corresponds more accurately to a known architectural pattern in the ancient world, since there are many examples of dining rooms being designed in this way whereas the proposed "bench" and "writing table" are unprecedented architecturally.[91] Donceel-Voûte's reconstruction of the arrangement of the furnishings suggests that the room could have held at least nine and possibly more reclining diners.[92] While the aspect of reclining is the common one for ancient banquets, it must be noted that the scrolls describe diners at the community meal as sitting (1QS 6:3–5). Donceel-Voûte's proposal has much in its favor, but it has not been widely accepted.[93]

In many ways participation in the common table symbolized membership in the Qumran community. There was a two-year trial period for each initiate before being accepted into full membership, during which time "he shall not touch the pure Meal of the Congregation until one full year is completed. . . . He shall not touch the Drink of the Congregation until he has completed a second year among the men of the Community" (1QS 6:16–17). Josephus adds: "Before he may touch the common food, he is made to swear tremendous oaths."[94] Similarly, exclusion from the meal for a specified time, usually a year, was a primary way in which members were disciplined (1QS 6:24–25; 7:15–16; 7:18–20).

This function of the meal as a boundary marker, setting the community apart from the outside world, is a feature it shared with meals in the culture at large. As we have noted elsewhere in this study, meals functioned as a central activity and focus for communal identity in groups of various kinds in the Greco-Roman world, such as clubs, funerary societies, and philosophical societies, as well other sectarian groups within Judaism, such as the Therapeutae, and, as we will see further below, the Christians.

There were also rules and regulations governing their behavior toward others within the community ("On joining the Community, this shall be their code of behavior with respect to all these precepts," 1QS 5:7). These rules represented the same kinds of concerns as were found in Greco-Roman clubs:

> They shall rebuke one another in truth, humility, and charity. Let no man address his companion with anger, or ill-temper, or obduracy, or

with envy prompted by the spirit of wickedness. Let him not hate him [because of his uncircumcised] heart, but let him rebuke him on the very same day lest he incur guilt because of him. And furthermore, let no man accuse his companion before the Congregation without having first admonished him in the presence of witnesses. (1QS 5:24—6:1)

> This is the Rule for an Assembly of the congregation. Each man shall sit in his place: the Priests shall sit first, and the elders second, and all the rest of the people according to their rank. And thus shall they be questioned concerning the Law, and concerning any counsel or matter coming before the Congregation, each man bringing his knowledge to the Council of the Community.
>
> No man shall interrupt a companion before his speech has ended, nor speak before a man of higher rank; each man shall speak in his turn. And in an Assembly of the Congregation no man shall speak without the consent of the Congregation, nor indeed of the Guardian of the Congregation. Should any man wish to speak to the Congregation, yet not be in a position to question the Council of the Community, let him rise to his feet and say: "I have something to say to the Congregation." If they command him to speak, he shall speak. (1QS 6:8–13)

Here we find parallels to the rules of Greco-Roman clubs.[95] Thus they are to abstain from speaking to one another in anger and from making frivolous accusations against another without bringing it to the community. In the assembly, each is to take his own place by rank and speak in turn in an orderly manner as directed by the chairman.

Another description of the community meal, this one from The Rule of the Congregation (1QSa), uses imagery from the motif of the messianic banquet.

> This shall be the assembly of the men of renown called to the meeting of the Council of the community when [the Priest-]Messiah shall summon them. He shall come [at] the head of the whole congregation of Israel with all [his brethren, the sons] of Aaron the Priests, [those called] to the assembly, the men of renown; and they shall sit [before him, each man] in the order of his dignity. And then [the Mess]iah of Israel shall [come], and the chiefs of the [clans of Israel] shall sit before him [each] in the order of his dignity, according to [his place] in their camps and marches. And before them shall sit all the heads of [family of the congreg]ation, and the wise men of [the holy congregation,] each in the order of his dignity.
>
> And [when] they shall gather for the common [tab]le, to eat and [to drink] new wine, when the common table shall be set for eating and the

new wine [poured] for drinking, let no man extend his hand over the
first-fruits of bread and wine before the Priest; for [it is he] who shall
bless the first-fruits of bread and wine, and shall be the first [to extend]
his hand over the bread. Thereafter, the Messiah of Israel shall extend his
hand over the bread, [and] all the Congregation of the Community
[shall utter a] blessing, [each man in the order] of his dignity. It is
according to this statute that they shall proceed at every me[al at which]
at least ten men are gathered together. (1QS28a 2:11–22)

Here the community meal is said to include not only the community, but
also "the Priest-Messiah," "the whole congregation of Israel," "the sons of
Aaron the Priests," "the chiefs of the clans of Israel," and "the Messiah of
Israel." The entire company processes in and sits "each in the order of his dignity." Then, after the priest says the benediction over the bread, "the Messiah
of Israel shall extend his hand over the bread, and all the congregation of the
Community shall utter a blessing, each man in the order of his dignity." This
text superimposes over the formula of the regular community meal a description of a banquet with the Messiah. The motif is that of the messianic or
eschatological banquet, the banquet of the end-time, a theme that is widely
reflected in biblical and extra-biblical tradition, as we will see further below.
Based on this text, Frank Moore Cross, among others, has suggested that the
Qumran community celebrated its common meals as a "liturgical anticipation of the Messianic banquet."[96] As I argue below, however, Cross's interpretation still leaves open how we might imagine the presence of the Messiah
liturgically realized at the Qumran meal.

The Qumran meal is often identified as a "sacred meal" analogous with
the Christian sacramental interpretation of the Lord's Supper. The closest
one gets to such a concept in the data is in Josephus's reference to the
Essenes entering the dining hall "as into some holy shrine" and practicing
silence at the table so as to appear "to those outside . . . like some awful mystery."[97] Notice, however, that Josephus is not referring to the meaning of
the meal per se, but rather to the effect it might have had on others outside
their community who observed them. It is a style of argument meant to
persuade the reader that these meals were not run-of-the-mill pagan affairs,
but rather had a form consistent with the strict rules of purity with which
they were circumscribed. The Essene meal was certainly one in which ritual
purity was sacrosanct, but to call it a sacred meal for that reason is not helpful, particularly since, as we have already seen, the term *sacred* when applied
to a meal in the ancient world can easily be used to apply to any Greco-
Roman banquet.[98]

Like the prototypical Greco-Roman banquet, the Essene meal functioned to define the boundaries of this community. By means of its rules of behavior largely derived from meal ethics and its use of the law as the banquet entertainment, it also functioned as a means to define the ethos of the community. In addition, its enhancement of the meal boundaries using purity laws and its enhancement of its connection with the divine through evoking the myth of the messianic banquet served to give a distinctive definition to its version of the Greco-Roman banquet.

Therapeutae

The *Therapeutae* were a sectarian group in Egypt known to us solely by means of a description found in Philo. Many aspects about his description are similar to what we know about the Essenes, leading to the hypothesis that the *Therapeutae* were related in some way to the Essene movement. Like the Essenes, they formed themselves into a separate community for the purpose of "contemplation" and communal living. Central to their communal activities were their gatherings for worship and common meals.[99]

Philo's description of their meals, like his description of the group as a whole, is clearly an idealization based on his desire to picture them as an ideal Jewish philosophical school. Thus it is not clear to what extent we may trust the picture he gives us. Several aspects appear valid; for example, the gathering for community meetings that included common meals in a large community room fits the pattern at Qumran. As to the form of those meals, Philo describes what is in effect his own idealization of what a "proper" meal should be, utilizing the traditions of the symposium as the model for his description:

> Among the banquets held in Greece there are two celebrated and highly notable examples, namely those in which Socrates took part. . . . That these deserve to be remembered was the judgment of men whose character and discourses showed them to be philosophers, Xenophon and Plato, who described them as worthy to be recorded, surmising that they would serve to posterity as models of the happily conducted banquet. . . . But since the story of these well-known banquets is full of such follies and they stand self-convicted in the eyes of any who do not regard conventional opinions and the widely circulated report which declares them to have been all that they should be, I will describe in contrast the festal meetings of those who have dedicated their own life and

themselves to knowledge and the contemplation of the verities of nature, following the truly sacred instructions of the prophet Moses.[100]

Philo's relation to the symposium tradition is seen by the emphases in his description. Thus he notes the special views of the *Therapeutae* on such traditional features as ranking at table, the presence of women at the table, why they eschew luxurious couches for austere ones, why free men rather than slaves serve, why water is served instead of wine, why no meat is served.[101] But especially, in contrast to the "unrestrained merry making" of Xenophon's account and the discussion on "common vulgar love" of Plato's account,[102] he notes that the *Therapeutae,* in a setting of appropriate solemnity, engage in a discourse on the highest level, on "some question arising in the Holy Scriptures,"[103] which is treated to the appropriate allegorical interpretation.[104] Philo thus uses symposium tradition itself as the source for his categories of the proper meal. Rather than refuting the symposium tradition, Philo embraces it, and thereby presents the *Therapeutae* as a group whose meal is modeled closely on the philosophical banquet tradition.[105]

THE BANQUET TRADITION AND JEWISH SEPARATISM

In order to gain such familiarity with Greco-Roman banquet traditions, Jews must have dined frequently with their Gentile neighbors. Yet Jewish dietary laws would seem to have made this unlikely. How was a Jew to negotiate dining at the table of a Gentile? In fact, this was an issue of great concern in much of Second Temple Jewish literature, such as the *Letter of Aristeas,* or Tobit, or *Joseph and Aseneth.* In contrast, however, as we have seen above, Ben Sira seemed unconcerned about this issue, since he made no mention of the dietary laws even in the midst of detailed instructions about table etiquette while at the table of a foreign dignitary. Such distinctions in the data only serve to reinforce the statement of Alan Segal, when he concludes: "We do not know exactly how ordinary Jews, as opposed to strict Pharisees, observed the dietary laws in the first century."[106]

Among the components of the dietary laws, the most central is the restriction regarding which animals can be eaten and which cannot.[107] This was such a widespread practice within Judaism that in the ancient world Jewish identity came to be synonymous with abstinence from pork. Also traditionally a part of dietary laws is the restriction against the consumption of blood, but it is not clear how widespread and in what form this would have been practiced at this period, particularly in diaspora Judaism. In addition, the category of "meat sacrificed to idols," which is discussed in Paul's letters and elsewhere in the New Testament,[108] would constitute another component of "dietary laws." These are the central dietary laws, but they do not exhaust the list.

An additional category of dietary laws is the ritual washing of the hands before meals, which is a practice attributed primarily to Pharisees and represents their application of Temple purity laws to the table. Jonathan Klawans, in a discussion of the debate on this issue between Jesus and the Pharisees as presented in Mark, suggests that the two views represented in this text, either for or against hand-washing before meals as a required ritual observance for all Jews, represent legitimate options within Jewish discourse of the first century.[109] Consequently, as suggested in this story in Mark, hand-washing as a ritual observance before meals was not universally practiced among Jews and could, in fact, be a boundary marker among Jews themselves.

There are also several versions of dietary law observance in this period that define Gentile food in general, especially wine and oil, as impure. Some data would even suggest that Gentiles as Gentiles were ritually defiling and so should simply be avoided, beyond the issue of specific food restrictions. In general, these variations on Gentile pollution were related to the issue of idolatry. Consequently, it is more appropriate to interpret the variations regarding specifically Gentile impurity as deriving from the perceived impurity inhering in the practice of idolatry.

The connection of idolatry with table practices may be noted as early as Deuteronomy, where the dietary laws are juxtaposed with restrictions against idolatry (Deuteronomy 13–14) and in the context are made to represent ways in which Israel becomes "a people holy to the Lord your God . . . out of all the peoples on earth" (Deut 14:2). Similarly, Ezek 33:25 equates idolatry with eating unclean foods ("you eat flesh with the blood and lift up your eyes to your idols") and Hos 9:3 connects unclean foods with the world of the Gentiles ("in Assyria they shall eat unclean food").

This connection of idolatry with impurity then influenced the dietary laws. In effect, the idea was that all Gentile food could be assumed to be tainted somehow through contact with idols. This was partly justified by the fact that at the Gentile table meat often came from the altar, and wine was usually offered in a libation before being drunk. Furthermore, prayers to the pagan deities were normal parts of Gentile meal customs. Under this interpretation, therefore, all food, including not only meat but also wine, bread, and vegetables, would be subsumed under the same category, as food deemed to be impure by reason of its having come from the Gentile world.[110]

Thus the question would arise whether a Jew could dine at a Gentile's table, or whether a Jew could invite a Gentile to his table. As Menahem Stern reminds us, Jews were widely known for their separatism throughout this period.[111] Shaye Cohen notes, however, that while the dietary laws "were a barrier to free social intercourse between Jews and Gentiles," nevertheless "we may not conclude that many or most diaspora Jews sought complete separation from their Gentile environment."[112] John Barclay adds that "the requirement of reciprocity in giving and receiving hospitality" in the ancient world would have made it quite difficult for Jews to interact with Gentiles according to recognized social conventions unless they were willing to accept and offer invitations to the table.[113] An observant Jew could dine with a Gentile and simply watch what he ate, an option often mentioned in the literature.[114] Indeed, Gentile discussions of Jewish food customs seem to assume just that, since Gentile knowledge of these customs would imply observing Jews at table.

The various dietary laws outlined above, including the issue of idolatry, should not be interpreted to mean that Gentiles were themselves ritually defiling, although that has often been suggested.[115] Rather, as Klawans strongly states: "It is an error to assume that Jews in ancient times generally considered Gentiles to be ritually defiling, and it is even more of an error to assume that such a conception would have been an impediment to Jewish-Gentile interaction."[116] Klawans cites as support for this view the *Letter of Aristeas,* in which, on the one hand, the issue of Jewish separatism because of food laws is strongly stated: "So that we should be polluted by none nor be infected with perversions by associating with worthless persons, he has hedged us about on all sides with prescribed purifications in matters of food and drink and touch and hearing and sight" (142). On the other hand, *Aristeas* provides instructions regarding the menu that allow the Jewish translators to eat at the king's table, which they do for seven consecutive nights (181–86). Klawans notes that it is not *ritual* impurity that is the problem, but rather *moral* impurity, most clearly associated with idolatry. Thus whenever the offensive foods are removed from the table, Jews and Gentiles can dine together.[117]

To the Gentile world, the Jewish abstinence from pork was the primary dietary law by which Jews were to be identified.[118] It became a standard feature of pagan characterization of Judaism, along with other customs such as circumcision and observation of the Sabbath. Generally speaking these were viewed as odd customs that set the Jews apart as a people, but it is incorrect to assume that they regularly produced among non-Jews hatred or animosity toward Jews.[119] Indeed, Greek and Roman ethnographers were fond of collecting bits of odd data about various ethnic groups in the Mediterranean world.[120] What is interesting about the discussions of Jewish abstinence from pork by the pagan writers is that they tend not to have a clear understanding of the reasoning behind it. They are only vaguely familiar with its connection with a wider system of dietary laws (e.g., Plutarch, *Table Talk* 669C: Jews abstain from "the most legitimate meat"; 670E: they also abstain from the hare). Furthermore, they generally do not assume that abstinence from pork means that Jews must also abstain from all table fellowship with non-Jews.

An especially helpful discussion is found in Plutarch's *Table Talk*. Here he has collected various items of trivia about meal customs that are useful for discussions at the symposium. Other subjects include: "Why old men are very fond of strong wine" (1.7), "Why fresh water instead of sea water is used to wash clothes" (1.9), "Why men become hungrier in autumn" (2.2), "Whether the hen or the egg came first" (2.3), "Why women are least liable to intoxication and old men most quickly liable" (3.3), "On those who are said to cast an evil eye" (5.7), and "Why the Pythagoreans used to abstain from fish more strictly than from any other living creature" (8.8). Among these varied subjects, one finds discussions of "Whether the Jews abstain from pork because of reverence or aversion for the pig" (4.5) and "Who the god of the Jews is" (4.6).

Here in Plutarch, the identity of the Jewish god is argued to be Dionysus, especially on the basis that Jews hold many sacred feasts that correspond in manner and season to those of Dionysus. The argument about pork takes a similar course. On the one hand, it is argued that the Jews honor the pig; if they abhorred it they would kill it rather than abstain from killing it. Another version of this argument is found in Petronius, who refers to a folk tradition that the Jews worship the pig. The other argument in Plutarch is that the Jews actually abhor the pig because it is a dirty and loathsome animal that is connected with the disease of leprosy.

Clearly there is very little direct experience with Jewish religious sensibilities among this group of Greco-Roman intellectuals. Indeed, their information appears to come largely from Greek ethnographic lore and traditions and is essentially neutral, without the rancor that developed in other areas where conflicts between Jews and Greeks had become more pronounced.

In other cases, however, references to the separatism of the Jews were more strident and negative. Tacitus, for example, enumerates a variety of specifics about Jewish beliefs and practices to support his view that their customs are "sinister and abominable and owe their vigor to their depravity," among which he lists the observation that "in dining and in sleeping, they keep themselves strictly apart."[121] Diodorus attributes their refusal to eat with Gentiles to their "hatred of humanity."[122]

Within Judaism itself, the issue of separatism was often strongly defended. Jewish literature of this period contains many examples of the literary idealization of the separate table. These stories are all examples of what has been called the *Diasporanovelle* because they are characterized as "tales which envisage situations in which exiled Jews were threatened with mortal danger, but in the end were dramatically delivered."[123] According to the standard motif, the heroes and heroines are individuals who either serve or are subjugated by a foreign king and must choose whether they will live by the laws of the king or by their own laws. The context for that decision tends to be a meal in the court of the king.

This is the case, for example, in Daniel, where the plot in the early part of the story revolves around the theme that the king wished to feed the chosen Israelite youths from the food of his own table. "But Daniel resolved that he would not defile himself with the royal rations of food and wine" (1:8). Rather, he asked that he and his companions be given vegetables and water. In the course of the story, his decision is confirmed by the greater health he and his companions exhibit versus those who ate the king's diet (1:9-16). What exactly is defiling about the king's food is not stated, but since it is wine as well as meat, it would appear that idolatry is the primary motif since wine derived its impurity from its use in idolatrous libations.

That connection is more clearly made in the Greek additions to Esther, in which she states, "I have not honored the king's feast or drunk the wine of libations" (14:17), making a more direct connection with idolatry as that which pollutes the food. Similarly, Judith refuses to eat the food and wine from the king's own table; rather, she eats what she has purposely brought with her (12:1-2,19). Tobit does the same when he is an exile in a foreign land. Whereas his countrymen had all committed the apostasy of idolatry (1:5), Tobit says of himself: "After I was carried away captive to Assyria and came as a captive to Nineveh, everyone of my kindred and my people ate the food of the Gentiles, but I kept myself from eating the food of the Gentiles. Because I was mindful of God with all my heart . . ." (1:10-12).[124] These texts all idealize Jewish heroes and heroines who abstain from Gentile food as a means of maintaining their Jewish identity. In all these cases the context is that of conflict with the Gentile world, and Gentile food in general is proscribed, notably even Gentile wine, along with the characteristic Gentile abomination, idolatry.

The story of the Maccabean revolt presents a classic case of a conflict over dietary laws. In the texts describing this event and glorifying the family of the Maccabees, the dietary laws emerge as a key to Jewish identity. The texts allude to a group within Judaism who had reached a compromise with the Seleucid king, Antiochus. They are described as having forsaken the law, especially signified by the fact that "they sacrificed to idols and profaned the Sabbath" (1 Macc 1:43). In contrast, the righteous ones are described as follows: "But many in Israel stood firm and were resolved in their hearts not to eat unclean food. They chose to die rather than to be defiled by food or to profane the holy covenant; and they did die" (1 Macc 1:62-63). Eventually the temple itself is profaned, symbolizing the fact that the conflict is one that involves the very center of the cult. Thus the eating of unclean food here becomes connected with the apostasy of idolatry and the profanation of the temple.

According to 2 Maccabees, the issue at the center of the conflict is whether "to partake of the sacrifices," which were made up of "unfit . . . abominable offerings that were forbidden by the laws" (6:4-5,7). Eventually, the Jewish leader Eleazar was tortured by being forced to eat swine's flesh, but he chose to die instead (6:18). The same story is repeated throughout this book, as seven brothers and their mother all face the same fate. They become martyrs for the faith of Judaism and an example for all Jews of this period, because they chose death rather than eat profaned food or "the flesh of the sacrificial meal" (6:21).

Joseph and Aseneth is another writing from this period that refers to dietary laws, but here the primary context is a story in which a Gentile becomes a Jew. Once more the story includes a reference to a court setting, since Joseph is at the court of Pharaoh. The text assumes that being Jewish means that one would not eat Gentile food; thus "Joseph never ate with the Egyptians, for this was an abomination to him" (7:1). Here also, the problem with Gentile food seems to be its connection with idolatry.[125]

All of the texts mentioned to this point present idealizations of Judaism. From their viewpoint, the definition of Judaism must include avoidance of Gentile food. These heroes and heroines of the faith exemplify that attitude, sometimes to the point of death, by refusing to eat even the food from the table of the king. Yet, as pointed out above in the illustration from *Aristeas,* if an appropriate menu was provided, then Jews could dine at a Gentile's table.

One way in which such menu provisions were defined was by means of the so-called Noahide Laws.[126] This refers to a tradition found in rabbinic literature that defines a set of laws intended for all humankind, not just Jews. These would represent the standards that God would require of all humanity, while the more specific commands of the Torah were given to the Jews alone. The most detailed version of this tradition is found in the Talmud, where various midrash traditions combine biblical texts, such as the promise of God to Noah, and the purity regulations designated for Gentiles who reside in Israelite territory (Leviticus 17–26).

The key text is Gen 9:1-17. Here God makes a covenant with "all flesh" that is signified by the rainbow (9:17). Included in that covenant are references to specific laws incumbent upon its recipients, including murder (9:6) and the eating of blood: "Only you shall not eat flesh with its life, that is, its blood" (9:4). This restriction against the eating of blood is repeated in the rules for "sojourners" ("aliens who reside among you") in Leviticus (17:10-16), along with other restrictions such as abstaining from idolatry (17:7-9) and incest (18:6-26). Later rabbinic tradition lists from six to as many as ten rules in this category, including especially the acknowledgment of the one true God, an idea that is implied in the restriction against idolatry in Leviticus. These lists do not include such essential items as circumcision or the full range of purity laws because they are specifically designated for righteous Gentiles. As is indicated in the category of "sojourners" in the land of Israel in Leviticus, the idea is to provide a minimum list of laws that will allow Jews and Gentiles to coexist and intermingle.

It is not known how early this interpretation developed. But a reference from the second century B.C.E. is found in *Jub.* 7:20-21, where Noah is said to have handed down certain laws: "But he bore witness to his sons so that they might do justice and cover the shame of their flesh and bless the one who created them and honor father and mother, and each one love his neighbor and preserve themselves from fornication and pollution and from all injustice."[127] Still another early reference to the righteousness required of Gentiles, this one from the first century, is found in the *Sibylline Oracles* 4:24–35:

> Happy will be those of mankind of earth who will love the great God,
> blessing him before drinking and eating, putting their trust in piety.

They will reject all temples when they see them, altars too, useless foundations of dumb stones (and stone statues and handmade images) defiled with blood of animate creatures, and sacrifices of four-footed animals. They will look to the great glory of the one God and commit no wicked murder, no deal in dishonest gain, which are most horrible things. Neither have they disgraceful desire for another's spouse or for hateful and repulsive abuse of a male.

Another well-known version from the late first or early second century c.e. is found in Acts 15. Here the issue is how to provide a means for Jews and Gentiles to intermingle in the same community. Here again there is recourse to a basic list of purity requirements connected with the Noahide Law tradition: "Therefore I have reached the decision that we should not trouble those Gentiles who are turning to God, but we should write to them to abstain only from things polluted by idols and from fornication and from whatever has been strangled and from blood" (Acts 15:19-20).[128]

Thus, although we cannot assume that the full-fledged rabbinic version of the Noahide Laws was extant in the time of Acts, there is clear evidence that there were some versions of this tradition to be found in various segments of Judaism. They provided a specific means to deal with the problem of food connected with idolatry when Gentiles and Jews dined together.

THE MESSIANIC BANQUET

An important metaphorical use of banquet ideology in Jewish thought is found in the tradition of the so-called messianic banquet. This was a widespread motif found in various stages and forms of Jewish literature and constitutes a significant contribution to the banquet ideology of the Greco-Roman period.[129]

As a beginning point, it might be best to define the term *messianic banquet* in the broadest possible way. This aids one in sifting through the data and represents best the variety of ways in which the term is used in scholarship. Rather than referring only to banquet imagery where there is specific reference to the Messiah, therefore, I will use the term to refer to the general symbolism of food and/or a festive meal to signify immortality and/or the joys of the end-time or afterlife. The terms *eschatological banquet* and *apocalyptic banquet* are often used in this more general sense.

As is suggested by this definition, the messianic banquet motif is especially associated with apocalyptic traditions in Judaism. However, like other apocalyptic motifs, the messianic banquet has its origins in a complex mythological heritage from the ancient Near East and is supplemented in the later periods by Hellenistic parallels.[130]

The Motif of Sacred Foods

One motif connected with the messianic banquet theme places the emphasis on the numinous quality of certain symbolic foods. The characteristic theme here is that of the "food of the gods," which confers immortality on anyone who eats it. A prominent motif expressing this idea in ancient Near Eastern mythology is the "tree of life," whose fruit is deemed to have special life-giving qualities (as in Gen 2:9).[131] There are echoes of this motif in the symbolism of the menorah in the biblical cult.[132] Apocalyptic literature utilizes it to represent the gift of eternal life to be given by God to the righteous at the end-time.[133] For the Greeks the "food of the gods" was ambrosia and the "drink of the gods" was nectar; these conferred immortality on all who partook of them.[134] In the Jewish work *Joseph and Aseneth,* a honeycomb is identified as the food of the angels that provides immortality to all who eat of it.[135]

The bestowal of "life" in the sense of immortality or eternal life at the end-time is connected with other symbolic foods as well. Prominent images include basic foods such as water, wine, bread, and fish.[136] In *Odes Sol.* 6:8-18, it is the "living water of eternity" that snatches the soul from death;[137] so also in John 4:10-14 the "living water" of Jesus is "a spring of water gushing up to eternal life." In Rev 22:1-2 and 17-19, the "water of life" is equated with the "tree of life" as a divine substance that imparts eternal life at the end-time.[138]

In the Greek tradition wine is considered to be the gift of the god Dionysus to mortals, and its effects, ranging from pleasure to literary inspiration, are viewed as the blessings of the god,[139] an idea that is echoed in some Jewish traditions as well.[140] One interpretation among the Greeks was the idea that in drinking wine one would thereby consume the god; furthermore, Dionysiac beliefs also included the promise of a happy afterlife, although this was not necessarily related specifically to wine-drinking.[141] In *Joseph and Aseneth,* however, the "cup of immortality" refers to a beverage that guarantees eternal life in heaven to those who drink it along with the "bread of life" and the "ointment of incorruptibility."[142]

Bread as a numinous food in biblical tradition is especially related to the miraculous bread from heaven, or manna, where it is also associated with the

miraculous water from the rock.[143] These miraculous foods take on numinous quality in a long and complex midrash tradition that is reflected
throughout our literature. The bread becomes "the bread of angels," an
apparent reference to the divine food eaten by angels,[144] and, as "bread of
life," it is a food that confers eternal life on those who eat it.[145] Philo interprets manna and rock to be types of the *logos,* or word and wisdom of God,
which nourish the soul.[146] For Paul, manna and water from the rock are
interpreted as "spiritual food" and "spiritual drink" and as symbolic of the
Christian Lord's Supper.[147]

Another creation theme that becomes a part of the messianic banquet tradition is the myth of Leviathan, one of the names given to the primordial sea
monster representing the power of the sea, whose defeat in a cosmic battle is
a constituent part of the combat motif in many ancient Near Eastern creation myths. In the Old Testament, the destruction of Leviathan by God represents God's power over chaos.[148] The idea that Leviathan is not only
destroyed but also provided as food becomes a symbol for the provision of
divine food for the righteous in the new age.[149] The widespread fish symbolism that occurs in Jewish and Christian art as well as in the New Testament
has been interpreted to signify fish as a numinous or eschatological food, an
idea developed at least partially from the Leviathan myth.[150]

The Motif of the Divine Banquet

This is the primary messianic banquet motif, since it places the emphasis on
the banquet itself, a banquet at which the Messiah is deemed to be present.
This theme has its apparent roots in another pattern found in certain ancient
Near Eastern creation myths. These myths tell of a great battle being waged
in the divine sphere. When the battle has been won, the gods assemble and
celebrate the victory with a great banquet.[151] Here the myth echoes the cultural tradition of the festive meal as the primary social institution for celebrating victory and deliverance.[152] Since apocalyptic literature takes up the
combat and victory motif, the banquet of celebration becomes a part of its
repertoire as well.[153]

This tradition is reflected in the description of the victory/coronation
banquet of David in 1 Chron 12:38-40, a passage with strong messianic
overtones. Here the warriors gather and celebrate with their new king, the
prototype of the Messiah. The nations come bearing gifts in tribute and
"there was joy in Israel" (v. 40). This description reflects the form of the banquet of the end-time, which is given a classic description in Isa 25:6-8:

On this mountain the Lord of hosts will make for all peoples a feast of rich food, a feast of well-aged wines, of rich food filled with marrow, of well-aged wines strained clear. And he will destroy on this mountain the shroud that is cast over all peoples, the sheet that is spread over all nations; he will swallow up death for ever. Then the Lord God will wipe away the tears from all faces, and the disgrace of his people he will take away from all the earth; for the Lord has spoken.

These texts provide a summary of the basic motifs that come to be associated with the messianic banquet: victory over the primordial enemies (e.g., death), eternal joyous celebration, abundance of food, the presence of the Messiah, judgment, and the pilgrimage of the nations.

Thus, for example, in *1 Enoch,* on that day when the Lord shall triumph over the kings and other rulers of the earth, they will be judged and will become victims of God's wrath. Then a "sacrifice" (for the banquet) will be provided and "the righteous and elect ones . . . shall eat and rest and rise with that Son of Man forever and ever" (62:12-14). Here judgment is expressed in terms of divine reversal; those who suffer now will rejoice "in that day"; those who hunger now will feast in the future. Others who may find a share at the table are those who give bread to the hungry in this life.[154] The table will be one with lavish provision of food and wine.[155] Indeed, it will be a table at which, when the "Messiah is revealed," the primordial representatives of chaos, the monsters Behemoth and Leviathan, will be eaten.[156]

The messianic banquet is sometimes represented as a wedding banquet, a motif that is closely related to the victory banquet in its mythological origins and connections with the themes of victory and kingship of the god.[157] More specifically, this motif is related to the theme of the "sacred marriage," a concept with a rich heritage from ancient Near Eastern myth and ritual.[158] This theme is especially prominent in biblical literature as a symbol for the relationship of God to the people of Israel,[159] or, in the New Testament, as a symbol for the relationship of Christ to the church.[160] The wedding banquet as a reflection of the sacred marriage theme is found in Song of Songs,[161] but more important for apocalyptic thought is Isa 54:5—55:5, where the theme of a divine marriage (54:5) is combined with a joyful feast characterized by abundance of food (55:1-2), vindication for the righteous (54:6-17), and the pilgrimage of the nations (55:5). This theme is then taken up in the New Testament, where it becomes a prominent image for the joys of the kingdom in the Gospel tradition, especially in the parables and the miracle at Cana.[162] In Revelation it is the primary motif for the messianic banquet.[163]

Among the Greeks and Romans, the festive banquet was utilized as a symbol for the joyous afterlife, a theme especially associated with Orphic and Dionysiac beliefs.[164] This idea is also associated with funerary reliefs that picture the deceased reclining at a festive meal, although there is some debate whether this motif is meant to refer to an eschatological banquet or whether it simply idealizes the past life of the deceased.[165]

The Evidence for Actual Communal Meals

The examples mentioned to this point represent the symbolic use of meal motifs in literature and art that sometimes, but not always, have some connection to actual meals. Some texts, however, are more explicit in connecting the theme of the messianic banquet to actual meals of a community. The communal meals at Qumran, for example, as we have already seen, seem to have been defined as a proleptic messianic banquet, since the description of the meal is heavily liturgical in form and, furthermore, includes the presence of the Messiah.[166] The interpretation of the Passover meal in Judaism also had eschatological overtones.[167]

Other examples are less clear. E. R. Goodenough, for example, has proposed the existence of a "mystic meal" in Hellenistic Judaism based especially on texts from Philo and meal symbolism found on Jewish monuments, but his conclusions are largely discredited today.[168] The meal references in *Joseph and Aseneth* have suggested to many interpreters that actual ritual meals with cultic significance were being referred to, but the data is complex and subject to varying interpretations.[169] From the world of the Greeks and Romans, the funerary banquet whereby the family and friends of the deceased would commemorate his death has been interpreted to signify in some sense the proleptic enjoyment of the eschatological banquet in the afterlife, but this interpretation is still much debated.[170] The ancient Near Eastern version of the funerary banquet, known as the *marzeah,* has also been interpreted to have eschatological overtones as well as connections with the sacred marriage theme.[171]

The Messianic Banquet as a Mythological Meal

In its role as a representation of the numinous being made available to humans, the messianic banquet is in its essence a mythological meal. It represents food and/or beings from a timeless, mythological world. To the extent that reference is made to real people and real history, such references are by definition made mythological as well. Indeed, the texts in which messianic banquets are presented are by and large literary idealizations. They do not describe real meals, but rather idealize meals on a divine plain.

For this reason, significant doubt must be raised as to the existence of a messianic banquet as a real meal. All of our references are in texts that have clearly idealized meals and represented them as participating in the mythological world. The Qumran messianic banquet text, for example, simply places the Messiah within the context of their normal community meal. How the presence of the Messiah was understood in that context is unclear from the text. Though the text can be read as a "liturgical anticipation" of the messianic banquet, as Cross carefully puts it, what that phrase actually means is left open. We simply do not know to what extent this concept, in which the meal was idealized as one at which the Messiah was present, was actually realized in liturgical form. Similar problems will be raised when we come to the Christian material. In general, it seems prudent to distinguish between literary idealizations of such meals and our reconstructions of how they may actually have been conducted and interpreted.

CONCLUSION

The meal traditions in Judaism are often studied as if they were a unique phenomenon. This study has attempted to place them in the broader world of the Greco-Roman banquet.

To be sure, there were distinctive features in the Jewish tradition, but the form taken by Jewish meals in the Greco-Roman period on any particular occasion or in any particular setting was that of the Greco-Roman banquet. Furthermore, the ideology of the meal was also that of the Greco-Roman banquet. Indeed, the literary tradition utilized to describe Jewish meals largely derived from the Greek symposium tradition. Especially notable is the way that meals functioned to define group identity within Judaism, as different groups distinguished themselves from the rest of Judaism by their table practices.

Nevertheless, there were some features that were distinctive to the Jewish banquet tradition. The dietary laws were such a feature, as was the tradition of the messianic banquet, although there were echoes of the latter in Greek tradition as well. Nevertheless, the dietary laws also represented a more precise and specific way in which meals functioned to define boundaries. So also, the messianic banquet represented a mythologization of the festive or joyous banquet that was a part of the common banquet tradition.

Jewish meals of the Second Temple period are seen to be embedded in the Greco-Roman banquet tradition in form, ideology, and literary descriptions. Though there were some distinctive aspects to Jewish meal traditions, these are best interpreted as subdivisions of the general banquet tradition and often can be seen as variations of common aspects of that tradition.

CHAPTER 7

THE BANQUET IN THE CHURCHES OF PAUL

But when Cephas came to Antioch I opposed him to his face, because he stood self-condemned; for until certain people came from James, he used to eat with the Gentiles. But after they came, he drew back and kept himself separate for fear of the circumcision faction. And the other Jews joined him in this hypocrisy, so that even Barnabas was led astray by their hypocrisy. But when I saw that they were not acting consistently with the truth of the gospel, I said to Cephas before them all, "If you, though a Jew, live like a Gentile and not like a Jew, how can you compel the Gentiles to live like Jews?"
—Gal 2:11-14

When you come together, it is not really to eat the Lord's supper. For when the time comes to eat, each of you goes ahead with your own supper, and one goes hungry and another becomes drunk. What! Do you not have homes to eat and drink in? Or do you show contempt for the church of God and humiliate those who have nothing? What should I say to you? Should I commend you? In this matter I do not commend you! . . . So then, my brothers and sisters, when you come together to eat, wait for one another. If you are hungry, eat at home, so that when you come together, it will not be for your condemnation.
—1 Cor 11:20-22, 33-34a

The only texts in the New Testament that specifically describe early Christian meals are the two quoted above. Both, of course, come from Paul. The first is his reference in his letter to the Galatians to an event that had taken place earlier at Antioch. The second is taken from his instructions to the Corinthians about how they should conduct their meal, which he terms the *Lord's supper*. Though only these texts actually describe early Christian meals, there are numerous allusions elsewhere in Paul's letters that allow us to fill out further details of the practices in his churches.

Even before Paul arrived on the scene, the Christian community already centered its communal gatherings around meals. How this practice developed has been explained in various ways, ranging from some form of Jewish meal to a specific type of Greco-Roman meal. This study provides what I argue is a more adequate explanation for the origin of early Christian meals. We have discovered that the very idea that sectarian groups should gather at meals was strongly embedded in Greco-Roman culture. When early Christians met for meals, they were engaging in a practice common to all religious people and sectarian groups in the ancient world. Like other such groups, they utilized the banquet institution with its rich symbolism and adapted it according to their own special needs and emphases. Thus the origin of early Christian meals is not to be found in any one type or originating event but rather in the prevailing custom in the ancient world for groups to gather at table.

I would also argue that the references in Paul to meals at Antioch and Corinth represent the same basic meal tradition. In other words, what Paul calls "the Lord's supper" at Corinth (1 Cor 11:20) is also what was being practiced at Antioch (Gal 2:11-12). Likewise the understanding Paul applied to the meal at Antioch would also inform his interpretation at Corinth. In addition, as I will argue below, we may assume that similar meal practices would have been common at other Pauline churches, including especially Galatia and Rome.

Not only did the meals and their attendant problems derive from banquet tradition, but, as I will argue, so did much of Paul's theological discourse in regard to the meaning and practice of the meal. This is consistent with the fact that, as scholars have often noted, Paul's theology does not develop in a vacuum but out of a dialogue with the situations that developed in his churches. As Paul faced problems at the meal, he was able to provide solutions that developed in dialogue with traditional banquet ideology. He took the pre-existing ideological structure of the proper banquet and recast it in Christian terms. But that should not surprise us, for he himself compared the pagan meal with the Christian meal, as if they were two sides of the same coin: "You cannot drink the cup of the Lord and the cup of demons. You cannot partake of the table of the Lord and the table of demons" (1 Cor 10:21).

A quick summary of my argument will illustrate how the meal texts in Paul are firmly embedded in banquet ideology. The meal controversies at both Antioch and Corinth (and Rome as well) derive from the nature of the meal to create *social boundaries*. At Antioch, Paul's dispute with Peter arises when Peter separates himself from the Gentile table, thus creating two tables within one community, one Jewish Christian, and the other Gentile Christian. For Paul, this contradicts "the truth of the gospel" (Gal 2:14) because it implies a separation within the community of faith, a community in which there is to be "neither Jew nor Greek" (Gal 3:28). At Corinth, Paul addresses an issue in which the community is eating separately rather than together. This has the effect of creating a collection of "individual meals" rather than one community meal. Only the latter can be called the "Lord's supper" (1 Cor 11:18-21). Thus Paul counsels that they should eat together rather than separately (1 Cor 11:33).

As Paul develops his arguments, he will refer to the power of the meal to create *social bonding* and define *social boundaries*. His arguments for social ethics within the community will draw on banquet traditions of *social obligation* toward one's meal companions. He will respond to issues of *social stratification* at the table but will especially develop the theme of *social equality*. In his discussion of early Christian worship, he will utilize many features from the rules of *banquet entertainment*, suggesting that worship took place at the community table. These themes also inform other sections of Paul's theology and ethics beyond the texts immediately concerned with the meals at Antioch and Corinth.

Let me clarify once more what is distinctive to my approach. Contrary to a large body of previous scholarship, I will not be arguing that Paul utilized a particular form of meal, such as the Passover meal or the meal of the mystery cults, as his model. I am instead referring to a generic meal model from the culture, one which, importantly, is utilized by groups throughout the Greco-Roman world, including Judaism and the mystery cults.

On the other hand, readers will also note that I have not taken the Lord's Supper tradition quoted by Paul at 1 Cor 11:23-26 to be the primary determinant for his meal theology. It is clearly a tradition that he derives from other sources; it is not one he creates. Furthermore, he quotes it as an authoritative resource. But it must be interpreted in order for it to have any meaning, and that is what Paul does. He gives it a singular interpretation that is his own and that derives from banquet ideology. Thus his overall discussion and model for the meal does not, in fact, come from the Lord's Supper tradition but from the generic banquet tradition. But once more that should not surprise us, for the Lord's Supper tradition is itself to be seen as a variation on generic banquet tradition; indeed, that is how Paul reads it.

THE COMMUNITY MEAL IN THE CHURCHES OF PAUL

The earliest reference to a Christian meal is at Antioch, a meal described in Paul's letter to the Galatians. The meal had taken place earlier and is brought into the discussion by Paul because he sees it as relevant to the issues at Galatia. As he describes the Antioch meal, it seems clear that the custom in Christian groups of eating a community meal together is presupposed, for Paul does not need to qualify or explain the practice to the Galatians. Furthermore, no question is raised as to its origins. Rather, it seems to be a tradition that predates Paul and that he accepts and continues to promote.

It is also clear that the Antioch meal was not a mere social occasion. Rather, it was a significant ritual event in the life of the church that carried important theological meaning. If this were not the case, Paul's argument would not make sense. Thus it can be called an early form of liturgy in the church.

Paul's description also suggests that a similar meal was common among Jerusalem Christians; otherwise the issue when the guests from Jerusalem arrived would not have been which table but why have a community table at all. Furthermore, though no meal practices of the church at Galatia are mentioned, it is fair to assume that they practiced communal meals similar to those at Antioch. Paul's use of the Antioch incident in the Galatian letter would then make more sense. As we analyze the Galatian letter below, further evidence will emerge to support this hypothesis. On the other hand, the burden of proof is not as great as one might think, for, as I have argued throughout this study, meals were so common for all groups in the ancient world that one can virtually assume that Christian groups would have met for meals unless there is evidence to the contrary.

In Corinth, the church also celebrated a community meal together. Here we again find evidence to suggest that such meals were regular components of their meetings. According to 1 Corinthians 11, the phrases "when you come together as a church" (1 Cor 11:17-18) and "when you come together to eat" (1 Cor 11:20-21, 33) tend to be synonymous. Consequently, we must assume that they regularly met at table. And since their meetings included some form of worship, we may also speculate that they worshipped at table, at least part of the time if not all of the time.

In 1 Corinthians the gathering is specifically called the "Lord's supper." Paul also refers for the first time to a Jesus tradition that has been passed on to him in which the Christian meal is defined as a "memorial meal" evoking the last supper of "the Lord" (1 Cor 11:23-25). Since Paul presents this tradition as one that was passed on to him,[1] he seems to assume its practice for all of the churches with which he is familiar. And the meal at Corinth in which this tradition is found is clearly a full banquet, sharing features much like the community meals being practiced in Jerusalem, Antioch, and Galatia. Consequently, the terminology "Lord's supper" and the invoking of the words of Jesus at the table were surely known also at Galatia, probably at Antioch, and perhaps at Jerusalem.

In Romans Paul also refers to a church fellowship meal. This can be seen by the way in which he describes the issues in Rom 14:1—15:13. Here a division has seemingly developed in the church over issues of dietary restrictions. Those who are "strong" in faith can eat anything, while "the weak" are following some form of dietary restrictions (14:1-4). Though other issues also divide these two groups, it is the differences over diet that get the most attention and that seem to be the focus for the problems. It seems most likely, therefore, that such ideological divisions came to the fore at the community meal. Since this is a church not founded by Paul, its traditions evidently developed independent of him. Furthermore, it is unclear how much he knew about them when he wrote. But when he mentions specific issues at the table, he seems either to be referring to actual problems or to what he suspected to be actual problems in their community.[2] Consequently, we can assume that they were practicing a regular fellowship meal, like the churches as Antioch and Corinth. And, based on Paul's discussion, the form and function of their meal was the same in its basic features as those in the other Pauline churches.

What do we know about how the meals in Paul's churches were conducted? First we must recall that Pauline churches, like virtually all early Christian groups, tended to be house churches. Paul frequently mentions the church meeting at someone's house.[3] The householders who hosted the church for its meetings functioned as patrons of the church.[4] The social event of meeting in a home would evoke the cultural practice of hospitality, a practice that centered on the meal one would give for one's guests.[5] It is hard to imagine meeting in a home without basic hospitality being practiced. Thus we should imagine Christian meetings taking place at table most if not all of the time, as they did at Antioch and Corinth.[6]

A home of sufficient size to accommodate the group of Christians would have to have contained a dining room, and it is in the dining room where the Christians would most likely have met. It has often been suggested that the gathering would have been too large for a typical dining room. Instead, the courtyard or atrium has been proposed as the most likely meeting place. L. Michael White argues, however, that such theories are based too much on presuppositions about the uniformity of dining rooms.[7] In fact, Greeks and Romans were accustomed to accommodating parties of various sizes in their homes and built dining rooms sufficient to hold them. Since the dining room is the one section of the house that was commonly set aside for entertaining guests, White's argument makes sense.

The community meal was a full-course dinner, as indicated by 1 Corinthians, in which the *deipnon,* or dinner course, is followed by the symposium. The same text also records the problem that some were getting too much to eat and drink while others were not getting enough. This tells us that the meal was intended, at least, to provide adequate food.

We do not know how the meal was arranged, but we can guess at some of its features. The householder/patron would presumably be the host. The food, however, may have been provided by everyone bringing a portion, somewhat like our potluck dinner today.[8] This is a format used in some Greco-Roman clubs and is suggested by the language of 1 Corinthians 14, where everyone is said to have brought as their contribution to the occasion not food but an expression of worship. It is also suggested by the phrase "one's own meal," which Paul uses to refer to the abuses at the banquet. How the meal could have devolved from a community meal to a meal of individuals is not clear, but one suggestion is that those who brought food for the community table ate it themselves instead of sharing it.[9]

The posture of the diners is indicated in only one text, and it is not specific to the meal setting. It is found in 1 Corinthians 14, where the participants at the worship service are said to be sitting. As I will argue shortly, the worship activities described in 1 Corinthians 14 most likely took place while they were still at the table. This would suggest that the posture at the table was sitting rather than reclining. If this was the case, it need not represent a wholesale departure from Greco-Roman banquet traditions. Most likely it represented a posture dictated by the size of the group—there was simply not room for all diners to recline.[10] We have some indication that large numbers were accommodated by sitting rather than reclining in some of the literature.[11] It should also be noted that the only other references to dining posture in the New Testament are found in the idealized descriptions of meals of Jesus in the Gospels. In these instances, the posture is always reclining.[12] Reclining is also indicated as the dining posture at the pagan temples (1 Cor 8:10).

Not only were these Christians gathering for a community meal, but they were also conducting their entire worship service at the table as well. This makes more sense of the data than the model often employed, whereby we picture their community meal as a mere appendage to the real meeting, much as a fellowship dinner is related to Christian worship today. But these were not "mere" fellowship dinners. Paul has attached too much importance to them.

Practically speaking, it makes sense that they would worship at table. If they ate when they gathered, and insisted that all eat together, why would they then adjourn to another room to worship? And what other rooms would be available? After all, the Greco-Roman house was designed so that hospitality and entertaining of guests all took place in one room, the *andron* or triclinium. Even if a gathering of Christians grew too large for the normal dining room and had to dine instead in the courtyard, since it was presumably the only space large enough to accommodate everyone, that would not change the conventions of hospitality.

Furthermore, as we have seen in this study, it was customary among various groups who gathered for meals to continue their meetings at table. The form of the meal lent itself to that. A full, formal banquet that included both a *deipnon* and a symposium, as the Corinth banquet surely did, would have to include some form of banquet entertainment during the symposium. The natural form of "entertainment" for this community would be communal worship. After all, clubs used the symposium for their meetings, philosophical discourses, and theological dramas. Jews used the symposium for discussion of the law. Singing of drinking songs, encomia, or hymns was also common. So Christians would have done the normal thing, namely, continue their meeting at table during the symposium. To cut the symposium short and adjourn to another location for worship would be the height of inhospitality. It would also be unnecessary, because worship as practiced by Christians, lacking any need for temples and altars, could be carried out quite well at the table. Furthermore, our primary description of early Christian worship, found in 1 Corinthians 14, reflects the ambience of the table setting, as I will argue below.

Of course, other models than the household table have been proposed for early Christian worship. The most often cited model is that of the synagogue.[13] However, synagogue architecture attests to a different practice. The standard synagogue structure contains a common assembly room with benches and a Torah shrine. Where provisions for communal dining are present, they are found separate from the assembly room.[14]

On the other hand, we know very little about what took place either in synagogue worship or in early Christian worship. The earliest reference to Christian worship is found in 1 Corinthians 14. The earliest reference to synagogue worship is found in Luke 4:16-30. These two texts seem poles apart in their descriptions of worship activities.

It is likely that there was not one single form of early Christian worship. And certainly we know it evolved over the generations and centuries to reach the form it had when the first Christian meeting houses were constructed. But the early groups who met in homes utilized a form of worship that correlated with their setting. We know it included a meal. It is therefore quite probable that the meal continued with worship at table.

This observation will become increasingly important as we analyze more closely Paul's theology and ethics and their interaction with banquet ideology. That this is the case should not surprise us. It has become a commonplace in New Testament scholarship to take into account how the letters and Gospels would have been first experienced. What we imagine is that they would have been read aloud to the community as it was gathered for worship. What we must now imagine is that they are likely gathered for worship at table when they hear the letter of Paul being read to them.[15]

JEWISH DIETARY LAWS AND THE CHURCHES OF PAUL

In three of the four churches mentioned above, namely, at Antioch, Corinth, and Rome, divisions at the table are a prime concern. And in all three cases, these divisions can be seen to be related to Jewish dietary laws. Recent studies by James D. G. Dunn, E. P. Sanders, and Alan F. Segal have given us a revised and more adequate understanding of Jewish dietary laws in this period as they relate to issues in the Pauline churches. I reviewed much of this material in chapter 6. Here I will summarize the relevant details.

Dietary laws in their strictest form did not refer specifically to Gentile food. They simply referred to unclean animals and blood. Vegetable items would not normally be included. But a secondary restriction had developed in regard to foodstuffs that had been sacrificed to pagan deities. This applied especially to meat but also, by extension, to wine and oil. It was in this way that Gentile wine came to be restricted. As Sanders notes, since "Greeks (and others) poured out a small libation whenever they drank wine, Jewish restrictions came to be applied to all Gentile wine."[16]

Dietary laws applied to the foodstuffs themselves, not to the people.[17] It is incorrect, therefore, to interpret dietary laws to mean that Jews could not eat with Gentiles at all. Indeed, Jews could and did associate with Gentiles extensively and must have eaten with them often. If such Jews followed any version of the dietary laws, they could simply choose a vegetarian diet when eating at a Gentile table.[18] This is the option chosen by some in the church at Rome (Rom 14:2).

Dietary laws, as well as circumcision, were of special significance in Jewish religious practice as boundary markers; that is to say, they set Jews apart from Gentiles. Dunn argues persuasively that when Paul contrasts "works of law" with "justification by faith," it is specifically the boundary, marking "works of law," namely, Sabbath observance, circumcision, and dietary laws, that he has in mind. These aspects of the law set the Jews apart and thus created the tension with which Paul was struggling.

With these observations in mind, let us now look at relevant texts in Paul.

The Incident at Antioch (Gal 2:11-14)

Why would the visitors from Jerusalem not eat with the Christians at Antioch? It seems clear that this incident refers to Jewish dietary laws. After all, it is the "circumcision party" from Jerusalem who refuse to eat with the predominately Gentile Christians in Antioch. What is not clear is what form of dietary laws is in question.

What must be taken into account here is the fact that the dietary laws had already been interpreted in different ways by different members of the Christian community. It is easy to account for the position of the "circumcision party," the group from Jerusalem. They would evidently have had a more pronounced sense of self-identity within Judaism as defined by the conservative orbit of Jerusalem. Their position on dietary laws would be consistent with their position on circumcision, since both may be seen as aspects of the Jewish law that specifically function as boundary markers, marking Jews off from Gentiles. What is not yet clear is the exact position on dietary laws that they would have held. Before addressing this, we need to examine the positions of the other parties in the debate.

The position of Peter and Paul, as well as the position of the Antioch community, prior to the arrival of the Jerusalem delegation is not as clear as one might think. After all, Paul identifies himself as a Pharisee by background, and Peter was closely associated with the church at Jerusalem. How is it that they feel free to dine with Gentiles while the Jerusalem visitors do not? It does not work to say that this represented a change in their understanding of Judaism since they became Christians. The nature of the debate at Antioch, and the earlier debate at the Jerusalem conference, works against this. Indeed, both Paul and Peter appear to have seen themselves as living a lifestyle consistent with their Jewish identity.

Why were they taken by surprise by the actions of the delegation from Jerusalem? If they knew how the visitors might react, why did they not set up the meal in such a way that it would meet dietary restrictions? I would suggest that what took place when the Jerusalem delegation arrived was a surprise precisely because it was atypical. In fact, the issue had probably not arisen at the Christian meals in Jerusalem. In a completely Jewish environment, when one's Jewish identity was not in question, it would not be a point of issue. But when the delegation of Jerusalemites came to the Gentile city of Antioch and were asked to eat with fellow Christians who happened to be uncircumcised Gentiles, suddenly questions of boundaries and identity became important.

Thus I would tend to follow Sanders in his interpretation of the issue behind the incident at Antioch. He notes his "doubt that biblical law was actually being transgressed." Rather, he suggests that this was an instance where association with Gentiles in itself was considered suspicious, without reference to any specific law.[19] This works to explain the incident best because it allows for an appropriate explanation for the positions of both Peter and Paul.

Idol Meat at Corinth

In 1 Corinthians 8 and 10, Paul refers to divisions in the community over whether it is appropriate to eat "meat sacrificed to idols." Although recent arguments have connected these issues with socioeconomic distinctions in the church, the terminology Paul uses is imbued with Jewish sensibilities. The key term is *eidōlothyton* ("meat sacrificed to idols"), a term that is likely to have arisen out of a traditional Jewish aversion to idolatry. A Gentile would be unlikely to use the term *idol* or to center his concern on the meat that came from the idol. Consequently, the terminology itself is best understood as having arisen out of Jewish dietary practices.[20]

However, 1 Cor 8:7 refers to the "weak," who now refuse to eat the idol meat, as those who were once accustomed to eating it. This seems difficult to reconcile with the idea that they were Jewish Christians. Most commentators, therefore, rule out the idea that the "weak" were Jewish Christians.[21]

The thesis that has clearly won the day is that of Gerd Theissen, who has presented a brilliant argument that the "strong" were the more wealthy members of the community and the "weak" were the lower-class members. Since meat was a rare and expensive commodity on the dinner table, the wealthy class would be more likely to be accustomed to eating meat on a regular basis. The lower classes, on the other hand, would not see meat except during festival season, when it would be provided by the city. They would then tend to associate meat only with religious festivals, whereas the wealthy would associate it with a normal meal. Thus the lower classes would fit Paul's definition of those who were formally accustomed to idols but now had "weak" consciences about eating meat.

What is the context for this tension within the community? Paul presents a hypothetical scenario in 8:10, whereby the "weak" might see the "strong" "eating in the temple of an idol" (8:10). Some have argued that this is the sole cause of the tension, and that "eating meat sacrificed to idols" therefore only refers to the practice at the pagan temple.[22] But the chance observance of someone at a "temple restaurant" does not seem to me to offer enough opportunity for conflict on this issue. I would rather argue that the context is, in fact, the communal meals of the Christian community. This would best explain how the tension between the two groups came to such an impasse. And it would fit better Paul's response to the situation in which he argues for unity within the community as his central point.

When the community gathered for its meal, therefore, there arose a split between two parties over the appropriateness of meat at the table. The issue was over whether meat from the meat market would have come from a temple sacrifice. The same situation is presented at 10:25-29, only in this case it is at the home of an unbeliever that the meal is held. Thus Paul counsels, "eat whatever is sold in the meat market" (10:25), thus indicating that the issue of "idol meat" is not only defined by the location of the meal at the temple, but also by the supposed origin of the meat wherever it might be eaten, whether at the table of an unbeliever (10:27-28) or, as I would argue, at the common table of the Christian community. In either case, Paul's advice to the "strong" is the same: abstain for the sake of the conscience of the other (8:13, 10:28-29).[23]

Weak and Strong at the Table in Rome

In Rom 14:1—15:13, Paul addresses an issue that is tantalizingly close to the one addressed in 1 Corinthians 8. Here also differences in regard to diet have been interpreted as differences between weak and strong and involve different interpretations about the appropriateness of eating meat. In Romans, however, there are more specific references to Jewish dietary laws and to the context of the issue in the fellowship meals of the Christian community. Thus Paul argues, "I know and am persuaded in the Lord Jesus that nothing is unclean in itself; but it is unclean for anyone who thinks it unclean" (14:14).[24] But in this context, some have chosen vegetarianism (14:2), while others who are "strong" are urged by Paul, "it is good not to eat meat or drink wine or do anything that makes your brother or sister stumble" (14:21). There are no hypothetical examples of dining separate from the community and being observed by a member of the community, like that found in 1 Cor 8:10. Rather, the implication of the argument throughout is that the context for the debate is that of the community meal.[25]

In all three cases, then, in Antioch, Corinth, and Rome, tensions arose at the table because of differing interpretations of Jewish dietary laws. At Antioch and Rome, the debate arose between Jewish Christians and Gentile Christians. At Corinth, it was a debate between two groups of Gentile Christians, one of which had adopted a Jewish theology about "idol meat." Out of this tension at the table Paul fashioned a distinctive theology of community.

BANQUET IDEOLOGY AND THE BIRTH OF CHRISTIAN COMMUNITY

Given the diversity that came to characterize Christian groups at a very early stage of development, how could a sense of cohesion have developed so easily? How could individuals from diverse ethnic, religious, and social backgrounds come to call one another "brothers and sisters"? How were these bonds created and experienced? The most likely locus for this development is the community meal, with its unparalleled power to define social boundaries and create social bonding.

We can see this development taking place especially in Paul. To be sure, the meal had already become a focus for communal identity prior to Paul. To meet for a meal was a natural thing to do, and to develop social bonds as a result was expected. Soon there developed a distinctive theological rationale for the community meal: it came to be defined as a memorial feast commemorating the death of Jesus. That was the shape of the meal that Paul inherited.

Now a new wrinkle was taking place with the wholesale inclusion of Gentiles in the Christian community. Up to this point, the "people of God" to whom one belonged was the people of Israel, a status indicated by the boundary markers of circumcision and some level of adherence to laws of purity. As long as the community was primarily drawn from a Jewish (and proselyte) constituency these could be assumed. But when Gentiles began to claim community membership as Gentiles, then something new was happening.

How could Gentiles make such claims? And even more important, how could they have possibly come to believe that they were part of God's people as Gentiles without circumcision? I believe it is participation in the meal that provided the catalyst for this development. First, it is the meal that created a sense of belonging, of social bonding with the community. And when this happened in a context in which dietary laws were not being practiced, then it was even more clear that they had been incorporated into the community as Gentiles. Thus the meal provided the occasion and ideology for a truly radical move in Christian history. And it was Paul who noted it and gave it a theological framework. In doing so he drew on the rich resources of Greco-Roman banquet ideology.

BANQUET IDEOLOGY AND PAULINE THEOLOGY

Spirit versus Flesh: The Issues at Antioch and Galatia

The first time Paul confronted problems at the community meal was at Antioch. He described the situation sometime later in his letter to the Galatians (2:11-14). His reference to this incident in the Galatian letter suggests significant parallels between the issues at Antioch and Galatia.

After rehearsing the events at Antioch and emphasizing how he had stood up to Peter, Paul then presents an excursus on "the truth of the gospel" (2:15-21). It is widely believed that at this point Paul is also summarizing his argument against Peter. But what he says applies not only to the situation at Antioch but also to the situation at Galatia. Indeed, this section serves as his transition from the Antioch anecdote to the realities addressed by the Galatian letter.

Paul characterizes himself and Peter as "Jews by birth" as opposed to all others, who are "Gentile sinners" (2:15). Yet he and Peter both practice an open table fellowship with Gentiles, which Paul characterizes as "living like a Gentile" as opposed to "living like a Jew" (2:14). By leaving the table of the Gentiles to join the "circumcision party," Peter in effect is implying that Gentiles must also "live like Jews." Or at least this is Paul's interpretation. Living like a Jew can therefore be narrowed down to those practices that define the boundaries between Jews and Gentiles, notably circumcision and dietary laws. Both issues were present at Antioch; both are also present at Galatia, though only circumcision is mentioned directly.[26]

As Dunn argues, the category "works of law" is best understood as a reference to those boundary-defining practices.[27] According to the logic of this text, a "Jewish way of life," as exemplified at a Jewish table, would define who were "the Jews" and who were "the Gentile sinners." Consequently, when Peter left the community table at Antioch to join the Jewish table, he in effect was identifying the community table as a table of "sinners." That is why "the truth of the gospel" was at stake, in Paul's opinion.

Following this interpretation, Paul's code language takes on a specific nuance appropriate to the table motif. "Justification" is to be understood as a term to refer to membership in the community of the people of God. This can be clearly seen in the overall process of Paul's reasoning, especially in his long argument in Galatians 3, in which he interprets the Abraham story so that Gentiles are included as "seed" of Abraham and thus heirs of the promise to Abraham. This is seen to counter the advantages of Judaism "by birth." Thus when Paul argues "in order that we might be justified by faith of Christ and not by works of law" (2:16b), and does so in reference to Peter's actions at the table in Antioch, he is referring to membership in the community through Christ rather than through circumcision and dietary laws, a membership that is therefore mediated by the community table (as well as by baptism, 3:27-20). He also points out that "if we seek to be justified in Christ," that is, as exemplified by sharing the community meal, but "are found to be sinners," as judged by Peter's actions in removing himself from the community table, then "Christ has become a servant of sin" (2:17). All of this from a simple disagreement at the table. But it is not a simple disagreement. What is at stake is the efficacy of the death of Christ, as Paul sees it, in establishing Gentiles as fellow heirs of the promise.

A key component of Paul's argument is found at 3:1-5. Here he argues that the Galatians must have been "bewitched," or, as we might say today, "brainwashed." How else can their behavior be explained, since, he argues, they have already received confirmation of their status as "children of God" by the fact that they have received "the spirit"? In other words, he argues from their experience, and he assumes they will immediately recognize the validity of his argument.

Most interpreters of this text seem to operate with a model of a revival meeting. Paul has swayed them with powerful preaching ("before your eyes

Christ was portrayed as crucified"), and they respond with ecstatic spiritual experiences ("you received the spirit"; "miracles [were worked] among you"). But there is a problem with this interpretation when one compares it with Paul's own criteria for the experience of the spirit. According to Paul: (1) The experience in Galatia must have been readily acknowledged by all in the community as verification of their new status; thus it must have been a community experience, not an individual experience. Whatever experience of the spirit is referred to here, it must be manifest in the community. (2) It must have functioned to clearly affirm membership among the people of God; otherwise the force of Paul's argument is lost. (3) It must have been easily identifiable as spirit of God. But ecstatic spiritual gifts are described by Paul in 1 Corinthians as tending toward individualism (chapters 12 and 14), easily mistaken for workings of other deities (12:2) and thus needing to be controlled by the receiver (14:32), and having little to do with community consciousness (chapter 14). Consequently, it is difficult to see how Paul can be arguing for the experience of ecstatic spiritual gifts as their experiential proof that they are "children of God."

But if we change the context to one in which the community was gathered at table, as suggested by the Antioch analogy Paul himself introduces, then the "experience" of the spirit takes on a different nuance. As Rudolf Bultmann has pointed out, in the Hellenistic church as well as in Paul, the spirit tends to be seen as a community possession and is experienced by the community at worship.[28] Rather than ecstatic gifts per se, then, I would suggest that Paul's argument refers to the experience of community itself as the gift of the spirit, an experience especially to be associated with the community meal (where they "drink of the spirit," 1 Cor 12:13), and one that was communicated with such power and clarity that it could only be attributed to the spirit. Thus Paul's move from 2:14 to 2:21 to 3:1-5 begins to make more sense. What he is saying is that the Galatians have already experienced through the community meal their inclusion in the community of God's people. Why should they then be attracted to a ritual of membership, namely, circumcision, as if they are outsiders rather than insiders? Bewitched, indeed!

The table context for the experience of the spirit makes Paul's argument much stronger than has previously been recognized. As I have emphasized throughout this study, the table was a prime and powerful image in Paul's world for boundary marking and community inclusion. He was simply using a powerful image available to him in the culture and mediated through Christian tradition. His contribution was to develop it even further.

The Body and Blood of the Martyr: The Pre-Pauline Memorial Meal
In 1 Corinthians 11, Paul quotes a meal tradition that has been passed on to
him:

> For I received from the Lord what I also handed on to you, that the Lord
> Jesus on the night when he was handed over [NRSV: "betrayed"] took a
> loaf of bread, and when he had given thanks, he broke it and said, "This
> is my body that is for you. Do this in remembrance of me." In the same
> way he took the cup also, after supper, saying, "This cup is the new
> covenant in my blood. Do this, as often as you drink it, in remembrance
> of me." For as often as you eat this bread and drink the cup, you pro-
> claim the Lord's death until he comes. (1 Cor 11:23-26)

A variation of the same tradition is found in Mark and will be discussed separately in the next chapter.

The following theses will guide our interpretation of this passage:

(1) The meal pictured here has the following features of a normal Greco-
Roman banquet: (a) benediction over the food, represented by the bread; (b)
the division of the meal into *deipnon* (mentioned in the text) followed by
symposium (implied by the wine blessing); (c) a benediction over the wine
marking the transition from *deipnon* to symposium. It is clear, therefore, that
the Greco-Roman banquet form provides the backdrop for this tradition.
Since that is the case, it is reasonable to expect that banquet ideology lies
behind the meal interpretation being presented here.

(2) The text is presented in the form of a Jesus story. The Gospels place it
within a narrative recounting the life of Jesus. Here, however, its narrative
context is strictly "on the night when he was handed over," that is, the night
he died. The term used here, *paradidonai,* simply means "handed over." Its
use with the meaning of "betray" is found in the Gospels, but that is a meaning that does not inhere in the term but in the context in which it is used. In
Rom 8:32, Paul presents his view that it is God who "handed over" *(paradidonai)* Jesus to be killed. It is therefore unlikely that the term *handed over* in
1 Corinthians is meant to refer to Judas's betrayal; rather, it refers to the theological concept of Jesus being handed over by God.

(3) The text is more likely to be etiological than historical in both form
and content. That is to say, it functions as a story that arose to explain a practice in the church. Meals were already being eaten and given significance specific to the Christian context. This story is told to give a particular meaning
to the practice, drawing on an interpretation of Jesus' death. How this interpretation developed is not clear here in Paul.

(4) The function of this text at Christian communal meals remains unclear. It cannot be read as a script for liturgical action, unless one can imagine someone in the community acting out the part of Jesus in some kind of divine drama, which seems unlikely. But in some sense it was nevertheless seen as a text defining the community meal.

This meal evokes several banquet models. It has overtones of the funerary banquet, for example, in which friends and family would gather to commemorate the death of a loved one. But such events were normally held on a yearly basis, on the birthday of the deceased, not on such a frequent basis as this. The funerary meal tradition certainly lent credence to the event for the participants, but it was not the sole model for the meal.

A variation of the funerary meal was the memorial meal, a form that is not widely attested but that this tradition certainly assumes. This seems to be the significance of the phrase "Do this in remembrance of me." The closest parallel is the memorial meal of the Epicureans, a meal that also had the same kind of etiological tradition connected with it. Like Jesus in this text, so also Epicurus was said to have founded the meal in his own honor just before his death.[29]

What is to be remembered is left somewhat vague. That is to say, presumably anyone's version of "the Christ story" could be substituted here. This is important to note since we too easily assume that the canonical gospel story was the universal story of Jesus. In Paul, however, we do not find a story of the life of Jesus. Indeed, as Charles B. Cousar notes, we do not even find speculation about the events leading to the death of Jesus, or who killed Jesus.[30] The Christ story for Paul operated on a mythic level. The phrase "Christ crucified" virtually summarizes the entire plot. For Paul it represented a negotiation between Jesus and God. Nowhere does he delineate any human actors in this drama.

This perspective of Paul seems to be present in his Lord's Supper text as well, for the meal pictured here is a meal of "the Lord Jesus." That phrase removes the text from any historical imagining. To call Jesus *kyrios* as Paul understood the term was to identify him within the panoply of the divine. This is clear in the christological hymn in Phil 2:6-11, another text Paul inherited that became foundational for his theology. Here in Phil 2:11, "Lord" is only pronounced over Jesus after his exaltation in the heavens; it is not a property of the historical Jesus (to the extent that Paul might have theologized about a historical Jesus).[31] Consequently, the meal being pictured here takes place on a mythological level, borrowing by implication the motif of the messianic banquet, a meal that takes place in the heavenly sphere.

But how could Jesus be "Lord" on the same night that he was "handed over" to die? Of such paradoxes are mythologies made. At least in Paul's mind we can see how it was not a paradox, for to him the Christ who dies on the cross is already a divine agent. After all, the story for Paul is one in which God "hands over" Jesus, hardly a historical detail, but a richly mythological/theological one.

The choice of bread and wine as elements to be interpreted is not remarkable in itself. Bread represented the food of the *deipnon,* and wine the drink of the symposium. That a benediction was said was also normal, and it is striking that Jesus words an unstated prayer over the bread. Listeners to the story from a Jewish background would imagine a Jewish benediction for the bread; pagan listeners might imagine a different prayer.

The words identifying the bread and wine with Jesus' death have presented problems for Christian interpreters throughout Christian history. What we must imagine is how those words would have had meaning at the early level of Christian faith represented by this tradition. Here the explanation that makes the most sense is that of the martyrological background. The language of "body for you" and "shedding of blood" had already become established as terminology for the death of the martyr. Jesus' death could easily have been interpreted very quickly as a martyrdom, and the evidence suggests that was the case.

What the saying of the words over the bread and wine represents is the idea that with the sharing of the bread and the wine one is sharing in the result brought about by that death. That result is the creation of the very community that is thus being circumscribed and affirmed by the act of sharing. Passing around the cup to be shared by all was common in wine ceremonies. This text suggests that a similar bread ceremony must have been common as well. Thus both parts of the meal are knit together with a focus on a single interpretation.

The language of covenant adds still another dimension to the tradition, for it is not in itself inherent to either the martyr or the memorial meal traditions. The term *new covenant* presumably derives from Jer 31:31. To Paul the new covenant idea would have had immediate application to the issues he was facing in all of his churches, namely, how the inclusion of the Gentiles was to be understood. Thus Paul would understand the "new covenant" to refer to this event itself. It could be that "new covenant" theology originated as a rationale for Gentile inclusion, but that seems unlikely given the nature of the controversy at Antioch, a controversy that could not have happened if all agreed that "new covenant" meant inclusion of the Gentiles.

In 1 Cor 11:20 Paul refers to the community meal as "Lord's supper" *(kyriakon deipnon)*. The term *Lord*, of course, gives the meal a sacred character of some sort. It signifies that in this meal Jesus is being memorialized as a divine figure. One might compare this terminology to that found in the Sarapis cult, where the meal is termed "the couch of the Lord Sarapis." Such terminology tends to mean that the meal functions in some kind of ritual context, most probably a sacrificial one.[32] Yet, as I have argued above, sacred meals tended to be merely variations on the generic Greco-Roman banquet. What was distinctive was the way in which the deity was perceived as a participant in the meal in some sense. Sarapis, for example, could be spoken of as "guest," "host," and "symposiarch" at his banquets.[33] In all such religious meals, there is a close tie between the ideology of the meal and the religious values to be expressed. That is, Sarapis, like the Christian "Lord," would provide banquets that met the highest ideals of the culture. They would be banquets at which equality, friendship, and joy would prevail over disputes at the meal.

Proclaiming Christ's Death: Meal and Community at Corinth

The issue that Paul addresses at 1 Cor 11:17-34 is that of "schisms" *(schismata,* 11:18) at the meal gatherings. These are characterized as consisting of each taking a "private supper" *(idion deipnon,* 11:21) as opposed to the "Lord's supper" *(kyriakon deipnon,* 11:20). The result is that "one goes hungry and another becomes drunk" (11:21), implying that there is an inequity in the distribution or availability of food. Paul then addresses this problem with an argument that begins by quoting the tradition by which the meal is to be interpreted (11:23-25). He next provides an interpretation of the tradition (11:26-32) that leads to his concluding advice: "So then, my brothers and sisters, when you come together to eat, wait for one another" (11:33).

Since Paul's instructions at 11:33 specify eating together, then the meal defined as "one's own supper" *(idion deipnon)* is to be understood as an "individual meal" as opposed to the communal meal, which is evidently the primary meaning intended by the term *Lord's supper.* The rhetoric of the text indicates that the Corinthians were calling their meal "Lord's supper." Paul then turns that terminology against them and creates a new term to define their meal. His term, *individual supper,* is thus a rhetorical twist he uses to make a point. The question that next arises is how he is able to define what they are doing at their meal so that it fits this terminology. In other words, what are they doing at their communal meal that turns it into an individual meal?

One traditional interpretation centers on the term *prolambanein* in verse 21. This term is translated "goes ahead with" in the NRSV. This gives the text the following meaning: "For when the time comes to eat, each of you goes ahead with your own supper [that is, before the Lord's Supper proper], and one goes hungry and another becomes drunk [at the Lord's Supper]." This correlates well with 11:33, where the advice is to wait for one another, and suggests that the main problem is that some were simply starting to eat before the others arrived.[34]

A more common meaning of *prolambanein* when its object is food is simply "to eat."[35] If one applies this sense to 11:21, then the "individual meal" would be consumed concurrently with the communal meal. The idea would then be that the eating was being conducted in such a way that it was being made a meal of individuals rather than a meal that enhanced community.[36]

In fact, in Greek philosophical tradition there was a great deal of discussion on this point. Plutarch, for example, remarks on the difference between a banquet in which portions are assigned and one in which the food is eaten from a common dish. He concludes: "But where each guest has his own private portion, companionship perishes." Here "his own" *(idion)* refers to "private" dishes, and it is criticized as detracting from the communal nature of the meal, a meal that is otherwise characterized as "common" *(koinon)*.[37]

In the context in Plutarch, the reply to this conclusion is: "This is true where there is not an equitable distribution." That is to say, what could make a meal with "private" dishes still function as a "common" meal would be the provision of "equal" portions, a custom that was not always practiced at Greek banquets. Indeed, the opposing argument continues, this would make the meal with private dishes superior to a meal with common dishes. The reasoning is as follows:

> Those who eat too much from the dishes that belong to all antagonize those who are slow . . . for suspicion, grabbing, snatching, and elbowing among the guests do not, I think, make a friendly and convivial prelude to a banquet. . . . Private possession in such matters [that is, portions] does not disturb the general fellowship, and this is due to the fact that the most important characteristics of a gathering and those worth more serious attention are in fact common, namely, conversation, toasts, and good fellowship.[38]

Thus in Plutarch a "common" meal would be one characterized by "equality" in terms of portions served and other activities. On the other hand, the opposite of this would be an "individual" meal, one in which portions are not equal and activities are not shared by all. According to these standards, then, the inequality signified by the situation at Corinth where "some are hungry and others are drunk" qualifies this meal as an "individual" one, just as Paul argues.

A communal meal could therefore be termed a "private" meal if equal sharing of portions and activities was not practiced. Theissen provides further examples of practices that could cause a meal to be termed "private." He points out, for example, that the food for the Christian meal at Corinth would probably have been provided by the hosts or patrons who provided the homes for the meetings, as well as by other wealthy members of the community. These individuals could then have eaten a greater quantity or a higher quality of food as their own private portion of the meal. They could do this in all good conscience because it was a generally accepted custom that ranking by status at any formal dining situation could be acknowledged by larger portions of food at the meal of the community where that status was held. In addition, differences in social class were sometimes acknowledged by serving a higher quality of food or wine to the upper classes. If it was the wealthy who were the real offenders in eating a private meal, then that would also explain why they could begin earlier than the others. The wealthy would have leisure time in the evening, whereas the working classes would arrive late to the meeting.[39]

Thus Theissen identifies social class as the central issue. He identifies the schism as one between "those who do not have [food]" (11:22) and those who have a "private meal" (11:21) at their disposal; between those who have houses (10:22) and those who do not. Indeed, house ownership can be assumed for several leaders in the Corinthian church, and implies a certain degree of wealth.[40] Thus Theissen interprets the conflict here as one between rich and poor. It is those who have houses who are guilty of humiliating those who do not have, and they do this by taking their own meal (11:21-22).[41]

However, Theissen's reconstruction of social class as the major explanation for schisms at Corinth needs to be examined more closely. He is correct to emphasize the importance of status at formal meals for, as we have seen, it was inherent in the institution to rank guests at a meal, either by position at the table, or by type or quantity of food served them, for example. But status is not equivalent to social class.[42] One's status in a community could indeed reflect one's status in society-at-large. But it could also be defined by the community itself. In fact, one of the functions commonly served by Greco-Roman clubs was to provide alternative means to status, since status within society was often not available to their membership because of their social class.[43] And the meal was very important in this process because its customs provided a highly visible means for acknowledging status.

On the other hand, even when status is imputed to social class in the literature, it should not always be taken at face value. For example, the conflict between rich and poor at a meal appears to have been a literary topos in the Greco-Roman world. Thus, whenever Plutarch's brother Timon spoke against "the rich lording it over the poor,"[44] he could not have been defining the banquet in which he was participating in literal terms, for the participants were all of the same social class. He rather was using a figure of speech or a topos. The contrast here is between "the rich man" and "the less well endowed." It is not a contrast between social classes but between extravagant wealth and an idealized sense of "the simple life." A related form of this literary topos is utilized by Plutarch elsewhere when he presents praise for the "frugal meal" as opposed to extravagant banquets in his fictionalized account of the "Banquet of the Seven Sages."[45]

That is not to say that meal customs did not provide for rigid distinctions among the guests according to their status. But these levels of status could all be within the same basic economic and cultural level, and often were. Of course, they did represent real distinctions on the social level, but not always in the stark terms of rich versus poor. Thus one might note that the "lower-class" guest at Pliny's dinner was a freedman.[46] So also in Petronius's *Satyricon*, Trimalchio the freedman was never quite accepted in cultural society although he was quite wealthy. Consequently, though he hosts a sumptuous banquet, he remains a boorish character in Petronius's account, illustrating that his true status in society was not what he himself might claim.

As for Paul's argument, note that 1 Cor 11:22 has a highly rhetorical style. Its short questions building one upon another are characteristic of the style of the diatribe.[47] It is a style in which hyperbole for rhetorical effect is quite appropriate.[48] If, indeed, the idea of rich versus poor was already a topos in discussions concerning status at meals, then Paul's reference to "those who do not have" need not be seen as a reference to poor people at the meal. This phrase can also be read "those who do not have houses," since it immediately follows the phrase "do you not have houses." Individuals who did not own houses would not necessarily be poverty-stricken. Notice also that it is the "hungry" who are told to eat at home (11:34); this suggests that they would indeed have food at home. The text does not necessarily speak of either poverty or homelessness. It implies that a question of status was under discussion, but it need not imply that that status was based entirely on economic standing nor that the social levels in Corinth were widely divergent.

This is not to say that social class did not contribute to the issue that developed. Indeed, it appears likely that it did. But the levels of social class cannot be assumed to be widely divergent. Indeed, since Paul's instructions do not address a problem of poverty, such as by providing for a distribution to the poor,[49] it would appear that the distinctions are not very great.

That different amounts of food were being consumed is the implication of 11:21, "For when the time comes to eat, each one of you goes ahead with your own supper, and one goes hungry and another becomes drunk." When one correlates this with the conclusion at 11:33 that they should "wait for one another," then the following reconstruction can be proposed: some arrived early and began eating from the food supplies they brought before the others arrived and the communal meal formally began. Thus they would be eating individual meals ("one's own meal"). It is inconsistent with 11:33-34 to interpret 11:21-22 as an example of the wealthy taking the prerogative by their superior status to eat a greater quantity and finer-quality food than the poor at the communal meal itself, as Theissen argues.[50] But it is conceivable that an inequity in individual food supplies could be *interpreted* as "the rich lording it over the poor," to use the language of Plutarch.[51] Thus it would reflect dissensions on the basis of a *perception* of class differences. It need not imply that rich and poor in a strictly economic or sociological sense are meant.

I would thus suggest that Theissen has overstated his case. Social stratification is certainly a regular feature of banquets, but it is incorrect to suggest that taking a larger portion or a better portion of food was de rigueur at pagan banquets and certainly incorrect to imply that Christians were operating by different rules at their banquets, as if the Christian banquet was unique. Theissen does not specifically argue for the uniqueness of the Christian banquet, but he implies as much, since he accounts for the divisions by drawing on pagan banquet customs, but when he accounts for Paul's response, he does so on the basis of Paul's theology, as if Paul is proposing a unique corrective to banquet customs. In fact, Paul's response is consistent with the arguments of other Greco-Roman moralists. So even though the problems at the Christian meal derive from banquet ideology, Paul's response does as well.

The idea that some were taking positions of rank and status derives especially from the references to "divisions" (*schismata*, 11:18) and "factions" (*haireseis*, 11:19) as opposed to those who are "genuine" or "just" (*dokimoi*,

11:19). Theissen proposes that here we have references to divisions into groups.[52] In light of the reference in 11:21 to "each taking his own meal," however, the reference is more likely to individual actions. Thus the use of "each" here would be the same as the usage at 14:26, "When you come together, each one has a hymn, a lesson, a revelation, a tongue, or an interpretation." In support of this interpretation, one may also note that "divisions" or "schisms" is also used to refer to matters of individual conduct that detract from the communal nature of the meal in the Guild of Zeus Hypsistos (lines 13–19).

Paul takes the position that all such actions are schismatic, including the imputing of rank to individual members. He does this because he is working with a model of unity as an inherent aspect of a communal meal. Consequently, his main argument in 11:17-34 is to provide that the meal truly be a communal one so that the discussion of unity can naturally follow and build on that fact. And whatever the problem with the "individual supper," Paul felt it could be resolved by eating together. Consequently, while the differentiations in food may have implied a difference in status connected with social class either because some were free to start eating earlier than others or because some simply brought more food for themselves, these differentiations were not of such gravity to be a concern in themselves. Rather, they were indicative of a more serious problem, in which a sense of status as applied especially to spiritual gifts was threatening Paul's concept of a proper meal community, which was characterized by unity.

The question of status at the meal is specifically implied in the term *genuine* (11:19). The schisms function to reveal these individuals, and the schisms in this context refer to the "individual supper." Consequently, it is at the meals that the "genuine" are revealed.

The term translated "genuine" *(dokimoi)* is related to forensic terminology. The root meaning of *dokimos,* meaning "testing," is not specifically forensic, but the verb cognate, *dokimazein,* is used as a technical term for official testing. Thus the court of the Areopagus is said to be made up of "those who have won approval" *(hoi dedokimasmenoi).*[53] Similarly, when one dishonored one's parents "the state . . . rejects him as unworthy of office" *(apodokimazein).*[54]

Forensic terminology is also found in Paul's discussion in 1 Corinthians 11, especially at 11:27-32.[55] Here, rather than being "genuine," one is in danger of being "guilty" *(enochos,* 11:27). One should therefore "examine" or "test" oneself *(dokimazein,* 11:28) lest one fall under "judgment" *(krima,* 11:29). This happens when one has not properly "discerned" or "judged" the body (*diakrinein*, 11:29). Thus Paul concludes: "But if we judged [*diekrinomen*] ourselves, we would not be judged [*ekrinometha*]. But when we are judged [*krinomenoi*] by the Lord, we are disciplined so that we may not be condemned [*katakrithōmen*] along with the world" (11:31-32).

It is notable that forensic terminology is used elsewhere in the context of assigning ranking at a meal. Thus in Plutarch's *Table Talk* discussion about assigning positions at table, when Timon presents an argument in opposition to assigned rankings, he characterizes the practice as making oneself a "judge" (*kritēs*) over one's friends. Such a one "instead of playing the host, makes himself a juryman and a judge over people who do not call upon him to decide an issue and are not on trial [*(krinomenōn*] as to who is better than who, or worse; for they have not entered a contest [*agōna*], but have come for dinner."[56] Consequently, the term *genuine (dokimoi)* in 1 Cor 11:19 derives its primary meaning from the politics of the table whereby rankings are to be assigned to those of higher status.

Paul, however, uses it in an ironic sense. The "genuine" to which he is referring are not those who have been given the formal positions of status, but instead they emerge when the individualized "factions" separate from them (11:19). The term, then, is being applied to the group that continues to cohere as a community though some have separated themselves. Their status is not one imputed by the community directly, but Paul implies that it is imputed indirectly nonetheless by the events. Indeed, theirs is a status imputed by God, for it is God who designates the true ranking at the "Lord's supper": "God has so arranged the body, giving the greater honor to the inferior member, that there may be no dissension within the body" (12:24-25). Thus the "genuine" are those judged by God to be of that category: "For it is not those who commend themselves that are approved ['genuine,' *dokimos*], but those whom the Lord commends" (2 Cor 10:18). And they are identified as such in this community by the fact that they continue to cohere as a community in the face of the separation of others into individual meals.

The term *genuine (dokimos)* is a favorite term of Paul's to refer to the attestation of the righteous by God. This concept often has eschatological overtones,[57] and that would be one of the meanings here. For one is certainly required to test oneself with a view toward the final judgment: "so that we may not be condemned along with the world" (11:32). But it also refers to activities at the meal itself. That is, the "genuine" would presumably be those who do not provoke schisms, whose attitudes and actions promote the communal nature of the meal, as is emphasized, for example, in the conclusion at 11:33. Thus those who test out to be "genuine" would be those who "examine [test] yourselves" (*dokimazein heauton,* 11:28) rather than judging others, who "discern the body" (*diakrinein to sōma,* 11:29), or community as a whole, rather than the individuals separately. When one tests oneself with a view to the community as a whole rather than with a sense of comparing oneself with others, then one gives proper regard to the unity of the community rather than succumbing to the divisiveness of individualism.

This may be compared with the rules of conduct at the meals of the Guild of Zeus Hypsistos. Here the proscription against "schisms" (*schismata,* line 13) not only includes restrictions about forsaking the community (line 14) but also prohibits various disagreements among the members (lines 15–19), including disagreements over their relative status (line 15). So also in the community of Christians at Corinth, similar perspectives were at work, most notably an injunction to conduct the meal with regard for the unity of the community as a whole. This means eating together, at the same time and in a "together" way; that is, in such a form that it is a community meal, not a set of individual meals. Only in this way, Paul says, will it be the "Lord's supper."

Paul's argument in 1 Corinthians follows some fairly traditional lines in popular philosophy. He has identified the question of status as a problem at the communal meal because, in effect, it makes two meals and creates schisms. Such schisms strike at the very nature of the communal meal to Paul. Thus he constructs an involved argument on the basis of the tradition in order to come to what may appear to be a mundane conclusion: eat together (11:33-34). But it is not mundane to Paul; it is essential to the meaning of the meal.[58] His interpretation of community ethics at the meal is based on the fact that the physical partaking of the food has to be done at the same time (11:33) and at the same place (11:34). Popular philosophy would have said that "the friend-making character of the meal" was destroyed by divisions. Paul interpreted the nature of the communal meal in the same way, but without using the terminology of friendship.

Paul's argument centers on the term *sōma,* or "body," which he takes from the bread saying in the tradition: "This is my body" (11:24).[59] This he interprets as the basis for unity: "Just as the body is one . . ." (12:12). Thus the proper eating of the meal is interpreted as properly "discerning the body" (11:29), an idea that leads to the conclusion at 11:33, "eat together." The connecting link for this interpretation appears to be found in the interpretation of the Christian meal at 10:17: "Because there is one bread, we who are many are one body, for we all partake of the one bread." In other words, the idea of unity at the meal is based on the metaphor of sharing food together. This was, of course, a common usage in popular philosophy as well.[60]

However, Paul does not center his argument on the food, but on the term that defines it in the liturgy, *sōma*. This term provides him with multiple metaphorical dimensions, for he can then extend his discussion into the parts of the body in order to define distinctions that exist in the unified body (12:4-6,12,27).[61] It also provides the basis whereby he can make a theological connection: the body is Christ's, so you are the body of Christ (12:12, 27). Thus unity comes to be founded ultimately on Christ, but it is brought to focus in the action of sharing food at the communal meal.

Paul's elaboration on the meaning of *sōma* develops as an interpretation of the Jesus tradition he quotes at 11:23-25. But that is not the only point where he interprets the tradition. He also adds an interpretive gloss at the end, at verse 26: "For as often as you eat this bread and drink the cup, you proclaim the Lord's death until he comes." This verse is clearly an addition to the original tradition because it represents a comment by a narrator, referring to the Lord in the third person, rather than being a quotation from the words of Jesus, in which he refers to himself in the first person. It could have been added prior to Paul, but since it presents a theology that fits Paul's thought and this context so well, it seems likely that it was added by Paul.

The "proclamation of the Lord's death" referred to here is best understood not in the sense of words that are said but as a reference to the act of eating and drinking itself. In other words, when the meal takes place in its proper form, then that in itself is a "proclamation of the Lord's death." It is that proper form that has been the focus of Paul's discussion. According to his argument, then, when the community eats with unity and equality, that is when they proclaim the death of the Lord.

For Paul, the purpose of the death of Christ was to create a saved community. More specifically, it resulted in the inclusion of the Gentiles into the community of the people of God. Over and over again, Paul argues that point, and more than once he refers to the meal as the locus for the experience of that community. At Antioch, the meal had to be inclusive of Gentiles or else "Christ died for nothing" (Gal 2:21). At Galatia, as I have argued above, it is at the community meal that they experienced "Jesus Christ publicly exhibited as crucified" (Gal 3:1). In Romans, Paul argues that Christians should "welcome one another . . . just as Christ has welcomed you" (Rom 15:7), thus emphasizing the interrelation between the inclusion into the community that the death of Christ provides and the acting out of that inclusion to others that the church should practice. The ritualization of that "welcome," as I argue below, would most likely have taken place at the community table. Here in 1 Cor 11:17-34 Paul finds the most profound meaning of the meal as "Lord's supper" in its ability to bring together a disparate people into one community. When this does not happen, then it is no longer the "Lord's supper." But when it does happen, then those ties that are created by the death of Christ, whereby they become a fictive family (1 Cor 8:11-12) and part of the heritage of Abraham (Gal 3:6-29), are acknowledged and experienced by the community gathered at table together. And it works so well because of the power of the banquet to create bonds and define boundaries. As in Gal 3:1-5, so also here it is the *experience* of justification that is Paul's focus. To experience inclusion in the community at the table, and to extend that experience to others, is in the most profound sense "to proclaim the Lord's death until he comes."

Worship and Rules of Table Talk in Corinth

After discussing problems at the meal (11:17-34), Paul apparently moves on to another subject ("Now concerning spiritual gifts . . .," 12:1). Yet the discussion of spiritual gifts throughout chapters 12 through 14 appears to be concerned primarily with activities at worship. Note, for example, the reference at 14:26, "when you come together." Indeed, the issue throughout these chapters has been concern for the community as opposed to the individual. Thus "prophecy" and "tongues" are defined according to their relative effectiveness within the gathered community at worship (14:1-25).

The question, then, is whether the text indicates that these worship activities are still being undertaken at table. Certainly there is something to be said for the fact that the multiple references to the "gathering" of the community use the same basic terminology. Thus the problems at the communal meal take place "when you come together" (*synerchēsthe*, 11:17), "when you come together as a church" (*synerchomenōn hymōn en ekklēsia*, 11:18), "when you come together . . . to eat the Lord's supper" (*synerchomenōn hymōn epi to auto kyriakon deipnon phagein*, 11:20), and "when you come together to eat . . . so that when you come together, it will not be for your condemnation" (*synerchomenoi eis to phagein hina mē eis krima synerchēsthe*, 11:33-34). Later in the same letter, then, when Paul refers to the occasion "when you come together" (*hotan synerchēsthe*, 14:26), at which various worship activities take place and during which they respond to one another as "the church" or "the assembly" (*ekklēsia*, 14:4, 5, 12, 19, 23, 28) and as "the body" (*sōma*, 12:12-31), it is reasonable to assume that he is talking about the same gathering that began with the meal in chapter 11.

Consequently, I propose that the worship activities described in chapters 12 and 14 take place at table. Indeed, these activities would have a logical connection with the meal, for they would take place "after supper" (*meta to deipnēsai,* 11:25) and during the symposium, at a time when meal customs designate an extended period of entertainment or conversation.

Notice, for example, that the form their worship took bears a marked similarity to the form taken by the activities at a symposium. Recall that a symposium in the philosophical model tended to consist of elevated conversation as the entertainment of the evening. So also here the subject of 1 Corinthians 12 and 14 is the problem of defining the proprieties of verbal participation in the Christian assemblies.

Furthermore, the form taken by the worship activities in 1 Corinthians 14 is that of an unstructured, undisciplined affair in which everyone is free to take part (as in, e.g., 14:27-33). In addition, the members are described as bringing contributions to the worship: "When you come together, each one has a hymn, a lesson, a revelation, a tongue, or an interpretation" (14:26). This is reminiscent of the philosophical banquets attended by Aulus Gellius where each guest brought a topic for discussion at the symposium.[62]

One might also compare Lucian's parody of the philosophical conversation in his *Symposium.* Here the participants compete in their various fields of expertise and eventually end up all talking at one time:

> Most of the company were drunk by then, and the room was full of uproar. Dionysodorus the rhetorician was making speeches, pleading first on one side and then on the other, and was getting applauded by the servants who stood behind him. Histiaeus the grammarian, who had the place next to him, was reciting verse. . . . But Zenothemis was reading aloud from a closely written book that he had taken from his attendant.[63]

To this might be compared Paul's reference to unruly drunkenness at the Christian meal at Corinth (11:21) and the problem he attempts to control in which individuals all want to speak at the same time (14:27-33).

It may also be noted that religious activities were common at any banquet, as evidenced in descriptions of philosophical symposia from Plato to Plutarch and in the utilization of the banquet form for various kinds of Jewish religious meals. Indeed, the clubs had tended to formalize this custom by placing their liturgical activities at table. So also, it would appear, did the Christians at Corinth.

As further support for this view, one can note how Paul's argument in this section draws on the imagery of the meal. For example, at 12:13 his argument for unity makes reference in a figurative expression to the symbolism of sharing a bowl of wine: "we were all made to drink of one spirit." Although the expression is figurative, the figure used has never made much sense in this context as traditionally interpreted.[64] But if we place it in the context of a discussion at table where drinking is taking place, then not only would it be appropriate to its setting, but it would also be identifiable with a common type of argument for unity in the setting of a meal.[65]

References to meals are found also at chapters 8 and 10, where the issue of meat sacrificed to idols and its relation to meal practices of Christians is discussed. Here it is not always clear whether communal meals of the church are in mind, especially since the hypothetical example given in chapter 8 is that of a Christian being observed by a fellow Christian dining at a pagan temple. Yet in chapter 10 we return to specific references to the Christian banquet, for here the reference is to the "table of the Lord" as the definitive symbol of the community, as opposed to the "table of demons" (10:21), and the sharing of bread together as the definitive symbol of unity (10:17). When one adds the reference to the assembly at 5:4, one can conclude that a major proportion of 1 Corinthians is concerned with activities of the church as an assembled community and that the center of most of those activities is the communal meal.

Although a majority of references to the gatherings of the community appear to refer explicitly or implicitly to meetings at table, the reference at 5:4 seems to be different. Here a judicial activity is apparently taking place. The text concerns one who is accused of "sexual immorality" (5:1). The judgment is to be as follows: "when you are assembled [*synachthentōn hymōn*] . . . you are to hand this man over to Satan" (5:4-5). Similarly the church is to act as a judicial body deciding inter-community disputes in chapter 6. Here they are to "take it to court . . . before the saints" (*krinesthai epi tōn hagiōn*, 6:1).

Thus we have the possibility of two types of meetings at Corinth, one a "business" meeting (5:1-8; 6:1-8) and the other a banquet meeting (10:1—14:40). A similar definition of the meetings of early Christians is described in Pliny's letter to Trajan about the Christians in Bithynia in the 90s C.E. There are two meetings mentioned, one in the morning and the other in the evening. The morning meeting included a "hymn to Christ" *(carmen Christo)* and an "oath" *(sacramentum)* not to be guilty of various immoral acts, including "fraud," "theft," "adultery," and "falsification of a trust." The proscription against "adultery" *(adulteria)* here is similar, of course, to that against "immorality" *(porneia)* in 1 Cor 5:1, and the term *sacramentum* could refer to a judicial setting. The evening meeting mentioned in Pliny is "to partake of food—but food of an ordinary and innocent kind." This corresponds to the banquet meeting, while the earlier meeting could be termed a "business" meeting. This distinction between two types of meetings was often practiced by Roman clubs, as we have already seen.[66] A further parallel is the fact that both Greek and Roman clubs also specified that intercommunity disputes were to be decided within the club rather than by civic authorities.[67]

On the other hand, we might notice the use of meal imagery in the proceedings described in 1 Corinthians 5. The act of excluding the immoral person, defined as "the old yeast," is described in terms of a metaphor of sharing a festival meal: "Therefore, let us celebrate the festival [meal] [*heortazōmen*], not with the old yeast, the yeast of malice and evil, but with the unleavened bread of sincerity and truth" (5:8). Indeed, the act of exclusion comes to focus especially at the communal meal: "do not associate with . . . do not even eat with such a one" (5:10-11). Thus the meeting described in 1 Corinthians 5 may have included a meal, but this is not certain. Nevertheless, it is striking that the imagery of the communal meal provides a basis for the definition of the community even in this context. Indeed, as practiced by various Greco-Roman clubs and as exemplified in the regulations of the Qumran community, exclusion from the community was especially effective when it was carried out at the communal banquet.

We should also note the extent to which the form of the Christian assembly and the literary traditions of the symposium have contributed to the form of Paul's letter. For example, after the specific references to the meal at 10:1-11:1 and 11:17-34, the discussion at 12:1—14:40 not only appears to be defining how worship should be conducted while at table but is doing so with a style and argumentation that derive from symposium traditions. This will be elaborated further below, but here the initial point to be made is that symposium literary traditions form a significant backdrop to the style and form of Paul's argumentation here. Like Plutarch, then, Paul would appear to have adopted the idea that when one talks about actual meals but does so in a written form, one should utilize the well-known patterns already established in the symposium literary tradition.[68]

After presenting his case for unity at the meal based on the doctrine of *sōma,* Paul then moves to arguments for proper behavior at the table. The transition is seen already in 12:7: "To each is given the manifestation of the Spirit for the common good." That is, whenever Paul speaks of the functions of the gifts within the community, he does so on the basis of the term *common good* or *to sympheron* and the related term *edification* or *oikodomē.* These terms function as ethical principles and constitute the real basis for the new ranking system in the community.

In philosophical literature, *sympheron* was used to refer to the social dimension of law and morality.[69] Thus Aristotle defined the purpose of law as "the common interest of all" *(tou koinē sympherontos pasin)*.[70] Epicurus defined justice in a similar way: "Natural justice is an expression of expediency [*tou sympherontos*] in order to prevent one man from harming or being harmed by another."[71] For Zeno, "all good is expedient" *(pan agathon sympheron einai)*.[72]

Paul used the term *sympheron* infrequently and tended to collapse its meaning into that of *oikodomē*. The two terms are used as synonyms at 10:23 with reference to the priority of community over individual needs: "'All things are lawful,' but not all things are beneficial [*sympherei*]. 'All things are lawful,' but not all things build up [*oikodomei*]." The basic ethical meaning of these terms is summarized at 10:24: "Do not seek your own advantage, but that of the other." The position referred to by the phrase "all things are lawful," as defined by Paul, represented an expression of the freedom of the individual over against the constraints of the community. The term *sympheron* served for him as an appropriate term to define the social dimension, or "social contract," inherent in ethical decisions.

But it is the term *oikodomē* that is even more important for Paul's view.[73] While *sympheron* indicates concern for the good of all, *oikodomē* denotes a more activist "building up" of the community. Its background prior to Paul includes metaphorical usages,[74] but it is Paul himself who seems to have developed it as an ethical term. It occurs in his earliest writing, in 1 Thess 5:11, in combination with "exhort" *(parakalein)*. Apparently, therefore, it is a term he had begun to utilize in his theological vocabulary fairly early. Furthermore, it must have been a term already known to the Corinthians, since it needs no explanation to them.[75] It is quite possible, therefore, that Paul had made use of the term in his earlier preaching in Corinth. In 1 Corinthians, especially chapter 14, it becomes a technical term used in reference to the idea of ethical responsibility to the community. In chapter 14 Paul is attempting to resolve a dispute about the relative value to be given to "prophecy" and speaking in tongues in the community. The argument here is a continuation of chapter 12 and functions to provide a commentary on the rankings of spiritual gifts with which chapter 12 ends.

"Prophecy" represents a form of spiritual communication directed to the community in contrast to the privatism of tongue speaking (14:4). As such it is understandable to all, whereas tongue speaking can only be understood if it is interpreted (14:2-5). Prophecy therefore functions for "upbuilding and encouragement and consolation" (*oikodomēn kai paraklēsin kai paramythian,* 14:3). This includes convicting unbelievers of their sins (14:24) because "the secrets of the unbeliever's heart are disclosed [by the prophet]" (14:25). Indeed, the prophet has spiritual insight not only into the secrets of human hearts but into the mysteries of God as well (13:2).

What form did this spiritual discourse take? On the one hand, it seems to be related to other known forms of ecstatic prophecy from this period.[76] So also here it clearly represents a recognizable and impressive demonstration of divine power, so much so that the unbeliever concludes that God is indeed present in the community ("in you [plural]," 14:25).[77] On the other hand, it can also be argued that the ecstatic aspect of prophecy is played down in 1 Corinthians. For example, prophets are classed together with apostles and teachers at 12:28, suggesting a comparative functional role in which ecstatic manifestations are not apparent. Consequently, it is not entirely clear what kind of phenomenon is being referred to with this terminology, other than to say that here in chapter 14 its function is primarily hortatory in nature.[78] What is clearly not indicated is that it has anything to do with predicting the future.

"Tongue speaking," however, was clearly an ecstatic phenomenon. It was unintelligible without an interpreter (14:2-19) and sounded like the ravings of a madman to an outsider (14:23). Similarly, in Acts 2:13 tongue speaking is compared to the ravings of a drunkard. In paganism such ecstatic utterances were especially associated with Dionysiac worship inspired by the god of wine.[79] It should be noted, however, that at the meetings of the Dionysiac association of the *Iobakchoi,* such utterances were not allowed.[80] Thus, as in Paul, so also here there was a provision for limiting religious expression in the community based on an ethical concern for what was best for the community as a whole.

Paul's primary ethical principle in chapter 14 is presented at verse 4: "Those who speak in a tongue build up themselves, but those who prophesy build up the church." "Edification" or *oikodomē,* then, becomes the principle on which ethical decisions are to be based. Here it means, on the one hand, that one is to speak out in the community worship service in such a way that all can understand and participate, that is, say the "Amen" to one's message (14:16). This is the kind of manifestation that prophecy represents; thus it is ranked first.

Tongue speaking, on the other hand, is not only judged as of less value, it is even judged to be detrimental. Thus if there is no one to interpret the tongue speaker, he or she is to remain silent: "But if there is no one to interpret, let them be silent in church and speak to themselves and to God" (14:28). Whatever the inherent religious value of the tongue speaking for the individual, unless it was a message in which all could participate, it was not to be spoken in the assembly. The ethics of the community take precedence: "strive to excel . . . for building up the church [assembly]" (*pros tēn oikodomēn tēs ekklēsias,* 14:12).

Oikodomē is also defined in the sense of speaking in an orderly manner. After summarizing the variety of activities at a worship service, Paul explains how they are to be conducted according to principles of social ethics: "When you come together, each one has a hymn, a lesson, a revelation, a tongue, or an interpretation. Let all things be done for building up [*pros oikodomēn*] . . . but all things should be done decently and in order [*panta euschēmonōs kai kata tax in ginesthō*]" (14:26,40). "Decently and in order" here function to define *oikodomē.* If "order" is the rule at the worship services, then "peace" (*eirēnē*) rather than "disorder" (*akatastasia*) should result (14:33). Paul's instructions defining these concepts in verses 16-33 specify that only three at the most from those representing each type of spiritual gift are to speak per service, that they are to speak in turn and not all at the same time, and that a tongue speaker is not to speak at all if there is no interpreter. Again, the sense is that there is no inherent value in these gifts for the community, no matter that they are spirit inspired, unless they contribute to the entire community.

Paul's concept of a proper worship service is clearly related to the concept of a proper symposium conversation as it was defined in clubs and associations. Note, for example, that the term *peace (eirēnē)* is used here in an ethical sense,[81] very much like the use of *peace (quietus)* in the Society of Diana and Antinous (line 24), where it also functions to define the basis for proper behavior at the community banquet. Also comparable is the usage of "good order and quietness" *(eukosmia kai hēsychia)* in the Society of the *Iobakchoi* (line 65). Here there is an emphasis on orderly behavior, just as in Paul "peace" is contrasted with "disorder" (14:33) and analogous to "decently and in order" (14:40). In the Society of the *Iobakchoi* one was not to speak without permission of the priest (lines 107–9), whereas in Paul there is no reference to a presiding official who was charged with keeping order.

Paul's ideas may also be compared with those of Plutarch. Plutarch also emphasized "good order" *(eutaxia)* as opposed to "lack of order" *(ataxia).* In the context of his discussion, "good order" was understood to be preserved by assigning guests to couches according to their proper rank in society. The prin ciple of "good order" was not to be applied only to the reclining arrangement, however. It was to be applied "in all details" *(peri panta)* of a drinking party. Only in that way would it be "a symposium that is as agreeable as possible."[82]

Thus when he referred to proper conversation at the banquet, he emphasized, as did Paul, that it should be of a type that all present could understand and participate in, and for this he used an analogy very much like Paul's. In 1 Cor 12:13, Paul spoke of unity based on the analogy of a shared cup of wine. Plutarch's argument states: "Indeed, just as the wine must be common to all, so too the conversation must be one in which all will share . . . [otherwise] . . . gone is the aim and end of the good fellowship of the party, and Dionysus is outraged."[83] Like Paul, Plutarch constructed an argument for a community bond on the basis of the shared wine, and this bond then determined the nature of the conversation. Also like Paul, what is to characterize the conversation is that it be participated in by all, just as the wine is.

For Paul "order" *(taxis)* refers to nothing more complicated than that everyone should speak in turn and not at the same time. The picture of Christian worship in Corinth as given here is of a loose, unstructured service, in which everyone participates at will, each with one or another type of message, "a hymn, a lesson, a revelation, a tongue, or an interpretation" (14:26). There is a particular emphasis on ecstatic utterance of such a sort that if an outsider were to witness it as the only aspect of the service, he would judge that they were all mad (14:23).

What Paul suggests to improve the service is not to do away with its free-spirited nature, but to impose order and communal participation on the varied verbal expressions. Thus the worship service after Paul's restructuring would still include ecstatic utterances. For example, he concludes, "do not forbid speaking in tongues" (14:39). He never denies the divine origin of this gift; indeed he was a tongue-speaker himself (14:18-19). Rather, he specified that this and all gifts and "contributions" (14:26) should be subject to the same rules: that they be expressed in an orderly fashion and in a form such that everyone could understand them and benefit from them. Inherent in this rule of order is the idea that each individual could control the spirit that possessed him, a principle he stated at 14:32: "The spirits of prophets are subject to the prophets."[84]

At the Christian assembly, the women must have been included as full participants in the communal meal just as were masters and slaves, rich and poor, Jews and Greeks. Indeed, their equal participation in the symposium discourse is clearly indicated in 11:2-16, for here they are seen to pray and prophesy just as the men do. The only question at this point for Paul is whether they are properly attired.

This assumption of participation by women at 11:2-16 is contradicted by 14:33b-36, where women are told to be silent at the assemblies. From the perspective of this study, 14:33b-36 stands out as an anomaly in its context. Silence had been recommended for particular individuals in the context of the discussion, but on the basis of the ethics of *oikodomē,* whereby each individual would be obligated to consider the effect of one's activities at worship on the community as a whole. The rule at 14:34 operates on a different principle, however, and has no apparent connection with the ethical foundation underlying the rest of the discussion.

To be sure, the position taken in 14:33b-36 is not uncommon in the culture. Indeed, women were still somewhat suspect as participants in a banquet. Furthermore, the style of legal language used here, as opposed to the ethical argument of the context, is similar to the form for rules in the inscribed statutes of Greek and Roman clubs. Yet this text is an abrupt departure in the context of Paul's argument and contradicts what he assumes in 11:2-16, namely, that women still speak at worship but dress differently. Paul had been careful to argue throughout 1 Corinthians on the basis of ethical principles that are to serve as the foundation for the social obligation of the individual to the community. Here in 14:33b-36 the perspective instead is that community law rather than social ethics is the determinative principle.

Because of these anomalies, the suggestion that makes the most sense is that this text is an interpolation added to Paul's letter from within the Christian community at a later time.[85] If this conclusion is not accepted, then this text must still be dealt with as an anomaly. The best explanations from that perspective are those that emphasize the unique nature of these instructions, suggesting that they apply to a specific situation in the community rather than to women as a whole.[86]

The fact that the Christian community included women as full participants in its communal meal was notable but not unique. The Greeks had a long-standing tradition that proper women did not attend banquets, particularly those with a traditional symposium. But there were many meal occasions, some festive, that involved the entire family. Whenever women and children were present at the table in a traditional Greek society, however, they were to sit rather than recline, thus indicating their secondary social status.

The Romans, on the other hand, had begun to allow women to recline at the table as full participants in a banquet. At the banquet of Trimalchio, for example, the host's wife reclines next to a woman friend, and they talk together and freely participate in the conversation at the table.[87] Indeed, Romans were aware of this difference between their customs and those of the Greeks and made much of it.[88]

Consequently, in the Roman period in Greece the customs appear to have been in flux. Undoubtedly many Greeks clung to the old ways. But there are also indications that other Greeks had adopted the Roman style. For example, in the second century C.E. Lucian of Samosata, in his satyrical *Symposium,* refers to women reclining at a marriage feast and symposium without remarking on it at all. They seem to have been placed at the lowest-ranking couches and are not mentioned as taking part in the conversation. For example, at one point they are addressed but do not reply. Later, however, when a brawl breaks out, they participate along with the men.[89]

This example from Lucian is an idealized, though satirical, view of what might be termed "high society" in Greece. Perhaps more germane to a discussion of early Christian communities would be the customs followed by the many Greek and Roman clubs. Here we find many examples of women, as well as slaves, listed as full members.[90] We must assume, therefore, that they would also have been full participants in the club banquets.

Since women were found at the table in certain contexts in the Greco-Roman world, the practice of Christians would not have been unique. But it would have been noticed. And the rationale for the inclusion of women, which was based on the concept of inclusion as the raison d'être of the Christian meal, would make this practice seem a necessary function of the meal, as necessary as inclusion of the Gentiles and other social and religious outsiders.

First Corinthians 8 and 10 also present discussions of meal ethics based on the concepts of "that which builds up" *(oikodomē)* and "that which is beneficial" *(sympheron).* Here, however, the issue is the eating of sacrificial meat at a communal meal. This had become a point of dispute between the "strong" and the "weak." For the "strong" the meat posed no problem. They knew that it had no real religious significance. To the "weak," however, the eating of such meat was understood to be an act of worship to the god to whom it was sacrificed. Thus whenever the "weak" brother or sister saw the "strong" brother or sister eating in a pagan temple, the conscience of the weak one was offended (8:10). And whenever a "strong" person ate meat in the house of an unbeliever who acknowledged it as sacrificial meat, then the unbeliever's conscience was offended also (10:28-29). The issue is not whether the meat has any efficacy—Paul acknowledges that it does not (8:4-6; 10:29-30)—but rather the issue is one of social obligation to a brother or sister or to an unbeliever with whom one happens to be sharing a meal.

In 8:1 the problem is stated in this way: "Now concerning food sacrificed to idols: we know that 'all of us possess knowledge.' Knowledge puffs up [causes pride in itself], but love builds up [reaches out to the other]." The knowledge that an idol has no power is not in itself wrong but has the wrong perspective. It is characterized by the individualism of "pride" (*physioun*), whereas Paul's perspective is that of "love" (*agapē*), which functions as a community ethic to "upbuild" or "edify" (*oikodomein*).

The terminology is quite similar at 10:23-24: "'All things are lawful,' but not all things are beneficial [*sympherei*]. 'All things are lawful,' but not all things build up [*oikodomei*]. Do not seek your own advantage, but that of the other." The phrase "all things are lawful" had evidently been the catchphrase of those identified as "strong." Here again Paul opposes this individualistic perspective in favor of a communal one. But in this instance, he applied the inter-community ethic in a missionary sense. The setting is a meal with an unbeliever, yet the Christian's actions are to be such that the unbeliever's conscience will not be offended, with the ultimate goal that he will be saved (10:33). This social obligation toward the unbeliever is defined by the same terms that are used to define ethics among brethren at the Christian communal meal, that is, "upbuilding" or *oikodomē* (10:23) and "beneficial" or *sympheron* (10:33). Clearly, the reason why the same sense of social obligation is extended to the unbeliever is because of the meal setting. The same missionary idea is found at 14:22-25, where the rules of inter-community ethics are applied to the unbeliever, but the implication of the context is that he has also shared the meal. Thus, because a meal is shared with an unbeliever, communal bonds are created that are comparable to those created among the Christian membership. Note also that to "seek . . . [the] advantage . . . of the other" (10:24,33; 14:4) in this context means seeking the neighbor's salvation, a concept that also applies in some cases when the ethics are between brothers and sisters (8:11-12).

What is apparent here is that the term *build up (oikodomē)* is consistently being used in connection with meal situations, though the setting varies from example to example. In chapter 8, the situation is described as a chance encounter with a brother or sister who is participating at a banquet in a temple dining room: "if others see you . . . eating in the temple of an idol" (8:10). This statement has about it the sense of a hypothetical example, albeit one that could very likely have happened.[91] The community dispute itself, then, would have arisen out of the known differences of the members in regard to dietary practices rather than out of the issue envisioned by the hypothetical example itself. Most likely it developed in the community meals themselves.

The example in chapter 10 should also be seen as hypothetical, though again it is an event that could very likely have happened. Here the believer is pictured as dining at the home of an unbeliever: "If an unbeliever invites you to a meal . . ." (10:27). In other cases implied in the text, it would appear that unbelievers had also appeared at the community table. Note that the community gathering ("when you come together," 11:20) included eating together and furthermore involved the presence of unbelievers (14:23).

The clearest definition of the ethical nature of *oikodomē* is found here at 10:24: "Do not seek your own advantage, but that of the other." Here the term is given an altruistic definition. A similar idea is found at 12:25, where the argument that the spiritual gifts do not cause schisms is based on the fact that "the members . . . have the same care for one another." The term *oikodomē* has been used throughout 1 Corinthians in a sense similar to the term *philia* ("friendship") in discussions of meal ethics in popular philosophy. The altruistic sense spotlighted here at 10:24 is not inconsistent with the friendship ethic.

A closer equivalent to the concept of friendship in Paul, and a term that seems to be used self-consciously in that sense, is the term *agapē* or "love." Paul presents *agapē* as the primary underpinning for *oikodomē* at 8:1: "Love builds up" *(hē agapē oikodomei)*. This phrase already points ahead to chapter 13, in which he presents *agapē* as the primary foundation for community ethics.

It is striking how closely the "hymn" to *agapē* in chapter 13 corresponds to the concept of friendship in popular philosophy.[92] First, it clearly relates to its context, for it takes its departure from the context of proper speaking at Christian assemblies: "If I speak in the tongues of mortals and of angels . . . if I have prophetic powers and understand all mysteries and all knowledge . . ." (13:1-2). Thus it functions here to define in more detail the ethical base for social obligation at the communal meal.

Second, it appears especially appropriate to a symposium context. Encomia or conversations in praise of love were in fact standard in the symposium tradition.[93] In popular philosophy the term for love in the banquet setting was *erōs*. Indeed, one of the most famous discourses on *erōs* in the ancient world was that at the table of Agathon in Plato's *Symposium,* where several speakers, including Socrates, speak in praise of *erōs*.[94] Here there is an emphasis on *erōs* as the virtue that creates harmony and fellowship at the meal, a type of argument that is attributed to friendship *(philia)* in other contexts in popular philosophy and to *agapē* in this context in 1 Corinthians. Thus the hymn to *agapē* instead of *erōs* in the context of a meal offers a striking and ingenious contrast to standard Greek tradition.[95]

Whenever the form of the text in 1 Corinthians 13 is analyzed, it is found to be closest to a particular kind of encomium to the greatest virtue. This seems to have been a stock subject for philosophical discourse, and often such praise was framed in a poetic form.

One speech in Plato's *Symposium* had such a form and is quite similar to 1 Corinthians 13. Among the attributes of *erōs* in this passage are the following:

> It is he [*Erōs*] who makes . . . peace among men. . . . He it is who casts alienation out, draws intimacy in; he brings us together in all such friendly gatherings as the present; at feasts and dances and sacrificial meals he makes himself our leader; politeness contriving, moroseness outdriving; kind giver of amity, giving no enmity . . . in toil and fear, in drink and discourse, our trustiest helmsman, boatswain, champion, deliverer. . . .[96]

There is clearly an emphasis here on *erōs* as the quality that creates harmony and fellowship at the meal, a type of argument that is attributed to friendship *(philia)* in other contexts in popular philosophy and to *agapē* in this context in 1 Corinthians.

Also close to Paul's argument is an encomium to truth in 1 Esd 4:34-40. Like Paul's encomium to *agapē,* it is also connected with a symposium context and is presented in a poetic style. Although it is not specifically concerned with social ethics, it approaches its subject in a style similar to Paul's. For example, in a passage reminiscent of 1 Cor 13:7-8 and 13, truth is described as "greater, and stronger than all things . . . truth endures and is strong for ever and lives and prevails for ever and ever" (4:35, 38).[97] This discourse takes place just after a banquet given by King Darius. The participants then propose to the king their views as to "what is strongest" (1 Esd 3:5). The encomium to truth is the response of Zarubbabel. The question is of a form that is typical of symposium discourses. For example, Plutarch presents such a formula in his fictional depiction of a symposium of the "seven sages":

> "What is the oldest thing?" "Time." What is the greatest?" "The universe." "What is the wisest?" "Truth."[98]

To this may be compared 1 Cor 12:31, in which *agapē* is called "the higher way," and 13:13, in which it is called the "greatest."[99]

Whether the hymn belongs in this context or whether it was even composed by Paul are points that have been rigorously debated.[100] It appears to be disruptive in its context since it is of a different style from the rest of the letter and seems to break into a text that could be construed as continuous from 12:31b to 14:1. From another perspective, however, it can be seen to fit quite well into its context. Note, for example, how well chapter 13 correlates with the themes of chapters 12 and 14. Furthermore, Paul had already alluded to the connection of *agapē* and *oikodomē* at 8:1. Here then he provides a poetic prelude to the practical ethical considerations of chapter 14. Thus *agapē* is the greatest virtue above prophecy and tongues (13:1-2). Indeed, all such gifts will cease, whereas *agapē* is of enduring value.

The function of the *agapē* hymn in its context in 1 Corinthians serves to emphasize the nature of the structure of social obligation that Paul is attempting to impose. For while he argues against the status system in effect at Corinth and appears to set up an alternative status system, in effect he has presented no status system at all but has overturned the idea of status itself. For example, Paul presents a goal for which one should strive, but that goal does not serve to enhance oneself but to serve others (taking 12:31 as an introduction to chapter 13). Similarly, the gift of prophecy is a worthy goal to seek, not because of worth inherent in itself but because it "upbuilds" the church (as in 14:1-5). Finally, love itself, as the ultimate ethical path, is not a path to glory but a path to service.

So also, whenever Paul speaks of ranking in the worship service, he consistently imputes the assigning of status to God and to the spirit. Whenever he speaks of order in the worship, he never speaks of a presiding officer or symposiarch. Rather, the purpose of the instructions, which are, after all, not addressed to the leaders but to the whole church, is to provide guidelines for which each individual is to take responsibility. See, for example, 1 Cor 11:28: "Examine yourselves." *Oikodomē* is an ethic defining the relationship of the individual to the community, not one by which the community governs the individual. Thus individuals are to be self-directed; whenever someone else is speaking, they are to remain seated and quiet. No fines are imposed for speaking out of turn; appeal is made only to their own individual sense of *oikodomē,* which is founded on the highest virtue of all, *agapē.*

It is interesting to note that the spirit appears to take no part in ordering the service. Rather, order at the gathering is up to the individual to whom the spirit is "subject" (14:32). It might be noted, however, that among the spiritual gifts enumerated by Paul at 12:28 are "forms of assistance" and "forms of leadership."[101] How these roles were carried out in community gatherings is not specified in the text.[102] One might be inclined to assume that they served a function similar to the "orderly officers" at club meetings or like the "presidents" at synagogue meetings and Christian meetings in a later period. But Paul's argument in chapter 14 appears not to allow for that possibility, since there is no reference to anyone who is charged with keeping order for the group as a whole.

Certainly, more is being claimed for *agapē* in 1 Corinthians 13 than is imputed to *oikodomē* in 1 Corinthians 14. But this kind of eloquence is in the nature of such a poetic interlude. It should also be noted that *agapē* is here a "way" of virtue (*hodos,* 12:31b).[103] As such, *agapē* is placed first, above faith and hope (13:13), precisely because it "builds up," whereas faith and hope are of value primarily to the individual. Thus the form, equating *agapē* with the highest virtue, further emphasizes Paul's definition of virtue as that which serves the community. The relative devaluation of faith and hope must be seen in this context and may be compared to the relative devaluation of tongue speaking as compared to prophecy.[104]

Indeed, as we have seen, Paul set about to define the proper meal according to popular morality, but with a uniquely Christian definition. He did not change the institution of the formal meal, but adopted and adapted it as the basis of his sense of community. It has often been noted that no reference to Christ is found in the hymn. That only emphasizes that Paul's definition of the "Lord's supper" as an *agapē* feast is derived from concepts in popular morality, although Paul anchors his discussion at least partially in the liturgical tradition (11:23-26).[105] Thus the hymn to *agapē* in this context represents a conscious effort on Paul's part to restructure symposium traditions and make of the institution a "Lord's supper" (11:20). Thus he altered the Platonic praise of *erōs* by applying the term *agapē* to the definition of "friendship" *(philia),* and thereby he created a new ethical terminology.

Welcome One Another: Hospitality at the Table in Romans

In Rom 14:1—15:13, Paul presents a discourse on community ethics that mirrors in many respects his discussion in 1 Corinthians 8–10. The problem once more is a situation of tension within the Christian community between the "weak" and the "strong." In both cases, "weak" and "strong" are defined by differences in diet, which in Romans especially is best understood as a reference to distinctions between Jewish and Gentile Christians over dietary laws.[106]

The context where the tensions would have come up is most likely to have been at the community table. Paul's primary concern is that the two sides "welcome" or "accept" one another. The term for *welcome (proslambanein)* carries the weight of reconciliation of tensions within the community. Stanley K. Stowers defines the term to mean "to take someone into a relation of mutual assistance, that is, ancient friendship."[107]

The question that then arises is how such acceptance was to be communicated. I would suggest that it was primarily at the table where this response was carried out. Just as the tensions arose at the table, so also would they be resolved at the table. The term *welcome* or *accept* can therefore be understood as embedded in the ancient concept of hospitality. In the language of Paul, it is a form of "building up" the community.

Was this a real situation in the church of Rome? It seems to me that Paul's language is too direct for this to be entirely hypothetical. With an increasing consensus of opinion that chapter 16 belongs to Paul's original letter,[108] we therefore have evidence that Paul was in conversation with individuals who were familiar with the church at Rome. In any case, Paul treats the issue as a real one, and, whether or not he got it entirely right in the case of Rome, it is not unlikely that it was common in more than one Christian community.

Why is his advice so different here than in Antioch and Corinth? In Antioch, he denounced the practice of dietary laws. In Corinth, and here, he urges tolerance for those who have dietary restrictions. What is consistent in the two cases is that Paul argues for the community to be held intact.

What we can imagine happening in Rome was that the "vegetarians" were individuals who were reluctant to eat meat that was not kosher; thus they ate no meat at all. This means that they remained a part of the meal fellowship, unlike the group in Antioch who separated themselves from the Gentile table. Consequently, Paul is dealing with dietary laws from another perspective. Now he can argue for tolerance, as long as community cohesion remains. And it is the common table that carries the primary force of conveying that cohesion.

Paul's strongest statement is at 15:7: "Welcome one another, therefore, just as Christ has welcomed you." This formula can be compared to other statements of Paul on the theological grounding of table ethics. For example, when Paul argued in 1 Corinthians 8 for the "strong" to accommodate themselves to the dietary scruples of the "weak" lest "by your knowledge those

weak believers for whom Christ died are destroyed" (8:11), he was basing
these ethical restraints on the bonds created by the death of Christ. On the
other hand, when he argued in Galatians that Peter was wrong to separate
himself from the table at Antioch to accommodate the dietary scruples of
"the circumcision faction," his argument was similar: "if justification comes
through the law, then Christ died for nothing" (2:21). In all three cases, the
communal bonds created by the death of Christ are to be kept intact by "welcoming one another as Christ also welcomed you" (Rom 15:7).

To welcome or accept the other, therefore, must be seen not as an intellectual acceptance, but as embodied in the ritual act of dining together at the
community table. The table was a common cultural symbol for membership
in a group. It was the ultimate expression of social bonding. Paul's advice to
the Romans drew on this cultural heritage and envisioned a way for Christians to experience the "welcome" of Christ as mediated by and ritualized at
the community table.

CONCLUSION

In summary, we have found: (1) that issues of the table are prominent in all
the major churches of Paul; (2) that these issues are best explained as having
arisen at the community meal; (3) that the conflict at Antioch and the resulting crystallization of Paul's theology should be taken as determinative for
defining the issues at all of Paul's churches; (4) that these issues involved Jewish dietary laws that resulted in divisions between Jews and Greeks at the
meal and thus in community life and theology; and (5) that the ideology of
the banquet as found in the culture formed the backdrop for the development of the issues and Paul's resulting theological, liturgical, and ethical
responses.

The aspects of the ideology of the banquet utilized by Paul include:

1) The significance of the meal to create social bonding. Thus Paul argues
to the Galatians that separate meals represent an overturning of the truth of
the gospel, since it symbolizes a distinction between Jews and Greeks. Similarly, separation at the table in Corinth causes the meal to deteriorate into
something less than the supper of the Lord. Rather, if they eat as one community, and thus symbolize that all are one before God, then they will
thereby "proclaim the Lord's death" (1 Cor 11:26), which, of course, is the
means whereby such unity among human beings has been established by
God.[109] When he addressed the Romans he took a somewhat different tack,

arguing that unity can be achieved at the same table even if a different menu is eaten (14:1—15:6).

2) The tradition whereby a meal symbolized social obligation within the community. Here Paul utilized traditional arguments from Greco-Roman meal ethics to define the basis for community identity and social ethics. This is especially to be seen in 1 Corinthians, where his arguments for unity, based on that which serves the community (or "builds up") rather than that which serves the individual, derive from traditional arguments for proper behavior at the banquet.

3) The dichotomy of social stratification versus social equality at the banquet. Here Paul argues consistently that equality before God is to be realized in community life by means of a community meal shared in common and equally among all. Yet at the same time, he must contend with customs that provide for normal social distinctions within a unified community. He seems to vacillate on this point, as does the Greco-Roman data, sometimes breaking down the barriers entirely and sometimes allowing distinctions to exist as long as the overall symbolism was one of unity.[110]

My conclusion, therefore, is that Paul's theology cannot be seen to exist as if in a vacuum or purely as an intellectual syllogism. Rather, it was understood, proclaimed, and practiced in the context of the life of the community. Just as the meal was central to the life of the community, so also it was central to the development of Paul's thought. For it was the community meal that provided not only the catalyst and context but also a social ideology for the development of Paul's theological, ethical, and liturgical formulations.

CHAPTER 8

THE BANQUET
IN THE GOSPELS

The kingdom of heaven may be compared to a king who gave a wedding banquet for his son . . .
—Matt 22:2 // Luke 14:16 // *Gos. Thom.* 64:1

For John came neither eating nor drinking, and they say, "He has a demon"; the Son of Man came eating and drinking, and they say, "Look, a glutton and a drunkard, a friend of tax collectors and sinners!"
—Matt 11:18-19 // Luke 7:31-35

Meals in the Gospels consistently reflect the Greco-Roman banquet tradition. For example, in all descriptions of meals of Jesus the posture is reclining. This is even true of the miraculous feedings that take place outdoors. The reclining motif is only the tip of the iceberg, however. As this study will show, the meal texts in the Jesus tradition have been constructed throughout with reference to the Greco-Roman banquet tradition and ideology.

The Jesus tradition is permeated with rich usages of the banquet motif, from its metaphorical use in the parables to stories about meals in which Jesus took part. What we are dealing with here is properly identified as a banquet motif. For these are narrative materials, and the banquet is a time-tested topos in various forms of literature functioning to typify the hero and his ideals. Consequently, in this literature the banquet is to be analyzed especially from a literary perspective.

The layers of the Jesus tradition are well known, but delineating them once more will help us identify the ways in which the banquet motif is functioning.

1) At the level of the historical Jesus, there are two usages commonly referred to in the literature. One is the banquet used as a motif within the preaching of Jesus, as, for example, in the parables. The excerpt quoted above from the parable of the great banquet is an example of this motif. The other type of historical Jesus data is a collection of references to meals held by or

participated in by Jesus. These types of meal texts are usually presented as a kind of "parabolic action," by means of which Jesus would proclaim a particular message. The second example quoted above refers to this type. The Last Supper text can also be placed in this category.

As I will argue below, the representations of meals of Jesus in the Gospel tradition function as idealizations of Jesus as hero. The extent to which the motif of Jesus at table accurately represented the historical Jesus is a complex issue. At minimum, however, it may be said that this data testifies to a Jesus who self-consciously chose a lifestyle that was positive toward the banquet table as compared with the ascetic lifestyle of John the Baptist.

2) At the level commonly referred to as "oral tradition," in the period after Jesus' death, early Christian preachers told stories about him in the context of the fledgling Christian communities. The banquet emerged as a useful motif for defining aspects of the hero, Jesus. During this period early Christian communities were also centering many of their communal religious activities on meals, which gave special meaning to stories of Jesus at table. At this point in the tradition, the typification of Jesus as a table companion of "tax collectors and sinners" became a symbol for the identity of early Christian groups.

3) The earliest written materials utilized these already existing motifs in the tradition and enlarge and expand on them, drawing especially upon the varied usages of the banquet motif in Greco-Roman literature. The Gospels continued this trend, so that the banquet became a stock literary motif to serve the theological interests of the individual Gospel writers. In addition, references to meal traditions in the Gospels served to enhance the communal meals being practiced in their communities.

The presentation of Jesus at table in the Gospels must be understood in relation to the overall plot of each Gospel. Each of the Gospel writers imagines the table where Jesus dined according to a particular idealized model, one that is consistent with the overall picture of Jesus presented in their particular stories. In addition, these idealized models can be seen to correlate with a plot motif used in each of the Gospels, the motif of irony. That is to say, the story of Jesus as told in the Gospels takes place on two levels. On one level, the values are those of the "world" that crucifies him. On the other level, the values are those of God, who "glorifies" him. The same is true when Jesus dines. What appears to be a normal meal setting is actually a "parabolic" presentation of a heavenly reality.

Therefore, throughout the various layers of the Jesus tradition, we are dealing with especially complex materials in which social reality and narrative world are significantly intertwined. It is clear that social reality is being represented in these texts and that the texts are true to the values of their social world. The question is where that social reality is to be located and how it is to be defined, that is, whether we are dealing primarily with the social reality of the storyteller or whether we have access to the social reality of the characters in the story, notably the social reality of the historical Jesus. The issues are complex, and nowhere are they more complex than when they relate to the historical Jesus.

THE BANQUET AND THE HISTORICAL JESUS[1]

Jesus obviously ate meals with various individuals in his lifetime, and many of those meals may have been memorable. But did Jesus use table fellowship as a mode of proclamation? A large number of scholars say he did, though they often disagree on how this was done and what message was communicated. Too often such conclusions have been drawn on the basis of inadequate data and untested presuppositions about the structure and social function of ancient meals. Utilizing the data and perspectives gathered in this study, we can come afresh at the issue of meals in the historical Jesus tradition.

A review of recent research on the historical Jesus must begin with Norman Perrin's influential book *Rediscovering the Teaching of Jesus*. Perrin's judgment on the table fellowship theme has been widely used by subsequent authors, sometimes in the same form and sometimes in a modified form. Perrin gave historical authenticity to the tradition that Jesus offered table fellowship to "outcasts," or "tax collectors and sinners," as especially recorded in Matt 11:16-19 ("Look, a glutton and a drunkard, a friend of tax collectors and sinners!"). Furthermore, according to Perrin, Jesus' table fellowship utilized the symbolism of the messianic banquet, as defined in Matt 8:11: "I tell you, many will come from east and west and will eat with Abraham and Isaac and Jacob in the kingdom of heaven" (= Luke 13:28-29). Both of these texts he judged to be "indubitably authentic."[2] His basic argument for authenticity in both cases was along the lines of the classic criterion of dissimilarity, that these texts represent perspectives more appropriate to Jesus' setting than to that of the early church.[3]

According to his interpretation, therefore, "a regular table fellowship" would have been held by Jesus and his followers that would have included "Jews who had made themselves as Gentiles," Perrin's interpretation of the meaning of "tax collectors and sinners." Utilizing the symbolism of the kingdom, especially as exemplified by the messianic banquet imagery that symbolized the anticipated final kingdom, Jesus' action in effect served "to welcome those people back into the community."[4]

According to Perrin, this reconstruction is seen as authentic because it explains how Jesus came to die: his actions defiled the boundaries of the community and thus functioned as an act of such offensiveness to Jewish sensibilities that Jewish leaders called for his death. It also explains how the early Christian community came to practice a communal meal together, a practice that came into existence so early that it must have been a continuation of the practice of Jesus himself.[5]

Subsequent scholarship has continued along these same lines. Thus, for example, the idea that Jesus offered the kingdom to outcasts by means of his table fellowship figures prominently, with some variation and elaboration, in the studies of James Breech, E. P. Sanders, Richard Horsley, Marcus Borg, John Dominic Crossan, Bruce Chilton, and John P. Meier.[6] This is not to say that they all come out at the same place; indeed, their reconstructions of the historical Jesus differ on significant points. Yet they all agree in giving prominence to the table fellowship theme. Indeed, for many scholars the theme of table fellowship with outcasts is primary and essential to any valid reconstruction of the historical Jesus. Crossan, for example, states emphatically: "My wager is that magic and meal or miracle and table . . . is the heart of Jesus' program. . . . If that is incorrect, this book will have to be redone."[7]

The question that needs to be asked is whether the picture of Jesus utilizing table fellowship with a symbolic meaning as part of his teaching program can be plausibly reconstructed as a real event in first-century Palestine. There is no doubt that it is a powerful image on the literary level. But the question remains whether it could function in the same way on the historical level in the time of Jesus.

The meals of Jesus as depicted in the Gospels contain typical elements of the Greco-Roman banquet and/or symposium tradition. These include such features as reclining (Mark 2:15; 6:39; 8:6; 14:3; 14:18 [and synoptic parallels]; Luke 7:36; 11:37; 14:7; 24:30),[8] washing of the feet prior to reclining (Luke 7:44; John 13:3-5), anointing the head with perfumes (Mark 14:3), saying prayers before the *deipnon* (Mark 6:41; 8:6-7; 14:22), ranking at the table (Luke 14:7) and at the symposium (Mark 14:23), sharing a wine libation around the table (Mark 14:23), discourse on appropriate themes during the symposium (Luke 14:7-24), ending the meal with a hymn (Mark 14:26), and a host of other literary features that will be discussed further in the analysis of Mark and Luke below. These and other motifs in the Jesus meal tradition derive from Greco-Roman meal customs as associated especially with the archetype of the formal meal, the banquet.

Since the Gospels are literary presentations of the Jesus story, they also utilized the common literary motifs of the banquet in the Greco-Roman world. Significant literary models include the literary form of the symposium or the idealization of the hero at table in folklore and literature. These literary models shape the telling of a banquet story and therefore complicate our quest for historical data.

There are four categories of meals of Jesus either alluded to or described in the data: (1) meals with Pharisees, (2) miraculous feedings, (3) meals with "tax collectors and sinners," and (4) meals with disciples. Of these, only three and four offer a high degree of historical probability. References to meals with Pharisees are found only in the Gospel of Luke and are clearly redactional.[9] The miraculous feeding stories, like other miracles in the Jesus tradition, are problematic if assumed to be historical events. Their function is to idealize Jesus, much as the meal texts in general do. Consequently, they will be analyzed as components of the literary motifs of the Gospel narratives.

The two categories that are the most fruitful for historical analysis are Jesus' meals with tax collectors and sinners and his meals with his disciples. The theme of meals with tax collectors and sinners is complicated on several levels. First, the question arises whether any of the stories that recount such meals could be reliable. Second, apart from the stories, could the sayings that characterized Jesus as eating with tax collectors and sinners represent reliable data about Jesus? Third, if there is something to this tradition, that is, if Jesus did eat frequently with tax collectors and sinners, what could such actions possibly mean?

Jesus must have had meals with his disciples. This we can assume. And it seems quite likely that they would have looked back on them later as full of meaning. But here the question is whether the Gospel narratives are reliable accounts of such meals. Furthermore, in all such cases of Jesus' meals, whether with disciples or tax collectors and sinners, even if one might conclude that such meals took place, the basic question would still remain, did Jesus use meals as a means of proclamation?

There are also isolated references in the Gospels in which seemingly incidental events take place at meals. In these instances, the meal provides the setting for the event, but the meal symbolism is secondary to the overall theme. Thus even if these references were judged to be historical, the meals themselves do not carry the symbolic weight to be judged parabolic actions of Jesus. The most important example from this group is the story of the anointing of Jesus at a meal, which occurs in various forms in the Gospels (Matt 26:6-13 = Mark 14:3-9 = Luke 7:36-50 = John 12:1-8). This story functions as a post-Easter interpretation of the death of Jesus and therefore most likely originated as a redaction by Mark.[10] Another text is the story of Martha and Mary at a meal setting, which is found only in Luke 10:38-42 and is best understood as another example of Luke's extensive use of the literary motif of table fellowship. This text will be discussed further below.

References to meal symbolism may also be found in the sayings of Jesus. Such sayings could have originated in a meal setting, such as in the "table talk" of Jesus. That would fit the pattern in ancient meals, as we have already seen, in which teaching could take place at table. But when these traditions were passed down, they tended to lack any specific context; most notably they lacked a meal context. At the least, these references show the pervasiveness of meal symbolism as a motif in folklore and literature. One need not assume that they refer in any way to actual meals of Jesus. Examples of such traditions may be listed as follows: (1) The Feast (Matt 22:2-13 = Luke14:16-23 = *Gos. Thom.* 64:1); (2) Blessed the Hungry (Matt 5:6 = Luke 6:21a = *Gos. Thom.* 69:2); (3) Salting the Salt (Matt 5:13 = Mark 9:50 = Luke 14:34-35); (4) Patches and Wineskins (Matt 9:16-17 = Mark 2:21-22 = Luke 5:36b-38 = *Gos. Thom.* 47:4); (5) Leader as Servant (Matt 20:25b-28 = Matt 23:11 = Mark 9:35b = Mark 10:42b-45 = Luke 9:48b = Luke 22:25-27 = John 13:14); and (6) Patriarchs and Gentiles (Matt 8:11-12 = Luke 13:28-29).[11]

There are various other meal references in the Gospels in which the primary motif is Jesus' opposition to certain interpretations of Jewish dietary laws. Some examples of these texts are as follows: 1) Unwashed Hands (Matt 15:1-9 = Mark 7:1-13); 2) What Goes In (Matt 15:11 = Mark 7:15 = *Gos. Thom.* 14:3); 3) Leaven of Pharisees (Matt 16:6, 11b = Mark 8:15b = Luke 12:1b); and 4) Inside and Outside (Matt 23:25-26 = Luke 11:39-41 = *Gos Thom* 89). In a recent analysis of the debate about hand-washing in Mark 7:1-15, Klawans has proposed that the Markan portrayal of the positions of Jesus and the Pharisees represented two legitimate opinions within Judaism of the day. That is to say, it was a matter of debate within Judaism of the day whether hand-washing as a temple purity rite should be required of all Jews.[12] Consequently, there is significant verisimilitude in this story of Mark; such debates were actually taking place in the first century. However, the larger question is whether this and other stories of debates with the Pharisees represent a reality in Jesus' day or a reality for the Jesus movement after the death of Jesus.[13]

The most highly elaborated description of a formal meal of Jesus with his disciples is that of the Last Supper. This tradition is attested in Mark, which was then used as a source by Matthew and Luke, and in 1 Cor 11:23-25.

The earliest Last Supper text is in 1 Cor 11:17-34. This text has a form that strongly suggests it took shape as an etiological legend. That is to say, it functions here to explain the meal, as etiological legends tend to do.[14] It was also adapted and interpreted by Paul to fit his needs in his context. Similarly, Mark has taken the Last Supper tradition and incorporated it creatively into his narrative. Indeed, Mark's passion narrative has been shown in recent research to be largely a creation of the Gospel writer.[15] Consequently, the basic story of the Last Supper as presented by both Paul and Mark was adapted in both cases to fit the needs and purposes of their writings. Neither author saw his version of the tradition to be invariable and inviolable. Furthermore, the variations between their two accounts regarding the words of Jesus are so distinct that a single original form cannot successfully be constructed, though many have tried. If the Last Supper is to be proposed as a historical event, then, it will have to be extrapolated from these two versions. One cannot simply read both of these accounts as historical and achieve a coherent result.

Those who support the historicity of the tradition in Mark often follow Mark's lead and interpret Jesus' last meal with his disciples as a Passover meal.[16] This thesis has not stood up to scrutiny, however. For example, there is very little relationship to a Passover meal in the Last Supper text at all, other than the introductory reference (Mark 14:12-16), and that is clearly Mark's creation.[17] Thus, even if Jesus did celebrate a Passover meal with his disciples as his last meal, we do not have a clear reminiscence of such a meal in the description we now have.

A historical reconstruction based on the Pauline text might point to the reference to these events taking place "on the night when he was handed over [*paradideto*; NRSV translates "betrayed"]" (1 Cor 11:23). Since the text says that this is the night when "the Lord" was handed over, however, it no longer claims to refer to historical memory, at least, not according to Paul's theology. "The Lord" is a christological category representing the risen Lord (Phil 2:9-11), and the theme of "handing over," while likely a reference to the crucifixion event, nevertheless defines it as an action of God (see Rom 8:32).[18] Of course, this text in Paul also witnesses to a pre-Pauline tradition that, at the least, apparently referred to a last meal of Jesus that included words of Jesus spoken over the bread and wine. Reconstructing a pre-Pauline historical Jesus tradition is problematic, however, not only because we cannot successfully reconstruct an original form, but also because Paul's theology is primarily concerned with interpreting the death of Jesus.

The question often raised by scholars is how much Jesus might have known about his own death. Some would argue that Jesus had a premonition that he would die soon. But the Last Supper tradition does more than simply predict his death. Rather, it provides a highly developed and ritualized interpretation of his death. To place the seeds of christological interpretation of Jesus in the thought and words of Jesus himself does not make good historical sense, though it is comforting theologically. Historical probability would suggest that such interpretations of Jesus' death developed in the years following his death, not before. After all, earliest Christian memory also testifies to the death of Jesus as a problem that the first disciples had to wrestle with.[19] Furthermore, some early Jesus groups seem to have given no particular theological meaning at all to the death of Jesus. This seems to be the case, for example, with the communities that lie behind the earliest sayings Gospels, Q and early Thomas.[20]

When Mark takes up the Last Supper text in his narrative of the life of Jesus, it becomes embedded in his larger theme in which Jesus has foreknowledge of his death and provides a soteriological interpretation of it. This literary and theological formula that originates in Mark is then taken up by all of the Gospels until it reaches its culmination in John.[21] Since the Last Supper story has no existence in our data apart from christological speculation, it quite likely originated as a form of christological speculation. Such a process of christological speculation, even in its earliest, originating form, is best understood as an attempt by the followers of Jesus to give him enduring significance after his death. To say that Jesus is the one who started such speculation about himself is to ignore the nature of the data, in which christological speculation is always a process under development. The process does not begin with certain knowledge or fact; rather, in its very beginning it is speculation, and as speculation it is subject to continuing reinterpretation.

Doing theology though storytelling, for which Mark is our first exemplar in Christian literature and whose method and content were followed closely by the other Gospel writers, also helped to shape how the story was told. A storyteller/theologian must embed his theology *within the story*. Mark does this by having *Jesus* explain the meaning of his death in his own words (10:45!), thus keeping the story viable as story while providing the theological interpretation of the storyteller at the same time. In addition, putting the interpretation in the mouth of Jesus lends it even greater authority. All of the

Gospel writers leave traces that they too have utilized such a method, for each one has Jesus explain his death in terms specific to that Gospel. When Jesus is made to say what, in fact, represents the theology of the storyteller, it is clear that we are not dealing with historical Jesus data.

There are still other pitfalls to be encountered when one attempts to interpret the Last Supper story as historical. Sometimes whenever scholars attempt to place the interpretive words of Jesus at the Last Supper within Jesus' own lifetime, they have to resort to interpretations that suggest Jesus was immediately misunderstood or else virtually ignored.[22] In such a case, one wonders what the value is in such a reconstruction. Sometimes it is asserted that the practice of the meal derived from the command of Jesus. That is, of course, what Paul's text says (but not Mark's). The problem here is that the tradition that stretches from before Paul to Paul to each of the Gospels in turn consistently and freely reinterprets the Last Supper tradition. Consequently, it would appear that the so-called command of Jesus was ironically preserved by successive generations who altered it. In fact, however, only the Pauline tradition referred to a command motif. The other strands of the tradition make no reference all to a dominical command (except Luke, of course, in a textual tradition clearly derived from Paul and quite likely added later to Luke). Consequently, the "command of the Lord" motif was neither widespread nor functionally significant in the tradition. It would appear to have functioned more as an apologetic device for certifying the interpretation of a particular interpreter rather than as "proof" that the church derived its authority for the Lord's Supper from the historical Jesus. Thus whatever might be proposed as the historical core of a meal or meals of Jesus with his disciples, it is not likely that it centered on an interpretation of Jesus' death. The Last Supper traditions simply do not provide adequate data to reconstruct a historical last meal of Jesus with his disciples. Crossan has provided a succinct conclusion on this issue that I think goes about as far as one can go: "Obviously, in such a situation, Jesus and those closest to him would have had a last supper, that is, a meal that later and in retrospect was recognized as having been their last one together. . . . I do not presume any distinctive meal known beforehand, designated specifically, or ritually programmed as final and forever."[23]

The final strand of data for historical investigation, and potentially the most fruitful, is the tradition that Jesus ate with tax collectors and sinners. There are two basic versions of this data: (1) a description of a meal of Jesus at the home of a tax collector and (2) a sayings tradition in which Jesus is criticized for eating with tax collectors and sinners. The meal tradition is found in its earliest form in Mark and the sayings tradition is found in its earliest form in Q.

Both texts can be understood as types of the *chreia* form. This form has been given extensive analysis and definition in recent research on the Gospel tradition.[24] The *chreia* was a form of rhetoric that is described in ancient literature and was taught in the schools. It is defined as "a saying or act that is well-aimed or apt, expressed concisely, attributed to a person, and regarded as useful for living."[25] Especially important in the definition for our study is that a *chreia* was normally utilized to characterize a famous person or hero.[26] *Chreiai* were therefore used extensively in the philosophical tradition to characterize famous philosophers.

At least two types can be singled out as widely used, namely, the Stoic *chreia* and the Cynic *chreia*. The Stoic *chreia* is characterized by its emphasis on moral teaching. The Cynic *chreia* "distinguishes itself by the odd, extreme, and often even burlesque action (or basic situation or final statement) of the central Sage-Hero that becomes the basis for a demonstration of Cynic ideals and values."[27] Recent studies have concluded that the *chreiai* in the Jesus tradition tend to be of the Cynic type.[28]

Mark's story of a meal of Jesus at the home of a tax collector fits the category of the Cynic *chreia* quite well. The text is as follows:

> And as he sat at dinner [Greek: "reclined"] in Levi's house, many tax collectors and sinners were also sitting with [Greek: "reclining with"] Jesus and his disciples—for there were many who followed him. When the scribes of the Pharisees saw that he was eating with sinners and tax collectors, they said to his disciples, "Why does he eat with tax collectors and sinners?" When Jesus heard this, he said to them, "Those who are well have no need of a physician, but those who are sick; I have come to call not the righteous but sinners." (Mark 2:15-17/Matt 9:10-13/Luke 5:29-32)

The basic, core *chreia* is reconstructed by Burton Mack as follows: "When asked why he ate with tax collectors and sinners, Jesus replied, 'Those who are well have no need of a physician, but those who are ill.'"[29] The logic of the text takes on a Cynic cast because it represents a counter-argument to the implied conventional logic of the objection. Furthermore, the saying about a physician is a conventional one and is especially congenial to the Cynic tradition, in which a comparison of the philosopher with a physician was widely used.[30] The core *chreia* has then been elaborated with data that relates it to its context in Mark, especially by identifying the setting as the home of the tax collector whom Jesus has just called to follow him and by identifying Jesus' detractors as "scribes of the Pharisees."

The text in its present form, therefore, represents a creation by Mark to coordinate with his own literary aims, in terms of both context and themes.[31] In addition, the form that the description takes has an air of unreality about it. It is difficult to imagine how Pharisees can be present in the dining room so that they can observe and comment without themselves being participants.[32] Such a feature cannot be made to fit conventional dining customs and settings, but obviously presents no problems to a narrator who is imagining a story world.

Another problematic phrase for historical reconstruction is: "I have come to call not the righteous but sinners." This saying represents an elaboration on the physician saying but also has an independent relation to the meal setting. The word *call (kalein)* is used here as a pun; the same term is the ordinary word meaning "invite" to a meal.[33] According to this saying, therefore, Jesus is being pictured not as the guest but as the host, the one who invites to the meal. Though this presents difficulties if the text is taken to be historical,[34] it works quite well on the literary level, where irony can have its full sway. Here, while the character in the story, Levi the tax collector, thinks he is the host who has invited Jesus, the reader perceives Jesus as the one who invites and his invitation is to that which the meal merely symbolizes here. Furthermore, the theme of calling is inherent to the context of Mark, where the meal is connected with a "call" story.[35] Thus the meal is made to symbolize redemption and calling to discipleship, a symbolism that works quite well in the literary context but is difficult to reconstruct in a historical setting. The meal description presented here, therefore, represents a literary idealization rather than a recalling of an actual event.

When taken out of its context in Mark and reduced to its basic form, as seen in Mack's reconstruction quoted above, the text as *chreia* does not present a description of a specific meal but rather presents a characterization of Jesus. The assumption behind the *chreia* is that Jesus characteristically dined with "tax collectors and sinners," that this was somehow indicative of his overall character, and furthermore that it was inherently an unconventional thing to do.[36]

The underlying logic behind the assumption that Jesus was engaging in an unconventional act by dining with such individuals appears to relate to traditional Jewish dietary laws and the assumption that Jesus would be transgressing those laws in some way by eating with such people.[37] But the logic of the text on the literary level is difficult to reconstruct on the historical level.

During Jesus' own lifetime, it is unlikely that he would be perceived to be making a statement like the one this text assumes merely by dining with questionable individuals. Rather, he would simply be making the statement that he is not a Pharisee. Furthermore, it may not be dietary laws per se that lie behind this characterization of "tax collectors and sinners." It is difficult to account for such individuals as being clearly in the unclean category.[38] In any case, in the text before us, the reconstructed basic *chreia,* these terms are already functioning with a symbolic sense, for the text assumes that these terms are to be understood as representative of a type rather than being reducible to only one set of historical figures.

This text also compares dining with Jesus with being healed by a physician. This is at best a subtle symbol, since it assumes that this apparent "parabolic action" of Jesus can be perceived as part of his teaching program. Such an interpretation is difficult to reconstruct on the level of social reality, although clearly it works well on a literary level. How could dining with Jesus alone represent an experience of "healing"? Since the *chreia* in its basic form represents an attempt to typify the teaching of Jesus utilizing a popular proverb about a physician, it has the form of a text created in a community that is idealizing its hero.

Thus the tradition represented in this text in both its elaborated form as found in Mark and in its basic *chreia* form can be seen to have its origin in the early church. There is one aspect of this tradition that deserves further investigation, however. Since both Mark and Q have independent versions of the motif that Jesus characteristically dined with "tax collectors and sinners," it clearly took shape in the tradition at a very early stage. In order to trace it further, we will now look at the form it took in Q.

The Q saying about Jesus' eating habits occurs in the larger context of an elaborated *chreia* in which Jesus is being contrasted with John the Baptist. The larger block of texts of which this text is a part includes Q (Luke) 7:1-10; 18–23; 24–26; 16:16; and 31–35. These texts all picture John and Jesus together as opposed to "this generation."[39] Our text in its immediate context is as follows:

> To what then will I compare the people of this generation, and what are they like? They are like children sitting in the market place and calling

to one another, "We played the flute for you, and you did not dance; we wailed, and you did not weep." For John the Baptist has come eating no bread and drinking no wine, and you say, "He has a demon"; the Son of Man has come eating and drinking, and you say, "Look, a glutton and a drunkard, a friend of tax collectors and sinners!" Nevertheless, wisdom is vindicated by all her children. (Luke 7:31-35 = Matt 11:16-19)

John Kloppenborg has defined three layers in the compositional history of Q. The earliest layer is made up of wisdom speeches, while the second layer represents the introduction of sayings that "adopted a critical and polemical stance with respect to Israel."[40] This text is located at the second or Q2 layer. It is part of a larger group of texts concerned with the theme of judgment and opposition to "this generation." Also characteristic of the stage represented by this text is the fact that Jesus and John are included together rather than being presented as rivals. Thus they are pictured here as allies against "this generation," as two types of "children" of wisdom.[41]

In terms of textual history, it seems apparent that the parable in v. 32 is independent of the saying in vv. 33-34, which has been attached as an explanation for the parable. Thus vv. 33-34 represent an independent saying.[42] Furthermore, the primary contrast here is between "fasting" and "feasting." The corollary added to the description of Jesus, that he is a "friend of tax collectors and sinners," since it has no parallel referent in the descriptive phrase referring to John, is secondary and must have been added at a later point.[43] It could have existed as an independent tradition, however, since table fellowship is a traditional motif for expressing the idea of friendship.[44]

Both of these text traditions at the *chreia* level function to provide identity to the followers of Jesus at a time of conflict. I have already noted how the *chreia* functioned to provide a "characterization" of Jesus. Both *chreiai* assume that what they celebrate provides not a single instance only but a characteristic of Jesus. By definition, they present an interpretation about Jesus in the words of a disciple, not in the words of Jesus himself. The social context in which such forms would be generated would most likely be the period in which Jesus was being preached about and interpreted, that is, in the period after Jesus' death. Furthermore, both of these *chreiai* function to provide justification for an issue of self-identity in the community by way of an anecdote about Jesus. Since both *chreiai* witness to a time of conflict in the life of the community, they are best dated to the time of the early Jesus movements after Jesus' death, namely, the period in which social formation of Jesus movements began to take place.

To this point we have analyzed the specific texts that are the most likely to represent table fellowship practices of the historical Jesus. We have presented arguments in each case that the social context and social world represented by these texts is most likely that of the early Jesus movements. It is also appropriate to look beyond the texts and ask if the motifs they utilize could be construed as historical. The best candidates for this are the two motifs, "dining with tax collectors and sinners" and "feasting versus fasting."

Dining with Tax Collectors and Sinners

In its basic meaning, this tradition is concerned with the regular practice of dining with people who are beneath one's own social status. In favor of this tradition as historical is its seeming consistency with other references in the historical Jesus database, for example, the concept that Jesus favored the less fortunate in the world (see, e.g., "Blessed are the poor," Q [Luke] 6:20). However, it should be pointed out that "tax collectors" would hardly be considered "less fortunate." Indeed, what is most scandalous about tax collectors could be said to be their exploitation of the poor. It is usually argued, therefore, that what is in common in the mix of "tax collectors," "sinners," and "poor" is their supposed social location on the fringes of Jewish society.[45] But Jesus is not said to have dined with the "poor." The symbolism of this meal is not that of a charity dinner. So what exactly is it that the tax collectors and sinners are supposed to be getting out of this meal?

First, let us look at the definition of the term *tax collectors and sinners*. Attempts to provide a historic definition to these characters that fits the story have proven to be problematic. In regard to "tax collectors," discussion has revolved around identifying who they were and what their offense was so that table fellowship with them would be scandalous. Distinctions have been made between tax collectors and toll collectors and the suggestion made that in the time of the Gospels only the latter would be found in Palestine.[46] As to their offense, it has been argued that they were hated because of their status as "quislings," that is to say, because they had consorted with the enemy, or because theirs was considered to be an occupation characterized by dishonesty. The scandal in dining with them could involve ritual purity, since they would be "Jews who had made themselves as Gentiles [by becoming quislings]," or, alternatively, could be a moral question, since they were by nature dishonest people.[47]

Sinners have been widely assumed to be the impure and thus roughly equivalent with the *'ammei ha-'arets* with whom the Pharisees presumably could not eat. Thus virtually every non-Pharisee could be included under this term.[48] More recently, however, E. P. Sanders has proposed that the term cannot refer to the ritually impure but only to "the wicked . . . those who sinned willfully and heinously and who did not repent."[49] Sanders concludes that Jesus' act consisted not in welcoming the impure into the kingdom, but rather in welcoming the "wicked" into his community. By thus offering his kingdom to them without first requiring repentance, he was engaging in an act contrary to Jewish tradition and therefore scandalous.[50] This, then, is Sanders's interpretation of the table fellowship texts: "His eating with tax collectors and sinners has, probably correctly, been seen as a proleptic indication that they would be included in the kingdom: the meal looks forward to the 'messianic banquet,' when many would come from east and west and dine with the patriarchs" (Matt. 8:11).[51] On the literary level, I think Sanders is right. This is the way this text functions in the Gospel narratives. I do not think it works, however, as a description of a plausible event in Jesus' ministry.

The category "tax collectors and sinners" is best understood as symbolic from the outset, from the very beginning of the formation of this *chreia* tradition. Furthermore, it must be seen as a characterization, as representative of a type, for the motif that Jesus associates/dines with such individuals is taken to represent a pattern for him, not a onetime individual activity. Thus the identity of the group so designated is not based so much on the actual as on the symbolic value of the terms. That is to say, at the earliest level of the tradition, *tax collector* and *sinner* go together and function as symbolic terms to define social position through the use of a set of apparently traditional terms of slander.

Indeed, *tax collector* had become synonymous with a variety of categories of despised people.[52] The term *sinner* is best interpreted along the same lines, not as a reference to a specific group in first-century Palestine but as a term of slander used in a sectarian context to define those outside one's own group.[53] So also the Gospels read the phrase "tax collectors and sinners" as symbolic, though primarily as a term of slander used against the Christian communities. Matthew, for example, expands it to the form "tax collectors and prostitutes" (21:31) and "Gentile and tax collector" (18:17). Luke's elaboration on the phrase, as will be seen further below, connects it with a wide variety of symbolic categories, including especially the category of "the poor." Consequently, neither actual tax collectors nor a specific social category of sinners is being singled out with the phrase. Rather, it is a term of slander used to define the boundaries between one's own group and those outside.

The story of Jesus dining with this group also assumes that those designated by the term *tax collectors and sinners* must be desirous of the table fellowship from which they are excluded. But why would tax collectors feel
excluded if certain sectarian Jews, such as *haverim* or Pharisees, refused to dine
with them?[54] After all, neither of these groups could be expected to dine with
anyone outside of their community anyway. Once again the question arises,
what is it that the "tax collectors and sinners" are supposed to get out of this?

One indication of the literary, or oral narrative, character of the motif is its
basic nature as an example of irony. That Jesus dines with "tax collectors and
sinners" functions as a criticism of Jesus and is understood to be a true statement. But to the "reader" or "listener" it would have a different meaning
than the one the critics in the story are applying to it. In truth, the motif
assumes, Jesus does characteristically dine with what appear to be unsavory
individuals, but these are in fact the types of individuals of which the kingdom is made up. Seen from this perspective, this motif would not be scandalous at the earliest level of its occurrence in this form. It would always have
represented a characterization of the companions of Jesus with which the
church would identify. It would serve as a theological rationalization in story
form to justify the situation in which the early Jesus movement found itself,
one in which it was living on the fringes of its society.

A further assumption of the story is that table fellowship with Jesus effectively breaks down barriers that are present in the social world. Thus the story
requires that Jesus be assumed by all parties involved, even his critics, to be
something more than just a normal teacher, that he somehow symbolized in
his person the presence of the "kingdom." A common explanation, and one
that is consistent with the Gospel narrative tradition, is that Jesus somehow
made table fellowship with him take on the aura of a messianic banquet. As
I have already noted, this idea works at a literary level but is difficult to envision at the historical level.

There are numerous problems with the idea that Jesus in his lifetime could
preside at a messianic banquet. Among other things, it requires that Jesus
somehow be in charge of the meal so that its form and structure be attribut-
able to him. While it is quite possible that Jesus did host meals,[55] the Gospel
texts make no such distinction. Rather, in the Gospels, the meals of Jesus
function primarily as literary events. Thus no matter who might ostensibly
host a meal in the Gospel narratives, if Jesus is present it takes on overtones
of a messianic banquet. The messianic banquet motif, therefore, does not
emerge in the Gospels as historical data but as part of the interpretive matrix
provided by the storyteller or Gospel narrator.

One might also ask how a messianic banquet can be envisioned to take place in real life. That is to say, such a meal requires the presence of a messiah, a "real" messiah who has full access to heavenly blessings, not a messianic pretender or someone in process of becoming a messiah. I do not find it plausible that the historical Jesus could have added that dimension to a meal simply by being present. Indeed, I find it highly unlikely that any historical figure could celebrate such a meal centered on himself. The messianic banquet is in its essence a mythological meal, a meal that takes place on a divine level with the participation of divine characters.[56] It functions well as a literary idealization of the apocalyptic consummation. There may even have been real communal meals that ritualized the presence of mythological forces or beings (the so-called proleptic messianic banquet).[57] But such a meal takes its form from its ritual character within the context of an eschatological community. These factors were not present at the meals of Jesus. Nor could there be a messianic banquet with Jesus until he had become a mythological character. This began to take place very early as part of the earliest christological speculation. It is already present in the Q text when it is stated, "The Son of Man has come eating and drinking . . ." (Luke 7:34 = Matt 11:19). But it was not present in Jesus' lifetime.

In my opinion, it is only in a narrative context that all of the conditions could be present to make this motif work. The motif in which Jesus dined with tax collectors and sinners and thus blessed them in some way would therefore originate in the form of a *chreia* functioning to characterize the self-consciousness of the early Christian community. It cannot work if placed in a real, historical context. It only works if presented in a literary context in which the presuppositions of the situation and characters can be carefully controlled. A prior motif, which in fact may be historical, would be that Jesus directed his preaching toward a critique of the norms of social stratification in his society. Early Christian preachers would then have taken up that tradition and created a *chreia* that utilized the stock motifs of the hero at table and the generic slanderous term *tax collectors and sinners*. In this way, Jesus was characterized as the sort of person who would do such a thing, and the *chreia* itself served as a theological justification for the self-identity of the community in which it originated.

Feasting versus Fasting

In favor of the historicity of this motif are the various classic arguments that have been proposed in past studies that this is a case of dissimilarity. Perrin's conclusion is typical: "The designation of Jesus as 'a glutton and a drunkard' belongs to the polemics of the controversy surrounding Jesus' earthly ministry during his lifetime, rather than to the circumstances of the controversies between the early Church and Judaism."[58]

What is not always emphasized, however, is the total meaning of the motif. That is, the primary motif includes the contrast of feasting with fasting as well as the contrast of Jesus with John the Baptist. Note, for example, that feasting in itself is not a revolutionary act; as indicated here, it only becomes a symbolic act when proposed in contrast to fasting. Furthermore, note that both fasting and feasting are constituent parts of Jewish piety. Thus to choose such actions does not necessarily set one apart from the group as a whole.

If this is to be taken as a historical reference to the ministry of Jesus, then it must not be separated from the connection with the John the Baptist tradition. There may, in fact, be a historical core here, designating Jesus as one who was known to have considered but rejected the monastic lifestyle of John. In the earliest form of the text, however, it presupposes a literary context. For here the lifestyles of Jesus and John are taken as wholes and placed side by side as two parts of a single message. Thus the text presents a characterization of Jesus and John in the form of a retrospect, one that can confidently sum up what Jesus and John were all about and how in the end neither one was successful in his mission to Israel.[59] The context for the formation of this motif, therefore, would most likely be the early church. While it may represent a reminiscence of an authentic characteristic of the historical Jesus, it only takes on the symbolism of a characterization of his ministry in the form that originates in the early church.

The Motif of the Hero at Table

According to the analysis presented to this point, the earliest meal texts in the Jesus tradition are *chreiai* that present idealizations of Jesus by means of traditional meal motifs. When we look at these materials more closely, we can detect a pattern. By and large, the type of characterization of the hero represented in these texts is roughly parallel to what we find in Cynic traditions. What many of these early texts have in common is a characterization of Jesus as one who parodied the institutions of society as a means of proclaiming his message, a message that therefore had a Cynic style to it.[60] Furthermore, the motifs present here are also common in Cynic tradition, such as the motif of the "hedonistic" Cynic or the use of the meal motif as a means of characterizing the Cynic hero.[61]

Thus the proposal that the early Jesus tradition is related to Cynic themes and motifs provides the best explanation for the context in which the table fellowship texts developed. This need not suggest that Jesus was himself a Cynic or identified with Cynic traditions. But it does suggest that certain early Christian communities utilized Cynic traditions to characterize and idealize Jesus as a hero.

This also means that there need be no other explanation for the development of these traditions than this. While authentic data may be utilized in the development of these *chreiai,* it is not necessary to propose any authenticity to the meal traditions to explain this data. Indeed, when it is noted that the meal data is utilized as a motif to characterize a particular aspect of Jesus' ministry, what emerges as prior and more important, perhaps, is not the motif itself but the characteristic that is illustrated thereby.

The Motif of "Open Commensality"

John Dominic Crossan has introduced a new motif into the discussion of table fellowship and the historical Jesus. He centers his argument on the text in which the disciples are sent out in a form that puts them in direct contrast with the Cynics. Whereas the Cynics carry a staff, bag, and food, the disciples are to carry none of these.[62] But the most important point is that they are to carry no food. "Take nothing for your journey, no staff, nor bag, nor bread, nor money; and do not have two tunics" (Mark 6:8-9 = Luke 9:3; see also Matt 10:10). When they arrived at a house, they were to "eat what is set before you; cure the sick who are there" (Luke 10:8-9 = *Gos. Thom.* 14:2) "for laborers deserve their food" (Matt 10:10). Thus, in contrast to the Cynic insistence on self-sufficiency, the disciples of Jesus would be insisting on social dependency.[63] Crossan combines this with the idea that Jesus was a peasant who was proposing a revolutionary social program. His program was characterized by social egalitarianism. The symbolic means for achieving this goal was by offering "open commensality" through his mission command. That is, when the disciples entered into a village and were to eat whatever was set before them, they were participating in a revolutionary act that was meant to change society, for they were symbolically participating in a table that had no boundaries.[64]

Crossan's reference to the theme of social egalitarianism in the original preaching of Jesus, such as in the parable of the great feast, is a strong point.[65] But when he ties it to an actual symbolic meal, particularly a meal in which the ones receiving the benefits are the ones acting as hosts, his thesis begins to lose its contact with historical probability. Also, in order that open commensality, which he defines as social egalitarianism at the table, could be experienced, there must be significant social stratification involved. Yet Crossan envisions Jesus and his hearers as all being part of the peasant class. Though he and his disciples would come as "magicians" who "share a miracle," they remain part of the same peasant class.[66] The strongest evidence for the open commensality theme in the Jesus tradition is the theme that Jesus ate with tax collectors and sinners. Yet this theme also works best if Jesus is not of the same social class with tax collectors and sinners. If all parties involved, including Jesus, are peasants, then the motif fails, for there is no experience of social stratification at the table.[67]

Consequently, while I think Crossan has made a strong argument for a theme of social egalitarianism in the preaching of Jesus, I think it is weakened by his identification of Jesus as a peasant. Furthermore, his view that Jesus had a "social program" to offer social egalitarianism to all by means of sharing open commensality at the table, a program initiated by Jesus and his disciples' arriving on the scene as itinerants without food, makes for a wonderful story on the literary level but becomes difficult to picture in actual practice.

In conclusion, we have found that none of the texts in which Jesus teaches by means of his table customs can be clearly affirmed as historical. Neither can it be affirmed that the cumulative effect of all these references implies a historical core, because one can explain the development of all these traditions merely by reference to existing oral and literary motifs. It is not necessary to posit that Jesus made use of meals in his overall teaching program in order to explain these texts.

On the other hand, it must be admitted that all of the characteristics of meals utilized in these texts are historically and socially valid. It *is* the case that meals defined community boundaries and, particularly in certain Jewish and Christian literary traditions, carried implications of the messianic kingdom. These factors are part of the function of meals among various social groups in the ancient world and were adopted into the myth and ritual of the early Christian communities. Thus these texts certainly represent social reality. The question is where that social reality is to be located.

My argument is that what is being identified as the historical Jesus at table is more likely the idealized characterization of Jesus at table produced in the early Christian community. The social realities of such meals are still being correctly assessed, but the one who presents parabolic messages by means of meal practices is more likely to be the idealized Jesus than the historical Jesus.

And the social realities defined by these meals, in which table fellowship is equated with a new community self-consciousness, are more likely those of an already developing early Christian community than those of the motley crowds who came to hear Jesus teach.

On the other hand, there could be some consistency between these traditions and the historical figure of Jesus. It is quite likely, for example, that Jesus was known to have chosen a lifestyle different from the monastic style of John and that this lifestyle was understood to be consistent with the tenor of his teachings as a whole. Consequently, since the ministry of Jesus was seen early on to function in tandem with that of John, for Jesus to accept feasting as opposed to fasting might have been a change worthy of note.

In the context of Jesus' ministry as we might reasonably imagine it, such actions would not likely be able to convey the offering of "his kingdom" to those with whom he dined, for then he would have to be one who actually hosted all of the banquets he attended. That would make him much more stationary a figure, namely, a homeowner, than we normally picture him to be. Rather, the meaning conveyed by Jesus' partaking of banquets would be that of one who, in contrast to John, existed in the urban world and affirmed that world.[68] Indeed, it is not too big a jump to see Jesus' preference for the urban world developing into the idea that he preferred the company of inappropriate people. Out of this context at some point the label "glutton and drunkard, friend [table companion] of tax collectors and sinners" could easily have developed. But it is a characterization that develops later, in the context of storytelling about Jesus.

It is in the Gospel narratives that the *chreia* traditions that characterize Jesus as a hero at table receive complex theological elaborations. Indeed, each Gospel writer takes this tradition and reworks it to fit his own theological agenda. In doing so, they provide evidence of the lively nature of the literary motif of the banquet. That is to say, each of them recognizes and is attracted to the powerful message to be found in this image, and each has the tools to expand on it out of the symbols already operative in their literary heritage. In the analyses that follow, I will give special attention to Mark and Luke as examples of the wide and complex use of the literary motif of the banquet. These two studies should be sufficient to establish the common patterns in the use of this motif.[69] I will conclude this section with brief comments on Matthew and John that will be suggestive of the patterns to be found in those Gospels.

THE BANQUET OF THE KING: MEAL AND IRONY IN MARK

In Mark's story of Jesus, Jesus dies as a king, but in an ironic mode.[70] The same is true of the meal scenes in Mark. When Jesus dines, since he is a king, he dines as a king. But only in an ironic mode. This is one of many instances in Mark where irony is essential to Mark's plot.[71] Theologically, irony in Mark connects with the apocalyptic emphasis.[72] Thus the other side of the ironic event, its "real" meaning as opposed to its apparent meaning, tends to be in the realm of apocalyptic. In relation to banquet imagery, this means that Mark works with an implicit model of the apocalyptic or messianic banquet.

The importance of the meal scenes in Mark has only recently begun to be noticed. Usually they have been related to other programs of analysis but have not been given extensive attention on their own.[73] Lee Klosinski's 1988 study, "The Meals in Mark," however, has now provided a preliminary presentation of the parameters of the data and has brought to our attention ways in which meals relate to significant themes in Mark.[74]

The primary meal scenes are well known. They include the meal with tax collectors and sinners at Levi's house (2:15-17), the two miraculous feeding stories (6:30-44; 8:1-9), the anointing at Bethany (14:3-9), and the Last Supper (14:12-25). There is also one actual banquet of a king in Mark's story, namely, the infamous banquet of Herod at which John is beheaded (6:21-29). In addition, there are numerous controversy stories in which Jesus disagrees with the scribes and Pharisees over eating customs, namely, in regard to dietary laws (2:23-28; 7:1-23) and fasting (2:18-22).

Each of the banquet scenes in Mark makes specific reference to the fact that the diners recline: at Levi's house (2:15), at Simon's house (14:3), in the "upstairs room" (14:15, 18), and, of course, at Herod's banquet (6:22, 26). In addition, when Jesus hosts the miraculous meals outdoors, they become reclining banquets as well (6:39, 40; 8:6).[75] Thus Mark consistently envisions these meal scenes as formal, luxurious banquets.

How much he knows about such banquets is another question, for he does not seem nearly as well read in symposium literature as is Luke, for example.[76] Yet he has a significant repertoire of meal traditions and motifs with which to work. Thus the Last Supper of Jesus has the traditional order of courses, *deipnon* followed by symposium, including the tradition of offering a prayer before each course (14:22-23).[77] When Jesus dines with Simon the leper, the motif of the servant anointing the guest of honor becomes the centerpiece of the story (14:3-9). And in Mark's picture of the banquet of Herod, he utilizes the motif of the rash, drunken king (6:21-28). These are but a few examples of Mark's rich sense for the basics of meal symbolism. Further examples will be given in the discussion below. And, although explicit references are rare, his understanding and appreciation of the messianic banquet motif will also prove to be quite significant.

Social Boundaries

When Jesus attends a meal in Mark, he is always the host, except in one instance when he is guest of honor at the home of Simon the leper in Bethany (14:3-9). The meals that Jesus hosts are consistently viewed in contrast to meals of his opponents. Thus, unlike the meals of the scribes and Pharisees, Jesus dines with tax collectors and sinners (2:15-17) and with a leper (14:3). Though the allusion is only a metaphorical one, he also does not rule out the presence of Gentiles at his table (7:28). Contrary to the customs of the scribes and Pharisees, he and his disciples pluck grain on the Sabbath (2:23-28), eat with unclean hands (7:1-8), disregard the dietary laws (7:14-23), and feast instead of fast (2:18-22).

The imagery is of two worlds, one where the banquets of Jesus are held, and the other where the banquets of his opponents are held. In the world of Jesus, unclean people and outcasts are welcome at the table, and dietary laws are abolished. The contrast is vivid and deliberate. For example, it is the Pharisees who appear like a Greek chorus and complain to his disciples about Jesus' eating with tax collectors and sinners (2:16).[78] This pericope is interwoven with the following pericopes in which the emphasis throughout is on Jesus' conflict with the Pharisees (2:1-3:6).[79] Included are other references to the different worlds of their meals: unlike the Pharisees, Jesus' disciples do not fast (2:18-22); contrary to the practice of the Pharisees, Jesus' disciples can gather food on the Sabbath (2:23-28) just as Jesus can heal on the Sabbath (3:1-6).

Jesus can break the Sabbath law because he is "lord of the Sabbath" (2:28). That is to say, in his world Jesus is king, though in an ironic sense. In the other world, Herod is king. "Give to the emperor the things that are the emperor's, and to God the things that are God's," Jesus says (12:17), thus indicating the division between the two realms. So it is that the banquet of Herod, at which he reclines together with his royal guests (*synanakeisthai*, 6:22) in the splendor of his palace (6:21-29), is intentionally placed in juxtaposition to the banquet of Jesus, at which he commands his guests to recline (*anaklinai, anapiptai,* 6:39, 40) in "a deserted place" (6:34-44).[80] These two images contrast further in that it is at Herod's banquet that John dies. So also when Jesus enters the world of Herod, though not specifically in a banquet setting, he too will die.

The world of Jesus is simply on a different plane; it partakes of the realities of the apocalyptic age. It is as the apocalyptic one, "the Son of Man," that Jesus is "lord of the Sabbath," the one who can break Sabbath laws and dietary laws. His disciples do not fast because they partake of the new age; they have "the bridegroom with them" (2:19). Jesus in effect offers the messianic banquet to those he invites to his table.[81] People come to his table from the ends of the earth: "Then he will send out the angels, and gather his elect from the four winds, from the ends of the earth to the ends of heaven" (13:27). This echoes the messianic banquet text in Isa 25:6-8:

> On this mountain the Lord of hosts will make for all peoples a feast of rich food, a feast of well-aged wines, of rich food filled with marrow, of well-aged wines strained clear. And he will destroy on this mountain the shroud that is cast over all peoples, the sheet that is spread over all nations; he will swallow up death for ever. Then the Lord God will wipe away the tears from all faces, and the disgrace of his people he will take away from all the earth; for the Lord has spoken.

So also at Jesus' table the banquet invitation doubles as a call to salvation. Thus Jesus justifies dining with tax collectors and sinners with the explanation: "I have come to call [invite; *kalein*] not the righteous but sinners" (2:17).

This dualistic perspective of Mark's story also defines the world of the disciples. It is they who were being called (or "invited") to Jesus' banquet. That call is a difficult one, so Jesus often has to prod them: "beware of the yeast of the Pharisees and the yeast of Herod" (8:15). The two banquet choices, either Jesus' or that of the Pharisees and Herod, represent the boundary divisions between the world of Jesus and the world of Herod. As this conflict is being played out in the story world of Mark, it echoes the conflicts within which Mark's community is living.

Social Bonding

Discipleship has often been recognized as a major theme in Mark. The importance of the banquet imagery in developing this theme has not always been given sufficient emphasis, however. First it should be noted that one of the primary ways in which boundary divisions and community identity were indicated was through the banquet. Certainly a primary way in which disciples are identified is as those who "follow" Jesus (1:16-20; 2:14; 10:52).[82] But when Mark wants to develop the image of a community gathered around Jesus, he utilizes most frequently the banquet motif. In doing so, he is drawing on the potent symbolism of the banquet as a sign of social bonding.

Thus when Jesus extends a general "call" to discipleship, it is by means of sharing food at the table (2:15-17). When by a single image Mark wants to designate that the crowd that follows Jesus has become a community, he does so with the banquet stories that we know as the miraculous feeding stories (6:30-44; 8:1-9). When the disciples gather as a community for the last two times before Jesus dies, it is at banquets (14:3-9; 14:12-25). By the time the disciples have accompanied Jesus to the garden, their numbers have already begun to dwindle.

A central image for social bonding used by Mark is one that is widespread in the culture. It is the image of sharing food together, most specifically sharing bread together. Whom you share bread with defines what group you are part of; thus the disciples are to avoid the "yeast of the Pharisees and of Herod" (8:15). Sharing discipleship with Jesus is defined not only as "taking up the cross" as Jesus did (8:34) but also as "drinking the cup" that Jesus drank (10:38-39). At the Last Supper, it is especially significant that the one who betrayed was the one who shared bread with Jesus (14:20). He is not alone, however, for all of the disciples share bread with Jesus (14:22), and they all eventually fall away. The stark contrast between sharing bread with Jesus and denying Jesus presents a strong message about discipleship in the face of persecution, one of the primary themes of Mark.

Social Obligation

Community formation represented by social bonding at the meal carries with it a sense of social obligation of the members to one another. This imagery is utilized by Mark in some of his most important sections on community ethics.

The overriding idea is that at the banquets of Jesus, where a new community is formed, new ideals consistent with the new age are present. The idea of a new age is symbolized by the connection of the banquet of Jesus with the abolition of dietary laws and the invitation of "the nations" and the unclean to the messianic banquet. So also the values of this new community are different from those of the earthly king:

> So Jesus called them and said to them, "You know that among the Gentiles those whom they recognize as their rulers lord it over them, and their great ones are tyrants over them. But it is not so among you; but whoever wishes to become great among you must

be your servant, and whoever wishes to be first among you must
be slave of all." (10:42-44)

Two different Greek terms are utilized here to refer to servanthood, *diakonos*
("servant") and *doulos* ("slave"). The term *diakonos* is a technical term for
table service, so it has often been proposed that that is the meaning here.
That this is Mark's preferred meaning for the term is especially indicated in
the story of the healing of Peter's mother-in-law:

> As soon as they left the synagogue, they entered the house of Simon and
> Andrew, with James and John. Now Simon's mother-in-law was in bed
> with a fever, and they told him about her at once. He came and took her
> by the hand and lifted her up. Then the fever left her, and she began to
> serve them. (1:29-31)

Here the term for *serve (diakonein)* is the verbal form of the term for *servant*
(diakonos). It is clearly table service that is meant here, since hospitality is
offered in the context of a household.

This text has a broader context of meaning in Mark than simply an incidental reference to what some might consider "women's work." Rather,
Simon's mother-in-law is presented as a model disciple, for her response to
the healing parallels the response of others elsewhere in Mark. Where they
are said to "follow," she is said to "serve." The significance is the same, but in
this case there is a further parallel to the teachings about servanthood in the
community in 10:42-44. What she exhibits, in fact, is an acting out of what
Jesus teaches to the disciples, who incidentally do not get the point, in 10:42-
44. Her story offers an instance of a case where a woman responds to Jesus
with true discipleship while the inner circle of disciples still struggles to
understand.

The same idea is present in the anointing story at 14:3-9. Here also, in
contrast to the male disciples, a woman disciple exhibits true discipleship,
primarily through her insight into the identity of Jesus. It is notable that here
true discipleship is indicated by the action of actual "table service," for in
anointing Jesus she does what a servant would normally do for the guests at
the banquet. This story, however, is so overladen with the symbolism of Jesus'
forthcoming death that its force as an example of servanthood to other members of the community has been muted. There are two occasions, by the way,
when the disciples do take the role of table servants, namely, in the two stories of the feeding of the multitudes (6:41, 8:6).

Table service, then, is presented as the dominant model for service to the community. One form this takes in Mark is in reference to hospitality. To the ancients "hospitality," which was represented as providing a meal to guests or strangers, was seen as a primary form of honoring one's neighbors. To provide hospitality was, in the social code of the banquet, to offer to them a place in one's social world, whether it be in one's family or one's community or one's polis. In Mark's story the offering of hospitality refers to the offering of community membership to the other. Within that framework are included other aspects of "serving" the needs of the other through sharing community with them.

Hospitality is the ethic practiced by Jesus on those occasions when the crowds follow him into the desert, where there is no food. Rather than sending them away to find food on their own, he provides it for them, thus proving himself to be a hospitable host as well as their benefactor. Hospitality is also the mode whereby the community is established. When Jesus invites tax collectors and sinners to his table, he is thereby extending hospitality to them (2:15-17).

Also connected with this theme is the story of the sending out of the disciples. Jesus instructs that they are to take no food nor other means of support (6:8-9). They therefore demand hospitality of the people in the cities they encounter, as a sign of their commitment to the kingdom: "Wherever you enter a house, stay there until you leave the place. If any place will not welcome you and they refuse to hear you, as you leave, shake off the dust that is on your feet as a testimony against them" (6:10-11). The terminology here clearly refers to the idea of hospitality. In the context of Mark, the situation whereby hospitality would be refused is not hard to envision. The disciples are unclean; consequently, those who practice the dietary laws would not offer them hospitality. This text therefore maintains a consistent reference to the plot of Mark: those opposed to the community of Jesus are those of "the yeast of the Pharisees and of Herod" (8:15). This point is made with stark emphasis at 9:40-41: "Whoever is not against us is for us. For truly I tell you, whoever gives you a cup of water to drink because you bear the name of Christ will by no means lose the reward." This text should be read not as a general reference to hospitality but as a reference to a specific issue, namely, the issue of table fellowship as a marker of the boundary between the community of Jesus and the community of "the yeast of the Pharisees and of Herod."[83]

The text at 10:42-44 is troublesome, however, because it seems to introduce the imagery of table service in a context in which other metaphors had been at work. Here the request of the disciples envisions the image of the throne room of the court rather than that of the banquet table ("Grant us to sit, one at your right hand and one at your left, in your glory," 10:37). The same can be said for the dominant image in the phrase "their rulers lord it over them, and their great ones are tyrants over them" (10:42), although in this case the imagery could work equally well at the banquet table.

What turns the tide is the occurrence of the phrase "table servant" at 10:43 ("Whoever wishes to be great among you must be your servant"). While this term does not necessarily have to refer to the table, it commonly does, and, as has been pointed out, it is so used elsewhere in Mark. What makes this point even stronger, however, is the cumulative effect of the argument I have been presenting to this point. When one considers the integral role in Mark's overall plot that is played by the symbolism of the banquet, then what would appear to be an isolated reference to table service is isolated no longer. It rather emerges as consistent with one of the dominant images for the community of Jesus' followers.

But what then does one do with the reference to court rather than banquet room at 10:37 ("Grant us to sit, one at your right hand and one at your left, in your glory")? While it is possible that the phrase "in your glory" is a reference to the messianic banquet,[84] I do not think that is its primary meaning. The emphasis here on "sitting" *(kathizein)* rather than "reclining" seems to me to represent an image of throne rather than banquet couch. This is consistent with the overall point, since the emphasis is on an image of rule and authority.

Jesus responds by presenting two counter-images referring to servanthood (10:43-44). One could be seen to be operative within the metaphorical world of the throne; rather than seeking to be "king," one is to seek to be "slave" *(doulos)*. The other figure presented by Jesus, that of "table servant" *(diakonos),* then injects a parallel image to that of the throne—namely, that of the banquet table of the king. Here one is likewise to seek not to be the guest of honor at the table but to be table servant.[85] This is in contrast to the other order of meals, that of the "yeast of the Pharisees and of Herod" (8:15), for in their world "the scribes . . . like . . . to have the best seats in the synagogues and places of honor at banquets" (12:38-39). Thus we have come full circle, and court and banquet table have been collapsed. It is at this point that one could say that a secondary meaning of "in your glory" (10:37) could then be as a reference to the messianic banquet. Indeed, we will find that court and banquet table are brought together in other aspects of Mark's plot as well.

Jesus' saying at 10:45 takes still another turn, however: "For the Son of Man came not to be served but to serve, and to give his life a ransom for many." Here he applies the table servant imagery to himself. He is to be a servant at the table, he says. Yet in none of the meals presented in Mark does Jesus take the role of servant. Nor does it seem appropriate, since he is the king at his banquets. In addition, in acting out the role of servant, he will give his life as a "ransom for many." This is not a normal action of a table servant. Yet the saying is presented with such sparseness and conciseness that it must have aroused the proper imagery in the minds of Mark's readers. What kind of table servant gives his life as a ransom? What traditional story motif is being referred to? In order to unpack this image, we must look more closely at the intricacies of the banquet imagery in the plot of Mark.

Banquet and Plot in Mark

Mark has been characterized as an "apocalyptic drama" and as a "myth of innocence."[86] What is being recognized in these characterizations is that the story Mark presents has a level of meaning that goes beyond a tracing of history, whether that history is presumed to be the history of Jesus or the history of the Markan community. Rather, Mark is presenting a story that sets forth a mythological framework for the self-understanding of his community.

The genre for this story is defined by Burton Mack, following George Nickelsburg, as that of "the wisdom story of the persecution and vindication of the righteous one."[87] It is a model derived from Hellenistic Jewish martyrology literature.

A significant indicator of this imagery is the definition of the death of Jesus given at 10:45: "For the Son of Man came not to be served but to serve, and to give his life a ransom [lytron] for many." Several themes in Mark converge at this point. Here we are specifically concerned with the apocalyptic figure, the "Son of Man." Jesus has presided at several tables to this point in Mark's story and has always functioned as host. Indeed, these banquets have had strong overtones of the messianic banquet. Now, however, a banquet is envisioned in which Jesus will be servant rather than host. Furthermore, at this banquet he will die as well. The imagery seems to be a "banquet" on a different plane from those he has attended to this point. At a command appearance in the world of Herod and the Pharisees, Jesus will, indeed, no longer be host nor even welcome guest. In effect, he will become as a slave. And there he will die as a "ransom."

A close parallel to this text in Jewish martyrological literature is found in 4 Macc 17:20-22:

> These, then, who have been consecrated for the sake of God, are hon-
> ored, not only with this honor, but also by the fact that because of them
> our enemies did not rule over our nation, the tyrant was punished, and
> the homeland purified—they having become, as it were, a ransom for
> the sin of our nation. And through the blood of those devout ones and
> their death as an atoning sacrifice, divine Providence preserved Israel
> that previously had been mistreated.

Here the term translated "ransom" in the NRSV is a different Greek term from
that in the text of Mark. But the context and meaning are similar.

The term translated "ransom" in 4 Maccabees is *antipsychon,* a term that
literally means "given for life." Its only other occurrence in the LXX is also in
4 Maccabees, at 6:29, in a text that also has significant parallels to the concept of martyrdom presented in Mark. Here the dying Eleazar interprets the
meaning of his death with his last words, expressed in a prayer to God: "You
know, O God, that though I might have saved myself, I am dying in burning
torments for the sake of the law. Be merciful to your people, and let our punishment suffice for them. Make my blood their purification, and take my life
in exchange [*antipsychon*] for theirs" (6:27-29).

The context of the martyr story in 4 Maccabees has other similarities to
Mark. Significant among these is the trial scene before the king. In 4 Maccabees, like the trial scene in Mark, the setting is envisioned as somewhere
within the throne room of the king. In 4 Maccabees, the trial proceeds by the
interrogators continuing to ask the prisoners to eat defiled food. Consequently, though it is a trial, there are also overtones here of a banquet setting.

Other Jewish martyr stories that center on the keeping of the dietary laws
also have allusions to the banquet table of the king (see further chapter 6).
The irony is that in Mark Jesus takes this role as one who opposes rather than
defends the dietary laws. In Mark's perspective, it is because he is the "Son of
Man," an authoritative apocalyptic figure, that this all makes sense. As the
one who inaugurates the apocalyptic age, he begins a new age in human history. This new age is one in which the nations will come to Zion. Consequently, those laws that kept the nations away until now, namely, the dietary
laws, are to be overruled.

The dangers involved in table fellowship in the world of the Pharisees and
Herod are passed on to the disciples. Thus they, too, will suffer. They will
"take up the cross and follow" (8:34). Jesus predicts their fate in words that
defined realities in Mark's own community: "They will hand you over to
councils; and you will be beaten in synagogues; and you will stand before

governors and kings because of me, as a testimony to them" (13:9). The primary imagery here is the alien worlds of the synagogue and the throne room of the king. But table fellowship imagery functions in this rhetoric as well.

A climactic text for the theme of discipleship in Mark is the Last Supper text. Here is a turning point, the last time all of the twelve are together with Jesus. It is a moment in which the themes of community (social boundaries) and intimacy with Jesus (social bonding) are at their most intense level. Yet from this point all of the disciples one by one will fall away, beginning with Judas and ending with Peter.

According to Mark's plot, the meal is a Passover meal (14:1-2; 14:12-16). Yet Passover motifs and themes are not present in the actual description of the meal. Rather, that description centers on the special ceremony connected with the eating of bread and drinking of wine. This ceremony, like every other narrative segment of Mark, has its primary meaning in the story world of Mark as a whole. What the disciples and Jesus do here is to be understood as connecting with the plot as a whole.

First let us look at the theme of bread in Mark. I have already noted how bread and the sharing of bread in Mark operates as a boundary marker. On the one hand, there is the bread that comes from the banquet world of Jesus. On the other hand, there is the bread that comes from the banquet world of the opponents. The disciples are specifically warned to "beware of the yeast of the Pharisees and of Herod" (8:15). This symbolizes the banquet world of Jesus' opponents; to partake of their "yeast" means to be a part of their community. The reference to bread as "yeast" *(zymē),* which occurs only here in Mark, may be utilized so as to provide an intentional contrast with the Last Supper meal that Jesus will offer his disciples, a meal where "unleavened bread" *(azymos)* is eaten (14:1,12).

The banquet world of Jesus offers a contrasting call and contrasting values. The wine he offers is new wine; it thus must be contained in fresh wineskins (2:22). So also the bread he offers is compared with the holy "bread of the presence" (2:26). This allusion can be connected with the miraculous bread fed to the multitudes. To eat this bread is to eat that which is considered unlawful and unclean, but "the Son of Man" is "lord of the Sabbath" (2:28), and is worthy to eat the bread of the presence as well as to "declare all foods clean" (7:19).

These allusions connect the bread of Jesus with the numinous food of the messianic banquet. Its numinous qualities are not what Mark develops, however. The connection of eating bread with the gaining of apocalyptic life is not made. Rather, life is connected with the theme of martyrdom. Bread, on the other hand, is consistently connected with the defining of community boundaries. Thus it is the sharing of the "bread of the children" (*ho artos tōn teknōn,* 7:27) that is Jesus' image for the sharing of the blessings of the community in his conversation with the Syrophoenician woman. On the other hand, the disciples participate in the banquet world of Jesus not only by the bread they eat but by how they eat it: "Now when the Pharisees and some of the scribes who had come from Jerusalem gathered around him, they noticed that some of his disciples were eating bread with defiled hands, that is, without washing them. . . . So the Pharisees and the scribes asked him, 'Why do your disciples not live according to the tradition of the elders, but eat with defiled hands?'" (7:1-2,5).[88]

Throughout Mark's story, the disciples are caught between those two worlds. Thus the reference at 6:8 that they are to "take no bread" on their mission, while it alludes to the theme of hospitality in its immediate context, has a further connection to later themes in the story. We recall that text when later the disciples decry the fact that "they had no bread" (8:16) in response to Jesus' warning about the bread of his opponents. The same is true in the feeding stories, where they complain that they cannot respond to the needs of the people because they have no bread (6:37; 8:4). The latter text is especially weighty with symbolism: "How can one feed these people with bread here in the desert?" The desert is the world of Jesus, yet the bread they desire is from the world of the opponents. They desire earthly bread, but Jesus offers miraculous bread. It is not the quality of the bread but the community identity and commitment that are at stake. That is the meaning of all the miracles, that the new age has come. But the disciples miss the point of Jesus' miracles, and missing the point can be summarized in this way: "They did not understand about the loaves, but their hearts were hardened" (6:52).

At the Last Supper, then, these themes come to a head. The sharing of bread becomes a primary symbol for discipleship; thus the departure of Judas, the "one who is dipping bread into the bowl with me" (14:20), becomes a story of betrayal. That story is repeated by each of the disciples, for each of them share bread with Jesus, and each eventually falls away.

The words over the bread, "Take; this is my body" (14:22), need explanation within the context of Mark's story. The term *body* apparently has a single meaning in Mark; it is the term for a corpse or a physical body that will be a corpse (5:29, 6:29, 14:8, 15:43). Consequently, Jesus is clearly referring to his death. But it is not the efficacy of his death that is the referent, for it is not "body" (*sōma*) but "life" (*psychē*) that is given as a "ransom" (10:45).

Rather, it is the manner of death that must be meant. The sharing of bread with Jesus by the disciples, then, means uniting with him in discipleship and, eventually, sharing in his fate. Yet the disciples soon fall away. Clearly, they continue to manifest the problem first defined at 6:52: "They did not understand about the loaves, but their hearts were hardened."

A parallel theme is developed in regard to the cup at the Last Supper. It is woven into the important section in Mark 8–10, in which the theme of discipleship is especially developed.[89] The section begins with Peter's confession, which, in the plot of Mark, represents the first time that the disciples show any sign of recognizing the significance of Jesus (8:27-30). This is followed by three separate programmatic texts in which Jesus predicts his death, the disciples reject the idea, and a lesson about discipleship is drawn (8:31-38; 9:30-37; 10:32-45). In one case, discipleship is described as to "take up their cross and follow me" (8:34). In another case, it is described in these terms: "The cup that I drink you will drink; and with the baptism with which I am baptized, you will be baptized" (10:39). In both cases, the reference is to the model of the death of Jesus as the death of a martyr.[90] Thus when Jesus prays in the garden on the eve of his death, he prays, "remove this cup from me" (14:36).

Therefore, when the cup is related to the "blood of the covenant" at the Last Supper and it is specifically said, "all of them drank from it" (Mark 14:23-24), we are to understand that it is the cup of martyrdom that they drink. In the memory of the church, though not in the story world of Mark, that is exactly the fate that awaits the faithful disciples. Therefore, although Mark ends his story with the disciples having failed to "follow" Jesus, he embeds in the Last Supper story the promise that, eventually, they will.

Banquet in Story and Community

A continuing debate in scholarship is the extent to which the social realities of the community of Mark can be derived from the story of Jesus that he writes. The Last Supper text is a case in point. For years this has been considered a representation of the form of Lord's Supper liturgy utilized in the Markan community. This conclusion was based on the fact that there were obviously such liturgical traditions floating around, since Paul includes a similar one in his letter to the Corinthians (1 Cor 11:23-25). More recently in Markan scholarship, however, it has been noted that the Last Supper text is not presented in any different way from any other story of Jesus in Mark. In particular, it does not include any exhortation that this ritual be repeated by the community, as Paul's tradition does (1 Cor 11:24, 25).

This means first that the Last Supper pericope in Mark must be interpreted in the context of Mark's overall story. It also means that we cannot go directly from this story to conclusions about the ritual life of Mark's community. For example, if this is to be taken as a liturgical text, what sets it apart from other stories about Jesus in Mark? And how would it have functioned in actual liturgical practice? Answers to these questions are not readily available.

There is another means toward this end, however. As I have argued throughout this book, it was a regular practice of groups in the ancient world to celebrate ritual meals together at which their group identity would be established and celebrated. This is true whether the groups were Greco-Roman, Jewish, or Christian. The cumulative effect of this program of research is to suggest with a high degree of assurance that the Markan community would have celebrated community meals together. But what else can we say about these meals?

To deal with this question more fully, we need to rehearse some of the points that have been made in recent studies about the relation of the story of Mark to the community of Mark. Mack has especially made the point that the community's own social formation lies behind the perspective promoted by the "myth of innocence" presented herein.[91] The point is that there was in the Markan community an experience of estrangement from Jewish tradition, brought about especially by the inclusion of Gentiles in their community. This factor in their identity led to a split with local Jewish leaders, who raised once more the specter that Jewish covenantal identity was to be associated with ritual boundary markers such as dietary laws. The Jesus story Mark presents proposes another worldview, one that lays claim to Jewish tradition in the face of their repudiation of dietary laws by means of a clever apocalyptic interpretation.

An apocalyptic approach commended itself to them for another reason as well. They interpreted their situation as one of persecution; indeed, they may have been experiencing this on a real level. Their self-identity thus became attached to that of the apocalyptic myth, that is, that the persecution they were enduring was but a sign of the end, when the suffering righteous ones would be vindicated by God.

Meanwhile, their situation was causing some weakening of the faith among the members. Consequently, Mark's story of Jesus presents a "myth of origins" that creates a world in which discipleship is defined by persecution and martyrdom. To embrace martyrdom is to take the path Jesus took. Their discipleship was in effect to complete the story begun but not finished by the disciples in Mark's story.

This sketch of the correlations between the probable social situation of Mark's community and the story of Mark thus establishes a context from which to pose again the question as to the probable form of their community meals. After coming at the question from a different perspective, one is able to arrive at a fairly traditional point; namely, that the Last Supper text in Mark reflects in some way a proposal as to the ritual practice at the community meals of the Markan community.

Here it should be said that just as Mark proposes a particular and paraenetic reading of the life of Jesus, so also he is proposing something somehow new in regard to their meals together. How they were celebrated prior to the writing of his Gospel is not known. Nor is it known whether they followed the model presented here. But we can outline a form and interpretation proposed by this Gospel.

The meals of the Markan community as promoted by this Gospel would have given special emphasis to the sharing of bread and wine on the model of Jesus' Last Supper. Whether any of Jesus' words were repeated in a ritual format is not clear. But the focus of the ceremony would have been along the lines emphasized in the story. That is to say, like the Passover meal in Judaism, their meal would reenact a midpoint in a continuing story. Like the disciples who gathered with Jesus, the community would share bread and wine in a pledge to discipleship and to the covenant of martyrdom. That this idea is being urged on them so forcefully points up the fact that they must have faced such a severe social crisis that their lives were literally at stake because of the faith they professed (see also 13:9-13). The liturgy at the meal can therefore be seen to represent a ritual response to their specific social situation.

THE PHILOSOPHICAL BANQUET: MEAL SYMBOLISM IN LUKE

Luke, as scholars have often noted, was probably the most literary of all the Gospel writers. One of Luke's literary devices that has been alluded to in previous studies is his use of the symposium motif of "table talk," whereby Jesus teaches while at a meal. This was what the philosophers often did in ancient literature. Thus such instances in Luke, notably 7:36-50; 11:37-54; and 14:1-24, can be related to the symposium genre.[92] These are not the only instances, however, in which Luke enriches his Gospel story with references to meal symbolism. Indeed, as I will show, the motif of table fellowship is one of his favorite literary devices. His use of this motif may be classified under the following categories:

1. Social Stratification: Ranking at Table as a Symbol of Status

As already noted in previous chapters, it was common at any formal meal in a Greek or Roman setting to assign rankings to the positions at table. As a feature of custom and etiquette, it also came to be translated into a literary theme. This point was elaborated in more detail in chapter 3. Here it might be useful to summarize some of those points for ease of comparison with Luke's usage.

Note, for example, that in Plutarch's imaginative description of the symposium of the legendary seven sages, he describes a discussion on the custom of ranking (*The Dinner of the Seven Wise Men* [*Septem sapientium convivium*] 148F–149F). The issue arises because a guest feels insulted at the position he was offered. The sage Thales counsels acceptance of one's position at table no matter what it is, for "a man that objects to his place at table is objecting to his neighbor rather than to his host, and he makes himself hateful to both."[93] Following his own advice, Thales then asks to be placed at the offensive position himself.[94]

Similarly, in *Table Talk* Plutarch takes up the topic of places at table as a part of the philosophical discussion. On one occasion, the topic of discussion was "Why the place at banquets called the consul's acquired honor."[95] On another occasion, Plutarch and his tablemates discussed the issue "Whether the host should arrange the placing of his guests or leave it to the guests themselves."

This last instance is introduced with an interesting anecdote. Plutarch relates how at a meal given by his brother Timon it was decided to break with custom and allow the guests to recline wherever they wished. Unfortunately, whenever an especially distinguished guest arrived late and discovered that no place worthy of his honor remained at the table, he was insulted and left angrily.[96]

These stories provide a clear relationship to the parable of the places at table, a parable found only in Luke, and one that Luke places in a banquet setting. While Jesus is reclining at the table of a Pharisee, he teaches the assembled guests:

> When he noticed how the guests chose the places of honor, he told them a parable. "When you are invited by someone to a wedding banquet, do not recline [*kataklinein*][97] at the place of honor, in case someone more distinguished than you has been invited by your host; and the host who invited both of you may come and say to you, 'Give this person your place,' and then in disgrace you would start to take the lowest place. But

when you are invited, go and recline [*anapiptein*] at the lowest place, so that when your host comes, he may say to you, 'Friend, move up higher'; then you will be honored in the presence of all who recline with you [*synanakeisthai*].[98] For all who exalt themselves will be humbled, and those who humble themselves will be exalted. . . ." (Luke 14:7-11)

Notice how the parable functions to symbolize how rankings will be assigned in the kingdom by reference to a recognized custom in the culture. The custom is obviously well understood and taken for granted; otherwise the parable would not work.

There are clearly literary themes present here as well, as a comparison with the Plutarch texts discussed above will show. First, it should be noted that in both examples from Plutarch and in the example from Luke, the subject of the discourse is introduced with a brief anecdote relating to the actual choosing of positions by the participants. Second, in both Luke and Plutarch's *Table Talk* the discussion centers on the motif of the late-arriving guest whose proper position at table has already been taken. Third, in all three examples the discussion then goes on to question the custom of ranking on the basis of other criteria derived from table fellowship ethics.

In Plutarch, the custom becomes the subject of the philosophical discussion of the evening. The diners debate the pros and cons of ranking at table. Their arguments are stated in terms of the traditional ethical categories that are often brought to play in popular philosophical discussions of ethics and etiquette at a meal. Thus one diner argues for the custom of ranking on the grounds that it is a mark of good order and good order is necessary for a pleasurable banquet. In this case, pleasure is the standard by which behavior at the banquet is to be judged.[99] Another diner argues that the custom should be abolished on the grounds that equality at the meal would enhance the "friendship" essential for the proper banquet.[100] Here friendship is the proper category for defining ethics at the table. The ethic of friendship is also implied by the statement of Thales quoted above that Plutarch attributes to Thales at the "Dinner of the Seven Wise Men." Indeed, friendship and pleasure are two of the most common ethical categories in the traditional philosophical discussions of ethics (or etiquette) at the table.[101]

To this may be compared Luke's emphasis. Here also the issue of ranking is resolved by reference to an ethical principle. To be sure, the principle is not the philosophical virtue, friendship, but rather is the "biblical" virtue, humility.[102] Yet, though the principles differ, the motifs are virtually the same.

Thus Luke utilizes literary motifs that are similar to those found in Plutarch. To be sure, Luke's relationship to Plutarch should not be overemphasized. Luke is clearly not writing a philosophical dialogue, nor is it probable that he is relying on Plutarch for his images. Rather, the similarities in the accounts of the two authors suggest that both are utilizing a literary motif that derives from popular literature in general and symposium traditions in particular.[103]

Luke makes another reference to the custom of ranking at table when he makes what appears to be an editorial revision in his source, which I take to be Mark. In Mark 10:35-45, the disciples James and John request of Jesus to be assigned positions of honor in the future kingdom: "Grant us to sit, one at your right hand and one at your left, in your glory" (10:37). The context is the travel section of Mark, so this request is made "on the road, going up to Jerusalem" (10:32). Luke utilizes much of Mark's travel section, including another pericope on ranking in the kingdom (Luke 9:46-48; Mark 9:33-37). But he moves this pericope on ranking in the kingdom (Mark 10:35-45) to another context: the setting of the Last Supper.

Thus, in Luke it is while the disciples are reclining at table, in a setting in which relative status is an ever-present reality, that the question concerning the ranking of the disciples in the kingdom comes up again: "A dispute also arose among them as to which one of them was to be regarded as the greatest" (Luke 22:24; see vv. 24-27 for the parallel to Mark). The question and Jesus' response are given added impact by the literary device of placing them in the meal setting.[104]

2. Social Bonding: Table Talk as a Mode of Teaching

Another prominent feature of symposium literature was its use of the table as a setting for philosophical discourse. The tradition derives especially from Plato's *Symposium,* in which the symposium becomes the setting for a philosophical discussion on "love" *(erōs).* The introduction to this discussion becomes a classic statement for the genre: "I [Eryximachus] next propose that the flute-girl who came in just now be dismissed. . . . Let us seek our entertainment today in conversation."[105] Thus Athenaeus could refer to philosophical banquets as characterized not by "intemperance" but by "decency and refinement,"[106] thereby referring to a tradition that these banquets place an emphasis on enlightened conversation.

As a corollary of this tradition, there developed the idea that certain topics or a certain form of speech was more appropriate for the table setting.[107]

Thus Plutarch describes his view of proper symposium conversation in this way: "Therefore subjects of discourse, like friends, should be admitted to dinners only if they are of proved quality."[108] He devotes several discussions to the theme of proper topics for symposium discussions. Among these topics are those described as "concerned with the proper business of drinking parties."[109] Included under this topic are discussions of the meal itself, such as meal etiquette, discourses on the types of food eaten, discourses on proper ethics at the table or the "friend-making" character of the meal, and so on.[110]

This tradition is clearly echoed in Luke's chapter 14, which begins with Jesus' being invited to a banquet in the house of a Pharisee. Much of the rest of the chapter is thus concerned with things that were said at table. The chapter is made up of a collection of sayings of Jesus about banquets, including the parable of the places at table (14:7-11), the parable of the banquet invitations (14:12-14), and the parable of the great banquet (14:15-24). Each of these pericopes uses the symbolism of the banquet to present a different teaching. All are tied together by the context as well; this is given emphasis by continual references to the table setting in the introductions to each pericope (14:7,12,14).

Thus chapter 14 is a highly structured literary unit with clear reference to the symposium genre. This point has been made in a study by X. de Meeûs.[111] He points out, for example, the structured nature of the chapter. That is, Jesus addresses successively the group of guests as a whole (14:7), the master of the house (14:12), and one of the guests who asks a question (14:15). These give the chapter a dialogue style similar to that of the symposium genre.[112] In addition, Luke includes characters that are typically included in the genre: the master of the house, the guest of honor and main speaker, the invited guests (14:7), and the uninvited (14:13, 24, 25; 15:1-2).[113]

Furthermore, de Meeûs notes how the underlying conflict that is present in Luke's account parallels the structure of Plato's *Symposium*. In Luke 14, one can argue that the participants at the meal are all Pharisees, taking the phrase "they were watching him closely" (14:1) to be referring to the Pharisees, who were also the participants. Thus one theme of the symposium section as a whole is the conflict between Jesus and the Pharisees. This is taken by de Meeûs to parallel the underlying conflict between Socrates and the Sophists that he finds to be present in the *Symposium*.[114] Thus the chapter begins with a Sabbath controversy (14:1-6). Then it moves to a contrast between the pride of the Pharisees versus the humility of Jesus (14:7-11). Next is the contrast between the community of the Pharisees and the community of Jesus (14:12-14; cf. 15:1-2). Then there is a contrast between the invited and the uninvited (14:15-24).[115]

But while chapter 14 is clearly related to the motif of philosophical table talk, it is not the only instance in Luke where such a reference is found. Indeed, Jesus often teaches while at table in Luke's Gospel.[116] Thus, in a passage derived from Mark, Jesus dines in the house of Levi the tax collector and, when he is criticized for eating with tax collectors and sinners, replies, "Those who are well have no need of a physician, but those who are sick; I have come to call not the righteous but sinners to repentance" (5:29-32). In a later passage that echoes this one, and that is found only in Luke, Jesus dines at the house of Simon the Pharisee, and, in response to the woman who washes his feet, teaches the parable of the two debtors (7:36-50). In 10:38-42, another passage found only in Luke, Jesus teaches in the house of Martha while Martha "serves"; the reference appears to be to service at a meal.[117]

In 11:37-41 Luke revises the reference in Mark that has Jesus and his disciples eating without first washing to include the reference that Jesus was dining in the house of a Pharisee. Thus the teachings that follow and that include a collection of sayings against the Pharisees are placed in the setting of a meal and, by means of this literary device, are tied together. Indeed, this entire section (11:37-54) can be shown to have been written according to the pattern of the symposium genre, much like chapter 14 as mentioned above.[118]

Finally, Luke has an extended section of teachings of Jesus at table on the occasion of the Last Supper (22:14-38). One of these has already been mentioned: the teaching to the disciples as to who will be the greatest in the kingdom. Other pericopes in this context also allude to the table fellowship theme, including 22:15-23 and 22:28-30. Of the four Gospels, only John has a longer section on the teachings of Jesus at table at the Last Supper (John 13–17).

3. The Idealized Model: Eating and Drinking as a Symbol of Luxury

Eating and drinking in a banquet setting in which one reclined and ate and drank at a leisurely pace took on in a very early period the sense of an activity symbolizing the life of luxury. As noted in chapter 2, this point has been brought to light especially by the studies of Jean-Marie Dentzer.[119] Dentzer points out how, from the beginning of its introduction as a custom in the Greek world, reclining carried with it the aura of royal luxury.

The upper-class imagery is carried out in the actual practices connected with the custom. For besides the accoutrements of luxurious pillows and couches, elaborate foods, and servants, those who banqueted were reminded of their standing in society by the fact that they reclined; for custom dictated that only free citizens were to recline; women, children, and slaves were to sit when they ate.

Luxury as a Negative Symbol

The image of luxury was often applied in a negative sense in literature throughout the Greco-Roman world. In Jewish literature, for example, the eighth-century-B.C.E. text from Amos contains a critique of the luxurious banquet of the wealthy utilizing the symbols of the banquet as evidence. Thus he decries their reclining "on beds of ivory," singing "idle songs to the sound of the harp," "drinking wine from bowls," and "anointing themselves with the finest oils" (6:4-7). Since Jewish tradition is not at all opposed to bountiful feasts, the reference here is clearly a motif utilized to characterize and criticize the wealthy.

Similarly, in Greek and Roman literature the luxury of the banquet was often used as a negative symbol. This was especially true in the tradition of satire. Indeed, one of the favorite devices of the satirist for criticizing society was the banquet. The typical form is illustrated by the banquet of Nasidienus described by the satirist Horace. The theme of the description is a critique of the excesses and bad taste of the newly rich as exhibited in the menu and other trappings of the banquet.[120] A similar theme is taken up by Petronius in the famous "Banquet of Trimalchio" section of his *Satyricon*. Here the freedman Trimalchio reaches a new low in vulgarity and boorishness with his exhibitions of excessive gluttony, drunkenness, and other forms of extreme behavior.[121]

This literary theme is echoed by Luke in a multitude of references to the negative imagery of the luxurious banquet. In general, these references tend to have eschatological overtones. Thus the luxurious meal functions as a symbol for the debauchery of "this age," which is due to be condemned in the future judgment. These texts thus function both as a warning and as an assurance to the faithful. They are assured that those who feast luxuriously now will eventually be judged, and they are warned lest they fall into the same trap.

Examples for this theme can be found in a number of parables. The parable of the rich fool in Luke 12:16-21 (a parable found elsewhere only in *Gospel of Thomas* 63, but without the meal imagery) uses the following terminology to describe the self-satisfaction of the rich man who had stored up huge amounts of food in his barns: "Soul, you have ample goods laid up for many years; relax, eat, drink, be merry" (v. 19).[122] The parable of the servant entrusted with supervision in Luke 12:42-46 (a parable also found in Q; see Matt 24:45-51) describes the faithlessness of the servant who has been set over the household with these words: "But if that slave says to himself, 'My master is delayed in coming,' and if he begins to beat the other slaves, men and women, and to eat and drink and get drunk, the master of that slave will come on a day when he does not expect him and at an hour that he does not know, and will cut him in pieces, and put him with the unfaithful" (Luke 12:45-46).

Besides parables, references to the negative imagery of the meal also occur in Luke's Gospel in the context of the general apocalyptic preaching of Jesus. For example, in Luke 17:26-29 (a Q text; see also Matt 24:37-39), the dissolute living that characterizes the "days of the Son of man" is described with meal symbolism: "They were eating and drinking . . ." (17:27,28). In another instance of eschatological preaching, in a text found only in Luke, a similar theme is presented: "Be on guard so that your hearts are not weighed down with dissipation and drunkenness and the worries of this life, and that day catch you unexpectedly" (Luke 21:34). Similarly, in Luke's sermon on the plain, those who "are rich . . . full . . . laughing . . . well spoken of" are singled out for the judgmental "woes" (Luke 6:24-25).

A showcase for this theme is perhaps Luke's parable of the rich man and Lazarus (Luke 16:19-31). Here one may note that the characteristic of the rich man, like the rich fool or those in the days of Noah or those characterized by Jesus' apocalyptic preaching elsewhere in Luke, is that he not only "was dressed in purple and fine linen" but also "feasted sumptuously every day" (v. 19).[123] And how does Lazarus differ? Lazarus "longed to satisfy his hunger with what fell from the rich man's table" (v. 21). Here we find a connection with our next theme. For when the situations of the two are reversed, this fact is illustrated by using the reverse of the same imagery. Lazarus, who hungered in earthly life, now rests on "Abraham's bosom" in the afterlife. Clearly this is a reference to a banquet scene in which the banqueters recline and thus rest on the bosom of the diner to their left. Lazarus is said to be on the bosom of Abraham in order to indicate that he is to the right of the host, Abraham, and therefore in a position of honor. The image is that of a sumptuous banquet, a potent image for the joys of heaven.[124] The rich man, meanwhile, in a true reversal of situations, begs for a single drop of water.

Thus here we have an example of the luxury of the banquet used in two different ways. In one case, it refers to a critique of riches and of a dissolute earthly life; in another case, it refers in a positive sense to the blessings of heaven. The latter is the well-known image of the messianic banquet, which, in fact, is another favorite image of Luke's. Indeed, the parallelism with the potent messianic banquet theme, as is illustrated by the parable of the rich man and Lazarus, may explain why Luke emphasized meal imagery in his depiction of the sins of this age.

The Luxury of the Banquet as a Positive Symbol

In apocalyptic literature, the theme of the messianic banquet, or the eschatological banquet, appears to be a widespread symbol used to refer to the joys of the new age.[125] When we come to Luke's Gospel, we find the image of the messianic banquet well established, without any need for Luke to explain it. It is obviously a part of the tradition Luke is using, and it is obviously well understood by Luke and his readers. Yet there is more than just a recording of traditional sayings on this subject in Luke. The theme is much too widespread and central to the focus of his Gospel. Indeed, it is apparent that Luke has incorporated this theme into his own theological enterprise and given it his own interpretations and emphases.

Besides the reference already mentioned in Luke's parable of the rich man and Lazarus, there are other specific references to the messianic banquet that are found only in Luke. For example, the introduction to the parable of the great banquet is clearly redactional. Here a guest at table is made to remark: "Blessed is anyone who will eat bread in the kingdom of God" (Luke 14:15). The parable given in response is clearly referring to the theme of the messianic banquet, so the introduction is not necessary for understanding it. Rather, this introduction serves to situate the parable in its literary context, and thereby the theme of the messianic banquet is correlated with the other meal references in this chapter. One may assume, then, that Jesus' meal with Pharisees in chapter 14 is being correlated with the themes of the parable. This is made even clearer in the context when the Pharisees note Jesus' normal preference for "tax collectors and sinners" at his table (15:1-2), a group that is obviously parallel to the group highlighted in the parable, namely, "the poor, the crippled, the blind, and the lame" (14:21).

Furthermore, the introduction serves as an effective counterpoint for the symbolic thrust of the parable, for the parable serves to emphasize not only the joys of those who will share the messianic banquet but also the theme of judgment: not everyone originally invited will eventually share the feast. In this regard, it serves as another variation of the divine reversal theme found also in the parable of the rich man and Lazarus (Luke 16:19-31). And it serves to enhance the judgment of the Pharisees that is implicit in both parables in their respective contexts.

In a similar way, another text from Q also functions in a judgment context:

> But he will say, "I do not know where you come from; go away from me, all you evildoers!" There will be weeping and gnashing of teeth when you see Abraham and Isaac and Jacob and all the prophets in the kingdom of God, and you yourselves thrown out. Then people will come from east and west, from north and south, and will recline [*anaklinein*][126] in the kingdom of God. Indeed, some are last who will be first, and some are first who will be last." (Luke 13:27-30)

This text, by the way, is placed by Luke at the conclusion of the parables of the narrow door and the closed door (13:23-26). Thus those who are locked out and who complain that they ate and drank in the presence of the door-keeper or Messiah (13:26) are told that others will take their place at the eschatological table. This undoubtedly correlates with the literary tendency in Luke to have Jesus dine quite often at the table of a Pharisee. Thus the condemnation of the Pharisees is indicated here, as it is in numerous other table fellowship references. Indeed, rather than the Pharisees, it is the disciples of Jesus who are told, as they share the last meal with Jesus, that they will "eat and drink at my table in my kingdom, and . . . sit on thrones judging the twelve tribes of Israel" (Luke 22:30).

It is at the Last Supper that the messianic banquet theme is given special prominence in Luke. Indeed, the entire Last Supper pericope shows signs of extensive editing by the author. This is evident not only in his unusual version of the meal itself (22:14-19a) but also in the extended "table talk" of Jesus during the meal (22:21-38).[127]

Luke's unusual version of the Last Supper has presented problems since earliest times, but it appears that the author had a reason for depicting it as he did. Here in 22:15-19a he has expanded on the Passover theme, reversed the order of cup and bread, and adapted and expanded the eschatological reference of Mark 14:25 so that it becomes his only interpretation of the meal (22:16,18). This interpretation makes this meal serve as another representation of the overall theme of table fellowship with Jesus in Luke, since the eschatological theme underlies most of these references. Thus the Last Supper of Jesus does not function as an isolated reference in Luke but as a final, and perhaps archetypal, example of a motif that has been developed throughout the Gospel. Indeed, since Luke's unique version of the meal at 22:15-19a coordinates so well with the meal themes and literary plan of Luke-Acts as a whole, it seems more likely that this so-called short version of his Eucharistic text, which is especially evidenced in the Western tradition of manuscripts, is more authentic than the long version (22:15-20), which is found in the majority of manuscripts.[128]

The Last Supper pericope in Luke thus derives its meaning from its location in the context of Luke-Acts. As a meal that is primarily eschatological in focus (22:16, 18, 30), it correlates with other eschatological or messianic banquet themes. For example, note that the messianic banquet tends to be connected with the theme of reversal, when the wealthy, the privileged, and especially the people of Israel (or Pharisees) will be judged (6:20-26; 13:25-30; 14:15-24; 16:19-31); so also here, during a traditional Jewish meal, a judgment is pronounced against Israel (22:28-30).

Luke's Last Supper also serves as a transition for the theme of table fellowship with Jesus from the "time of Jesus" to the "time of the church." This idea is indicated by Jesus' vow that he will not eat and drink again until "it is fulfilled in the kingdom of God" (22:16,18). Thus table fellowship with Jesus then becomes associated exclusively with the messianic banquet at which he will be the host as he is here. Furthermore, the idea of Jesus being present with his disciples becomes focused on the meal. Thus, whenever the presence of the risen Lord is to be experienced in the church, it is to be associated especially with the communal meal. The combination of Jesus' unusual interpretation of the Last Supper in 22:15-19a and the Lukan resurrection story of the appearance to the disciples on the road to Emmaus, in which the disciples are hindered from recognizing him until "he had been made known to them in the breaking of the bread" (24:35), clearly indicates the nature of this transition.[129] Thus whenever the church celebrates the "breaking of bread" (Acts 2:42, 46; 20:7), which is a peculiarly Lukan designation for the communal meal, the indication is that this is a continuation of this same theme, in which the risen Lord is known to them especially in the meal and in which they look forward to the future blessings of the messianic banquet.[130]

Social Obligation: Table Service as a Symbol for Community Service

In the context of a formal banquet at which one reclined, there is a natural requirement that there be servants who serve. Indeed, customs and etiquette had become rather rigid and formal in regard to the entire table ritual from the arrival of the guests to their departure.

In Luke's Gospel, the custom of serving at table is made into a symbol for community service as a whole. The use of this motif is illustrated in the parable of the servant entrusted with supervision (Luke 12:42-46; Matt 24:45-51). Here the duty assigned to the servant is to care for the household, that is, "to give them their allowance of food at the proper time" (12:42), rather than eating, drinking, and being merry himself (12:45). This text surely correlates with the reference in Acts 6:1-6 to actual table service in the early church. In addition, however, it can be interpreted as a symbol of servant-hood as a whole.

The most significant reference to the servant theme is the one that, as has already been noted, Luke moves from the Markan context to the Last Supper context (Luke 22:24-27; Mark 10:35-45). Indeed, in this pericope, several themes that we have discussed are brought together. Thus, whenever the disciples bring up the question as to their ranking in the kingdom, Jesus' response is two-pronged. Yes, they will take positions of honor at the eschatological table and judge the twelve tribes of Israel (22:30). But their idea of ranking needs modification. Much like the advice to take the position at the lower end of the table so as to receive the invitation to "move up higher" (14:7-11), so also here Jesus says:

> The kings of the Gentiles lord it over them; and those in authority over them are called benefactors. But not so with you; rather the greatest among you must become like the youngest, and the leader like one who serves. For who is greater, the one who reclines at table [*anakeisthai*],[131] or the one who serves? Is it not the one who reclines at table? But I am among you as one who serves. (Luke 22:25-27)

An important question raised by Luke's version of this saying is how Jesus fulfills this phrase that he is "among you as one who serves." In the other Gospels, this is made clearer. In Mark, for example, the very next phrase, which Luke omits, makes clear what is intended by the servant symbol: "For the Son of man also came not to be served but to serve, and to give his life as a ransom for many" (Mark 10:45). Thus here the servant theme refers to the death of Jesus.

In the Gospel of John, although Luke's saying is not found, the same idea is presented in the same context as Luke's, that is, at the Last Supper (John 13:1-20). Thus whereas in Luke Jesus speaks of himself as servant at the meal, in John Jesus acts out the role of servant by washing the feet of the disciples. This action appears to be interpreted in two ways in John. One interpretation, which is close to that of Mark, is that this action symbolizes the meaning of Jesus' death.[132] Another interpretation, which is similar to Luke's, is that by this action Jesus presents himself as the model of servanthood.[133]

Yet, unlike both Mark and John, Luke does not make explicit what meaning he intends by this reference. This is surprising in two respects. First, while Luke is not likely to have known of the option utilized by John, whereby Jesus actually acts out the role of servant,[134] he surely knew of Mark's interpretation, yet he chose not to use it. Second, as we have seen, Luke is especially conscious of the meal imagery in general and appears to make lavish use of it in putting together his Gospel. This strongly suggests that Luke must have something specific in mind as his interpretation of this text. Furthermore, given his redactional skills, he must have put together this section so as to bring out the exact meaning he intended. Thus, if the meaning of this text appears to be ambiguous or overly subtle, then we must assume that Luke intended that it be so.

I would suggest two reasons that Luke omits Mark's reference to the death of Jesus at this point.[135] The first is that the saying in Mark, especially the phrase "the Son of man also came not to be served but to serve" (Mark 10:45), is too limiting for the symbolism of servanthood. In Luke, as we will see, one of the significant usages of the table service motif is service offered to Jesus. Second, Luke seems to prefer ambiguity here, as in other meal texts, in order that the symbolism may be capable of multiple interpretations. Thus, for example, Jesus is depicted as both host (22:17,19) and servant (22:27) at the table.

The first interpretation that may be suggested is that Jesus presents himself as the example of servanthood for the church to follow. This correlates with the various texts that place exemplary disciples in the same position as Jesus, as servants at the table. It also correlates with the servanthood theme in Luke in general.

The second interpretation for the text is suggested by a parable found elsewhere in Luke:

> Be dressed for action and have your lamps lit; be like those who are waiting for their master to return from the wedding banquet, so that they may open the door for him as soon as he comes and knocks. Blessed are those slaves whom the master finds alert when he comes; truly, I tell you, he will fasten his belt and have them recline at table [*anaklinein*],[136] and he will come and serve them [*diakonein*]. (Luke 12:35-37)

Here the master takes the role of servant in order to reward the servants. The image is that of the messianic banquet, but here the messiah is servant rather than host. But there is an internal consistency in the use of this image in this parable, for here it is those who themselves were "faithful servants" who are then rewarded by being served.

This parable then provides another possible interpretation of the Last Supper text (22:25-27). Jesus' presentation of himself as host/servant at the Last Supper is thus seen as prefiguring his role as host/servant at the messianic banquet. This of course correlates quite well with the eschatological emphasis presented in the Last Supper pericope as a whole.

This theme of Jesus as host/servant at the banquet appears to be reflected in another set of texts whereby Jesus' entire ministry is characterized as one in which he feeds the hungry. This is presented in Mary's Magnificat: "he has filled the hungry with good things" (Luke 1:53). It is also a major theme of the Beatitudes (Luke 6:21, 25). Furthermore, it is an underlying theme of the multiplication of the loaves story (Luke 9:10-17). Although a formal table setting is not explicit in these texts, they can nevertheless be seen as extensions of the messianic banquet theme and related to the theme of Jesus as both host and servant.

Another way in which the table service theme functions in Luke is illustrated by the text in 7:36-50. Here is found Luke's version of the story of Jesus being anointed by a woman while at table. In Luke's version, Jesus has been invited to dine at the house of a Pharisee. While he is reclining, a woman of the streets comes in and, standing behind his couch, washes his feet with her own tears. She thus gives to Jesus the proper treatment one should receive from a servant, whereas Jesus criticizes his host for not providing the usual amenities by providing a servant to wash his feet.

Here the image is that of serving Jesus at table as a symbol for true worship. Thus the table symbolism functions again as an image for the true community of Jesus. But unlike other such references, in which the true followers of Jesus are his table companions (as in, e.g., 5:27-32), here his true follower has taken the position of servant. This, of course, functions in the story to contrast with the failure of the host and table companion to exhibit true regard for Jesus. Nevertheless, the servant theme in the Gospel of Luke as a whole gives added value to the image of the servant in this pericope.

The same motif is utilized in other references, such as the unusual story whereby Martha serves Jesus at table while Mary listens (Luke 10:38-42). Though the story seems to function primarily to legitimate Mary's role as a listener rather than a servant at the table, yet it also by implication assumes the legitimacy of the role of Martha to serve.[137] Similarly, whenever Peter's mother-in-law is healed, she rises to serve them (Luke 4:38-39; Mark 1:29-31).[138]

Finally, the same theme is presented in the parable of the servant's reward, which is found only in Luke:

> Who among you would say to your slave who has just come in from plowing or tending sheep in the field, "Come here at once and recline at table [*anapiptein*]?"[139] Will you not rather say to him, "Prepare supper for me, put on your apron and serve me while I eat and drink; later you may eat and drink?" Do you thank the slave for doing what was commanded? So you also, when you have done all that you were ordered to do, say, "We are worthless slaves; we have done only what we ought to have done!" (Luke 17:7-10)

Most probably these various interpretations of the table service theme are not meant to be seen at cross-purposes with one another but are meant to resonate together. The theme of Jesus as table servant functions as a symbol of his ministry; it also functions as a symbol of the blessings he will offer at the end-time. One can be seen as interrelated with and as an anticipation of the other. The joys of the end are proleptically realized in table fellowship with Jesus now; thus his ministry offers bread to the hungry, just as his table fellowship offers forgiveness to the penitent.

Jesus as table servant also serves as an example to his disciples. They, too, are called to serve, and they will be rewarded by being served. Their service is presented to others, but is thereby a service presented to Jesus himself.

Table Fellowship as a Symbol for Community Fellowship

A ubiquitous symbol of the table was its function to designate a special relationship between the participants at the meal. In the Greco-Roman world, whenever groups organized themselves as funerary clubs, trade associations, religious parties, or philosophical schools, more often than not the central social activity that served to exemplify group identity and solidarity was the communal meal.[140] The same was true in the case of several Jewish groups that had an identifiable and separate social identity.[141] Indeed, any gathering of friends around the table was seen as an event that created a special tie among the diners. This aura of social bonding connected with the meal was ancient and extended across cultures. Nevertheless, there were specific aspects of the phenomenon of table fellowship that were characteristic of the Greco-Roman period.

One such characteristic was the philosophical tradition whereby certain ethical categories were assigned to the social setting of the meal. Thus whenever ethics at the table was discussed, categories such as "pleasure," "love," and especially "friendship" were invoked as guiding principles.

Plato, for example, discussed rules at the table under the category of "symposium laws," which had as their goal to make the participants friends rather than enemies.[142] Plutarch, again, reflects his relationship to this philosophical tradition, for "friendship" is one of the primary categories he uses in his discussions of table ethics. Thus he refers to "the friend-making character of the table."[143] That is, friendship is central to the entire occasion: "A guest comes to share not only meat, wine, and dessert, but conversation, fun, and the amiability that leads to friendship."[144] Thus, whenever discussions take place concerning such questions as proper conversation at the table,[145] or whether guests should be ranked,[146] and so on, one of the primary ethical categories utilized was friendship.[147]

For example, Plutarch attributed to Timon, his brother, the following argument in favor of abolishing ranking at table:

> If in other matters we are to preserve equality among men, why not begin with this first and accustom them to take their places with each other without vanity and ostentation, because they understand as soon as they enter the door that the dinner is a democratic affair and has no outstanding place like an acropolis where the rich man is to recline and lord it over meaner folk?[148]

What is especially noticeable here is the use of the categories of "meaner folk" and "rich" to designate barriers that should be abolished at the table.

Clearly, Plutarch and his brother were not social revolutionaries. They were not calling for the liberation of the poor. Indeed, the distinction between the "meaner folk" and the "rich" is not that great. After all, the fact that they all recline together and share the same meal indicates that they are all part of the same privileged class.

Nevertheless, there were commonly practiced methods for distinguishing the relative status of those who were accepted in the table fellowship. Besides the practice of ranking referred to here, one could also distinguish between the elite and the rest of the guests by providing a different quantity or quality of food.[149] These practices led to criticisms by a number of moralists of the age who argued along similar lines as Timon in the text quoted above from Plutarch. That is, to distinguish between the guests in this way worked against the central meaning of table fellowship, or "the friend-making character of the table."[150]

Thus both the social custom and the corresponding moral critique had become virtual commonplaces leading to their development as literary motifs. For example, the fact that Timon refers to "rich" and "meaner folk" to define those who are separated by ranking at the meal, when, in fact, wealth had not been an explicit category for designating ranking (other categories could be used), suggests that the terms have taken on a catchall symbolic meaning. They refer in a general sense to the variety of ways in which social distinctions could be drawn in such a setting in the ancient world. The terms, then, refer to a literary motif whereby the banquet is again seen as a symbol of luxury and wealth, and as promoting a distinction between "rich" and "poor," but in this case the emphasis is not on the distinction between the diners and the outside world but rather on the distinctions among the diners themselves. Furthermore, the arguments that are presented in regard to this phenomenon draw upon traditional motifs and categories.

It is this collection of traditional motifs and categories that appears to be related to Luke's extensive use of the table fellowship theme to develop his argument as a whole. That is, a central theme of Luke's theology is that salvation has come to the "poor," a term that he uses as a symbol for social outcasts in general.[151] A primary means whereby Luke presents this theme is by means of the image of table fellowship, for it is characteristic of Jesus' ministry that "he eats with tax collectors and sinners" (5:27-32; 7:34; 15:2), a category of outcasts with which the "poor" came to be associated as well.

To be sure, the critique that Jesus "eats with tax collectors and sinners" is given prominence in the tradition Luke inherits. The meal at Levi's house derives from Mark (2:13-17). Indeed, there is even a connection with the Greek philosophical tradition of friendship at table present in Q, for it is Jesus' table fellowship with them that allows him to be called a "friend [*philos*] of tax collectors and sinners" (Luke 7:34; Matt 11:19).

But Luke expands on this theme far beyond its significance in the tradition. For in Luke Jesus' entire ministry is characterized as one to the poor, the captives, the blind, the oppressed (Luke 4:18-19; see also 6:20-26; 7:22; 14:15-24; and so forth). This formula recurs often in Luke, and, although it can be expressed in a variety of ways, the idea is always the same: Jesus' ministry is to society's outcasts. As Luke develops this theme in his Gospel, the imagery of the meal serves as one major means for conveying it.[152]

Thus the meal at Levi's house with tax collectors and sinners is interpreted by Jesus' saying, "I have come to call not the righteous but sinners to repentance" (Luke 5:32). A few chapters later, when Jesus is at table in the house of a "righteous one" (that is, the house of Simon the Pharisee), it is a woman who is a "sinner" who extends the proper amenities of the table to him and who receives in return true fellowship with him (that is, forgiveness).

The same themes are recalled in the story of Zacchaeus (Luke 19:1-9). Zacchaeus is a tax collector who is also rich (v. 2). When Jesus consents to be a guest in his home (vv. 5-7), the scene is intended to be reminiscent of the meal at Levi's house (5:27-32). Thus the detractors note that Zacchaeus is a "sinner" (v. 7), and the story concludes with a parallel saying of Jesus (v. 10; cp. 5:32). This story adds a new element, however, in that Zacchaeus is also rich. But unlike the wealthy who are ostentatious at table, he is redeemed by his almsgiving (v. 8).

The symbolic references to outcasts are expanded to include not only the poor, but also the blind, lame, lepers, deaf, and so forth (see, e.g., 7:22). Thus, in the parable of the great banquet, those who finally attend are identified with terminology that is highly significant in Luke's Gospel; here Jesus' table companions at the messianic banquet are defined as "the poor, the crippled, the blind, and the lame" (14:21).

This same symbolism is also utilized in Luke's version of the Sermon on the Plain. Notice that it is the poor, the hungry, the mournful, and the excluded who are singled out for blessing; the rich, the well-fed, the joyful, and the socially accepted are singled out for woes. As in the parable of the rich man and Lazarus so also here: roles will be reversed, and those who suffer now will receive the kingdom, characterized by satisfaction of hunger, joyfulness, and acceptance into fellowship with God; in short, all of the blessings of the messianic banquet.

Furthermore, his followers are to continue that same ministry of Jesus. His servanthood, in the sense that he fills the hungry, is to be followed by the community of his disciples. Now the symbolism changes, the meal becomes symbolic not of Jesus' ministry but of that of the church as a whole, or, better, it becomes a symbol of the church itself. Notice how this idea is presented in the following parable:

> When you give a luncheon or a dinner, do not invite your friends or your brothers or your relatives or rich neighbors, in case they may invite you in return, and you would be repaid. But when you give a banquet, invite the poor, the crippled, the lame, and the blind. And you will be blessed, because they cannot repay you, for you will be repaid at the resurrection of the righteous. (Luke 14:12-14)

Lest the connection be missed, this parable is placed back to back with the parable of the great banquet, a parable that clearly refers to Jesus' ministry and invitation to the same outcasts. Thus the church is to follow Jesus' lead by extending its fellowship (or its meal invitation) to society's outcasts just as Jesus did (and will do at the end-time).[153]

The same theme can also be illustrated in the parable of the prodigal son (Luke 15:11-32). Here the prodigal son serves as a paradigm for the "outcast." The parable describes his "lost" state by reference to the hunger he experiences. His redeemed state is illustrated by the great feast of celebration that the father gives upon his return. An additional point of the parable is made by means of the episode involving the elder son (15:25-32). He resents that the feast is being given for his prodigal brother. He is chastened, however, with a plea that he join in the celebration (15:28). The elder brother thus serves as a paradigm for the "righteous" who have here been entreated to join in the feast celebrating the return of the "sinner."

The meal imagery contributes a certain richness to this theme. The message is not one of simple evangelism, of basic acknowledgment of the existence of outcasts, nor is it a message that one is only to feed and clothe the needy (although this idea is included in the overall theme in Luke). Rather, the table fellowship imagery forces upon the theme a stronger meaning. For it is fellowship of the most intimate kind that is envisioned here. The richness of the meal imagery in popular culture and literature, whereby sharing a meal meant sharing a relationship of a special kind, is here applied to a definition of the Christian community. In essence, the church is being challenged to take on itself the same scandal Jesus took on himself: "He eats with tax collectors and sinners."

In conclusion, the table fellowship theme is clearly a prominent literary motif for Luke. Some of the references and symbols are derived from the tradition he inherits, but Luke has significantly expanded on the theme. In his usage he appears to refer to a common pool of ideas and motifs from popular literature. His references are often rather subtle, but he expects Theophilus and his peers to catch them because their ears are attuned to the literature of the day and thus to the literary usage of meal symbolism.

The heritage that Luke draws on is a rich one, both from the side of Christian tradition and from that of popular literature. His use of these varied traditions is also rich, imaginative, and sometimes quite complex. Indeed, he appears to prefer complex rather than simple images, multiple rather than single meanings. Thus sometimes Jesus is presented as host of the meal, sometimes as guest, sometimes as servant. Sometimes he dines with the "righteous" (Pharisees), sometimes with "sinners," sometimes with the "crowd" (Luke 9:16). Similarly, sometimes the reader is to see himself or herself as guest (e.g., 5:27-32), sometimes as host (e.g., 14:12-14), sometimes as servant (e.g., 12:42-46; 22:24-27). Yet the meal imagery is so pervasive that it appears to make a significant contribution not only to the literary organization of Luke's Gospel but also to its central theological themes.

MEAL AND IRONY IN MATTHEW AND JOHN

The use of the literary motif of the banquet continues in Matthew and John, following the same lines as developed first in Mark. In both cases, Jesus is portrayed as the hero at table and the table is made to symbolize the kingdom. In addition, each author develops this theme individually and integrates it into his own literary and theological program.

Matthew incorporates Mark's meal imagery into his Gospel and expands and adapts it.[154] He enlarges on the theme of Jesus as King and its ironic development in the story of Jesus. Consequently, like Mark, Matthew envisions the banquet of Jesus as the banquet of a king. But a central image for Matthew's development of this idea is exemplified by his version of the great banquet parable. This parable provides a window into Matthew's special use of meal imagery and incorporation of this imagery into his plot.

> Once more Jesus spoke to them in parables, saying: "The kingdom of heaven may be compared to a king who gave a wedding banquet for his son. He sent his slaves to call those who had been invited to the wedding banquet, but they would not come. Again he sent other slaves, saying, 'Tell those who have been invited: Look, I have prepared my dinner, my oxen and my fat calves have been slaughtered, and everything is ready; come to the wedding banquet.' But they made light of it and went away, one to his farm, another to his business, while the rest seized his slaves, mistreated them, and killed them. The king was enraged. He sent his troops, destroyed those murderers, and burned their city. Then he said to his slaves, 'The wedding is ready, but those invited were not worthy. Go therefore into the main streets, and invite everyone you find to the wedding banquet.' Those slaves went out into the streets and gathered all whom they found, both good and bad; so the wedding hall was filled with guests. But when the king came in to see the guests, he noticed a man there who was not wearing a wedding robe, and he said to him,

'Friend, how did you get in here without a wedding robe?' And he was speechless. Then the king said to the attendants, 'Bind him hand and foot, and throw him into the outer darkness, where there will be weeping and gnashing of teeth.' For many are called, but few are chosen." (Matt 22:1-14)

This parable derives from Q and is found in a less elaborated form in Luke 14 and in Thomas. It is Matthew who has made it into a wedding banquet, made the host a king, and introduced the episode of the guest without a wedding robe. Like Luke, Matthew interprets this parable as a reference to the theme of the messianic banquet. Luke makes the connection in his introduction (Luke 14:15); Matthew does it more subtly by simply changing it to a wedding banquet, a frequent theme of messianic banquet imagery. Utilizing the wedding banquet imagery also allows him to make a connection with other sayings that refer to Jesus as the bridegroom (9:15; 25:1ff.) and with the parable of the foolish bridesmaids (25:1-13).

The messianic banquet as depicted here speaks of the gathering of "good and bad" to the table. This correlates with Matthew's emphasis on the apocalyptic gathering of the nations, namely, Gentiles, to the table (8:11-12, in the context of the healing of the centurion's servant; 12:15-21), an event that lies in the immediate future for this community (28:19).

Consequently, the theme of Jesus at table functions in an ironic mode in Matthew, just as it does in the rest of the Gospels. "Jesus is the royal Son of God in whom God's end-time Rule is a present, albeit hidden, reality," as Jack Dean Kingsbury notes.[155] Furthermore, the banquet in Matthew represents the drawing of boundaries between the community and its opponents. This is embedded in the plot Matthew adopts from Mark and is further elaborated in his expansions to that plot.

In John, a special emphasis is placed on the food Jesus offers. It is miraculous wine (2:1-11), living water/water of life (4:10-14), bread from heaven (6:31ff.), bread of life (6:35, 48), flesh and blood (6:53-54), and miraculous fish (21:1-14). In short, it is numinous food, the food of the gods. Yet the world is not ready for it. Thus Jesus responds, "my time has not come," when asked to provide for the wedding banquet (2:4) or attend the festival (7:8). In these contexts, it means that the time of the heavenly banquet, the banquet of Jesus, is not yet here because the world is not yet ready. Indeed, Jesus goes away to prepare a place for the banquet (14:2-4). Meanwhile, the disciples are to "feed the sheep" (21:15-17; see also 6:1-14).

John, of course, has a last supper, but it is very different from the Last Supper in the synoptics (see 13:1—17:26). There are no references to words of Jesus over bread and wine, and it is not a Passover meal. Yet it is a meal that refers symbolically to the death of Jesus and includes a command that the disciples do as he has done (13:14-15). The meal utilizes a motif from banquet tradition for its symbolic reference. The motif is the washing of the feet of the guests by a servant before the meal is to begin. Here Jesus moves from his position as a table participant, puts aside his clothing, and takes on the dress and role of the servant who washes the feet (13:4-12).[156] It is a powerful symbol for the servant image of Jesus, a symbol first used to interpret the death of Jesus in Mark (10:45), then placed in a table-talk scene at the Last Supper by Luke (22:24-27), and now elaborated further by John.[157] It carries a dual symbolism in John, as an interpretation of the death of Jesus (13:6-9) and as a model of servanthood for the disciples to follow (13:12-16).[158]

Although John does not have a traditional Last Supper scene, he does have words of Jesus over bread and wine. This is the enigmatic text at 6:53-54: "Very truly, I tell you, unless you eat the flesh of the Son of Man and drink his blood, you have no life in you. Those who eat my flesh and drink my blood have eternal life, and I will raise them up on the last day." This text is embedded in the lengthy and highly significant bread of life discourse that begins with the multiplication of the loaves (6:1-14), where Jesus blesses the bread and distributes it in a manner reminiscent of the synoptic Last Supper ritual (6:11).[159] The discourse concludes with the saying at 6:53-54 and its aftermath.

Clearly, the bread of life discourse plays a major role in the plot and theology of John.[160] And, of course, it is imbued with meal symbolism, primarily from the messianic banquet tradition. The text at 6:51b-57 represents a change in focus in the discourse, in which the bread of life becomes no longer a christological symbol for Jesus, following the pattern for all of the "I am" sayings. At v. 51b, the bread becomes the "flesh" of Jesus that one is to eat, and the "blood" of Jesus is added at v. 53 as the drink at this morbid meal.

This change of symbolic reference has resulted in the proposal that vv. 51b-57 were added later and represent an imposition of a "sacramental" tradition to the text of John.[161] These verses do seem clearly to have been added at a later point. The interesting question to raise, however, is what meaning the text now has with this addition.

Instead of a sacramental interpretation, I would suggest a contextual interpretation. The theme of eating the flesh of Jesus, which is introduced at

v. 51b, leads to a heightened level of tension in the plot. "The Jews" then question, "How can this man give us his flesh to eat?" (6:52). To this, Jesus responds that *only* those who eat his flesh and drink his blood can "have life" (6:53). The troublesome text (v. 51bff.) represents a line drawn in the sand, a boundary marker. The climax comes when "many of his disciples" say, "This teaching is difficult; who can accept it?" (6:60). The result is that "because of this many of his disciples turned back and no long went about with him" (6:66). But at this point in John's narrative, Peter steps forward with John's version of Peter's great confession. To the question of Jesus, "Do you also wish to go away?" Peter responds, "Lord, to whom can we go? You have the words of eternal life" (6:67-69).

Consequently, I see the meal of "flesh and blood" as a secondary-level elaboration on the theme of symbolic food that is so central to John. During the development of the text of John, when this elaboration of the bread of life discourse took shape (namely, the addition of 6:51bff.), the symbolic emphasis was still operative but developed in a new form. It was produced in the context of the increasing tension of the community with the Jewish world out of which it had come.[162] The reference to "eating flesh and drinking blood" represents in the story the radical boundary now drawn between the Johannine community and its neighboring synagogue community, here envisioned as two different meal communities. Clearly, from the point of view of the Johannine community, now no longer a synagogue community but rather a meal community, it is the meal that constitutes a new boundary marker between the two communities, effectively supplementing, if not replacing, the synagogue as the boundary marker.

CONCLUSION

At the beginning of this chapter, I sketched out an outline of the layers of tradition to be found in the Gospels. In that sketch, I started with the earliest layer and worked forward. Now that we have reached the conclusion of the study, I will start at the latest layer, the Gospels, and work backward.

As we have seen, the Gospel narratives make a rich use of the literary motif of the banquet in telling their stories of Jesus. He is idealized along the model of the hero at table, much like other heroes in ancient literature. Wherever he dines, the table takes on the aura of a festive meal, a common category for ritual meals in the culture, and defined here in terms of the messianic banquet. His table is one in which the normal categories of social stratification are being critiqued and the category of social equality is being enhanced, much as we find in popular literature of the day. It is a table where social boundaries are drawn and a new community is in process of formation. Indeed, the table of Jesus becomes a primary symbol for the kingdom itself.

But the table of Jesus as sketched in the Gospels is a literary phenomenon. And the Gospel writers all recognize it as such and develop this theme to fit their own theological agendas. Indeed, as we have seen exemplified in our studies of Mark and Luke, the Gospel writers extend the banquet motif far beyond references to specific meals of Jesus. Rather, they extend their use of the motif to the extent that it becomes woven into the very fabric of the plot of each Gospel narrative. The Gospel writers are all accomplished story-tellers, and the banquet is a stock motif for storytelling.

Given the extent to which the meal stories and traditions in the Gospels are literary in nature, and the extent to which these traditions participate in the general program of the Gospels to present an idealized portrait of Jesus, the question of history behind these stories becomes more acute. As is well recognized in Gospel research today, there are at least two levels to the question of history in the Gospels. On one level is the history of the community out of which or for which the Gospel narrative is presented. On another level is the history the stories purport to tell, namely, the story of Jesus.

What do the meal stories and traditions tell us about the Gospel communities? Did they practice meals using these stories as their models? Or, to put it in more specific terms, did they practice a "Lord's Supper" using the Last Supper narrative as a model, much as the Pauline communities seem to have done? The problem with the latter question is that the Gospel traditions, save for a disputed section of Luke and a reference in John to another type of meal, do not contain the command to repeat the meal. Consequently, the Last Supper as narrated in the Gospels functions simply as another Jesus story, without clear indication that it was a model for a ritual activity in the life of the community any more than any other Jesus story was.

But there is another way to approach this issue. Based on my analysis of community formation in the Greco-Roman world as presented throughout this study, I would suggest that it was highly likely that the Gospel communities did celebrate meals together and that those meals were significant moments for the formation of community identity. Therefore, a more fruitful way to define the ritual life of the Gospel communities would be to take into account the entirety of the meal theology in each of the Gospels. This is not to say that one should read the Gospel narrative as an exact model for the

Gospel community. Rather, it is to say that the foundation story for each Gospel community, namely, the story told in its Gospel narrative, would have functioned to provide an idealized model for the life of the community as it should be. And since they can be assumed to have gathered for meals, those meals would have been to some extent reflective of the idealized model for meals presented in the story.

The Jesus tradition inherited by the Gospel writers already exhibited a sophisticated use of traditional meal narrative motifs. That is to say, as stories of Jesus were told at the oral level, common storytelling motifs from the culture were utilized. We identified at least one type of storytelling motif when we isolated the Cynic *chreia* form as the basic form lying behind meal stories and meal sayings in the Jesus tradition. These observations should not come as a surprise. Stories of Jesus were told in order to idealize Jesus. Such stories would utilize the storytelling models of the day; one such model was the idealization of the hero at table. Our conclusion is that the Jesus meal stories and traditions, therefore, most likely originated as traditional motifs to characterize Jesus.

It is the Jesus that is so characterized who becomes a candidate for historical possibility. That is to say, it is not the picture of Jesus at table that can be defined as historical; that picture is derived from a storytelling motif. But it is the picture of Jesus that is *characterized* by such a story that qualifies for historical query. Thus the picture of Jesus at table with tax collectors and sinners may be evidence for a historical Jesus who preferred the company of individuals who were of a questionable social identity for a person like Jesus (a category that also needs defining) to associate with. So also the saying that Jesus was a "glutton and a drunkard" in contrast to John the Baptist may be evidence for a historical Jesus who preferred the urban world with all of its questionable associations.

There is more to this data than the historical Jesus question, however. What I have attempted to show here is the richness of the literary motif of the banquet to be found at all levels of the Jesus tradition. This is the point I have emphasized in this chapter, as supported by the mass of data collected in the previous chapters. It is this data that should be taken into account in all future discussions of the table fellowship motif in the Gospel narratives and Gospel traditions.

CHAPTER 9

THE BANQUET AND CHRISTIAN THEOLOGY

Why did early Christians meet at a meal? Various theories have been proposed by historians of early Christianity to explain this phenomenon. This study proposes a simple answer. Early Christians met at a meal because that is what groups in the ancient world did. Christians were simply following a pattern found throughout their world.

What kind of meal did the early Christians celebrate? Once more a variety of proposals have come forth from historians. Once more this study proposes a simple answer. Early Christians celebrated a meal based on the banquet model found commonly in their world.

No further explanation for the origin of early Christian meals is needed. In particular, theories that propose a single origin in the teachings and/or practices of Jesus are especially to be ruled out, as are explanations that locate the background of the Christian meal either in a particular Jewish tradition, such as the Passover meal, or in a particular Greco-Roman tradition, such as the mystery cult meal. Rather, this study has shown that all of these presumably distinct meal types derive from the same banquet tradition.

The Greco-Roman banquet tradition contributed more to early Christianity, however, than simply the form of the meal. The banquet was a social institution of the first order and as such was a carrier of a social code, the ideology of the banquet. Earliest Christian theology developed out of the models for religious thinking of its day, and one such model was the ideology of the banquet. Banquet ideology provided a model for creating community, defining behavior within the community, sharing values, and connecting with the divine. It was also embedded in a social practice and so provided a means for the ideology to be confirmed through a shared experience. Since early Christian groups first created and experienced community by means of table fellowship, banquet ideology is also the foundation for the development of early Christian liturgy.

A third component of the banquet tradition, besides the form of the meal and the ideology of the meal, is the literary form within which both form and ideology were communicated. Literary descriptions of banquets, which purported to describe the meal as practiced, were actually idealizations based on literary models. As such, they defined the ideal form of the "proper meal" as understood by the culture. Consequently, the literary descriptions could also become prescriptive and provide a model for how a meal should be practiced, especially by setting the meal within a larger context of an idealized meal tradition.

Literary descriptions are rich with data about meal ideology and cultural values. But they do not provide an exact description of how meals were practiced. Rather, they provide descriptions according to literary prototypes. We must extrapolate from these descriptions in order to get at the actual practice of meals. This is the distinction I have loosely defined as the "narrative world" versus the "real world." This perspective provides an important qualification for historical reconstruction of meal practice and a more appropriate means to assess the real value of literary descriptions as sources of information about meal ideology.

The foundation resource for banquet tradition is the symposium. To be sure, the symposium as a social institution had a distinctive function particular to Greek culture. But one can also trace the influence of the symposium tradition as the prototype for the banquet throughout the Greco-Roman world. Plato's *Symposium* alone was of enormous influence as a model for the form and ideology of the banquet as well as for the literary form in which a banquet was to be described.

Symposium literature as a genre began with Plato and Xenophon and continued throughout the Roman period. It provided a model for describing a meal, as noted by Plutarch. The model had a narrative component, in which the meal was described using stock figures such as the uninvited guest, the late-arriving guest, and the drunkard, and stock plot structures, such as the discourse couched in a competitive framework. These narrative components show up in later literary works of various kinds, some of which simply continue the genre, as is found in Plutarch and Lucian, and some of which respond to the components of the genre without fully adopting the genre itself, as is found in Philo's description of the Therapeutae or in the earliest written form of the Passover haggadah or in the organization of the discussion in 1 Corinthians 11–14. Echoes of the genre also occur in motifs derived from what I would call popular storytelling tradition. For example, the motif of the late-arriving guest, which was part of the symposia of Plato and

Xenophon, was utilized in a variety of forms in the popular meal tradition and came to be included as well in the Jesus tradition (Luke 14:8-11).

In addition to the narrative component of the symposium genre, there was also a discourse component. This tradition is traced especially to Plato's archetype, in which the decision was made to dismiss the flute girl and spend the evening in philosophical discourse. Following Plato's lead, philosophical discourse became a substitute form of banquet entertainment. It is important to note, however, that the setting is still the banquet. Consequently, the discourse at table was expected to follow patterns that fit the ambience of the occasion, such as a shared conversation and a topic appropriate to a table discussion. Among those topics were the features of the meal itself. Thus it was here where the form and values of the meal were discussed according to philosophical categories. Plutarch especially devotes many of his table-talk discourses in *Quaestiones convivales* to meal customs and etiquette.

The symposium genre called for such philosophical discussion to take place in discourse form. The philosophical discourse on meal etiquette was influential beyond the genre, however. The values connected with the meal as defined in the philosophical tradition provided a standard for discussions of meal etiquette in a variety of other forms and genres, ranging from the statutes of clubs and associations to the rules for Christian worship outlined by Paul in 1 Corinthians 14. What especially connects this data with the symposium tradition is the way in which the rules for banquet behavior are based in ethical principles that are parallel to those of the philosophical tradition.

The symposium literary tradition also provided an important elaboration on the symposium as a part of the form of the meal. Technically, the symposium was the second course of the meal, the *deipnon* being the first course. According to the cultural definition of the meal, the symposium was the time in which extended drinking of wine and the entertainment of the evening took place. Traditional entertainment was provided by a flute girl, party games, such as *kottabos,* dramatic presentations, or even more prurient activities. But the philosophical symposium, as described in the symposium literary tradition, centered its banquet entertainment on enlightened philosophical discourse. From this tradition, there developed variations in a number of contexts, especially in the Jewish and Christian traditions, in which discourse on the law or the biblical tradition was designated as the appropriate topic for table fellowship gatherings.

Here is located the foundation for early Christian worship. It is almost a matter of connecting the dots. Early Christians met in homes, hosted by those who served as patrons of the Christian community. The dining room is the one area in the ancient house where one offered hospitality to one's guests; that is to say, hospitality took place at table. When we then look at the data in the Pauline letters, particularly in 1 Corinthians, we find that when the church gathered together for worship, they also came together to eat. It fits the cultural pattern. And when we find Paul describing worship in 1 Corinthians 14 using motifs from symposium discourse tradition, we know we are dealing with the common banquet tradition. Consequently, early Christians worshipped at table, and when they did so, they utilized the already existing patterns for the form and ideology of the meal.

The form of the meal prescribed that the guests of status would recline and would be given positions appropriate to their status. Such a meal required servants to provide the amenities of the table. There must be a specified number of formal courses of the meal (*deipnon* and *symposium*) with special prayers before each course. These are among the expectations for any banquet that any host in the Greco-Roman world would be expected to provide. This form came with its supportive banquet ideology. As early Christians developed their distinct form of community identity, they simply adapted the common banquet tradition to fit their purposes. The adoption and adaptation of banquet ideology was a significant factor in the development of early Christian theology.

For example, the banquet provided the ideology for social boundaries. For clubs and associations, and similar groups such as the Essenes at Qumran, the boundaries of the community were defined by membership at the table. To be expelled from the table was to be expelled from the community. Such groups often had membership rolls and dues to indicate membership boundaries. The Essenes had even stricter boundary markers, including purificatory rites before entrance into the "pure meal." But the experience of community formation and solidarity was when the community was gathered at table. The New Testament texts are imbued with references to the boundary-making function of the table, from Paul's discussions of the distinctions between "the table of the Lord" and "the table of demons" to the elaborate development of the literary motif of the boundary of the table in the Gospels.

To share bread and wine together at a formal banquet was considered a powerful form of social bonding. Plutarch spoke in the highest terms of the bonds created by the shared wine bowl. His words are echoed by Paul, who spoke of the sharing of bread and wine as the act that created the one "body," that is to say, it was a community-creating ritual. The power of the ritual was not contained in the essence of the bread or wine, but in the context of the meal and the accompanying ritual by which it was shared. Indeed, it was in the context of the meal that the earliest Christians experienced the bonding event that made them into a fictive family, in which they could call one another brothers and sisters and think of themselves as part of the family of God. In this sense the meal became the means for community formation, or, to put it differently, the theology of community came to be intertwined with and brought to experience by the ritual.

The meal provided a resource for elaboration on social stratification versus social equality. It is often argued that earliest Christianity was especially marked by its creation of a community of equals and that this was part of its attraction. But where did such an idea come from and how could it be envisioned and acted out? I would contend that banquet tradition already provided a model for such a discourse and early Christians simply made use of that model. Certainly the meal was built around the social stratification of the day, whereby each individual was assigned a position according to rank. The earliest Christian groups also had their hierarchical rankings, with apostles and prophets highly ranked, of course, but also such individuals as the patron, or host, receiving a high rank as well.

On the other hand, there was an inherent pull toward equality at the banquet dating from at least the time of Homer, and this was remarked on in great detail in philosophical discourse as well as in popular morality, as evidenced in satire. The meal was an occasion when the outside world was to be set aside and a new community of equals to be established. Indeed, significant components of meal ideology, most especially the etiquette or social obligation at the meal, required that equality be present. Without the aura of equality, it could not be a proper meal. Thus there was a constant debate between the two opposite values of social stratification and social equality. Early Christian groups joined this debate and utilized the resources from banquet ideology to develop their own discourse on these themes.

Ethics in early Christianity was largely social ethics, and social ethics discourse was founded primarily on banquet ideology. The philosophical discourse on behavior at the meal, based in such ethical principles as friendship and pleasure, was quite complex and influential across a wide spectrum of the ancient world. In essence, one was to conduct oneself in such a way as to think of the other first and put the good of the community first. The principles for such behavior were based on the idealized proper meal. Since the meal was an occasion in which community was the focus, behavior was defined according to that which enhanced the community as a whole. Categories such as friendship and pleasure, both basic components of the proper banquet, were invoked as the basis for appropriate behavior. The ideology of social obligation at the banquet became the foundation for all banquet rules of order, from clubs and associations to Ben Sira to Paul. It was a prime component of social ethics discourse per se, since it was a primary and singular context in which the principal ethical category, friendship, functioned. Paul's ethical discourse was also primarily about social ethics, and his theology of community followed the logic of the friendship discourse in philosophical ethics. Paul did not use the category of friendship, however; instead he developed his own categories, namely, "edification" or "building up" of the other, the "common good" of the community, and especially *agapē* or altruistic love. But the emphasis on putting the other first and the community first, and the description of the kind of behavior that would do this, paralleled closely the philosophical discussion of meal ethics.

Another basic "value" connected with the banquet is what I have called festive joy, a translation of the term *euphrosynē*. It reminds us that a meal was always a festive occasion. As a *value* connected with the meal, it defined behavior as well. That is to say, one should conduct oneself in such a way as to enhance the festive joy of the community as a whole. This category shows up especially in meals connected with religious festivals and is viewed there as a prime religious value, as a gift of the god. It is paralleled in the ancient biblical definition of the festival meal in which one was commanded to "rejoice before the Lord" (e.g., Deut 16:11-14). It can be seen as a parallel term to "pleasure" in philosophical discourse.

The category of festive joy is also represented in the Jewish and Christian tradition by the messianic banquet tradition. In this tradition the joys of the end-time are symbolized as a great and bountiful banquet. The central meaning of the symbol is that it is a time of festive joy, when the entire community of God gathers not in a temple, synagogue, or church, for example, but in a great banqueting hall and celebrates a great festive party with tables that overflow with food and wine. It is a symbol that lies behind each of the meal stories in the Jesus tradition. It provides the ideology of the numinous for early Christian meals, for it is when the community forms itself in anticipation of the messianic banquet that it experiences the presence of the divine.

The symposium tradition provided a means to idealize a hero, as Socrates was idealized in Plato's *Symposium*. So also in the Gospels, Jesus was idealized as the hero at table. Wherever Jesus dined, the messianic banquet lay somewhere in the background. One of the more interesting meals of Jesus is the wedding feast at Cana, found only in John's Gospel. Here the components of the meal are all present, including the wine, which is essential for the festivities. What is remarkable about the story, which occupies a prime position in John as the "first sign" or miracle of Jesus, is what the miracle consists of. What Jesus does by changing water into wine is, in effect, to guarantee that the festivities will continue, and for a long time too, considering how much wine is provided. The value being reinforced here is the festive nature of the messianic banquet.

The classic story defining the table of Jesus is the Markan story of the meal at Levi's house. Jesus takes on the aura of host; he is the one who "invites" or "calls," and his "invitation" is to a meal on a different plane, namely, the messianic banquet. The controversy is over the boundaries of the table, and Jesus, true to the values of the messianic age, has opened the doors to everyone. The guests all recline, befitting a festive meal, and Jesus and the outcasts are found to be reclining together, indicating the equality at work at the meal of Jesus. It is the richness of the banquet tradition that makes this story work.

The picture of the earliest Christian communities that emerges from this study, then, is of communities that were formed sociologically and theologically by the table ritual and banquet ideology. This was simply the way groups formed in the Greco-Roman world. But over the generations, Christianity began to take on new forms and develop new supportive theologies.

When the form of the meal changed, that is, when it moved from house to meeting hall to basilica, then worship was no longer at table, and liturgy moved from symposium discussion to church order. The community that began its existence in private homes around a banquet table evolved into a church that met in a meeting hall before an altar.

Early on, however, there are signs that this process had already begun. The form of meal known as the *agapē* or "love feast" seems to have developed along with, or perhaps more appropriately, alongside, the Eucharist. It is unclear when the two became separate strands of tradition. In the time of Paul, as we have seen, the Lord's Supper is one and the same with the communal meal. In Jude 12, however, and in Ignatius (e.g., *Rom.* 7:3 and *Smyrn.* 8:2) the *agapē* is already being mentioned, so that by the end of the first century c.e. we know that there was such a meal, though it is still unclear in what way it was related to the still developing forms of the Eucharist. The Eucharist, meanwhile, developed into a stylized symbolic meal governed by church order traditions that specified the prayers and the appropriate order and hierarchical leadership.

Michael White points to the turn of the third century as a time of transition in this development.[1] He cites as evidence the *Apostolic Tradition* of Hippolytus of Rome (217–235), which refers to two meals, a morning meal at worship, which by then is a stylized Eucharist, and an evening communal meal, still designated as "Lord's Supper" but lacking the sacral overtones of the morning meal. In the same period, Clement of Alexandria refers to the separation of the Eucharist from the communal meal or *agapē*.[2] So at least by this time, the Eucharist and *agapē* had become separate meals, and the Eucharist had clearly lost its relationship to the communal meal tradition. What is unclear is to what extent the Eucharist was developing a new form even earlier.

White goes on to connect the literary data exemplified by Hippolytus and Clement with the archaeological data, particularly the evidence from Dura Europos.[3] Here is found our earliest and best-preserved example of a house church, and it documents the transition from house church to what White identifies as a "hall of assembly." It is unclear whether the Christian community of Dura Europos met in the building when it was still in the form of a private house. But in ca. 242 C.E. the building was renovated by taking out the wall between the dining room and the room next to it in order to create a larger room designed for assembly purposes. In the process the building lost its dining room. White concludes that "the separation of the eucharist from the agape meal [the communal meal] coincided with a fundamental shift in the physical locus and social pattern of Christian assembly when renovation of church edifices began to develop into halls of assembly."[4] In other words, the change from house church to assembly hall coincided with the relocation of worship from dining room to assembly hall. And this coincided with the change of the meal from a communal supper to "a stylized and ritualized meal" no longer resembling a real meal or banquet but now "reduced to schematic and symbolic elements." As White notes, this change in physical space also introduced a change in "social pattern."[5] With a change in social pattern came a change in social code.

Church historians today have come to recognize the need to rethink the origins of the Eucharist.[6] Previously it had been widely assumed in scholarship that a straight line could be drawn from the earliest Christian meals, perhaps even the last meal of Jesus, to the fourth-century Eucharist. This assumption must now be rethought. We can no longer draw such a line. The earliest evidence testifies to significant local variations in early Christian communal meal practices. In addition, the change from communal meal to the fourth-century form of the Eucharist is too severe.

It is the severity of that change that must especially be confronted. On the one hand, we are now challenged to reimagine the course of development of the Eucharist. We must give full recognition to the fact that in that development the essence of the liturgical event changed in form, focus, and theology. This new understanding of Eucharistic origins should produce a greater awareness and appreciation of its historical foundations, theological grounding, and social code.

On the other hand, the thesis of this study, that earliest Christian meals developed out of the model of the Greco-Roman banquet, can provide a surer basis for historical reconstruction of Christian origins. This will allow a greater appreciation for the diversity of early Christian social formation and theological elaboration. Furthermore, if we take full account of the richness of the earliest Christian meal tradition, we can find in it models for renewal of Christian theology and liturgy today toward a greater focus on community.

The primary change from symposium to Eucharist is the evolution of the ritual from the dining table to the altar and from the social world of the banquet to that of church order. This change began to take place rather quickly, as documented in early Christian literature and supported by archaeological evidence. It represented a transition from the social code of the banquet to another social code. The banquet tradition was carried on somewhat longer in the form of the *agapē*, or fellowship meal. This ritual meal coexisted with the Eucharist for some time and tended to carry the traditions of the banquet. The Eucharist, on the other hand, soon lost its connection with banquet traditions. New Testament texts still maintain that connection, however, and provide a means for the church ever and again to reexamine its origins and renew its theology by recapturing and reconfiguring its own traditions.

ABBREVIATIONS

AB	Anchor Bible
ABD	*Anchor Bible Dictionary.* Edited by D. N. Freedman. 6 vols. New York, 1992.
ABRL	Anchor Bible Reference Library
Ael.	Aelian
Var. hist.	*Varia historia*
Aesch.	Aeschylus
Ag.	*Agamemnon*
AION	*Annali dell'Istituto Orientale di Napoli*
AJA	*American Journal of Archaeology*
AJSR	*Association for Jewish Studies Review*
ANET	*Ancient Near Eastern Texts Relating to the Old Testament.* Edited by J. B. Pritchard. 3d ed. Princeton, 1969.
ANRW	*Aufstieg und Niedergang der römischen Welt: Geschichte und Kultur Roms im Spiegel der neueren Forschung.* Edited by H. Temporini and W. Haase. Berlin, 1972–.
Apul.	Apuleius
Metam.	*Metamorphoses*
ArchEph	*Archaiologikē Ephēmeris*
Aristophanes	
Vesp.	*Vespae*
Aristotle	
Eth. Nic.	*Ethica Nichomachea*
Ath.	Athenaeus
AthMitt	*Mitteilungen des deutschen archäologischen Instituts, Athenische Abteilung,* 1876–.
ATR	*Anglican Theological Review*
b.	Babylonian tractate
BAGD	Bauer, W., W. F. Arndt, F. W. Gingrich, and F. W. Danker. *Greek-English Lexicon of the New Testament and Other Early Christian Literature.* 2d ed. Chicago, 1979.
BCH	*Bulletin de correspondance hellénique*
Ber.	*Berakot*

BGU	*Aegyptische Urkunden aus den Königlichen Staatlichen Museen zu Berlin, Griechische Urkunden.* 15 vols. Berlin, 1895–1983.
BSA	*Annual of the British School at Athens,* 1895–.
CBQ	*Catholic Biblical Quarterly*
Cic.	Cicero
Att.	*Epistulae ad Atticum*
Fin.	*De finibus*
Sen.	*De senectute*
Tusc.	*Tusculanae disputationes*
Verr.	*In Verrem*
CIL	*Corpus inscriptionum latinarum*
Clem. Al.	Clement of Alexandria
Paed.	*Paedagogus*
cp.	compare
CP	*Classical Philology*
CQ	*Classical Quarterly*
CR	*Classical Review*
DarSag	C. Daremberg and E. Saglio, *Dictionnaire des antiquités grecques et romaines d'après les textes et les monuments* (1877–1919)
Dio Chrysostom	
Or.	*Orationes*
Diog. Laert.	Diogenes Laertius
EFATM	École française d'Athènes, Travaux et mémoires des anciens membres étrangers de l'école et de divers savants
EncyDSS	*Encyclopedia of the Dead Sea Scrolls,* ed. L. H. Schiffman and J. C. VanderKam (2 vols.; Oxford: Oxford University Press, 2000).
Epict.	Epictetus
Diatr.	*Diatribai (Dissertationes)*
EPRO	Études préliminaires aux religions orientales dans l'empire romain
ETL	*Ephemerides theologicae lovanienses*
Eur.	Euripedes
Bacch.	*Bacchae*
FBBS	Facet Books, Biblical Series
FRLANT	Forschungen zur Religion und Literatur des Alten und Neuen Testaments
Gell.	Aulus Gellius
NA	*Noctes Atticae (Attic Nights)*
GGR	*Geschichte der griechischen Religion.* HKAW 5.2.1–2. 2 vols. Munich: Beck, 1967 (vol. 1, 3rd ed.), 1961 (vol. 2, 2nd ed.)
Gos. Thom.	*Gospel of Thomas*
GRBS	*Greek, Roman, and Byzantine Studies*

HBD	*HarperCollins Bible Dictionary.* Edited by P. J. Achtemeier et al. 2nd ed. San Francisco, 1996.
HDR	Harvard Dissertations in Religion
Hellenica	*Hellenica: Recueil d'épigraphie, de numismatique et d'antiquités grecques*
Hesperia	*Hesperia: Journal of the American School of Classical Studies at Athens*
HKAW	Handbuch der Klassischen Altertumswissenschaft
Hom.	Homer
Il.	*The Iliad*
Od.	*The Odyssey*
Hor.	Horace
Sat.	*Satirae*
HTR	*Harvard Theological Review*
IDB	*The Interpreter's Dictionary of the Bible.* Edited by G. A. Buttrick. 4 vols. Nashville, 1962.
IDBSup	*The Interpreter's Dictionary of the Bible: Supplementary Volume.* Edited by K. Crim. Nashville, 1976.
IG	*Inscriptiones graecae.* Editio minor. Berlin, 1924–.
Ignatius	
Rom.	*To the Romans*
Smyrn.	*To the Smyrnaeans*
ILS	*Inscriptiones Latinae Selectae,* ed. H. Dessau
JBL	*Journal of Biblical Literature*
JEA	*Journal of Egyptian Archaeology*
JHS	*Journal of Hellenic Studies*
Jos.	Josephus
J.W.	*Jewish War*
Jos. Asen.	*Joseph and Aseneth*
JRS	*Journal of Roman Studies*
KEK	Kritisch-exegetischer Kommentar über das Neue Testament (Meyer-Kommentar)
LCL	Loeb Classical Library
LGS	*Leges Graecorum sacrae e titulis collectae,* ed. J. von Prott and L. Ziehen. Fasc. 1, pars 1–2. 2 vols. Leipzig: Teubner, 1896–1906.
LSG	*Lois sacrées des cités grecques,* ed. F. Sokolowski. EFATM 18. Paris; De Boccard, 1969.
LSJ	Liddell, H. G., R. Scott, H. S. Jones, *A Greek-English Lexicon.* 9th ed. with revised supplement. Oxford, 1996.
LSS	*Lois sacrées des cités grecques, Supplément,* ed. F. Sokolowski. EFATM 11. Paris: De Boccard, 1962.

Lucian
    Hist. conscr.   *Quomodo historia conscribenda sit*
    Nav.   *Navigium*
    Salt.   *De saltatione*
    Sat.   *Saturnalia*
    Symp.   *Symposium*
Lucr.   Lucretius
LXX   Septuagint
m.   Mishnah tractate
MAAR   Memoirs of the American Academy in Rome
Macrob.   Macrobius
    Sat.   *Saturnalia*
Mart.   Martial
    Epig.   *Epigrams*
NICNT   New International Commentary on the New Testament
NIGTC   New International Greek Testament Commentary
NovT   *Novum Testamentum*
NovTSup   Novum Testamentum Supplements
NRSV   New Revised Standard Version
NT   New Testament
NTS   *New Testament Studies*
OCD   *Oxford Classical Dictionary.* Edited by S. Hornblower and A. Spawforth. 3rd ed. Oxford, 1996.
Odes Sol.   *Odes of Solomon*
OTP   *Old Testament Pseudepigrapha.* Edited by J. H. Charlesworth. 2 vols. New York, 1983.
Ovid
    Fast.   *Fasti*
Papyri
    PColon   Köllner Papyri [= PKöln]
    PColumbia   Columbia Papyri
    PMich.   Michigan Papyri
    POsl.   Papyri Osloenses
    POxy.   Oxyrhynchus Papyri
    PYale   Yale Papyri
Petron.   Petronius
    Sat.   *Satyricon*
Philo
    Contempl.   *De vita contemplativa*
    Ios.   *De Iosepho*
    Flacc.   *In Flaccum*

Leg.	*Legum allegoriae*
Spec.	*De specialibus legibus*
Philostr.	Philostratus
Vit. Apoll.	*Vita Apollonii*
Vit. soph.	*Vitae sophistarum*
Pind.	Pindar
Isthm.	*Isthmionikai*
Plato	
Leg.	*Leges*
Resp.	*Respublica*
Symp.	*Symposium*
Plaut.	Plautus
Curc.	*Curculio*
Men.	*Menaechmi*
Pliny the Elder	
Nat.	*Naturalis historia*
Pliny the Younger	
Ep.	*Epistulae*
Plut.	Plutarch
An virt.	*An virtus doceri possit*
Cat. Mai.	*Cato Maior*
Conj. praec.	*Conjugalia praecepta*
Quaest. conv.	*Quaestiones convivales*
Sept. sap. conv.	*Septem sapientium convivium*
PPF	*Poetarum philosophorum fragmenta,* ed. Diels
Pseudo-Dem.	Pseudo-Demosthenes
Ps.-Philo	*Pseudo-Philo*
PW	Pauly, A. F. *Paulys Realencyclopädie der classischen Altertumswissenschaft.* New edition. G. Wissowa. 49 vols. Munich, 1980.
QS	Qumran Scroll
RAC	*Reallexikon für Antike und Christentum.* Edited by T. Kluser et al. Stuttgart, 1950–.
RB	*Revue biblique*
REG	*Revue des études grecques*
RelSRev	*Religious Studies Review*
RevQ	*Revue de Qumran*
RVV	Religionsgeschichtliche Versuche und Vorarbeiten
SBL	Society of Biblical Literature
SBLDS	Society of Biblical Literature Dissertation Series
SBLMS	Society of Biblical Literature Monograph Series
SBLSBS	Society of Biblical Literature Sources for Biblical Study

SBLTT	Society of Biblical Literature Texts and Translations
SBT	Studies in Biblical Theology
SEG	*Supplementum epigraphicum graecum*
Sen.	Seneca
Ben.	*De beneficiis*
Ep.	*Epistulae morales*
S.H.A.	Scriptores Historiae Augustae
Alex. Sev.	*Alexander Severus*
SIG	*Sylloge inscriptionum graecarum.* Edited by W. Dittenberger. 4 vols. 3d ed. Leipzig, 1915–1924.
SJLA	Studies in Judaism in Late Antiquity
Suet.	Suetonius
Jul.	*Divus Julius*
SUNT	Studien zur Umwelt des Neuen Testaments
t.	Tosefta tractate
Tac.	Tacitus
Ann.	*Annales*
Hist.	*Historiae*
TAPA	*Transactions of the American Philological Association*
TDNT	*Theological Dictionary of the New Testament.* Edited by G. Kittle and G. Friedrich. Translated by G. W. Bromiley. 10 vols. Grand Rapids, 1964–1976.
Tertullian	
Apol.	*Apologeticus*
Theophrastus	
Char.	*Characteres*
TRE	*Theologische Realenzyklopädie.* Edited by G. Krause and G. Müller. Berlin, 1977–.
Val. Max.	Valerius Maximus
WBC	Word Biblical Commentary
Xen.	Xenophon
An.	*Anabasis*
Cyr.	*Cyropaedia*
Hell.	*Hellenica*
Mem.	*Memorabilia*
Symp.	*Symposium*
ZNW	*Zeitschrift für die neutestamentliche Wissenschaft und die Kunde der älteren Kirche*
ZPE	*Zeitschrift für Papyrologie und Epigraphik*

NOTES

1. THE BANQUET AS SOCIAL INSTITUTION

1. A similar thesis has now been advanced by Matthias Klinghardt, *Gemeind-schaftsmahl und Mahlgemeindschaft: Soziologie und Liturgie frühchristlicher Mahlfeiern* (Texte und Arbeiten zum neutestamentlichen Zeitalter 13; Tübingen: Francke Verlag, 1996). His study parallels mine in many respects and independently confirms the principal thesis here advanced, that the Greco-Roman banquet was a single social institution found throughout the Greco-Roman world and was adapted for use in different contexts.

2. See, e.g., Hans-Josef Klauck, *Herrenmahl und hellenistischer Kult: Eine religions-geschichtliche Untersuchung zum ersten Korintherbrief* (Neutestamentliche Abhand-lungen, N. F., 15; Münster: Aschendorff, 1982), and Åke V. Ström, "Abendmahl I: Das sakrale Mahl in den Religionen der Welt," *TRE* 1 (1977): 43–47.

3. Note that the symposium is certainly a social and literary phenomenon in its own right. What I want to emphasize here, however, is the function of the symposium tradition as an archetype for the common Greco-Roman banquet tradition.

4. Joachim Jeremias, *The Eucharistic Words of Jesus* (3rd ed.; New York: Scribner's, 1966), and Hans Lietzmann, *Mass and Lord's Supper* (Leiden: Brill, 1953–55).

5. Jeremias's identification of the Last Supper as a Passover meal has been refuted on the basis of the NT text by Eduard Schweizer (*The Lord's Supper According to the New Testament* [FBBS 18; Philadelphia: Fortress Press, 1967]). Furthermore, more recent studies of Mark have demonstrated the redactional nature of the Last Supper narrative, including such details as the Passover setting; see esp. Vernon Robbins, "Last Meal: Preparation, Betrayal, and Absence (Mark 14:12-25)," in *The Passion in Mark: Studies on Mark 14–16,* ed. Werner H. Kelber (Philadelphia: Fortress Press, 1976), 21–40. Nevertheless, Jeremias's Passover thesis has continued to dominate much of the discussion, as seen by such varied studies as I. Howard Marshall, *Last Supper and Lord's Supper* (Grand Rapids: Eerdmans, 1980), and Gillian Feeley-Harnik, *The Lord's Table: Eucharist and Passover in Early Christianity* (Philadelphia: University of Pennsylvania Press, 1981).

6. Lietzmann, *Mass and Lord's Supper,* 172–215.

7. To simplify my argument, I have referred to Lietzmann's categories as "type A" and "type B." He defines his two types in this way: the first is the liturgy of

Hippolytus, which he traces to Paul; the second is the liturgy of Sarapion, which he traces to the *Didache*. The Pauline tradition emphasizes the commemoration of the death of Jesus. The *Didache* tradition, which he also identifies with the early Jerusalem tradition, commemorated the table fellowship of Jesus with his disciples without reference to his death. See Lietzmann, *Mass and Lord's Supper,* 195–208. This position has been reformulated in Burton L. Mack's *A Myth of Innocence: Mark and Christian Origins* (Philadelphia: Fortress Press, 1988).

8. The classic formulation of the thesis of diversity in early Christianity was set forth in Walter Bauer's *Orthodoxy and Heresy in Earliest Christianity* (Philadelphia: Fortress Press, 1971), and especially promoted in more recent years in the collection of essays by James M. Robinson and Helmut Koester, eds., *Trajectories through Early Christianity* (Philadelphia: Fortress Press, 1971). It is now a standard perspective in studies on Christian origins and has received special prominence in recent debates on Christian origins, as exemplified in Burton L. Mack, *Who Wrote the New Testament? The Making of the Christian Myth* (San Francisco: HarperSanFrancisco, 1995), and idem, *The Christian Myth: Origins, Logic, and Legacy* (New York: Continuum, 2001). On diversity in early Christian Lord's Supper practices, see Dennis E. Smith and Hal E. Taussig, *Many Tables: The Eucharist in the New Testament and Liturgy Today* (Philadelphia: Trinity Press International, 1990), 36–69. Recent studies on the history of liturgy have now begun to emphasize the diversity found at the earliest levels in both Christian and Jewish worship traditions; see Paul F. Bradshaw and Lawrence A. Hoffman, eds., *The Making of Jewish and Christian Worship* (Notre Dame, Ind.: University of Notre Dame Press, 1991); Paul F. Bradshaw, *The Search for the Origins of Christian Worship: Sources and Methods for the Study of Early Liturgy* (New York: Oxford University Press, 1992); and Andrew McGowan, *Ascetic Eucharists: Food and Drink in Early Christian Ritual Meals* (Oxford Early Christian Studies; Oxford: Clarendon, 1999).

9. The "sacramental" meal became a dominant motif in anthropological studies beginning with the classic work of William Robertson Smith (*The Religion of the Semites: The Fundamental Institutions* [3rd ed. repr.; New York: KTAV, 1969]) and continuing in the works of James George Frazer (*The Golden Bough: A Study in Magic and Religion,* 12 vols. [3rd ed.; New York: Macmillan, 1935]); Jane E. Harrison (*Prolegomena to the Study of Greek Religion* [3rd ed.; Cleveland: World, 1922] and *Themis: A Study of the Social Origins of Greek Religion* [2nd ed., repr. of 1927 ed.; Cleveland: World, 1962]); and, in the study of Greek religion, E. R. Dodds (*The Greeks and the Irrational* [Berkeley: University of California Press, 1951]). It still recurs as a basic category for the analysis of ancient sacred meals, although recent studies have begun to question its occurrence in Greek religion; see, e.g., J. P. Kane, "The Mithraic Cult Meal in its Greek and Roman Environment," in *Mithraic Studies,* 2 vols., ed. John R. Hinnells (Proceedings of the First International Congress of Mithraic Studies; Manchester: Manchester University, 1975), 2.313–51, and Albert

Heinrichs, "Human Sacrifice in Greek Religion: Three Case Studies," in *Le sacrifice dans l'antiquité* (Fondation Hardt pour l'étude de l'antiquité classique, entretiens tome 27; Geneva: Fondation Hardt, 1980), 195–235. Further discussion and critique of this issue will be provided in chapter 4. See also my article, "Sacred Meals (Greco-Roman)," *ABD*, 4.650–53.

10. Émile Durkheim, *The Elementary Forms of the Religious Life* (repr.; London: Allen and Unwin, 1976). See also Mircea Eliade, *The Sacred and the Profane* (New York: Harcourt, 1959). On sacred and secular at the banquet, see also S. Stein, "The Influence of Symposia Literature on the Literary Form of the Pesah Haggadah," in *Essays in Greco-Roman and Related Talmudic Literature*, ed. Henry A. Fischel (New York: KTAV, 1977), 26.

11. See also Pauline Schmitt-Pantel, "Sacrificial Meal and *Symposion*: Two Models of Civic Institutions in the Archaic City?" in *Sympotica: A Symposium on the Symposium*, ed. Oswyn Murray (Oxford: Clarendon, 1990), 24: "A number of writers still talk of 'sacred' and 'profane' meals. . . . The 'insertion of the religious element' is clear in all the collective practices which interest us here, whether *symposion*, meal of hospitality, or sacrificial banquet, and the sacred-profane distinction seems to me inapplicable here." Also in idem, "Collective Activities and the Political in the Greek City," in *The Greek City from Homer to Alexander*, ed. Oswyn Murray and Simon Price (Oxford: Clarendon, 1990), 200: "the Greek city knows no separation between sacred and profane."

12. Petron. *Sat.* 26.7–78.8, also known as the *Cena Trimalchionis* or "Banquet of Trimalchio."

13. See also Ezio Pellizer, "Outlines of a Morphology of Sympotic Entertainment," in *Sympotica*, ed. Murray, 180–81, who notes the distinction between literary data and reality. Also see François Lissarrague, "Around the *Krater*: An Aspect of Banquet Imagery," in *Sympotica*, ed. Murray, 196, who points out that artistic representations, such as vase paintings, are not to be taken as "photographic images" of everyday life but as "a system of signs" that provides "evidence for what one might call the social imagination, that is to say the code, the system of values, through which a society sees itself at a particular moment in its history." These are obvious points but nevertheless often overlooked in historical reconstructions.

14. In anthropology, attempts are made to address these issues by distinguishing between the "etic" perspective, in which phenomena are defined according to the investigator's categories, and the "emic" perspective, in which the categories of the people being studied are utilized. See further Susan R. Garrett, "Sociology of Early Christianity," *ABD*, 6:89–99.

15. In New Testament studies, Norman Petersen has especially addressed this issue in his *Rediscovering Paul: Philemon and the Sociology of Paul's Narrative World* (Philadelphia: Fortress Press, 1985).

16. Lucian, *Hist. conscr.*, 50.

17. See, e.g., Mary Douglas, *Purity and Danger: An Analysis of Pollution and Taboo* (New York: Praeger, 1966); "Deciphering a Meal," *Daedalus* 101 (1972): 61–81; and *Natural Symbols: Explorations in Cosmology* (2nd ed.; London: Barrie & Jenkins, 1973).

18. See especially Claude Lévi-Strauss, *The Raw and the Cooked* (New York: Harper & Row, 1969).

19. Douglas, "Deciphering a Meal," 62.

20. See Clifford Geertz, "Thick Description: Toward an Interpretive Theory of Culture," in *The Interpretation of Cultures* (New York: Basic, 1973), 26–27.

21. See the essays collected by P. E. Easterling and J. V. Muir, eds., in *Greek Religion and Society* (Cambridge: Cambridge University Press, 1985), esp. "Foreword" by Moses Finley and "On Making Sense of Greek Religion" by John Gould.

22. See the reviews of scholarship and issues in *Interpretation* 37 (1982); Carolyn A. Osiek, *What Are They Saying about the Social Setting of the New Testament?* (2nd ed.; Mahwah, N.J.: Paulist, 1992); Howard Clark Kee, "Sociology of the New Testament," *HBD*, 961–68; Stanley K. Stowers, "The Social Sciences and the Study of Early Christianity," in *Approaches to Ancient Judaism*, ed. W. S. Green (Brown Judaic Studies 32; Atlanta: Scholars, 1985), 5:149–81; and Susan R. Garrett, "Sociology of Early Christianity," *ABD*, 6:89–99.

23. For a sense of the debate, compare Bruce J. Malina's review of Meeks's *First Urban Christians* (*JBL* 104 [1985]: 346–49) with Susan R. Garrett's review of Malina's *Christian Origins and Cultural Anthropology* (*JBL* 107 [1988]: 532–34). Malina represents the "social science perspective" and Meeks and Garrett the "social history perspective."

24. Studies that collect all biblical references to a particular motif and present them together make this assumption. For an example, see J. F. Ross's article "Meals," in *IDB* 3 (1962): 315–18.

25. Douglas, "Deciphering a Meal," 61.

26. Ibid.

27. As I discuss later, variations developed in these customs particularly in the Roman period, when we find women reclining at the table. Nevertheless, the act of reclining still carried an elitist symbolism.

28. See John H. Elliott, "Patronage and Clientism in Early Christian Society: A Short Reading Guide," *Forum* 3:4 (December 1987): 39–48, for a review of issues and literature. See also L. Michael White, *The Social Origins of Christian Architecture*, vol. 1: *Building God's House in the Roman World* (Harvard Theological Studies 42; Valley Forge, Pa.: Trinity Press International, 1997), who gives special attention to the institution of patronage in relation to religious organizations and the building of religious structures in the Greco-Roman world.

29. Meeks makes a similar point about status inconsistency in early Christian groups in *The First Urban Christians,* 191. On Greek and Roman clubs and associations, see chapter 5 below.

30. Gregory Nagy, *The Best of the Achaeans: Concepts of the Hero in Archaic Greek Poetry* (Baltimore: Johns Hopkins University Press, 1979), 128 §14 n. 4.

31. Jack Goody, *Cooking, Cuisine and Class: A Study in Comparative Sociology* (Cambridge: Cambridge University Press, 1982), 191. Goody's conclusions are similar to those of Mary Douglas, although he disagrees with Douglas's approach (Goody, *Cooking*, 29–32).

32. Portions of the argument in this chapter appeared in an earlier, abbreviated form in Smith and Taussig, *Many Tables*, 21–35.

2. THE GRECO-ROMAN BANQUET

1. Oswyn Murray, "Sympotic History," in *Sympotica: A Symposium on the Symposium*, ed. Oswyn Murray (Oxford: Clarendon, 1990), 11. Murray has revived the study of the symposium in classical scholarship in a collection of essays that began to appear in the 1980s. *Sympotica* is an important collection of studies by a variety of scholars devoted to this topic.

2. See, e.g., Mary Douglas, *Purity and Danger: An Analysis of Pollution and Taboo* (New York: Praeger, 1966); "Deciphering a Meal," *Daedalus* 101 (1972): 61–81; *Implicit Meanings: Essays in Anthropology* (London: Routledge & Kegan Paul, 1975); *Natural Symbols: Explorations in Cosmology* (2nd ed.; London: Barrie & Jenkins, 1973); and *Food in the Social Order: Studies of Food and Festivities in Three American Communities* (New York: Russell Sage Foundation, 1984).

3. For Greek evidence, see Jean-Marie Dentzer, "Aux origines de l'iconographie du banquet couché," *Revue Archéologique* (1971): 215–58. For Roman evidence, see Ovid, *Fast.* 301: "It used to be the custom of old to sit on long benches in front of the hearth," cited in Annette Rathje, "The Adoption of the Homeric Banquet in Central Italy in the Orientalizing Period," in *Sympotica,* ed. Murray, 285. See also Ath. 1.17f: "In their gatherings at dinner the heroes [in Homer] sit instead of reclining." In Jewish tradition, see Philo, *Ios.* 203, who refers to sitting as the ancient custom instead of reclining.

4. See Dentzer, "Aux origines de l'iconographie," and idem, *Le motif du banquet couché dans le proche-orient et le monde grec du VII⁰ au IV⁰ siècle avant J.-C.* (Bibliothèque des écoles françaises d'Athènes et de Rome 246; Rome: École française de Rome, 1982).

5. Dentzer, "Aux origines de l'iconographie," 215–17, 250–58.

6. See Katherine M. D. Dunbabin, "Triclinium and Stibadium," in *Dining in a Classical Context,* ed. W. J. Slater (Ann Arbor: University of Michigan Press, 1991), 136 and fig. 36, who refers to a late fourth-century-C.E. mosaic from Carthage that illustrates a sitting banquet in a luxurious setting.

7. See Dentzer, "Aux origines de l'iconographie," and idem, *Le motif du banquet couché.*

8. Standard works on Greek meal customs include: W. A. Becker and Hermann Göll, *Charikles* (8th ed.; London: Longmans, Green, 1889), 89–108; Hugo Blümner,

The Home Life of the Ancient Greeks (London: Cassell, 1893), 202–332; Victor Ehrenberg, *The People of Aristophanes* (3rd ed.; New York: Schocken, 1962), 102–4; Robert Flacelière, *Daily Life in Greece at the Time of Pericles* (New York: Macmillan, 1966), 167–81; E. A. Gardner, "Food and Drink: Meals, Cooking, and Entertainments," in *A Companion to Greek Studies*, ed. Leonard Whibley (4th ed.; Cambridge: Cambridge University Press, 1931), 639–43; Charles Burton Gulick, *The Life of the Ancient Greeks* (New York: D. Appleton, 1902), 143–52, 179–87; A. Mau, "Convivium," PW 4 (1900): 1201–8; C. Morel and E. Saglio, "Coena," DarSag 1.2 (1877): 1269–82; Iwan von Müller, *Die griechischen Privataltertümer* (Handbuch der klassischen Altertumswissenschaft 4.1.2; 2nd ed.; München: Beck, 1893), 118–31, 264–68; and Michael Vickers, *Greek Symposia* (London: Joint Association of Classical Teachers, 1978).

9. On Homeric meal customs, see especially Gerda Bruns, "Küchenwesen und Mahlzeiten," in *Archaeologia Homerica II,* ed. F. Matz and H. G. Buchholz (Göttingen: Vandenhoeck and Ruprecht, 1970), chapter Q; Morel and Saglio, "Coena," 1269–72; and Ath. 1.8e–14d.

10. Ath. 1.11–12, 17–18. See also Hom. *Il.* 9.200, 218; 24.472–73; *Od.* 3.32–39, 428–29. For further references and discussion, see Bruns, "Küchenwesen und Mahlzeiten," 49–50; and Dentzer, "Aux origines de l'iconographie," 244–45. See also Rathje, "Adoption of the Homeric Banquet."

11. Bruns, "Küchenwesen und Mahlzeiten," 57–60; Morel and Saglio, "Coena," 1269.

12. On the terms for meals in the classical and post-classical periods, see Ath. 1.11b-f and Plut. *Quaest. conv.* 8.6 (726B–F).

13. On Roman meal customs, see J. P. V. D. Balsdon, *Life and Leisure in Ancient Rome* (New York: McGraw-Hill, 1969), 19–54; W. A. Becker, *Gallus* (repr. of 1849 ed., 2nd ed.; London: Longmans, Green, 1915), 451–504; Hugo Blümner, *Die römische Privataltertümer* (Handbuch der Klassischen Altertumswissenschaft 4.2.2; Munich: Beck, 1911), 385–419; Jérôme Carcopino, *Daily Life in Ancient Rome* (New Haven, Conn.: Yale University Press, 1940), 263–76; Ludwig Friedländer, *Roman Life and Manners under the Early Empire* (New York: Barnes & Noble, 1968), 2.146–64; Joachim Marquardt, *Das Privatleben der Römer* (Handbuch der römischen Alterthümer 7; 2nd ed.; Leipzig: Hirzel, 1886), 1.297–340; and Morel and Saglio, "Coena," 1276–82.

14. See, e.g., Mart. *Epig.* 8.67.10, 14.223; see also Balsdon, *Life and Leisure in Ancient Rome,* 20; Becker, *Gallus,* 453; Marquardt, *Das Privatleben der Römer,* 1.267–68.

15. E.g. Sen. *Ep.* 82; Apul. *Metam.* 1.18.

16. S.H.A. *Alex. Sev.* 30.

17. Mart. *Epig.* 4.8.4.

18. E.g., Plaut. *Curc.* 2.344.

19. Compare Pliny the Younger *Ep.* 3.5.10.

20. Sen. *Ep.* 122.6; Plaut. *Men.* 208, *Curc.* 323.

21. See, e.g., Macrob. *Sat.* 3.17.6.

22. Balsdon, *Life and Leisure in Ancient Rome,* 19, 33.

23. Ibid., 26; see, e.g., Galen 6.757–58. This custom is reflected in one of the major texts providing the idealized description of the banquet, the *Symposium* of Plato. Here Socrates is intercepted on his way to the baths and invited to the banquet at the home of Agathon (*Symp.* 174A).

24. Balsdon, *Life and Leisure in Ancient Rome,* 34.

25. Chan Hie Kim, "The Papyrus Invitation," *JBL* 94 (1975): 392, 398–401.

26. J. R. Gilliam, "Invitations to the *Kline* of Sarapis," in *Collectanea Papyrologica: Texts Published in Honor of H. C. Youtie,* ed. Ann Ellis Hanson (Papyrologische Texte und Abhandlungen 19; Bonn: Rudolf Habelt, 1976), 1.315–24.

27. POxy. 110, second century C.E.

28. Kim, "The Papyrus Invitation," 397.

29. Gilliam, "Invitations to the *Kline* of Sarapis," 319.

30. POxy. 2678, third century C.E.

31. POxy. 111, third century C.E.

32. POxy. 2791; second century C.E.; text corrected. Other invitations to birthday feasts are BGU 333 (3rd–4th C.E.), POxy. 112 (3rd–4th C.E.), and POxy. 1214 (5th C.E.); from Kim, "The Papyrus Invitation," 398. See also the discussion of birthday feasts later in this chapter.

33. Gell. *NA* 13.11.3. See also Gell. *NA* 13.11.2: "Now he [Varro] says that the number of the guests ought to begin with that of the Graces and end with that of the Muses; that is, it should begin with three and stop at nine, so that when the guests are fewest, they should not be less than three, when they are most numerous, not more than nine." On a preference for a maximum of nine, see also Cic. *Att.* 13.52; Suet. *Jul.* 48. Note that the standard triclinium arrangement would provide space for nine guests to dine comfortably at three per couch, as illustrated in figure 4 (p. 17).

34. Plut. *Quaest. conv.* 5.5.

35. *Quaest. conv.* 678D. See also the argument attributed to Plutarch's grandfather Lamprias at *Quaest. conv.* 678 E–F.

36. *Quaest. conv.* 679A–B.

37. *Quaest. conv.* 679B–C.

38. See Dunbabin, "Triclinium and Stibadium," for a convenient summary of the Greek and Roman evidence.

39. So argued by Birgitta Bergquist, "Sympotic Space: A Functional Aspect of Greek Dining-Rooms," in *Sympotica,* ed. Murray, 37–65. For the dining arrangements at the *asklepieion* at Troizen, see Gabriel Welter, *Troizen und Kalaureia* (Berlin: Gebr. Mann, 1941), 1, 12, 14. For Corinth, see Carl Roebuck, *Corinth XIV: The Asklepieion and Lerna* (Princeton, N.J.: American School of Classical Studies at Athens, 1951), plan C. At Troizen there is a "dining hall" with separate dining rooms, each forming a dining arrangement for nine to seventeen diners. At Corinth,

three dining rooms of eleven couches each are arranged side by side. See also figures 1–3 in this chapter (pp. 15–16).

40. The term derives from Xen. *Symp.* 1.4; see Michael Jameson, "Private Space and the Greek City," in *The Greek City from Homer to Alexander,* ed. Oswyn Murray and Simon Price (Oxford: Clarendon, 1990), 188.

41. Ibid., 172, 187–91. It is Vitruvius who described a distinct separation between "men's quarters" and "women's quarters" in the Greek house. His model has been widely accepted in scholarship, recently, for example, by Susan Walker, "Women and Housing in Classical Greek: The Archaeological Evidence," in *Images of Women in Antiquity,* ed. Averil Cameron and Amélie Kuhrt (Detroit: Wayne State University Press, 1983), 81–91. Jameson argues that "Vitruvius' description of the houses of the Greeks corresponds to nothing that has been discovered from the Classical period of Greece" ("Domestic Space in the Greek City-State," in *Domestic Architecture and the Use of Space,* ed. Susan Kent [Cambridge: Cambridge University Press, 1990], 92). Rather, he argues, the *andronitis* ("men's quarters") and *gynaikonitis* ("women's quarters") that are attested in the literature refer to "two areas defined by use, not fixed by the design of the house" ("Private Space and the Greek City," 187). The only part of the house that was so fixed by design was the *andron,* or dining room, which Jameson terms "an enclave within the largely female space of the private house where representatives of other *oikoi* were admitted" (ibid., 191). Andrew Wallace-Hadrill makes a similar observation regarding the Roman house: "Of course, individual rooms in houses would have been used in appropriate circumstances by women, and there must have been gender distinctions to observe; but to identify whole areas as set apart for exclusive female use is arbitrary and unjustified" (*Houses and Society in Pompeii and Herculaneum* [Princeton, N.J.: Princeton University Press, 1994], 9).

42. D. M. Robinson and J. W. Graham, *Excavations at Olynthus, Part VIII: The Hellenic House* (Baltimore: Johns Hopkins University Press, 1938), esp. 55–63, 171–85, pl. 85; see also Stephen G. Miller, *The Prytaneion: Its Function and Architectural Form* (Berkeley: University of California Press, 1978), 219–24.

43. The issues involved in identifying a dining room in a Greek structure are nicely summarized in Miller, *The Prytaneion,* 219–24. See also figures 2–3 (pp. 15–16) in this chapter.

44. Ibid. On off-center doorways, see also R. A. Tomlinson, "Two Buildings in Sanctuaries of Asklepios," *JHS* 89 (1969): 106–9.

45. Roebuck, *Corinth XIV,* 51–57; 52 fig. 13, plan C. See also figure 1 (p. 15) in this chapter.

46. There were still some discernible differences, however. See Gisela M. A. Richter, *The Furniture of the Greeks, Etruscans, and Romans* (London: Phaidon, 1966); Boardman, "Symposium Furniture," in *Sympotica,* ed. Murray, 122–131; and Miller, *The Prytaneion,* 222 n. 7.

47. See especially Katherine M. D. Dunbabin, "*Ut Graeco More Biberetur:* Greeks and Romans on the Dining Couch," in *Meals in a Social Context: Aspects of the Communal Meal in the Hellenistic and Roman World,* ed. I. Nielsen and H. S. Nielsen (Aarhus Studies in Mediterranean Antiquity I; Aarhus: Aarhus University Press, 1998), 81–101, who notes the differences between Greek and Roman reclining practices, especially in terms of the arrangement and design of couches in the dining room and the location of the first ranked position. She emphasizes that the data regarding Greek and Roman dining customs is complex and should not be collapsed into one Greco-Roman form. I agree that the data is complex, but wish to center this study on a different level of abstraction, in which nevertheless there were significant aspects of the dining customs held in common. For example, everyone was reclining, but they arranged the couches differently.

48. See diagram in Marquardt, *Das Privatleben der Römer,* 304. The term *Pi shape* is derived from Dunbabin ("*Ut Graeco More Biberetur,*" 88–89). See also figure 4 (p. 17).

49. Poland, "*Stibadeion,*" PW 3A (1929): 2481. For a discussion of further variations in Roman dining practices, see Katherine M. D. Dunbabin, "Convivial Spaces: Dining and Entertainment in the Roman Villa," *Journal of Roman Archaeology* 9 (1996): 66–80.

50. Athenaeus quotes Phylarchus of Athens (third century B.C.E.) to the effect that the *propoma* existed in earlier periods in Greece: "An appetizer [*propoma*] was handed round before dinner, as had been the custom in the beginning" (2.58c). He also provides an extended discussion of various food items that were served as appetizers (2.58b–60b). Plutarch, however, disputes the antiquity of this custom: "The serving of the so-called aperitives [*propoma*] is a great change, too. The ancients did not even drink water before the dessert course [*entragein*]" (*Quaest. conv.* 734A). See also Becker and Göll, *Charikles,* 325.

51. Mart. *Epig.* 10.31.

52. See, e.g., Gell. *NA* 13.11.6; S.H.A. *Alex. Sev.* 37.10.

53. Gell. *NA* 13.11.6–7 speaks of the *bellaria* at the *secundae mensae* and equates it with the Greek term *tragēmata,* thus indicating that the term *bellaria* included more than just sweet cakes, but also the general tidbits of the dessert course; e.g., in S.H.A. *Alex. Sev.* 37.10 fruit is included.

54. Balsdon, *Life and Leisure in Ancient Rome,* 44–50, esp. 44–47; see also Becker, *Gallus,* 485–504, and Marquardt, *Das Privatleben der Römer,* 331–40.

55. Mart. *Epig.* 11.31.4–7.

56. Plato *Symp.* 175A. See further on the pre-meal rituals of washing, perfuming, etc., in Becker and Göll, *Charikles,* 318–20.

57. Ath. 14.641d, quoted from Aristophanes (*Vesp.* 1216); see also Ath. 2.60a, 4.156e.

58. Becker and Göll, *Charikles,* 236–37, 320. On the use of a spoon, see Ath. 3.126a–f. On training the young to eat with the proper etiquette, see Plut.

An virt. 439D–E and especially 439F: "to touch salt fish with but one finger, but fresh fish, bread, and meat with two."

59. Note the presence of dogs as a regular feature in artistic representations of banquets; see examples in Richter, *The Furniture of the Greeks, Etruscans, and Romans*, plates 294, 317, 363, 416.

60. Ath. 4.146f–147a.

61. Ath. 4.149d, quoting Theopompus, ca. 410–370 B.C.E.

62. Lucian *Symp.* 43.

63. Ath. 11.462c–d, quoting Xenophanes of Colophon, sixth century B.C.E.

64. Plato *Symp.* 176A.

65. Xen. *Symp.* 2.1.

66. See the discussion in Athenaeus on the disagreement in the sources as to the proper designation for this libation. Some dedicate the cup to the "Good Deity," others to the "goddess of health" *(Hygieia); see* Ath. 11.486f–487b. See also 15.692f–693f. Karl Kircher, however, distinguishes two customs here and shows that the cup to *Hygieia* is not a libation (*Die sacrale Bedeutung des Weines* [RVV 9.2; Giessen: A. Töpelmann, 1910], 16–17).

67. Ath. 15.675b–c, quoted from Philonides the physician.

68. Ath. 2.38d, quoted from Philochorus, late fourth century B.C.E.

69. Thus Martin P. Nilsson, *Geschichte der griechischen Religion* (HKAW 5.2.1–2; Munich: Beck, 1961, 1967) 1.414–16, 2.213–18; idem, "Die Götter des Symposions," in *Opuscula selecta* (Lund: Gleerup, 1951), 1.438–42. See also Kircher, *Die sacrale Bedeutung des Weines,* 24–34.

70. Pind. *Isthm.* 6.10, cited in Kircher, *Die sacrale Bedeutung des Weines,* 18 n. 1; translation mine. See also ibid., 17–19; Gulick, *The Life of the Ancient Greeks,* 183; Blümner, *The Home Life of the Ancient Greeks,* 212.

71. W. W. Tarn, "The Hellenistic Ruler-Cult and the Daemon," *JHS* 48 (1928): 210–13. See also Kircher, *Die sacrale Bedeutung des Weines,* 13–21, 24–38, 40–42.

72. Plato *Symp.* 176A.

73. On the use of salt with wine, see Plut. *Quaest. conv.* 4.4 (669B). See also Becker-Göll, *Charikles,* 330–32; Gulick, *The Life of the Ancient Greeks,* 148.

74. Ath. 14.641d–e; Loeb translation adapted by the author.

75. Plut. *Quaest. conv.* 612E–F.

76. Flacelière, *Daily Life in Greece,* 173.

77. For standard data on the Greek and Roman diet, see Becker-Göll, *Charikles,* 322–25; Blümner, *Home Life,* 206–8; Don R. Brothwell, "Foodstuffs, Cooking, and Drugs," in *Civilization of the Ancient Mediterranean: Greece and Rome,* ed. M. Grant and R. Kitzinger (New York: Scribner's, 1988), 1.247–61; Don R. Brothwell and Patricia Brothwell, *Food in Antiquity: A Survey of the Diet of Early Peoples* (New York: Praeger, 1969); R. J. Forbes, "Fermented Beverages 500 B.C.–1500 A.D.," in *Studies in Ancient Technology* (Leiden: Brill, 1965), 3.111–37, and idem, "Food in Classical Antiquity," in *Studies in Ancient Technology,* 3.86–110; Reay Tannahill,

Food in History (rev. ed.; New York: Crown, 1988), 60–91; and Kenneth D. White, "Farming and Animal Husbandry," in Grant and Kitzinger, eds., *Civilization of the Ancient Mediterranean,* 1.211–45.

78. On the varieties of breads, see Ath. 3.109b–116a.

79. See Ath. 7.281–330.

80. Jean Casabona, *Recherches sur le vocabulaire des sacrifices en Grec, des origines à la fin de l'époque classique* (Paris: Ophrys, 1966), 28–38.

81. Apicius, *De Re Coquinaria,* compiled ca. fourth century C.E.

82. Thus see Plato *Leg.* 1.637, Ael. *Var. hist.* 2.37, Plut. *Quaest. conv.* 678B; drinking unmixed wine is called a Scythian custom, thus a barbarism, in Ath. 10.427a-c.

83. Plut. *Conj. praec.* 140F.

84. Ath. 10.426d.

85. Plut. *Quaest. conv.* 3.9.

86. "Greek wine was a natural fermentation and yet remained sweet: since it failed to eliminate all the sugar, we may assume that it reached close to the upper limit for natural fermentation, of 16 to 17 percent alcohol by volume; diluted 1 part of wine to 2 or 3 of water, this is roughly equivalent in terms of both liquid intake and alcoholic strength to the range of modern beers" (Murray, "War and the Symposium," in *Dining,* ed. Slater, 101 n. 24).

87. For example, see the collection of references to fine wines in Jasper Griffin, *Latin Poets and Roman Life* (Chapel Hill: University of North Carolina Press, 1986), 65–69; on ancient wine production and trade, see Michal Dayagi-Mendels, *Drink and Be Merry: Wine and Beer in Ancient Times* (Jerusalem: The Israel Museum, 1999).

88. Noted also by Emily Gowers, *The Loaded Table: Representations of Food in Roman Literature* (Oxford: Clarendon, 1993), 7.

89. See Richard I. Pervo, "Wisdom and Power: Petronius' *Satyricon* and the Social World of Early Christianity," *ATR* 67 (1985): 307–25.

90. Plato *Symp.* 176E, 177D.

91. Plato *Symp.* 213E.

92. Plut. *Quaest. conv.* 620A.

93. On the iconography of the *krater* in Greek vase painting, see François Lissarrague, "Around the *Krater:* An Aspect of Banquet Imagery," in *Sympotica,* ed. Murray, 196–209.

94. See, e.g., Diog. Laert. 1.104.

95. Cic. *Tusc.* 1.40.96, *Verr.* 2.2.26.

96. Plato *Symp.* 222E. See also 214A–D.

97. See, e.g., Plut. *Quaest. conv.* 711D.

98. For a general description of the sport, see Brian A. Sparkes, "Kottabos: An Athenian After-Dinner Game," *Archaeology* 13 (1960): 202–7.

99. Ath. 782B, cited in Ross Scaife, "From *Kottabos* to War in Aristophanes' *Acharnians,*" *GRBS* 33 (1992): 33.

100. Ibid., 27–30. Scaife cites as evidence the erotic themes in vase paintings illustrating *kottabos* as well as literary references such as the fragment from Sophocles found in Ath. 487D: "Here is tickling and the peck of kisses: I establish these as prizes of victory for the man who casts the *kottabos* most pleasingly and strikes the bronze head" (28 n. 7).

101. On the various games, see Becker and Göll, *Charikles,* 344–55; Ehrenberg, *The People of Aristophanes,* 103; Flacelière, *Daily Life in Greece,* 181; Gulick, *The Life of the Ancient Greeks,* 185.

102. Scaife, "From *Kottabos* to War in Aristophanes' *Acharnians,*" 31–32.

103. See, e.g., Plut. *Quaest. conv.* 7.7: "Whether the music of flute girls is proper after-dinner entertainment." The issue revolved around the banishment of the flute girl in Plato's *Symposium* (176E) so that the guests could concentrate on conversation.

104. Lucian *Symp.* 46.

105. See, e.g., the references collected by Ath. 13.607a–608, where flute girls are classed with dancing girls and other harlots. On the subject in general, see Chester G. Starr, "An Evening with the Flute Girls," *La parola del passato* 33 (1978): 401–10. On sexual stereotypes in ancient art and literature, see John Boswell's note on the stereotypical portrayal of one of the partners in a representation of a homosexual encounter as a youth. He notes that such representations should not be seen as normative for social life, but rather as normative for artistic stereotypical representations (*The Kindness of Strangers: The Abandonment of Children in Western Europe from Late Antiquity to the Renaissance* [New York: Pantheon, 1988], 28–29 n. 58).

106. Plut. *Quaest. conv.* 712F–713A.

107. Ibid. 713A–B.

108. "Il simposio greco arcaico e classico come spettacolo a se stesso" (L. E. Rossi, *Spettacoli conviviali dall' antichità classica alle corti italiane del '400: Atti del VII convegno di studio* [Viterbo, 1983], 44), quoted by Ezio Pellizer, "Outlines of a Morphology of Sympotic Entertainment," in *Sympotica,* ed. Murray, 177.

109. Plato *Symp.* 176E.

110. Xen. *Symp.* 9.7.

111. See, e.g., Richter, *Furniture of the Greeks, Etruscans, and Romans,* plates 282, 296, 311, 368.

112. Among recent studies of the subject, see especially Jan N. Bremmer, "Adolescents, *Symposion,* and Pederasty," in *Sympotica,* ed. Murray, 135–48. In a study of erotic themes on vases in general, where the scenes depicted do not necessarily picture a banquet, H. A. Shapiro notes a commonly held perception: "The most reasonable scenario is that erotic vases were used at all-male symposia, or drinking parties, the Athenian version of a stag party" ("Eros in Love: Pederasty and Pornography in Greece," in Amy Richlin, ed., *Pornography and Representation in Greece and Rome* [Oxford: Oxford University Press, 1992], 53).

113. Jameson, "Private Space and the Greek City," 190. See also Pauline Schmitt-Pantel, "Collective Activities and the Political in the Greek City," in *The Greek City*, ed. Murray and Price, 199–213.

114. Plut. *Quaest. conv.* 710C.

115. Plato *Symp.* 223B–D.

116. Lucian *Symp.* 17, 43–48.

117. See the examples cited in Balsdon, *Life and Leisure in Ancient Rome*, 36–42.

118. See, e.g., Pliny the Elder's sermon against drunkenness, *Nat.* 14.28.

119. For a summary of these laws, see Gell. *NA* 2.24.

120. Plato *Symp.* 176E.

121. Plut. *Quaest. conv.* 7.7.

122. Ibid., 708D.

123. Ath. 5.186a.

124. Pliny the Younger *Ep.* 3.5.13: "In summer he rose from dinner while it was still light, in winter as soon as darkness fell, as if some law compelled him." A winter meal lasting until dark would still last two to three hours. See also Balsdon, *Life and Leisure in Ancient Rome*, 19.

125. Cic. *Sen.* 13.45–14.46.

126. Ibid., 13.44.

127. Plut. *Quaest. conv.* 1.10.1 (628A), 2.4.1 (638B), 4.1.1 (660D).

128. Kathryn Argetsinger, "Birthday Rituals: Friends and Patrons in Roman Poetry and Cult," *Classical Antiquity* 11 (1992): 175–93. See also Wilhelm Schmidt, *Geburtstag im Altertum* (RVV 7.1; Giessen: A. Töpelmann, 1908), and Argetsinger's critique of Schmidt in "Birthday Rituals," 175 n. 1.

129. Horace *Ode* 4.11.17–18; quoted in Argetsinger, "Birthday Rituals," 186.

130. See especially John H. Oakley and Rebecca H. Sinos, *The Wedding in Ancient Athens* (Wisconsin Studies in Classics; Madison: University of Wisconsin Press, 1993), and Noel Robertson, "The Betrothal Symposium in Early Greece," in *Dining*, ed. Slater, 25–57.

131. Plut. *Quaest. conv.* 666F–67A.

132. Ibid., 666D.

133. Oakley and Sinos, *Wedding*, 22, who cite Menander's *Dyskolos* and *Samia* for the latter type.

134. Plut. *Quaest. conv.* 666E.

135. Oakley and Sinos, *Wedding*, 22, citing Ath. 6.245a.

136. Ibid., 23.

137. Ibid., 22–23.

138. Ibid., 22.

139. Lucian *Symp.* 8.

140. Robert Garland, *The Greek Way of Death* (Ithaca, N.Y.: Cornell University Press, 1985), 21–37; see also Donna C. Kurtz and John Boardman, *Greek Burial*

Customs (Aspects of Greek and Roman Life; London: Thames and Hudson, 1971), 141–46. A helpful annotated bibliography on all aspects of burial rites in antiquity is found in Ian Morris, *Death-Ritual and Social Structure in Classical Antiquity* (Key Themes in Ancient History; Cambridge: Cambridge University Press, 1992), 205–10.

141. Hegesippos, *Adelphoi* 11–16, as quoted in Kurtz and Boardman, *Greek Burial Customs,* 146.

142. The *totenmahl* (funerary banquet) reliefs have been extensively studied by Dentzer, who draws the conclusions given above. See Dentzer, "Aux origines de l'iconographie," and *Le motif du banquet couché.*

143. Garland, *The Greek Way of Death,* 114.

144. Fragment 1009 as quoted in Murray, "Death and the Symposion," *AION* 10 (1988): 240.

145. Theognis 973–78. Ibid., 241.

146. Ibid., 254.

147. J. M. C. Toynbee, *Death and Burial in the Roman World* (Aspects of Greek and Roman Life; London: Thames and Hudson, 1971), 37, 50–51, 137.

148. Ibid., 50–51, 61–64; see also Richard Jones, "Burial Customs of Rome and the Provinces," in *The Roman World,* ed. John Wacher (London: Routledge & Kegan Paul, 1987), 2:813–14.

149. Like the Assyrian reliefs, which show the king surrounded by submissive figures, so also the Greek grave reliefs that copy this motif show the deceased reclining and often accompanied by a servant and the deceased's wife, who is shown sitting. Thus see Dentzer, "Aux origines de l'iconographie," 215–17, 240–46.

150. Joan B. Burton, "The Function of the Symposium Theme in Theocritus' *Idyll* 14," *GRBS* 33 (1992): 228–29.

151. Ibid., 230. Violence against women is a theme of vase paintings of sympotic scenes in early-fifth-century Greece, as noted in Robert F. Sutton Jr., "Pornography and Persuasion on Attic Pottery," in Richlin, ed., *Pornography and Representation,* 11–12.

152. Burton, "Function of the Symposium Theme." See also Joan Burton, "Women's Commensality in the Ancient Greek World," *Greece and Rome* 45:2 (October 1998): 143–65.

153. Burton, "Function of the Symposium Theme," 230. See Diog. Laert. 8.41.

154. Ibid., 230–32.

155. Ibid., 234–35.

156. See Val. Max. 2.1.2, Petron. *Sat.* 67–69.

157. Cornelius Nepos, *De viris illustribus, praef.* as quoted in Tenney Frank, *Aspects of Social Behavior in Ancient Rome* (Cambridge, Mass.: Harvard University Press, 1932), 3.

158. Lucian *Symp.* 8.

159. Ibid., 13.

160. See especially Kathleen E. Corley, *Private Women, Public Meals: Social Conflict in the Synoptic Tradition* (Peabody, Mass.: Hendrickson, 1993), 24–66. Corley

has amassed a wealth of evidence on the sexual stereotyping of women at banquets in the Greco-Roman period.

161. As seen, e.g., in Plato's *Symposium:* as each guest arrived, Agathon ordered his servants to attend to his needs (175A, 213B).

162. As in Lucian's *Symposium:* here the servants of the host served the meal, but the servants of the individual guests evidently stood behind them in order to provide for their individual needs. Thus one of the guests stealthily passes food to his servant standing behind him so that he may slip out with an extra portion (11).

163. As seen in Plutarch's discussion of the different ways in which Greeks, Romans, Persians, and others designate the place of honor at the table (*Quaest. conv.* 1.3, esp. 619B).

164. This is the issue in Plutarch's symposiac discussion, "Whether the host should arrange the placing of his guests or leave it to the guests themselves" (*Quaest. conv.* 1.2). The discussion centers on determining which option would contribute most to the friendship and pleasure of the event. See further on this text in chapter 3 below.

165. In Plutarch's discussion mentioned in the previous note, such an incident is noted, in which a guest arrives late and then leaves in disgust when he observes that there is no place left at table worthy of his status in society (ibid., 615C–D).

166. See, for example, Ath. 9.372a (quoting from Polemon the geographer): "It is ordained among the Delphians that whosoever shall bring for the festival of the Theoxenia the largest horn onion to Leto shall receive a portion from the table." Note also that priests were regularly honored with special portions for services rendered, as will be discussed further in chapter 4 below.

167. Mart. *Epig.* 3.60. See further ibid., 1.20, 3.49, 4.85, 6.11, 10.49.

168. Pliny the Younger *Ep.* 2.6.

169. Ibid., 2.6.4.

170. Ibid., 2.6.3.

171. Ibid., 2.6.5–6.

172. See also Pellizer, "Outlines of a Morphology of Sympotic Entertainment," 181: "Probably the use of the *symposion* was not limited to aristocratic or tyrannical circles (therefore élites), but must have been practised also in wider strata of society such as the mercantile, artisan, or peasant classes, as one can deduce from certain hints in Aristophanes and from the proliferation of sympotic scenes in vase painting." See also this conclusion by Paul Veyne: "Without couches, there could be no real feast, even among the poor" ("The Roman Empire," in *A History of Private Life I: From Pagan Rome to Byzantium* [Cambridge, Mass.: Belknap Press of Harvard University Press, 1987], 188).

173. Plut. *Quaest. conv.* 673A.

3. THE PHILOSOPHICAL BANQUET

1. The depiction of various gatherings of the "seven wise men" was a part of Greek tradition and a motif used by both Plato and Xenophon. These individuals, who

were viewed as the intellectual forefathers of Greek thought, lived several centuries before Plato and Xenophon in the sixth century B.C.E. For a detailed discussion of Plutarch's version of this story, see David E. Aune, "Septem sapientium convivium," in *Plutarch's Ethical Writings and Early Christian Literature,* ed. Hans Dieter Betz (Leiden: Brill, 1978), 51–105.

2. See, e.g., Konrat Ziegler, "Plutarchos von Chaironeia," PW 21 (1951): 636–962, who considers Plutarch's descriptions to be generally reliable reminiscences of actual meals although nevertheless influenced by literary models. On Plutarch's family and circle of friends, see also ibid., 641–51, 665–96; and Christopher P. Jones, *Plutarch and Rome* (Oxford: Clarendon, 1971), 39–64.

3. "Therefore subjects of discourse, like friends, should be admitted to dinners only if they are of proved quality. . . . Permission is given to use as criteria the examples whose seventh set of ten this book comprises" (Plut. *Quaest. conv.* 697E).

4. Josef Martin, *Symposion: Die Geschichte einer literarischen Form* (Paderborn: F. Schöningh, 1931).

5. Plato *Symp.* 176E.

6. Ath. 5.186a.

7. Plut. *Quaest. conv.* 629C–D.

8. Ibid., 629C.

9. Gell. *NA* 15.2.

10. Ibid., 17.8.

11. "*Utiles delectabilesque sermones*" (ibid., 15.2.3.).

12. Ibid., 7.13.4. Compare Plut. *Quaest. conv.* 614D.

13. Gell. *NA* 7.13.5.

14. Ibid., 7.13.7–11.

15. Ibid., 7.13.12.

16. Plut. *Quaest. conv.* 672E.

17. Ibid., 1.1.

18. Ibid., 613A.

19. Ibid., 613B–C.

20. Ibid., 613E–F.

21. Ibid., 614A–B.

22. Ibid., 614B.

23. Ibid., 716E–F.

24. Ibid., 717A.

25. Ibid., 614D.

26. Ibid., 615A.

27. Ibid., 614D–E.

28. Ibid., 614E.

29. Ibid., 615A.

30. Ibid., 644C. The topic of Plutarch's discourse here is: "Whether people of old did better with portions served to each, or people of today, who dine from a common

supply" (ibid., 642F). Compare Diog. Laert. 8.35, where the "friends" in Pythagore-anism had as the symbol of their unity the sharing of "one bread"; compare also 1 Cor 10:17, discussed below in chapter 8.

31. Plut. *Quaest. conv.* 643A.

32. Ibid., 612D.

33. Ibid., 660B.

34. See esp. Jean-Claude Fraisse, *Philia: La notion d'amitié dans la philosophie antique* (Paris: Vrin, 1974), and, more recently, John T. Fitzgerald, ed., *Greco-Roman Perspectives on Friendship* (SBLSBS 34; Atlanta: Scholars, 1997).

35. Plato *Leg.* 2.671C–72A.

36. Plut. *Quaest. conv.* 1.2 (615C–619A).

37. Ibid., 615E.

38. See Martin, *Symposion,* 174–75.

39. Plut. *Quaest. conv.* 616B.

40. Ibid., 615F.

41. Ibid., 616C.

42. Ibid., 616D.

43. Ibid., 616E–F.

44. Ibid., 616F–617E.

45. Ibid., 617A.

46. Ibid., 617F–619A.

47. Ibid., 618A.

48. Ibid., 616B.

49. Ibid., 617C.

50. Ibid., 616B.

51. Ibid., 617A.

52. Ibid., 617C.

53. On the importance of status in Greco-Roman society, see Ramsay Mac-Mullen, *Roman Social Relations 50 B.C. to A.D. 284* (New Haven, Conn.: Yale University Press, 1974), 59–62, 76–77, 88–120. On the relation of the formal meal and its accoutrements to one's social class in society, see Jean-Marie Dentzer, "Aux origines de l'iconographie du banquet couché," *Revue Archéologique* (1971): 250–55.

54. Plut., *Quaest. conv.* 616D.

55. Ibid., 616F.

56. Ibid., 616D.

57. Ibid., 616C, 616E.

58. On the connection of "friendship" *(philia)* with "equality" *(isotēs),* see Fraisse, *Philia,* 63–66 (Pythagoreans), 202–13, 246–47, 269–71 (Aristotle), and 181 (Plato). Aristotle, for example, allowed for a kind of friendship in unequal relationships (as in parent to child) but primarily argued that equality was essential for friendship in its proper sense (*Eth. Nic.* 8.6.7–8.8.7). Plutarch appears to argue from an Aristotelian position when he defines the proper guests at a dinner party as

"friends and intimates of one another who will enjoy being together," that is, they are "those who share the same culture and same beliefs" (*Quaest. conv.* 708D). See also the phrase "equality of friends" *(isotēs philotēs)* as a phrase from ancient wisdom in, e.g., Plato *Leg.* 6.757a, Aristotle *Eth. Nic.* 8.7 (1157b, 34–36); cited in Stählin, *"Philos,"* *TDNT* 9 (1974): 152–53.

59. On membership of women and slaves, see Diog. Laert. 10.4–7; A.-J. Festugière, *Epicurus and His Gods* (Cambridge, Mass.: Harvard University Press, 1956), 29–30; J. M. Rist, *Epicurus: An Introduction* (Cambridge: Cambridge University Press, 1972), 10–11. Some women members were married, such as Themista, wife of Leonteus of Lampsacus, but many were courtesans, often with nicknames indicating their servile origin, such as Leontion, Mammarion, Hedeia, Erotion, Nikidion, and Demelata (Festugière, *Epicurus and His Gods,* 43 n. 17). A summary of Epicurus's teaching on women and sexual relations is found in Diog. Laert. 10.118–19: "As regards women, he [the wise man] will submit to the restrictions imposed by the law. . . . The Epicureans do not suffer the wise man to fall in love. . . . No one was ever the better for sexual indulgence, and it is well if he be not the worse. . . . Nor, again, will the wise man marry and rear a family." On attitudes to servants: "Nor will he punish his servants; rather he will pity them and make allowance on occasion for those who are of good character" (10.118). On attitudes to public esteem and wealth, see further below.

60. Diog. Laert. 10.18.

61. See references in Cic. *Fin.* 2.101, Pliny the Elder *Nat.* 35.5.

62. Diog. Laert. 10.128–29. See also Diog. Laert. 10.6.11, Ath. 12.546f.

63. Ath. 12.546f; translation from Bailey, *Epicurus: The Extant Remains* (Oxford: Clarendon, 1926), 5.59.

64. See, e.g., Diog. Laert. 10.85, 128, 131; Festugière, *Epicurus and His Gods,* 32–33.

65. See, e.g.: "The flesh cries out to be saved from hunger, thirst, and cold. For if a man both have and hope to have these things, he might rival even Zeus in happiness" (Bailey, *Epicurus: The Extant Remains,* A.33; translation adapted).

66. Rist, *Epicurus: An Introduction,* 105.

67. Diog. Laert. 10.144.

68. Ibid., 10.149. The concept of "static" and "active" pleasures derives from Aristotle, e.g., *Eth. Nic.* 7.15.8; see Rist, *Epicurus: An Introduction,* 101–2, 170–72.

69. See Rist, *Epicurus: An Introduction,* 103. Note also the technical use of *euphrosynē* as a term for "a joyous feast" as discussed in chapter 4 below.

70. A scholiast is an ancient editor; here the term refers to an ancient editor of Epicurus.

71. Diog. Laert. 10.149.

72. Ibid. 10.131–32. The full quotations is as follows: "It [pleasure] is not an unbroken succession of drinking-bouts and of revelry, not sexual love, not the enjoyment of the fish and other delicacies of a luxurious table, which produce a pleasant life; it is sober reasoning." In his *Symposium,* which is not extant, Epicurus is reputed

to have said that a wise man will not "babble when drunken" (*lērein,* Diog. Laert. 10.119). Compare the discussion of proper symposium conversation in Plutarch, where "babbling" *(lērein)* is proscribed. This term is also used by the Stoics to describe in negative terms the kind of talk that takes place at drinking parties (H. von Arnim, *Stoicorum veterum fragmenta* [Leipzig, 1903–24], 3.643).

73. Achille Vogliano, ed., *Epicuri et Epicureorum scripta in Herculanensibus papyris servata* (Berlin: Weidmann, 1928), frag. 8, col. 1, p. 70. The fragment is from a work on Epicurus by Philodemus, an Epicurean who lived ca. 110 to ca. 40/35 B.C.E. For a brief commentary on this fragment, see Festugière, *Epicurus and His Gods,* 22–23, 26. This translation is mine, adapted from that of Festugière.

74. Festugière suggests that the sentence may have begun: "[Those who live a dissolute life must not be admitted,] nor those who groan in anxiety of soul . . ." (*Epicurus and His Gods,* 22).

75. Bailey, *Epicurus: The Extant Fragments,* V.41; see also Hermann Usener, ed., *Epicurea* (Leipzig: Teubner, 1987), frag. 394: "if it is necessary to laugh in [doing] philosophy."

76. Compare "illusory opinion" *(kenē doxa)* in Diog. Laert. 10.149 (quoted above, p. 59), which is defined as "desires for crowns and the erection of statues in one's honor." Compare also the argument of Timon in Plut. *Quaest. conv.* 616D (quoted above, p. 56), who also contrasts "empty fame [*kenē doxa*] from market place and theater" with the equality that should prevail at the banquet.

77. Diog. Laert. 1.141 (*Basic Doctrines* 7).

78. See Usener, *Epicurea,* frags. 551–60.

79. See Dugas, *L'amitié antique;* Fraisse, *Philia;* K. Treu, "Freundschaft" *RAC* 8 (1969): 418–34; Fitzgerald, *Greco-Roman Perspectives.*

80. See Carlo Diano, "Epicure: La philosophie du plaisir et la société des amis," *Les études philosophiques* 22 (1967): 173–84; Festugière, *Epicurus and His Gods,* 27–28; Fraisse, *Philia,* 307–17; and Rist, *Epicurus: An Introduction,* 127–29, 139. Part of Epicurus's argument was to separate "sexual love" *(erōs)* from "friendship" *(philia),* contrary to Plato but in agreement with Aristotle. *Erōs* was seen to be accompanied by "agony and distress" (Usener, *Epicurea,* frag. 483) whereas *philia* brings "security" (Diog. Laert. 10.148).

81. Diog. Laert. 10.120. See also Diog. Laert. 10.148.

82. Thus Festugière, *Epicurus and His Gods,* 36–42. See also Diano, "Epicure: La philosophie du plaisir et la société des amis," and Wolfgang Schmid, "Epicur," *RAC* 5 (1961): 746–55.

83. Diog. Laert. 10.120. See also Diog. Laert. 10.144, Lucr. 5.11.

84. See, e.g., Diog. Laert. 1.9–10, where, after several criticisms of Epicurus and his thought have been recounted, appeal is made to "the abundance of witnesses who attest to his unsurpassed good will to all men . . . his friends, so many in number that they could hardly be counted as whole cities . . . his gratitude to his parents, his generosity to his brothers, his gentleness to his servants . . . and in general his benevolence

to all humankind." See also Festugière, *Epicurus and His Gods,* 21–23, 42; Rist, *Epicurus: An Introduction,* 11–12, 136–38.

85. Diog. Laert. 10.120; however, notice the Epicurean disdain for death, e.g., 10.124–26. Compare John 15:13, "Greater love has no man than this, that a man lay down his life for his friends."

86. See, e.g., the summary of three different views of friendship among Epicureans in Cicero *Fin.* 1.65–70. Compare Rist, *Epicurus: An Introduction,* 29–31.

87. Plutarch wrote ten moral essays on anti-Epicurean themes, three of which are extant. On the other hand, he, like other anti-Epicurean writers such as Cicero, often found Epicurean ideas compatible with his thought. See C. W. Chilton, *Diogenes of Oenoanda: The Fragments* (London: Oxford University, 1971), xxiii; see also Betz, ed., *Plutarch's Ethical Writings,* 223–24, 291–98, 406–7; Fraisse, *Philia,* 434–45.

88. Philip Merlan, "Greek Philosophy from Plato to Plotinus," in *The Cambridge History of Later Greek and Early Medieval Philosophy,* ed. A. H. Armstrong (Cambridge: Cambridge University Press, 1970), 63 n. 1. In contrast, Albrecht Dihle discounts Epicurean influence on philosophical ethics of the Roman period, but his conclusion is perhaps stated too strongly ("Ethik," *RAC* 6 [1966]: 670–72). Rather, the Epicurean school appears to have been very much alive and well during the Roman period and up to the third century c.e., as suggested in Chilton, *Diogenes of Oenoanda,* xii–xxviii; cf. Diog. Laert. 10.9. But even more significant, Epicurean thought was often taken over by non-Epicurean writers, even those who wrote anti-Epicurean tracts, such as Cicero and Plutarch. This is only to be expected, since the dialogue between schools evidenced by the myriad of anti-Epicurean writings not only affected the inner debates within the school itself but also influenced those on the other side of the debate. On the issue of friendship, for example, the Epicurean speculation could not go unnoticed nor did it fail to have its effect; see Fraisse, *Philia,* 325–30, 421–45; see also Schmid, "Epikur," 767–74. Norman W. DeWitt (*Epicurus and his Philosophy* [Minneapolis: University of Minnesota Press, 1954] and *St. Paul and Epicurus* [Minneapolis: University of Minnesota Press, 1954]) has championed the influence of Epicurean thought in later centuries but, as others have noted, he tends to overstate his case.

89. K. J. Dover, *Greek Popular Morality in the Time of Plato and Aristotle* (Berkeley: University of California Press, 1974). See also Lionel I. C. Pearson, *Popular Ethics in Ancient Greece* (Stanford: Stanford University Press, 1962).

90. Ibid., 1–8.

91. On Plutarch's relation to popular morality, see Betz, "Introduction," in *Plutarch's Ethical Writing.*

92. On the genre of Latin satire, see Michael Coffey, *Roman Satire* (New York: Barnes & Noble, 1976); J. Wight Duff, *Roman Satire: Its Outlook on Social Life* (Berkeley: University of California Press, 1936); Ulrich Knoche, *Roman Satire* (Bloomington: Indiana University Press, 1975); Edwin S. Ramage, David L. Sigsbee, and Sigmund C. Fredericks, *Roman Satirists and Their Satire* (Park Ridge, N.J.:

Noyes, 1974); Niall Rudd, *Themes in Roman Satire* (Norman: University of Oklahoma Press, 1986); and Charles Witke, *Latin Satire: The Structure of Persuasion* (Leiden: Brill, 1970).

93. See esp. C. W. Mendell, "Satire as Popular Philosophy," *CP* 15 (1920): 138–57.

94. On the banquet theme in satire, see Niall Rudd, *The Satires of Horace* (2nd ed.; Berkeley: University of California Press, 1982), 213ff.; L. R. Shero, "The *Cena* in Roman Satire," *CP* 18 (1923): 126–43; Martin, *Symposion,* 211–40.

95. Ramage, Sigsbee, and Fredericks, *Roman Satirists and Their Satire,* 9–10.

96. Ibid., 39; see Lucilius 30.1019–37 for fragments from the banquet of Troginus. He presents a scene of gluttony, drunkenness, and lewdity that burlesques refined dining.

97. Ibid., 84; Martin, *Symposion,* 216–19; Shero, "The *Cena* in Roman Satire."

98. Martin, *Symposion,* 216–19; Ramage, Sigsbee, and Fredericks, *Roman Satirists and Their Satire,* 99–106, 111–13. Shero ("The *Cena* in Roman Satire," 134–39) presents a detailed argument for the dependence of Petronius on the themes of Horace. For a less enthusiastic view, see Martin S. Smith, ed., *Petronius: Cena Trimalchionis* (Oxford: Clarendon, 1975), xix–xx, who emphasizes the originality of Petronius. See also Richard I. Pervo, "Wisdom and Power: Petronius' Satyricon and the Social World of Early Christianity," *ATR* 67 (1985): 307–25, for a study of the "social code" of food in Petronius.

99. For a summary of the debate about the genre of Petronius's *Satyricon,* see Smith, ed., *Cena Trimalchionis,* xv–xviii.

100. See Ramage, Sigsbee, and Fredericks, *Roman Satirists and Their Satire,* 172–73. Menippean satire is a mixture of prose and verse that perhaps originated with Menippus in the third century B.C.E. His satires are not extant but are known secondhand from later writers who referred to them and copied them. He promoted a Cynic point of view and seems to have used the banquet theme in several works. Menippean satire was a style used by Varro, Seneca, Petronius, and Lucian, as well as others. See ibid., 53–63, 89–113; Martin, *Symposion,* 211–40.

101. Martin, *Symposion,* 222–28. See also R. Bracht Branham, *Unruly Eloquence: Lucian and the Comedy of Traditions* (Cambridge, Mass.: Harvard University Press, 1989), 104–23, esp. 108, where he points out Lucian's combination of mythical wedding feast with philosophical symposium.

102. The motif of the brawl occurs also in Lucilius, Horace, and Petronius. Lucian also makes use of other stock features of symposium literature, such as the uninvited guest and the late guest; indeed, he makes some reference to nearly all of the regular literary motifs. See Martin, *Symposion,* 222–28; see also 33–116, 127–39.

103. Lucian *Symp.* 48.

4. THE SACRIFICIAL BANQUET

1. Stanley K. Stowers, "Greeks Who Sacrifice and Those Who Don't: Toward an Anthropology of Greek Religion," in *The Social World of the First Christians: Essays in*

Honor of Wayne A. Meeks, ed. L. Michael White and O. Larry Yarbrough (Minneapolis: Fortress Press, 1995), 293–333, makes a strong case for the centrality to the concept of eating at a sacrifice of the roasting of the *splachna* at the altar, which was only available to the male elites. His point is a good one. My concern, however, is for the gathering in the dining room, and I will be referring to that event throughout this study.

2. Hom. *Il.* 2.426–31. See also *Il.* 4:48–49.

3. See Jean Casabona, *Recherches sur le vocabulaire des sacrifices en Grec, des origines à la fin de l'époque classique* (Paris: Ophrys, 1966).

4. Ibid., 132–34, 164–67, 176–78, 186–87.

5. Ibid., 84, 132–34.

6. Plato *Symp.* 174C.

7. Plato *Leg.* 809D.

8. Xen. *Hell.* 2.4.20. Translation mine, adapted from Casabona, *Recherches,* 9.

9. Ibid., 130–34.

10. Ibid., 134.

11. Aesch. *Ag.* 150.

12. Plut. *Quaest. conv.* 693E–694A.

13. Ibid. 693F.

14. Stephen G. Miller, *The Prytaneion: Its Function and Architectural Form* (Berkeley: University of California Press, 1978). See also Michael J. Osborne, "Entertainment in the Prytaneion at Athens," *ZPE* 41 (1981): 153–70.

15. Pausanias 2.27.1.

16. See especially Ludwig Ziehen, "Opfer," PW 18 (1939): 621–22.

17. Diog. Laert. 2.40.

18. *SIG* 1004.31; from Oropos, the cult of Amphiaraos.

19. *LSS* 88a.3–4 (also repeated at 88b.4–5); from Lindos, the cult of Zeus and Athena, fourth and second centuries B.C.E.

20. Ibid., 94.13; from Camiros, cult of Poseidon, third century B.C.E.

21. Ziehen, "Opfer," 621–22.

22. Sterling Dow, "The Greater Demarkhia of Erkhia," *BCH* 89 (1965): 180–213. The inscription on which Dow's study is based is published in Georges Daux, "La Grande Démarchie: Un nouveau calendrier sacrificiel d'Attique (Erchia)," *BCH* 87 (1963): 603–34. See also *SEG* 21.541.

23. Dow, "The Greater Demarkhia of Erkhia," 205–10.

24. Ibid., 210.

25. Thus Walter Burkert, "Greek Tragedy and Sacrificial Ritual," *GRBS* 7 (1966): 104 n. 36.

26. Michael Jameson notes "the process of moving from the ordinary, profane world to the special, supernatural world. . . . The place of ritual, if a sanctuary, was already separated from the profane world outside or it would be marked off by preliminary rites to create a symbolic circle into which the participants entered. At its

center was an altar" ("Sacrifice and Ritual: Greece," in *Civilization of the Ancient Mediterranean*, ed. Michael Grant and Rachel Kitzinger [New York: Scribner's, 1988], 2.967–68.

27. Birgitta Bergquist, *The Archaic Greek Temenos* (Acta Instituti Atheniensis Regni Sueciae 4.13; Lund: Gleerup, 1967), 125.

28. Ibid.

29. Ibid., 133–35.

30. Ibid., 130–31.

31. A classic example of dining rooms at a temple complex is found at the Asklepieion at Corinth, illustrated in figures 1–3 (pp. 15–16). See also the multiple dining rooms at the *hestiatorian* or dining hall of the Asklepieion at Troizen (Gabriel Welter, *Troizen und Kalaureia* [Berlin: Gebr. Mann, 1941], 25–36), at the Demeter sanctuary at Corinth (Nancy Bookidis and Ronald S. Stroud, *Corinth XVII, Part III: The Sanctuary of Demeter and Kore, Topography and Architecture* [Princeton, N.J.: The American School of Classical Studies at Athens, 1997], 393–412), at the sanctuary of Hera at Perachora (R. A. Tomlinson, "Perachora: The Remains outside the Two Sanctuaries," *BSA* 64 [1969]: 164–72), and at the Asklepios sanctuaries at Athens and at Epidaurus (R. A. Tomlinson, "Two Buildings in Sanctuaries of Asklepios," *JHS* 89 [1969]: 106–9). Other examples are found at temple structures throughout the Greek world (see, e.g., A. Frickenhaus, "Griechische Banketthaüser," *Jahrbuch des Deutschen Archaeologischen Instituts* 32 [1917]: 114–33). See also the recent review of literature on the subject in Bookidis and Stroud, *Corinth XVII*, 393–412.

32. On temporary dining structures at Greek sanctuaries, see M. S. Goldstein, "The Setting of the Ritual Meal in Greek Sanctuaries: 600–300 B.C." (Ph.D. diss., University of California, Berkeley, 1979).

33. On meals in Roman temples, see John E. Stambaugh, "The Functions of Roman Temples," *ANRW* 2.16.1 (1978): 570.

34. Jameson, "Sacrifice and Ritual: Greece," 962, 972.

35. Helene P. Foley, *Ritual Irony: Poetry and Sacrifice in Euripides* (Ithaca, N.Y.: Cornell University Press, 1985), 33. See also Walter Burkert's discussion of the "holy" in Greek religion, where, however, he does not address the issue of sacrificial meat (*Greek Religion* [Cambridge, Mass.: Harvard University Press, 1985], 269–71).

36. Quoted from the *Vita Aesopi* in M. Isenberg, "The Sale of Sacrificial Meat," *CP* 70 (1975): 271.

37. Ibid., 272–73.

38. J. Grafton Milne, "The *Kline* of Sarapis," *JEA* 11 (1925): 6–9; Herbert C. Youtie, "The *Kline* of Sarapis," *HTR* 41 (1948): 9–29; Mariangela Vandoni, *Feste pubbliche e private nei documenti greci* (Testi e documenti per lo studio dell'antichita, serie papirologica 8; Milan: Instituto Editoriale Cisalpino, 1964), nos. 138, 140, 142, 143, 145; Ludwig Koenen, "Eine Einladung zur *Kline* des Sarapis," *ZPE* 1 (1967): 121–26; J. R. Gilliam, "Invitations to the *Kline* of Sarapis," in *Collectanea Papyrologica: Texts Published in Honor of H. C. Youtie*, 2 vols., ed. Ann Ellis Hanson

(Papyrologische Texte und Abhandlungen 19; Bonn: Rudolf Habelt, 1976), 1.315–24; Chan-Hie Kim, "The Papyrus Invitation," *JBL* 94 (1975): 391–402; and G. H. R. Horsley, ed., *New Documents Illustrating Early Christianity* (Sydney, Aus.: The Ancient History Documentary Research Centre, Macquarie University, 1981), 1.5–9, 2.75.

39. Respectively, POxy. 2678 (third century C.E.) and POxy. 2791 (second century C.E.), both of which are quoted in chapter 2.

40. POxy. 110, second century C.E., also quoted in chapter 2.

41. POxy. 2592 (late first to early second century C.E.) and Olga Giannini, "Nuovi papiri fiorentini, 7. Invito ad una festa," *Annali della scuola normale superiore di Pisa* 2.35 (1966): 18–19. To these one can compare POxy. 1485: "The dream-interpreter invites you to dinner in the *Demetrion* [sanctuary of Demeter]."

42. POxy. 1755 (= Vandoni, *Feste*, 145) and PColumbia inv. 550a; the latter is published in Gilliam, "Invitations to the *Kline* of Sarapis," 322–24.

43. Ibid., 323, n. 27.

44. PColumbia inv. 548a, in ibid., 320–22. The word translated "birth-house" *(lochion)* is not attested elsewhere in Greek. Gilliam defends his translation on the basis of the similarity of the term to an epithet connected with Artemis, *lochia*, which refers to her role as protector of women in childbirth, a role applied to Isis (the consort of Sarapis) in the Hellenistic Isis and Sarapis cult.

45. POxy. 1484 and PColon inv. 2555, the latter published by Koenen, "Eine Einladung zur *Kline* des Sarapis." Koenen argues for the connection of Thoeris with Isis and Sarapis. PColon. inv. 2555 is especially distinctive in that the god himself extends the invitation, a form that will also be found in the Panamara inscriptions discussed below. The text reads: "The god invites you to the banquet which takes place in the sanctuary of Thoeris."

46. POxy. 523 (= Vandoni, *Feste*, 142, second century C.E.), POsl. 157 (= Vandoni, *Feste*, 143, second century C.E.), PYale 85 (late second century C.E.). See also Gilliam, "Invitations to the *Kline* of Sarapis," 319; Kim, "The Papyrus Invitation," 398–401.

47. Youtie, "The *Kline* of Sarapis," 13–17, 22–23. The letter Youtie is interpreting is PMich. inv. 4686. The excerpt quoted above is from lines 11–21.

48. Youtie, "The *Kline* of Sarapis."

49. Milne, "The *Kline* of Sarapis."

50. See, e.g., David Gill, "*Trapezomata*: A Neglected Aspect of Greek Sacrifice," *HTR* 67 (1974): 117–37; Louise Bruit, "The Meal at the Hyakinthia: Ritual Consumption and Offering," in *Sympotica: A Symposium on the Symposium*, ed. Oswyn Murray (Oxford: Clarendon, 1990), 170–71; Michael Jameson, "Theoxenia," in *Ancient Greek Cult Practice from the Archaeological Evidence*, ed. Robin Hägg (Proceedings of the Fourth International Seminar on Ancient Greek Cult, organized by the Swedish Institute at Athens, October 22–24, 1993; Stockholm: Svenska Institutet i Athen; P. Åströms, 1998), 35–57.

51. Jameson, "Sacrifice and Ritual: Greece," 966–67.

52. Ibid., 972: "In a larger sense the gods were the hosts in their sanctuary and the meal came from the animal given to the gods."

53. Xen. *An.* 5.3.7–13.

54. See, e.g., E. R. Dodds, "Introduction," in *The Plays of Euripides: Bacchae* (2nd ed.; Oxford: Clarendon, 1960), xvi–xx.

55. See, e.g., J. P. Kane, "The Mithraic Cult Meal in its Greek and Roman Environment," in *Mithraic Studies,* Proceedings of the First International Congress of Mithraic Studies, ed. John R. Hinnells (Manchester: Manchester University, 1975), esp. 2.334–39.

56. Albert Henrichs, "Human Sacrifice in Greek Religion: Three Case Studies," in *Le sacrifice dans l'antiquité* (Fondation Hardt pour l'étude de l'antiquité classique, entretiens tome 27; Geneva: Fondation Hardt, 1980), 230 and n. 3.

57. Henrichs, incidentally, acknowledges this (ibid., 230–31).

58. *PPF* 20, as quoted in LSJ, s.v.

59. Thus Louis Robert, "Epigramme de Thasos," *Hellenica* 2 (1946): 117–18.

60. For examples, see Robert, "Epigramme de Thasos."

61. *SEG* 1.248.19–20; see also Louis Robert and Jeanne Robert, "Bulletin épigraphique," *REG* 71 (1958), nos. 108 and 421.

62. Louis Robert, "Villes et monnaies de Lycie," *Hellenica* 10 (1955): 199–200; see also idem, "Sur un papyrus de Paris glossaire latin-grec," *Hellenica* 11–12 (1960): 13 n. 1.

63. Dio Chrysostom *Or.* 3.91–99.

64. J. Hatzfeld, "Inscriptions de Panamara," *BCH* 51 (1927): 57–122. On Zeus Panamaros, see also Alfred Laumonier, *Les cultes indigènes en Carie* (Paris: De Boccard, 1958), chapter 5; Hans Oppermann, *Zeus Panamaros* (Giessen: A. Töpelmann, 1924); and Pierre Roussel, "Le miracle de Zeus Panamaros," *BCH* 55 (1931): 70–116.

65. On the date of these inscriptions, see Pierre Roussel, "Les mystères de Panamara," *BCH* 51 (1927): 136. The phenomenon of invitations being inscribed on stone may be compared to other types of cultic propaganda being so inscribed, such as "proclamations" or "notices," which were inscriptions by which a priest would announce his liberality on a festive day (ibid., 128 nn. 3 and 4). On the propaganda function of such inscriptions, see ibid., 130–31.

66. Hatzfeld, "Inscriptions de Panamara," 74:14, lines 2, 5–6. My translation.

67. Ibid., 73–74:11, lines 2–4, 7–8. My translation.

68. Ibid., lines 5–7. My translation.

69. Thus Roussel, "Les mystères de Panamara," 129–32.

70. Roussel connects this universalistic appeal to the general spirit of the age and to a common characteristic of Asiatic deities at this period (ibid., 131–32, 136). Note also this example from another invitation: "Since the ancestral god invites all humanity to the feast daily to share his philanthropy . . ." (Hatzfeld, "Inscriptions de

Panamara," no. 20). Here it is the "philanthropy" of the god that is extended to all humanity.

71. Roussel argues that the invitations were extended to cities as political units; thus each city was promised "equality" with other cities ("Les mystères de Panamara," 129–30). I take the view of Hatzfeld, however, who argues that the invitations were being extended to the individual citizens of a city, so that "equality" would refer to the status of each individual at the table ("Inscriptions de Panamara," 72–73).

72. Lucian *Sat.* 13.

73. Ibid., 17.

74. For a defense of Lucian's social conscience, see Barry Baldwin, "Lucian as Social Satirist," *CQ* 11 (1961): 199–208. See also Edwin S. Ramage, David L. Sigsbee, and Sigmund C. Fredericks, *Roman Satirists and Their Satire* (Park Ridge, N.J.: Noyes, 1974), 4–7, on the relation of the satirist to his society as a literary stance; also Niall Rudd, *Themes in Roman Satire* (Norman: University of Oklahoma Press, 1986).

75. Hatzfeld, "Inscriptions de Panamara," 12. My translation.

76. Thus Roussel, "Les mystères de Panamara," 132. He refers also to a decree from Caria in which a priest is praised for "celebrating the mysteries with all reverence and festive joy," a text quoted by Roussel from *BCH* 18 (1894): 39 n. 4.

77. Hatzfeld, "Inscriptions de Panamara," no. 68.

78. G. Cousin and G. Deschamps, "Inscriptions du temple de Zeus Panamaros," *BCH* 15 (1891): 179; quoted by Roussel, "Les mystères de Panamara," 132–33.

79. Roussel, "Les mystères de Panamara," 131–35. He especially cautions: "In a general sense, it is absurd to deny all pious significance to these public feasts or to the corporation feasts which are so numerous in the Roman epoch" (ibid., 133).

80. Thus Hatzfeld, "Inscriptions de Panamara," 72. In opposition to this view, Roussel identifies the references to "festive joy" in the Panamara invitations to represent "only the sentiment of cheerfulness which accompanies the celebration of a banquet," which he deems to be "of a terrestrial order" rather than mystic in some way ("Les mystères de Panamara," 134–35).

81. This has become something of a truism in scholarship on Greco-Roman philosophy; see, for example, A. H. Armstrong, ed., *Cambridge History of Later Greek and Early Medieval Philosophy* (Cambridge: Cambridge University Press, 1970), 4–6.

82. Plut. *Quaest. conv.* 6.8.

5. THE CLUB BANQUET

1. This text is bracketed in the Loeb Classical Library edition, indicating the view that it appears to be "an interpolated fragment of a parallel version." See LCL text, 489 n. b.

2. On the phenomenon of clubs and associations in general, see the recent study edited by John S. Kloppenborg and Stephen G. Wilson, *Voluntary Associations in the*

Graeco-Roman World (New York: Routledge, 1996), esp. the essay by Kloppenborg ("Collegia and *Thiasoi*," 16–30).

3. Standard works on Greek clubs include: Paul Foucart, *Des associations religieuses chez les Grecs* (Paris: Klincksieck, 1873); Erich Ziebarth, *Das griechische Vereinswesen* (Fürstlich Jablonowski'schen Gesellschaft zu Leipzig, Priesschriften 34; Leipzig: S. Hirzel, 1896); Franz Poland, *Geschichte des griechischen Vereinswesens* (Leipzig: Teubner, 1909); W. S. Ferguson, "The Attic Orgeones," *HTR* 37 (1944): 61–140; and A. D. Nock, "The Cult of Heroes," *HTR* 37 (1944): 141–74.

4. Ferguson, "The Attic Orgeones," 61–62, 67–73.

5. *Digesta* 47.22.4, cited in ibid., 64–68. Ferguson dates this law to 594 B.C.E. He also refers to archaeological evidence for the existence of such organizations prior to Solon (68 n. 7).

6. Poland, *Geschichte*, 8–33.

7. E.g., *Od.* 1.227, 11.415; see also Ch. Morel and E. Saglio, "Coena," DarSag 1.2 (1877): 1269.

8. Ferguson, "The Attic Orgeones," 70–71 n. 12.

9. Ath. 362e.

10. Poland, *Geschichte*, 33–46 (cultic names), 49–56 (names indicating social relationships), 57–70 (names derived from the name of a deity), 152–68 (general collective names), 73–86 (names derived from personal and place-names).

11. Henri Seyrig, "Quatre cultes de Thasos," *BCH* 51 (1927): 220.

12. See the statutes of the "Guild of Zeus Hypsistos," lines 8, 15, 16, 18, quoted below.

13. Poland, *Geschichte*, 152, 259–66, 392–95 (on functional titles); 465–66 (on expenditures for meal furnishings).

14. The entire inscription, with the translation printed here, was first published by Benjamin D. Meritt, "A Decree of Orgeones," *Hesperia* 11 (1942): 283. On the dating of the two parts, see ibid. and Ferguson, "The Attic Orgeones," 76.

15. This phrase is reconstructed on the basis of the occurrence of these two terms elsewhere in the inscription; see Meritt, "A Decree of Orgeones," 283–84.

16. Ferguson, "The Attic Orgeones," 62; see also 131–32 on the etymology of the term.

17. Ibid., 95–122.

18. *IG* 22, part 1, 1259, 1–5.

19. See Jean Casabona, *Recherches sur le vocabulaire des sacrifices en Grec, des origines à la fin de l'époque classique* (Paris: Ophrys, 1966), 130–34, and discussion in chapter 4 above.

20. Ferguson, "The Attic Orgeones," 95. On the "host," see also 82–83 and 85–86.

21. Ibid., 78–79.

22. Ibid.

23. Meritt, "A Decree of Orgeones," 287 and n. 28.

24. *LSS,* 56.

25. Sterling Dow and David H. Gill, "The Greek Cult Table," *AJA* 69 (1965): 103–14.

26. Ibid., 112.

27. *LSG* 47 (= *SIG* 1097 = *IG* 22.2499 = *LGS* 43), lines 24–30. Also discussed in Ferguson, "The Attic Orgeones," 80–81. The *cella* in a temple was the room reserved for the image of the deity.

28. *LSG,* 87; Ferguson, "The Attic Orgeones," 80; *SIG* 3.249.

29. See earlier discussion in chapter 2.

30. Examples are cited in Ferguson, "The Attic Orgeones," 80 n. 27.

31. Ferguson, "The Attic Orgeones," 122.

32. See, for example, the statement of Poland, *Geschichte,* 259: "One can especially discern in [the banquets'] increasing importance the inner decay of the Greek association's communal life."

33. The standard reference work on Roman *collegia* is still Jean-Pierre Waltzing's four-volume work *Étude historique sur les corporations professionnelles chez les Romains* (Louvain: Peeters, 1895–1900). Volumes 1 and 2 contain his analysis of *collegia;* volume 3 is a comprehensive collection of inscriptions; and volume 4 is a collation of the evidence according to various subjects: a list of all known colleges, types of internal organization, principal character, finances, and so forth. Waltzing uses and largely supplants previous works on the subject, including Theodor Mommsen, *De collegiis et sodaliciis Romanorum* (Kiliae: Libraria Schwersiana, 1843), and Wilhelm Liebenam, *Zur Geschichte und Organisation des römischen Vereinswesens: Drei Untersuchungen* (Leipzig: Teubner, 1890). Other studies include Samuel Dill, *Roman Society from Nero to Marcus Aurelius* (repr. of 1904 ed.; New York: World, 1956), 251–86; E. Kornemann, "Collegium" PW 4.1 (1900): 380–480; Francesco Maria de Robertis, *Il fenomeno associativo nel mondo romano* (Naples: Libreria scientifica editrace, 1955); Russell Meiggs, *Roman Ostia* (2nd ed.; Oxford: Clarendon, 1973), 311–36; Ramsay MacMullen, *Enemies of the Roman Order* (Cambridge, Mass.: Harvard University Press, 1966), 173–79; and idem, *Roman Social Relations 50 B.C. to A.D. 284* (New Haven, Conn.: Yale University Press, 1974), 73–87.

34. Waltzing, *Étude historique sur les corporations,* 1.32–33.

35. On religious colleges in general, see ibid., 1.33–48, 195–255, 4.180–226. Waltzing notes that most private religious colleges were primarily burial clubs (1.262).

36. MacMullen, *Roman Social Relations,* 76–77.

37. Waltzing, *Étude historique sur les corporations,* 1.52–59; see esp. 57: "The professional corporations, formed on the Roman model, were unknown [in Greece] during the independence of Greece."

38. Ibid., 1.42–48; J. M. C. Toynbee, *Death and Burial in the Roman World* (Aspects of Greek and Roman Life; London: Thames and Hudson, 1971), 54–55.

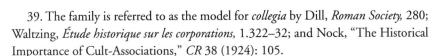

39. The family is referred to as the model for *collegia* by Dill, *Roman Society,* 280; Waltzing, *Étude historique sur les corporations,* 1.322–32; and Nock, "The Historical Importance of Cult-Associations," *CR* 38 (1924): 105.

40. Note that officials of *collegia* are modeled after municipal officials and especially military officials; see Waltzing, *Étude historique sur les corporations,* 1.357–68; Dill, *Roman Society,* 263.

41. MacMullen, *Enemies of the Roman Order,* 174.

42. Waltzing, *Étude historique sur les corporations,* 3.117 (#387 = *CIL* 4.581).

43. Ibid., 1.323 n. 2.

44. Ibid., 1.326.

45. Ibid., 1.325–28; MacMullen, *Roman Social Relations,* 77–78, 178 n. 74. On the moralists and satirists, see esp. chapter 3 above.

46. Tac. *Ann.* 14.17. See MacMullen, *Enemies of the Roman Order,* 169, and, for other examples of political unrest connected with *collegia,* 173–79.

47. Justinian *Digesta* 47.22.3.1. Text from Waltzing, *Étude historique sur les corporations,* 155–57; translation from Naphtali Lewis and Meyer Reinhold, *Roman Civilization* (New York: Harper, 1966), 2.271.

48. This inscription was first printed in its entirety by Mommsen, *De collegiis et sodaliciis Romanorum,* appendix; he also provides a commentary, 98–115. See also Waltzing, *Étude historique sur les corporations,* passim (see index); Dill, *Roman Society,* 260–61; and MacMullen, *Roman Social Relations,* 78–79.

49. Justinian *Digesta* 47.22.1.1. The law on *collegia* summarized in this sixth-century-C.E. document is thought to be the same as the one that is excerpted in the inscription above.

50. Waltzing, *Étude historique sur les corporations,* 1.152.

51. Justinian *Digesta* 47.22.1.

52. Ibid., 47.22.3.2.

53. See Joachim Marquardt, *Das Privatleben der Römer* (2nd ed.; Handbuch der römischen Alterthümer 7; Leipzig: Hirzel, 1886), 1.207–12; Waltzing, *Étude historique sur les corporations,* 4.685–99; J. P. V. D. Balsdon, *Life and Leisure in Ancient Rome* (New York: McGraw-Hill, 1969), 22.

54. Plut. *Cat. Mai.* 18.3, quoted in MacMullen, *Roman Social Relations,* 62; see also 76–77 and A. R. Hands, *Charities and Social Aid* (Aspects of Greek and Roman Life; Ithaca, N.Y.: Cornell University Press, 1968), 36–37, 52–53, 60.

55. Examples in Waltzing, *Étude historique sur les corporations,* 4.678–85.

56. Ibid., 1.236. See also Wilhelm Schmidt, *Geburtstag im Altertum* (RVV 7.1; Giessen: A. Töpelmann, 1908).

57. Suggested by Waltzing, *Étude historique sur les corporations,* 4.635.

58. Ibid., 1.233–36. See also the celebration of the "birthday of the society" *(natalis collegi)* of the society of Aesculapius and Hygieia, which is also probably the date of the dedication of the cult statue; ibid., 3.269 (#1083 = *CIL* 6.10234), lines 11–12.

59. On the offices of *scriba* and *viator,* see ibid., 1.385–405, 415–16.

60. On the office of *magister cenarum,* see ibid., 1.420–22.

61. Compare the *hilaria,* or "joyous festival" of Cybele, mentioned in Macrob. *Sat.* 2.21.10.

62. Waltzing, *Étude historique sur les corporations,* 3.166 (# 608 = *CIL* 5.7906) 3, 8–9.

63. Ibid., 1.211. On meals in Roman temples, see John E. Stambaugh, "The Functions of Roman Temples," *ANRW* 2.16.1 (1978): 570.

64. Waltzing, *Étude historique sur les corporations,* 3.268 (# 1081 = *CIL* 6.10231).

65. Ibid., 1.229–30 and sources cited there.

66. Ibid., 1.225–27.

67. Meiggs, *Roman Ostia,* esp. 243, 324–29.

68. See James E. Packer, *The Insulae of Imperial Ostia* (MAAR 31; Rome: American Academy in Rome, 1971), 157–60 and plan 15, p. 100, on the "Caseggiato dei Triclini" ("Insula of the Triclinia"). The estimate of the height of the structure is based on the width of the lower walls. Capacity of the rooms is estimated on the basis of formal tendencies in the Ostian *insulae* in general. The estimate of a "highly congested tenement" is enforced by the rather large latrine facilities (rooms 17 and 23A) (ibid., esp. 159–60).

69. On the date, see G. Calza and G. Becatti, *Scavi di Ostia I: Topografia Generale* (Rome: La Libreria dello Stato, 1953), 132, 217, 235.

70. *CIL* 14 (suppl.) #4569 and commentary pp. 678–79; see also Meiggs, *Roman Ostia,* 324; Packer, *Insulae of Imperial Ostia,* 160 n. 5. The inscription does not give the name of the club whose members are listed; it merely refers to the list as "a list of common soldiers in 16 divisions" (*numerus caligatorum decuriarum XVI,* column 1, lines 13–14). This same description is applied to the College of the Carpenters in two other Ostian Inscriptions; e.g., *CIL* 14.160.8–11: "a list of common soldiers in 16 divisions of the College of the Builders in Wood of Ostia" (*numerus caligatorum decuriarum XVI collegii fabrum tignuariorum).* See also Waltzing, *Étude historique sur les corporations,* 2.357–68 on the military organization of *collegia,* and 1.382 and 2.351 on the social distinctions between *caligati* and *honorati.*

71. The fact that the rooms around the courtyard are all individual rooms rather than being interconnected in any way is unusual at Ostia (see nos. 8–13, 24–27) . This led to the suggestion that the structure was originally an inn; see Kleberg, *Hôtels, restaurants et cabarets dans l'antiquité romaine* (Uppsala, Swe.: Almqvist and Wiksells, 1957), 45; see also Packer, *Insulae of Imperial Ostia,* 67–68.

72. Packer, *Insulae of Imperial Ostia,* 159; Meiggs, *Roman Ostia,* 324. Meiggs names five dining rooms besides the chapel, but does not specify which they are. He also refers to a kitchen, whereas Packer implies there is none.

73. For an example of this form of dining room, see figure 4 (p. 17).

74. McKay, *Houses, Villas, and Palaces,* 94. On sizes of *collegia* in general, see MacMullen, *Enemies of the Roman Order,* 341–42 n. 14.

75. Waltzing, *Étude historique sur les corporations*, 1.217–18.

76. On the political activity of trade associations, see MacMullen, *Enemies of the Roman Order*, 173–79; idem, *Roman Social Relations*, 75–76.

77. Waltzing, *Étude historique sur les corporations*, 1.210–17.

78. Ibid., 3.268–71 (# 1083 = *CIL* 6.10234 = *ILS* 7213), lines 1–4.

79. The evidence is summarized in Phillippe Bruneau, *Recherches sur les cultes de Délos à l'époque hellénistique et à l'époque impériale* (Bibliothèque des écoles françaises d'Athènes et de Rome, fasc. 217; Paris: De Boccard, 1970), especially chapters 17 and 18, 585–638. See also Waltzing, *Étude historique sur les corporations*, 3.18–115 and 669 on *collegia* in Asia and Greece.

80. Bruneau, *Recherches sur les cultes*, 623, 627–28.

81. Suggested by J. Starcky, "Autour d'une dédicace palmyrénienne à Sadrafa et à du Anat, 6: Salles de banquets rituels dans les sanctuaires orientaux," *Syria* 26 (1949): 62–63.

82. See the evidence for "semitic thiasoi in the Roman age" collected by J. T. Milik, *Recherches d'épigraphie proche-orientale I: Dédicaces faites par des dieux (Palmyre, Hatra, Tyr) et des thiases sémitiques à l'époque romaine* (Institut français d'archéologie de Beyrouth, bibliothèque archéologique et historique, 92; Paris: Librairie orientaliste Paul Geuthner, 1972).

83. See especially Martin Hengel, *Judaism and Hellenism* (Philadelphia: Fortress Press, 1974), 1.243.7; Dombrowski, "*Hyḥd* in I QS and *to koinon*: An Instance of Early Greek and Jewish Synthesis," *HTR* 59 (1966): 293–307.

84. See Robert L. Wilken, "Collegia, Philosophical Schools, and Theology," in *The Catacombs and the Colosseum*, ed. Stephen Benko and John J. O'Rourke (Valley Forge, Pa.: Judson, 1971), 268–91, and Abraham J. Malherbe, *Social Aspects of Early Christianity* (2nd ed., enl.; Philadelphia: Fortress Press, 1983), 87–91, for bibliographies and summaries of the discussion relating early Christianity to Greek and Roman clubs. To the works cited there should be added Bo Reicke, *Diakonie, Festfreude und Zelos in Verbindung mit der altchristlichen Agapenfeier* (Uppsala Universitets Årsskrift 1951:5; Uppsala: A.-B. Lundequistska, 1951).

85. See, e.g., Pliny the Younger's legal classification of Christianity as a *hetaeria* (*Ep.* 10.96) and Tertullian's defense of Christianity as a legal *factio* (*Apol.* 38–40).

86. Philo *Flacc.* 136. See also Waltzing, *Étude historique sur les corporations*, 3, 355–92, and 678 on *collegia* in Africa.

87. Strabo 17.1.8 (c. 794).

88. See especially Mariano San Nicolo, *Aegyptisches Vereinswesen zur Zeit der Ptolemäer und Römer* (2nd ed.; Münchener Beiträge zur papyrusforschung und antiken Rechtsgeschichte 2.1; Munich: Beck, 1972); idem, "Zur Vereinsgerichtsbarkeit im hellenistischen Ägypten," in *Eritymbion: Heinrich Swoboda dargebracht* (Reichenberg: Gebrüder Stiepel, 1927), 255–300; and A. E. R. Boak, "The Organization of Guilds in Greco-Roman Egypt," *TAPA* 68 (1937): 212–20. See also the references in the following note.

89. Text, translation, notes, and commentary in Colin Roberts, T. C. Skeat, and A. D. Nock, "The Gild of Zeus Hypsistos," *HTR* 29 (1936): 39–88.

90. Ibid., 42, 45, 69.

91. Ibid., 40–42.

92. Note the reference to a statue to Zeus Hypsistos in Corinth (Pausanias 2.2.8); see further ibid., 44–72.

93. Philo *Flacc.* 136. For other examples of "synods" see Poland, *Geschichte*, 158–63; for "synods" in Egypt see San Nicolo, *Aegyptisches*, 1.17–29, 207–11, 2.43 n. 5; and Skeat, Roberts, and Nock, "Gild of Zeus Hypsistos," 72–74.

94. Skeat, Roberts, and Nock, "Gild of Zeus Hypsistos," 75–79.

95. Ibid., 79–87.

96. Ibid., 47, 53.

97. Ibid., 51; see also San Nicolo, *Aegyptisches*, 41–53.

98. Philodemus *De Musica* 110.

99. Ath. 8.365c.

100. Thus San Nicolo, *Aegyptisches*, 42–43. See further on these terms: Poland, *Geschichte*, 155–56, 247–48, 232–33, 272.

101. Skeat, Roberts, and Nock, "Gild of Zeus Hypsistos," 51.

102. Ibid., 85–86.

103. Plato *Symp.* 176A.

104. Compare the banquet rites of the Society of Diana and Antinous, lines 2.29–30, as discussed earlier. Note, however, that Nock makes much of the fact that Zeus Hypsistos is not mentioned here as the object of worship. He suggests this as a sign of the increasing secularization of such clubs ("Gild of Zeus Hypsistos," 86).

105. The term *brotherhood (phratra)* properly refers to an ancient religious unit at Athens. Since such a Greek form of civic organization did not exist in Egypt, the term must be interpreted as a general term for an association and thus as basically parallel in meaning to *synod (synodos)* (ibid., 52).

106. Of course, it must be admitted that prohibitions against leaving the fellowship and rules specifying full participation for the full year that the club is organized serve the added and purely practical purpose of ensuring that the membership dues continue to be paid.

107. Compare Theophrastus, *Char.*, 28.1–2, who defines "abusive speech" *(kakologia)* as "a bent of the mind toward the worse in all a man says" and characterizes the "abusive speaker" *(kakologos)* as one who talks about other people like "the genealogists"; that is, he seeks to find the worst in people by examining their pedigrees. See further Skeat, Roberts, and Nock, "Gild of Zeus Hypsistos," 52–53.

108. See further on "the late-arriving guest" in chapter 3; similar rules are found in the statutes of the *Iobachkoi* as discussed below.

109. Skeat, Roberts, and Nock, "Gild of Zeus Hypsistos," 48.

110. Skeat, Roberts, and Nock (ibid., 47) note that usually in the papyri, *andrōn* refers to the living room in an Egyptian house, whereas *symposion* is used to refer to

the dining room, which is usually located upstairs. The term *andrōn,* however, has a long history in Greek and Roman writings with the meaning "dining room" or "banqueting hall" (Herodotus to Vitruvius, see LSJ, s.v.). Thus that is the preferred meaning I would apply to the text here.

111. See examples in Skeat, Roberts, and Nock, "Gild of Zeus Hypsistos," 77–79.

112. Skeat and Roberts contend that "the practice of drinking together limited effective membership" (ibid., 52). They note that Demotic lists indicate that membership rolls of Egyptian clubs rarely went beyond forty. Compare this with the membership lists for *collegia* in Italy; these averaged ca. 150, but went as high as 1200 to 1500 (MacMullen, *Enemies of the Roman Order,* 342).

113. Louis Robert, "Deux décrets d'une association à Athènes," *ArchEph* (1969): 7–14.

114. Ibid., 8–9; see also Waltzing, *Étude historique sur les corporations,* 1.521.

115. Robert, "Deux décrets," 14.

116. This festival is mentioned in the oath the priestesses of Dionysus swore at the *Anthesterion* (Pseudo-Dem. 59.78). See Sam Wide, "Inschrift der Iobakchen," *AthMitt* 19 (1894): 266; Ludwig Deubner, *Attische Feste* (2nd ed.; Hildesheim: Georg Olms, 1969), 100; Martin P. Nilsson, *The Dionysiac Mysteries of the Hellenistic and Roman Age* (Lund: Gleerup, 1957), 55. See also A.-J. Festugière, "Les Mystères de Dionysos," *RB* 44 (1935): 201 n. 3, who refers to the month *Iobakchion* at Astypalaea and at Amorgos, both of which are islands in the Aegean; Thomas L. Robinson, "Dionysos in Athens," (unpublished seminar paper; Harvard Divinity School, Dec. 11, 1972), 9 n. 12, who refers to the cry *"iō Bakchai, iō Bakchai"* in Eur. *Bacch.* 578.

117. The inscription dates from the archonship of Arrius Epaphroditus, whose dates are unknown. Most attempts at dating it are based on the probable identification of "the most excellent Claudius Herodes" (line 9) as either the famous Athenian orator Herodes Atticus or a descendant of his, either a son or a grandson. Those who take the former position date the inscription shortly before 187 C.E., the date of Atticus's death. Thus Ernst Maass, *Orpheus* (Munich: Beck, 1895), 32–41; *SIG* 268 n. 8; *IG* 22 1368; Sokolowski, *LSG,* 99. For the latter view, see Wide, "Inschrift der Iobakchen," 248, 261–62, 266–67 (230–240 C.E.); W. Kroll, "Iobakchoi," PW 9 (1916): 1829 (2nd or 3rd century C.E.); Nilsson, *Dionysiac Mysteries,* 46 (early 3rd century C.E.).

118. Note that the statutes are being restored, suggesting that they previously existed but were not being enforced. "Restore the statutes" (*anaktēsai ta dogmata,* lines 14–15) is the cry of the membership.

119. Thus Maass, *Orpheus,* 22 n. 3.

120. Thus Wide, "Inschrift der Iobakchen," 275; Ludwig Ziehen, *LGS,* 137; Deubner, *Attische Feste,* 149.

121. Kroll, "Iobakchoi," 1830; Deubner, *Attische Feste,* 138–42.

122. Kroll, "Iobakchoi," 1829.

123. Deubner, *Attische Feste,* 149–51.

124. Franz Poland, "*Stibas*," PW 3A (1929): 2482.

125. Ath. 4.138f.

126. Poland, "*Stibas*," 2481.

127. Ibid., 2482–83; Nilsson, *Dionysiac Mysteries*, 63.

128. Philostr. *Vit. soph.* 2.3; quoted in Poland, "*Stibas*," 2482.

129. On the Dionysiac grotto, see Nilsson, *Dionysiac Mysteries*, 61–62.

130. See *SIG* 1109, note 52, on this reading of the term *stibas* in this context.

131. See also Poland, *Geschichte*, 263; Robinson, "Dionysos in Athens," 9 n. 16.

132. Lines 159–63: a wreath and a memorial drinking party were provided in honor of a deceased member. This is rather less than what a Roman funerary society might provide, suggesting that the *Iobakchoi* are not to be identified primarily as a funerary society.

133. A yearly sacrifice is consistent with the practices of the earlier Dionysiac associations who met *only* for that purpose, according to Nilsson, *Dionysiac Mysteries*, 64.

134. Wide, "Inschrift der Iobakchen," 270.

135. Ziehen, *LGS*, 135, reads *tamias Boukolikos* together as one office instead of two ("cowherd-treasurer"), taking the adjective *Boukolikos* ("cowherd") with the previous title in the list. This suggestion has not been well received by other editors, however. No other text prints Ziehen's reading; rather, all read "cowherd" as a separate title. See, e.g., Kroll, "Iobakchoi," 1829.

136. On the common Dionysiac title *Boukolos* ("cowherd"), see Nilsson, *Dionysiac Mysteries*, 48, 52–55, 59, and discussion below of the ritual at the *stibas* of the Iobakchoi. See also the famous Agrippinilla inscription from Torre Nova near Rome. Here there is an elaborate hierarchy that includes three *archiBoukoloi* ("chief cowherds"), seven *Boukoloi hieroi* ("priest cowherds"), and eleven *Boukoloi* ("cowherds") (Nilsson, *Dionysiac Mysteries*, 52). For the inscription, see Achille Vogliano, "La grande inscrizione bacchica del metropolitan museum," *AJA* 37 (1933): 215–31, and Franz Cumont, "La grande inscription bachique du Metropolitan Museum, II: Commentaire religieux de l'inscription," *AJA* 37 (1933): 232–63. A fragment from a late Hellenistic altar was found in Pergamon with the inscription: "To Dionysos Kathegemon, [dedicated by] Herodes the Archiboukolos" (Machteld J. Mellink, "Archaeology in Asia Minor," *AJA* 83 (1979): 340–41 and pl. 54, fig. 6).

137. Proteurythmos is otherwise unknown. Maass (*Orpheus*, 62–66) suggests that it is a mystic representation of Orpheus, since the term *eurythmos* ("rhythmical") is associated with music as is Orpheus. Following this suggestion, but with less emphasis on the mystical, are Poland ("patron of the art of music"; *Geschichte*, 213) and Nilsson ("it may be guessed that he was Orphic or a god of the dance; we know nothing for certain"; *Dionysiac Mysteries*, 60–61). Kroll, however, rejects Maass's idea with the unsatisfying explanation that this was merely a new personification ("Iobakchoi," 1831). Palaimon was a sea-god who had mysteries on the Isthmus (Nilsson, *Dionysiac Mysteries*, 60; see also idem, *GGR* 2.350). Kore is, of course, connected

with Demeter and the Eleusinian mysteries. The form of the list here suggests that Dionysus was paired with Kore and Palaimon with Aphrodite. Dionysus was normally paired with Ariadne, however, so the connection here with Aphrodite is rather unusual. For an analysis of the relationships of these deities to the Dionysiac cult, see Wide, "Inschrift der Iobakchen," 277–80.

Note that among the deities who were being portrayed by the members are two goddesses, Kore and Aphrodite, yet it is normally assumed that the Iobakchoi had only male members. Other Dionysiac associations, notably the one headed by the priestess Agrippinilla in Torre Nova (see previous note), had female members and officers. For discussions of female participation in the Dionysiac cult of the Roman period, see C. Kerényi, *Dionysos* (Princeton, N.J.: Princeton University Press, 1976), 349–88; see also Ross S. Kraemer, *Her Share of the Blessings: Women's Religions among Pagans, Jews, and Christians in the Greco-Roman World* (New York: Oxford University Press, 1992), 36–49.

138. See Arthur Pickard-Cambridge, *The Dramatic Festivals of Athens* (2nd ed.; Oxford: Clarendon, 1968), 8, 12; for Ephesus, see Maass, *Orpheus*, 56–57.

139. Nilsson, *GGR* 1.582–85; Deubner, *Attische Feste*, 103–4.

140. Plut. *Quaest. conv.* 3.7 (655E).

141. Philostr. *Vit. Apoll.* 4.21.

142. Thus Adolf Deissmann, *Bible Studies* (Edinburgh: T. & T. Clark, 1901), 231–32; idem, *Light from the Ancient East* (repr., Grand Rapids: Baker, 1965), 348–49; Poland, *Geschichte des griechischen Vereinswesens*, 399.

143. Thus Kroll, "Iobakchoi," 1830; see also Nilsson, *Dionysiac Mysteries*, 138–39.

144. Wide, "Inschrift der Iobakchen," 276. Maass, *Orpheus*, 54–71 and 123–25, tries to identify the association and its rites as primarily Orphic in character, but most scholars reject this interpretation. See, for example, O. Kern, "Mysterien," PW 16 (1935): 1297: "The Orphic hymn book knows no Dionysos Iobakchos and no Iobakchoi." See also Nilsson, *Dionysiac Mysteries*, 46 n. 2.

145. Thus Kroll, "Iobakchoi," 1831. Nilsson, however, thinks that the names of the officials also represent roles played by the members in the drama (*Dionysiac Mysteries*, 64).

146. Xen. *Symp.* 9.2–7.

147. Nilsson, *Dionysiac Mysteries*, 59–61.

148. Ibid., 59.

149. Ibid., 64; Festugière, "Les Mystères de Dionysos," 194, 206–7.

150. Nilsson, *Dionysiac Mysteries*, 46.

151. Compare this regulation from another Greek association: "No one is permitted to enter into the most august assembly of the *eranistai* before he is approved to be pure and pious and good," quoted in Wide, "Inschrift der Iobakchen," 269; Robinson, "Dionysos in Athens," 9 n. 14.

152. Compare the *rhabdophoroi* ("rod bearers"), who kept order in the theater. The *thyrsos* was a "wand wreathed in ivy and vine-leaves with a pine cone at the top, carried by the devotees of Dionysus" (LSJ).

153. Maass, *Orpheus,* 28 n. 2, 29–30 n. 10.

154. Suggested by Robinson, "Dionysos in Athens," 17 n. 54.

155. Lucian *Symp.* 8–9, 38, 43.

156. Compare similar rules for the Guild of Zeus Hypsistos (line 17) and the Corinthian Christians (1 Cor 6:1-8).

157. See Nilsson, *Dionysiac Mysteries,* 63; Festugière, "Les Mystères de Dionysos," 201 n. 9.

158. Ibid.

159. See further the earlier discussion of this festival.

160. W. Dörpfeld, "Die Ausgrabungen am Westabhange der Akropolis," *AthMitt* 20 (1895): esp. 176–80; see also John Travlos, *Pictorial Dictionary of Ancient Athens* (New York: Praeger, 1971), 274–77.

161. The following description is derived from Dörpfeld, "Die Ausgrabungen," 176–80.

162. Poland, *Geschichte,* 469–70.

163. Nilsson, *Dionysiac Mysteries,* 64.

164. MacMullen, *Enemies of the Roman Order,* 174.

165. John S. Kloppenborg also acknowledges this but seems to devalue it ("Collegia and *Thiasoi*").

166. Plut. *Quaest. conv.* 1 (612 C–D).

167. Plut. *Quaest. conv.* 2 (629 C–E).

6. THE JEWISH BANQUET

1. Translation from Jon D. Levenson, *Sinai and Zion: An Entry into the Jewish Bible* (New York: Harper & Row, 1987), 181.

2. These developments are traced in Jean-Marie Dentzer, *Le motif du banquet couché dans le proche-orient et le monde grec du VIIe au IVe siècle avant J.-C.* (Bibliothèque des écoles françaises d'Athènes et de Rome 246; Rome: École française de Rome, 1982).

3. See especially Martin Hengel's statement: "the influence of Greek conventions can be seen in Sirach's extensive account of dining customs" (*Judaism and Hellenism* [Philadelphia: Fortress Press, 1974], 2.150).

4. Ben Sira 39:4; 34:9–12; see also George W. E. Nickelsburg, *Jewish Literature between the Bible and the Mishnah* (Philadelphia: Fortress Press, 1981), 56.

5. See Plato *Symp.* 174A and E, 213 A; see also Xen. *Symp.* 3–4 and the discussion in chapter 3.

6. Discussed in chapter 4.

7. See also Ben Sira 19:1–3; 23:6; 31:25–30; 37:27–31.

8. For a discussion of this passage and the Near Eastern context from which it derives, see Hans Walter Wolff, *Joel and Amos* (Hermeneia; Philadelphia: Fortress Press, 1977), 272–77; Shalom Paul, *Amos* (Hermeneia; Minneapolis: Fortress Press, 1991), 199–212.

9. John G. Snaith, *Ecclesiasticus, or the Wisdom of Jesus Son of Sirach* (London: Cambridge University Press, 1974), 155.

10. See, e.g., Jean-Marie Dentzer ("Aux origines de l'iconographie du banquet couché," *Revue Archéologique* [1971]: 215–58), who points out that the Greek custom of reclining, for example, which was always accompanied by various accoutrements of wealth and luxury, tended to denote that one was a member of a privileged class (240–58).

11. Plato *Symp.* 175C, 222E; W. A. Becker and Hermann Göll, *Charikles* (8th ed.; London: Longmans, Green, 1889), 318; see also chapter 2.

12. Note that both the Hebrew and Greek traditions are familiar with the custom of providing "crowns" for the drinkers at a symposium; see Isa 28:1-4 and Becker and Göll, *Charikles*, 329.

13. See, e.g., Alexander A. Di Lella, *The Wisdom of Ben Sira* (AB 39; New York: Doubleday, 1987), 391.

14. See discussion in chapter 2.

15. Wolff, *Joel and Amos*, 271–77.

16. See discussion in chapter 2.

17. Plato *Symp.* 176E.

18. See Plutarch's debate in the second century c.e. on the issue whether this reference in Plato is meant to be taken as a general rule for philosophical discussions in his own day (*Quaest. conv.* 7.7).

19. There are several texts that specifically mention sitting at meals (9:9, 31:12, 31:18, 32:1). In many cases there are variant readings, however, that appear to refer to the practice of reclining (see especially Rudolf Smend, *Die Weisheit des Jesus Sirach Erklärt* [Berlin: Georg Reimer, 1906], 85–86 [on 9:9]). Still other texts clearly refer to reclining, especially 32:2, as noted above.

20. On the custom of reclining in the ancient world in general, see Dentzer, "Aux origines de l'iconographie"; on the practice of reclining in rabbinic literature, see Samuel Krauss, *Talmudische Archaeologie* (Leipzig: Gustav Fock, 1912), 3.43–45. See also the discussion in chapter 2.

21. See e.g. 1 Esd 4:10; Tob 9:6.

22. Smend, *Die Weisheit*, 85–86.

23. See especially Plato *Symp.* 176E: "'Since it has been resolved, then,' said Eryximachus, 'that we are to drink only so much as each desires, with no constraint on any, . . . next propose that the flute-girl who came in just now be dismissed: let her pipe to herself or, if she likes, to the women-folk within, but let us seek our entertainment today in conversation.'" On the general tradition of conversation at philosophical banquets, see the discussion in chapter 3.

24. To this may be compared *m. 'Abot* 3.4: "Rabbi Simeon says: 'When three eat at one table and do not speak words of Torah there, it is as though they had eaten of the sacrifices of the dead. . . . But when three eat at one table and do speak words of Torah there, it is as though they have eaten from the table of God.'"

25. Nickelsburg, *Jewish Literature*, 56.

26. Victor Tcherikover, *Hellenistic Civilization and the Jews* (Philadelphia: Jewish Publication Society of America, 1966), 142–51; see also Hengel, *Judaism and Hellenism*, 137.

27. See Snaith, *Ecclesiasticus*, 176ff.

28. See also Ben Sira 13:1–26, et al.

29. Identified as "hellenizers" by Hengel, *Judaism and Hellenism*, 131–53, but Nickelsburg, *Jewish Literature*, 64, disagrees and points to Ben Sira's lack of polemic against Hellenism and the influence of Hellenistic philosophy on his thought.

30. On this text and other parallels between Ben Sira and Egyptian wisdom traditions, see Jack T. Sanders, *Ben Sira and Demotic Wisdom* (SBLMS 28; Chico, Calif.: Scholars, 1983), esp. 92–93.

31. On symposium literature in general, see Josef Martin, *Symposion: Die Geschichte einer literarischen Form* (Paderborn: F. Schöningh, 1931); on the influence of symposium literature on literary forms in the Talmud, see S. Stein, "The Influence of Symposia Literature on the Literary Form of the Pesah Haggadah," in *Essays in Greco-Roman and Related Talmudic Literature*, ed. Henry A. Fischel (New York: KTAV, 1977), 13–44.

32. See especially the discussions on subjects such as this in Plutarch's *Table Talk* (*Quaest. conv.*). Although Plutarch writes much later than Ben Sira, he makes a conscious effort to write in the symposium tradition of the great philosophers who have gone before, as he says at 612C–E. Thus he devotes treatises to the discussion of wine (623D–625C), music (704C–706E, 710B–711A), and the office of symposiarch (620A–622D). To be sure, Plutarch writes in a style very different from that of Ben Sira. Closer to the literary form in which Ben Sira wrote is the sixth-century-B.C.E. Greek poet Theognis, whose poems, many of which were on symposiac topics, were evidently intended to be sung at the symposium. Many of his themes are similar to themes found in Ben Sira; these have been noted and discussed in Th. Middendorp, *Die Stellung Jesu Ben Siras zwischen Judentum und Hellenismus* (Leiden: Brill, 1973), 7–26.

33. See also Werner Jaeger, *Paideia: The Ideals of Greek Culture* (New York: Oxford University Press, 1943), 2.177.

34. See, e.g., George Foote Moore, *Judaism* (Cambridge, Mass.: Harvard University Press, 1927), 1.308–12.

35. See textual notes in Di Lella, *The Wisdom of Ben Sira*, 575; on the possible relation of the rabbinical schools to the philosophical schools in a later period, see Shaye J. D. Cohen, "Patriarchs and Scholarchs," *Proceedings of the American Academy for Jewish Research* 48 (1981): 57–85.

36. See, e.g., Plato's "Symposium Laws" in *Leg.* 2.671C; Jaeger, *Paideia*, 2.174–97; see also chapter 3 in this volume.

37. Georg Bertram, "*Paideuō*," *TDNT* 5 (1968): 603–12.

38. *t. Ber.* 4, 8, 98. Translation from Gordon J. Bahr, "The Seder of Passover and the Eucharistic Words," in *Essays,* ed. Fischel, 474.

39. The origin of the custom of sitting in the vestibule for appetizers and reclining in the dining room for the meal is unknown to me. The only other parallel I know of is the possible parallel at Ben Sira 32:1-2 discussed above. But since the rabbinic text quoted here is from a late period, and quite likely from a time when the custom of reclining in the culture was changing or had changed to sitting, I would interpret the combination of sitting and reclining as a mark of that transition period. Reclining would thus represent an anachronistic use of an old tradition, much as it continued to be in later versions of the Passover liturgy.

40. Thus Bahr, "The Seder of Passover," in Fischel, ed., *Essays,* 483.

41. *m. Ber.* 6.5.

42. *m. Ber.* 5.6, cited later in this chapter. Bahr proposes a different reconstruction of the order of the service: First course (appetizers): first cup; second course (main course): second cup, meal, third cup; third course (dessert): fourth cup (ibid., 480). His reconstruction is based partly on his analysis of the hand-washing ritual and the assumption that the second such ritual comes before the meal (485–86). I would instead point to the ceremonial cup of wine and ceremonial washing of the hands as consistent with the Greco-Roman ritual beginning the symposium, as, e.g., in Ath. 11.462c–d; Plato *Symp.* 176A. See also chapter 2.

43. *m. Ber.* 6.6.

44. See also Bahr, "The Seder of Passover," in Fischel, ed., *Essays,* 481.

45. See, e.g., *Quaest. conv.* 614E and discussion in chapter 3.

46. *m. Ber.* 6.1.

47. This idea is well established in scholarship on Second Temple Judaism; see e.g. Stein, "The Influence of Symposia Literature," in Fischel, ed., *Essays,* 200–201] and sources cited there; S. Safrai and M. Stern, eds., *The Jewish People in the First Century* (Compendia Rerum Iudaicarum ad Novum Testamentum; Philadelphia: Fortress Press, 1976), 2.736–43, 808–10.

48. Philo emphasizes lay participation in the Passover sacrifice, *Spec.* 2.145, cited in J. B. Segal, *The Hebrew Passover: From Earliest Times to A.C. 79* (London Oriental Series 12; London: Oxford University Press, 1963), 26; see also Safrai and Stern, *Jewish People,* 2.892. On the importance of the priest for the manipulation of the blood in Hebrew sacrificial ritual, see Segal, *The Hebrew Passover,* 29; Jacob Milgrom, *IDBSup,* 765.

49. Stein, "The Influence of Symposia Literature," in Fischel, ed., *Essays,* 200.

50. Ibid.

51. *m. Pesaḥ* 10.1–9. Translation from Bahr, "The Seder of Passover," in Fischel, ed., *Essays,* 475–77.

52. Ibid., 491.

53. Ibid., 480–82; Stein, "The Influence of Symposia Literature," in Fischel, ed., *Essays,* 201.

54. Compare to Bahr's position; see also my earlier discussion of the festal meal.

55. Stein, "The Influence of Symposia Literature." Baruch Bokser (*The Origins of the Seder: The Passover Rite and Early Rabbinic Judaism* [Berkeley: University of California Press, 1984], 50–66) argues against Stein's thesis, but his arguments are unconvincing, especially since he works from too narrow a definition of the idea of the symposium and takes at face value the various Jewish texts that protest that Jewish banquets are fundamentally different from pagan banquets.

56. See esp. Stein, "The Influence of Symposia Literature," in Fischel, ed., *Essays,* 201–2, 210–11.

57. Thus, e.g., when Plutarch describes conversations at meals he attended, he does so in conscious imitation of symposium literature (*Quaest. conv.* 612D–E); see also chapter 3 of this volume. Similarly, Philo describes the meals of the Therapeutae in contrast to, and therefore in a form imitative of, the literary symposia; see further on the Therapeutae below.

58. Stein, "The Influence of Symposia Literature," in Fischel, ed., *Essays,* 217–18, 221–28.

59. Ibid., 210–13.

60. Ibid., 213–17; see also chapter 3.

61. Stephen G. Wilson ("Voluntary Associations: An Overview," in *Voluntary Associations in the Graeco-Roman World,* ed. John S. Kloppenborg and Stephen G. Wilson [New York: Routledge, 1996], 6) appropriately questions the usefulness of the terms *sect* and *sectarian* for ancient groups, including Jewish groups, for which he would propose the term *voluntary association.* He notes, correctly, that the term *sect* was originally developed to define "church/sect" relationships in the United States, in which a sect is defined over against "a larger, mainstream entity" with a "universalist vision." His point is well taken, yet the term *voluntary association* does not quite capture the phenomenon of these Jewish groups and their self-identity in relation to other Jews. I agree with Anthony J. Saldarini ("Sectarianism," in *EncyDSS,* 853–57) that *sect* is still a useful term for the Jewish groups here described.

62. Jacob Neusner, *The Idea of Purity in Ancient Judaism* (SJLA 1; Leiden: Brill, 1973), 64–71.

63. Ibid., 67; idem, *From Politics to Piety: The Emergence of Pharisaic Judaism* (Englewood Cliffs, N.J.: Prentice-Hall, 1973), 87; idem, "Two Pictures of the Pharisees: Philosophical Circle or Eating Club," *ATR* 64 (1982): 535.

64. *b. Ber.* 55a; quoted in Neusner, *The Idea of Purity,* 70.

65. Neusner, *The Idea of Purity,* 66.

66. Ibid., 65–66, 117.

67. Ibid., 65.

68. E. P. Sanders, *Jewish Law from Jesus to the Mishnah: Five Studies* (Philadelphia: Trinity Press International, 1990), 197, 209; Hannah K. Harrington, *The Impurity Systems of Qumran and the Rabbis: Biblical Foundations* (SBLDS 143; Atlanta: Scholars, 1993), summarizes Sanders's position on p. 268.

69. Harrington, *The Impurity Systems,* 281; for her complete argument, see pp. 267–81.

70. The *ḥaverim* texts are conveniently collected and translated in Emil Schürer, *The History of the Jewish People in the Age of Jesus Christ,* ed. Geza Vermes, Fergus Millar, and Matthew Black (rev. ed.; Edinburgh: T. & T. Clark, 1973–87), 2.386–87.

71. Thus ibid., 2.398–99; see also Joachim Jeremias, who translates *ḥaver* as "Pharisee" (*New Testament Theology: The Proclamation of Jesus* [New York: Scribner's, 1971], 118; cited by E. P. Sanders, *Jesus and Judaism* [Philadelphia: Fortress Press, 1985], 187–88). Neusner (*From Politics to Piety,* 87) speaks of *ḥaverot* as "fellowship groups" formed within Pharisaism; his arguments have been taken to imply an equation of Pharisees and *ḥaverim* (esp. by Sanders; see following note); see, e.g., Neusner, *The Idea of Purity,* 64–71, where he seems to speak of Pharisees and *ḥaverim* as equivalent.

72. Implied in Alan F. Segal, *Rebecca's Children: Judaism and Christianity in the Roman World* (Cambridge, Mass.: Harvard University Press, 1986), 125–26, which is also his reading of Neusner. Sanders argues strongly against Jeremias, Schürer, and Neusner, but does acknowledge a probable overlap between Pharisees and *ḥaverim* (*Jesus and Judaism,* 187–88, 388–89 nn. 59–60). Ellis Rivkin argues that *ḥaverim* were not connected with Pharisaism (*A Hidden Revolution: The Pharisees' Search for the Kingdom Within* [Nashville: Abingdon, 1978], 173–75). Shaye J. D. Cohen is also skeptical of the connection between Pharisees and *ḥaverim* but he is ultimately noncommittal (*From the Maccabees to the Mishnah* [Library of Early Christianity; Philadelphia: Westminster, 1987], 118–19).

73. Schürer, *The History of the Jewish People,* 2.386–87, 398–400.

74. Aharon Oppenheimer, "Ḥaverim," in *EncyDSS,* 1333–36, esp. 1334.

75. See esp. chapter 5.

76. Josephus compares the Jewish "sects" to philosophical schools; see also Morton Smith, "Palestinian Judaism in the First Century," in Fischel, ed., *Essays,* 183–97.

77. This section is a revised and enlarged version of my article on "Meals" in *EncyDSS,* 530–32. On the Essene meal in general, see also Todd S. Beall, *Josephus' Description of the Essenes Illustrated by the Dead Sea Scrolls* (Cambridge: Cambridge University Press, 1988), 52–64; K. G. Kuhn, "The Lord's Supper and the Communal Meal at Qumran," in *The Scrolls and the New Testament,* ed. Krister Stendahl (London: SCM, 1958), 63–93; Lawrence H. Schiffman, *Reclaiming the Dead Sea Scrolls* (Philadelphia: Jewish Publication Society, 1994), 333–38; James C. VanderKam, *The Dead Sea Scrolls Today* (Grand Rapids: Eerdmans, 1994), 84–86, 173–75; and Matthias Klinghardt, *Gemeinschaftsmahl und Mahlgemeinschaft: Soziologie und Liturgie frühchristlicher Mahlfeiern* (Texte und Arbeiten zum neutestamentlichen Zeitalter 13; Tübingen: Francke Verlag, 1996), 217–49.

78. For a review of the arguments, see VanderKam, *The Dead Sea Scrolls Today,* 71–98.

79. Harrington, "Purity," in *EncyDSS,* 2.724.

80. Jos. *J. W.* 2.129–32.

81. Ibid., 2.120–21.

82. Ibid., 2.130.

83. Ibid., 2.131.

84. See esp. chapter 3.

85. Jos. *J. W.* 2.130.

86. Roland de Vaux, *Archaeology and the Dead Sea Scrolls* (London: Oxford University Press, 1973), 12–14.

87. Ibid. Schiffman, *Reclaiming the Dead Sea Scrolls,* 337–38, suggests the bones might have been buried to keep dogs from scattering them and thereby defiling the camp.

88. De Vaux, *Archaeology and the Dead Sea Scrolls,* 11–12.

89. See Pauline H. E. Donceel-Voûte, "'Coenaculum': La salle à l'étage du *locus* 30 à Khirbet Qumrân sur la mer morte," *Banquets d'Orient (Res Orientales)* 4 (1992): 61–84, and Robert Donceel and Pauline H. E. Donceel-Voûte, "The Archaeology of Khirbet Qumran," in *Methods of Investigation of the Dead Sea Scrolls and the Khirbet Qumran Site: Present Realities and Future Prospects,* ed. Michael O. Wise et al. (Annals of the New York Academy of Sciences, vol. 722; New York: New York Academy of Sciences, 1994), 1–31.

90. De Vaux, *Archaeology and the Dead Sea Scrolls,* 29–33, pl. XXIa.

91. Acknowledged by de Vaux, *Archaeology and the Dead Sea Scrolls,* 30–33.

92. Donceel-Vaûte, "'Coenaculum,'" 82–83, fig. 12.

93. See the critiques by Eric Myers in Wise, ed., *Methods of Investigation,* and by Joseph Patrick in *EncyDSS,* 60.

94. Jos. *J. W.* 2.139.

95. On the relation of the Qumran community to Greco-Roman clubs and associations, see also M. Delcor, "Repas culturels esseniens et therapeutes," *RevQ* 6 (1969): 401–25; Dombrowski, "*Hyḥd* in I QS and *to koinon*: An Instance of Early Greek and Jewish Synthesis," *HTR* 59 (1966): 293–307; Moshe Weinfeld, *Organizational Pattern and the Penal Code of the Qumran Sect: A Comparison with Guilds and Religious Associations of the Hellenistic-Roman Period* (Novum Testamentum et Orbis Antiquus 2; Göttingen: Vandenhoeck and Ruprecht, 1986), 22–43; and Klinghardt, *Gemeinschaftsmahl,* 227–44. Erik W. Larson, however, is skeptical (Schiffman and VanderKam, eds., *Encyclopedia of the Dead Sea Scrolls,* 321–23).

96. Frank Moore Cross Jr., *The Ancient Library of Qumran and Modern Biblical Studies* (Garden City, N.Y.: Doubleday, 1961), 77.

97. Jos. *J. W.* 2.129, 133.

98. See Schiffman, *Reclaiming the Dead Sea Scrolls,* 333–38, who also disputes the idea that the Essene meal was a sacred meal.

99. See esp. Schürer, *The History of the Jewish People,* 2.591–97.

100. Philo *Contempl.* 57, 64.

101. Ibid., 67–74.

102. Ibid., 58, 60.

103. Ibid., 75.

104. Ibid., 78.

105. For a more extensive discussion of the meal of the Therapeutae in the context of the Greco-Roman banquet tradition, see Klinghardt, *Gemeinschaftsmahl,* 183–216.

106. Alan F. Segal, "Romans 7 and Jewish Dietary Laws," in *The Other Judaisms of Late Antiquity* (Brown Judaic Studies 127; Atlanta: Scholars, 1987), 175. Cp. J. D. G. Dunn, *Jesus, Paul, and the Law: Studies in Mark and Galatians* (Louisville, Ky.: Westminster John Knox, 1990), 181: "There was a spectrum of law observance regarding table-fellowship within Judaism. That is to say, there were those who observed the dietary, tithing and purity rulings with a greater degree of scrupulosity. And there were many others who were less scrupulous." See also E. P. Sanders, *Jewish Law from Jesus to the Mishnah,* 281, who posits a type of Judaism, perhaps represented by Paul in 1 Cor 10:27-29, in which one would simply dine at a Gentile table without asking about the food.

107. Lev 11:1-47; Deut 14:4-21; for a thorough discussion, see Jacob Milgrom, *Leviticus 1–16* (AB 3; New York: Doubleday, 1991), 641–742.

108. 1 Cor 8:1-13; 10:14-33; see also Acts 15:29; Rev 2:14, 20.

109. Jonathan Klawans, *Impurity and Sin in Ancient Judaism* (New York: Oxford University Press, 2000), 147.

110. See the discussion of Segal on this point, "Romans 7 and Jewish Dietary Laws," esp. 176–77.

111. Menahem Stern, *Greek and Latin Authors on Jews and Judaism* (Fontes ad res Judaicus spectantes; Jerusalem: Israel Academy of Sciences and Humanities, 1974–84), 2.39–40.

112. Shaye J. D. Cohen, *The Beginnings of Jewishness: Boundaries, Varieties, Uncertainties* (Berkeley: University of California Press, 1999), 54.

113. John M. G. Barclay, *Jews in the Mediterranean Diaspora: From Alexander to Trajan (323 BCE–117 CE)* (Berkeley: University of California Press, 1996), 435.

114. The various options are summarized in Barclay, *Jews in the Mediterranean Diaspora,* 435 n. 50.

115. This is a view held by, among others, G. Alon, "The Levitical Uncleanness of Gentiles," in *Jews, Judaism and the Classical World* (Jerusalem: Magnes, 1977), 146–89, and, more recently Dunn, *Jesus, Paul, and the Law,* 129–82.

116. Klawans, "Gentile Impurity," 288.

117. Ibid., 296–97.

118. Examples in Menahem Stern, ed., *Greek and Latin Authors on Jews and Judaism,* 3 vols. (Fontes ad res Judaicus spectantes; Jerusalem: Israel Academy of Sciences and Humanities, 1974–84), nos. 176, 253, 281, 334.

119. Thus John G. Gager, *The Origins of Anti-Semitism: Attitudes toward Judaism in Pagan and Christian Antiquity* (New York: Oxford University Press, 1983), esp. 82–88; on the positive acceptance of Jews and Jewish customs by Gentiles in general, see Louis H. Feldman, *Jew and Gentile in the Ancient World* (Princeton, N.J.: Princeton University Press, 1993).

120. See the references to the customs of the Jews collected in Stern, *Greek and Latin Authors.*

121. Tacitus *Histories* 5.4–5, as quoted in Margaret H. Williams, *The Jews among the Greeks and Romans: A Diasporan Sourcebook* (Baltimore: Johns Hopkins University Press, 1998), 162–63; see also Stern, *Greek and Latin Authors,* no. 281.

122. Diodorus 34.1.2, as quoted in Barclay, *Jews in the Mediterranean Diaspora,* 436; see also Stern, *Greek and Latin Authors,* 2.39.

123. Collins, *Between Athens and Jerusalem,* 88; see also 87–89 for brief discussion of this form with references to relevant literature.

124. While of the same form as the other documents cited here, Tobit is dated to an earlier period, prior to the persecutions of Antiochus (Nickelsburg, *Jewish Literature,* 35). The other documents can be dated to the Hasmonean period; see ibid., 19 (Daniel, final composition), 173 (Greek additions to Esther), 109 (Judith); see also John J. Collins, *Between Athens and Jerusalem: Jewish Identity in the Hellenistic Diaspora* (New York: Crossroad, 1983), 87–89 (Daniel 1–6, Greek additions to Esther).

125. C. Burchard, "Joseph and Aseneth," *OTP* 2:210 n.d.

126. Samuel Sandmel, *Judaism and Christian Beginnings* (New York: Oxford University Press, 1978), 180; Segal, *Rebecca's Children,* 165–71; idem, *Paul the Convert: The Apostolate and Apostasy of Saul the Pharisee* (New Haven, Conn.: Yale University Press, 1990), 194–201.

127. *Jubilees* dates from ca. 169 to 140 B.C.E. and is connected especially with the interpretive tradition of the Essenes (Nickelsburg, *Jewish Literature,* 79–79; Neusner, *The Idea of Purity,* 55–58). This text and the following from the Sibylline Oracles are emphasized in the discussions of Segal cited earlier.

128. Segal notes that *Didache* 6:3, with its rule against eating food offered to idols, agrees with the position presented in the "apostolic decree" in Acts ("Romans 7 and Jewish Dietary Laws," 181). See further idem, "Acts 15 as Jewish and Christian History," *Forum* 4.1 (forthcoming).

129. This section is a revision of my essay "The Messianic Banquet Reconsidered," in *The Future of Early Christianity: Essays in Honor of Helmut Koester,* ed. B. A. Pearson (Minneapolis: Fortress Press, 1991), 64–73, and my article "Messianic Banquet," *ABD,* 4.788–91.

130. Klinghardt, *Gemeinschaftsmahl,* identifies the idealized, utopian meal as a significant feature in Greco-Roman "meal theology," which he classifies under the category *charis* as a term referring to this concept as a "meal value." His analysis supplements mine with additional Greco-Roman parallels to the messianic banquet.

131. Gen 2:9; T. H. Gaster, *Myth, Legend, and Custom in the Old Testament* (New York: Harper, 1969), 29–34, 336–38.

132. Carol L. Meyers, *The Tabernacle Menorah: A Synthetic Study of a Symbol from the Biblical Cult* (Missoula, Mont.: Scholars, 1976), 95–202.

133. *1 En.* 24:4-25:7; *T. Levi* 18:11; *4 Ezra* 8:52; Rev 2:7; 22:2, 14, 19.

134. Hom. *Od.* 5.93; *Il.* 5.335–42, 19.38–39.

135. *Jos. Asen.* 16:14. Also identified with "bread of life" and manna; see Burchard, "Joseph and Aseneth," 228 n. f.

136. E. R. Goodenough, *Jewish Symbols in the Greco-Roman Period* (New York: Pantheon, 1953–68), vols. 5 and 6, 12.94–131; Joachim Jeremias, *The Eucharistic Words of Jesus* (3rd ed.; New York: Scribner's, 1966), 233–34.

137. Cp. *Odes Sol.* 11:7–8, 30:1–7.

138. See also Rev 7:17; 21:6.

139. Albert Henrichs, "Changing Dionysiac Identities," in Ben F. Meyer and E. P. Sanders, eds., *Jewish and Christian Self-Definition*, vol. 3: *Self-Definition in the Greco-Roman World* (Philadelphia: Fortress Press, 1982), 140–43.

140. Morton Smith, "On the Wine God in Palestine," in *Salo Wittmayer Baron Jubilee Volume* (Jerusalem: Central Press for the American Academy for Jewish Research, 1974), 815–29.

141. Henrichs, "Changing Dionysiac Identities," 159–60.

142. C. Burchard, "The Importance of Joseph and Aseneth for the Study of the New Testament: A General Survey and a Fresh Look at the Lord's Supper," *NTS* 33 (1987): 109–17.

143. Exod 16:1—17:7; Num 11:7-9; 20:2-13.

144. Ps 78:25; Wis 16:20; *4 Ezra* 1:19.

145. *Jos. Asen.* 16:8, 14-16; John 6:25-59.

146. Philo *Leg.* 2.86, 3.166–70.

147. 1 Cor 10:1-13.

148. Ps 104:26; Job 40–44; see also Rev 12:3-9; 21:1.

149. *2 Bar.* 29:1-4; *1 En.* 60:7-10, 24; *4 Ezra* 6:49-52; see also rabbinic references in Louis Ginzburg, *Legends of the Jews* (Philadelphia: Jewish Publication Society of America, 1909–38), 1.27–28, 5.41–46; Hermann L. Strack and Paul Billerbeck, *Kommentar zum Neuen Testament aus Talmud und Midrasch* (Munich: Beck, 1922–61), 4.1156–65.

150. New Testament references include: Matt 14:13-21 = Mark 6:32-44 = Luke 9:10-17 = John 6:1-15; Matt 15:32-39 = Mark 8:1-10; Luke 24:42-43; John 21:9-14. For Jewish art, see Goodenough, *Jewish Symbols,* 5.3–61. For Christian art, see Graydon F. Snyder, *Ante Pacem: Archaeological Evidence of Church Life before Constantine* (Macon, Ga.: Mercer University Press, 1985), 24–26, 64–65. On the relation of fish to the Leviathan myth, see Goodenough, *Jewish Symbols,* 6:3–61.

151. *Enuma Elish* VI:69–94 [*ANET* 69]; Isa 34:5-7; Zech 9:15; Gaster, *Thespis: Ritual, Myth, and Drama in the Ancient Near East* (Garden City, N.Y.: Doubleday,

1961), 93–94; Paul D. Hanson, "Zechariah 9 and the Recapitulation of an Ancient Ritual Pattern," *JBL* 92 (1973): 46 n. 25, 53–55.

152. As in 3 Macc 6:30-41; *Ps.-Philo* 27:9.

153. Paul D. Hanson, *The Dawn of Apocalyptic* (Philadelphia: Fortress Press, 1975), 300–322; Adela Yarbro Collins, *The Combat Myth in the Book of Revelation* (HDR 9; Missoula, Mont.: Scholars, 1976), 207–9, 224–30.

154. *t. Isaac* 6:13.

155. As in Isa 25:6-8 quoted above; see also Joel 2:24-26, 3:18; cp. the "unfailing table" of *4 Ezra* 9:19.

156. *2 Bar.* 29:1-4; see also the reference to death being swallowed in Isa 25:8 quoted above.

157. Adela Yarbro Collins, *Combat Myth*, 223–24.

158. S. Smith, "The Practice of Kingship in Early Semitic Kingdoms," in *Myth, Ritual and Kingship*, ed. S. H. Hooke (Oxford: Oxford University Press, 1958), 32–71.

159. Hos 2:1-23; Isa 54:4-8; Ezek 16:7-8.

160. John 3:39; 2 Cor 11:2; Eph 5:23-32.

161. Song 2:4, 5:1; see esp. Marvin H. Pope, *Song of Songs* (AB 7C; Garden City, N.Y.: Doubleday, 1977), 374–75, 504–10.

162. Matt 9:15 = Mark 2:19-20 = Luke 5:34-35; Matt 22:1-14; 25:1-13; Luke 14:7-11; John 1:1-11. Cp. John 3:29; *Gos. Thom.* 104.

163. Rev 19:7-9; 21:2, 9; 22:17; Adela Yarbro Collins, *Combat Myth*, 223–31.

164. Plato *Resp.* 2.363.c–d; Richmond Lattimore, *Themes in Greek and Latin Epitaphs* (Urbana: University of Illinois Press, 1962), 52. On Orphic and Dionysiac beliefs, see Henrichs, "Changing Dionysiac Identities," 160.

165. Franz Cumont, *Recherches sur le symbolisme funéraire des Romains* (Haut-Commissariat de l'État français en Syrie et au Liban, service des antiquités, bibliothèque archéologique et historique 35; Paris: Geuthner, 1942), 417–22; A. D. Nock, "Sarcophagi and Symbolism," in *Essays on Religion and the Ancient World*, ed. Zeph Stewart (Cambridge, Mass.: Harvard University Press, 1972), 2.613; and Dentzer, *Le motif du banquet couché*, 530–32.

166. 1QSa II.11–22; Cross, *Ancient Library of Qumran*, 85–91.

167. Jeremias, *Eucharistic Words of Jesus*, 59.

168. E. R. Goodenough, *Jewish Symbols*, 12.94–105, 126–31, 190–98. For a critique of Goodenough, see M. Smith, "Goodenough's *Jewish Symbols* in Retrospect," *JBL* 86 (1967): 57–59.

169. Burchard, "Joseph and Aseneth," 211–12 n. i; idem, "The Importance of Joseph and Aseneth," 113.

170. Franz Cumont, *After Life in Roman Paganism* (New Haven, Conn.: Yale University Press, 1922), 199–206; J. P. Kane, "The Mithraic Cult Meal in Its Greek and Roman Environment," in *Mithraic Studies*, Proceedings of the First International Congress of Mithraic Studies, ed. John R. Hinnells (Manchester: Manchester University, 1975), 342–43.

171. Bezalel Porten, *Archives from Elephantine: The Life of an Ancient Jewish Military Colony* (Berkeley: University of California Press, 1968), 183; Pope, *Song of Songs,* 210–29.

7. THE BANQUET IN THE CHURCHES OF PAUL

1. When Paul says, "I received from the Lord" (1 Cor 11:23), he is using a standard expression for the passing on of traditional material within a religious community. It is not a phrase denoting direct revelation to Paul from Jesus but rather means that the tradition is deemed to have the authority of the Lord behind it. For a review of the evidence for this interpretation, see Hans Conzelmann, *1 Corinthians* (Hermeneia; Philadelphia: Fortress Press, 1975), 195–96; and Gordon D. Fee, *The First Epistle to the Corinthians* (NICNT; Grand Rapids: Eerdmans, 1987), 548–49.

2. J. D. G. Dunn, *Romans 9–16* (WBC 38B; Dallas: Word, 1988), 795.

3. Examples abound. A typical reference is found in Paul's closing greetings, such as in Rom 16:5: "Greet also the church in their [Prisca and Aquila's] house." For other examples, see 1 Cor 16:19 ("Aquila and Prisca, together with the church in their house, greet you warmly in the Lord") and Philemon 2 ("to the church in your [Philemon's] house"). On the house church in Paul and early Christianity, see especially Gerd Theissen, "Social Stratification in the Corinthian Community: A Contribution to the Sociology of Early Hellenistic Christianity," in idem, *The Social Setting of Pauline Christianity: Essays on Corinth,* ed. and trans. John H. Schütz (Philadelphia: Fortress Press, 1982), 83–91; Abraham J. Malherbe, *Social Aspects of Early Christianity* (2nd ed., enl.; Philadelphia: Fortress Press, 1983), 60–112; Hans-Josef Klauck, *Hausgemeinde und Hauskirche im frühen Christentum* (Stuttgarter Bibelstudien 103; Stuttgart: Katholisches Bibelwerk, 1981); Wayne A. Meeks, *The First Urban Christians: The Social World of the Apostle Paul* (New Haven, Conn.: Yale University Press, 1983), 75–77; Robert Banks, *Paul's Idea of Community* (rev. ed.; Peabody, Mass.: Hendrickson, 1994), 26–36; L. Michael White, *The Social Origins of Christian Architecture,* vol. 1: *Building God's House in the Roman World* (Harvard Theological Studies 42; Valley Forge, Pa.: Trinity Press International, 1997), 11–25, 102–23, 145–47.

4. See Rom 16:23, in which Paul describes Gaius as "host to me and to the whole church," indicating that he was the householder who had provided the meeting place for the church. On the potential misuse of the position of host, see Abraham J. Malherbe's interpretation of 3 John 1:10 in "The Inhospitality of Diotrephes" (*Social Aspects of Early Christianity* [2nd ed., enl.; Philadelphia: Fortress Press, 1983]). He argues that Diotrephes had abused his position as host by denying entrance to the assembly to certain individuals.

5. For a general study of the subject, see John Koenig, *New Testament Hospitality: Partnership with Strangers as Promise and Mission* (Overtures to Biblical Theology; Philadelphia: Fortress Press, 1985).

6. See White, *Building God's House,* 119: "In Paul's day and into the second century the primary setting for assembly had been the communal meal in the dining room of the house."

7. Ibid., 107.

8. Peter Lampe makes a persuasive argument that the meal at Corinth was organized like a pagan *eranos,* which was the ancient equivalent of a potluck dinner. See Lampe, "Das korinthische Herrenmahl im Schnittpunkt hellenistisch-römischer Mahlpraxis und paulinischer Theologia Crucis (1 Kor 11,17-34)," *ZNW* 82 (1991): 192–98, and "The Corinthian Eucharistic Dinner Party: Exegesis of a Cultural Context (1 Cor. 11:17-34)," *Affirmation* 4:2 (1991): 1–15.

9. Lampe, "The Corinthian Eucharistic Dinner Party." See also Gerd Theissen, "Social Integration and Sacramental Activity: An Analysis of 1 Cor. 11:17-34," in *The Social Setting of Pauline Christianity,* 151–52, 160–63.

10. Jerome Murphy-O'Connor (*St. Paul's Corinth: Texts and Archaeology* [Good News Studies 6; Wilmington, Del.: Glazier, 1983], 158–59) argues that the wealthy would have gathered early in the dining room where there were facilities for reclining, and the latecomers, or the non-wealthy, would then have had to spill over into the atrium, where they would have to sit. This would have been one of the causes of the divisions at the meal, since these two dining areas would have been physically separated; furthermore, they would have indicated status by the fact that reclining would be allowed for some and sitting for others. This argument is somewhat weakened by the fact that 1 Corinthians 14 seems to refer to the entire assembly, not just part of it. Lampe also attributes the sitting posture to an overflow crowd that has probably moved to the atrium for the symposium. He proposes that the posture and movement to another room would not detract from the connection of the events of 1 Corinthians 14 with the symposium tradition because the types of activities described in 1 Corinthians 14 fit the symposium tradition so well. Thus these activities would be understood as "Symposionsersatz" or as a "symposium equivalent" ("Das korinthische Herrenmahl," 190–91).

11. See, e.g., Lucian *Symp.* 13.

12. See examples collected in the next chapter.

13. See discussion in Meeks, *First Urban Christians,* 80–81.

14. See White, *Building God's House,* 60–101, esp. 69, 176 n. 24.

15. See, for example, J. Louis Martyn's reference to the idea that the church would have experienced the public reading of the Galatian letter when gathered for worship. He does not, however, elaborate on what the worship setting might have been—namely, whether it would have been worship at table. This is rarely done by scholars who attempt to analyze the reading of the letter as an "aural event," as Martyn calls it ("Events in Galatia: Modified Covenantal Nomism versus God's Invasion of the Cosmos in the Singular Gospel: A Response to J. D. G. Dunn and B. R. Gaventa," in *Pauline Theology,* vol. 1: *Thessalonians, Philippians, Galatians, Philemon,* ed. Jouette M. Bassler [Minneapolis: Fortress Press, 1991], 161).

16. E. P. Sanders, "Jewish Association with Gentiles and Galatians 2:11-14," in *The Conversation Continues: Studies in Paul and John in Honor of J. Louis Martyn,* ed. Robert T. Fortna and Beverly R. Gaventa (Nashville: Abingdon, 1990), 178.

17. Ibid., 176.

18. Sanders, "Jewish Association," 176–80; Alan F. Segal, *Paul the Convert: The Apostolate and Apostasy of Saul the Pharisee* (New Haven, Conn.: Yale University Press, 1990), 232–33.

19. Sanders, "Jewish Association," 186.

20. As Barrett points out, the normal Greek term would be *hierothyton,* meaning "sacrificed for sacred purposes," a term Paul uses at 10:28 (*The First Epistle to the Corinthians,* 188). See also Conzelmann, *1 Corinthians,* 139: *eidōlothyton* "is a Jewish term, constructed with a polemical edge against the Greek *hierothyton.*"

21. See C. K. Barrett, *A Commentary on the First Epistle to the Corinthians* (2nd ed.; London: Black, 1971), 194; Conzelmann, *1 Corinthians,* 137–38, 147; Wendell Lee Willis, *Idol Meat in Corinth: The Pauline Argument in 1 Corinthians 8 and 10* (SBLDS 68; Chico, Calif.: Scholars, 1985), 93.

22. Fee, *The First Epistle to the Corinthians,* 358–63.

23. Note that the issue in 8:10 is not whether the weak might be tempted to eat in a temple but rather that they might be tempted to eat "idol meat." And Paul's response is not that he will abstain from temple restaurants but abstain from meat for the sake of the conscience of the "weak" (8:13).

24. See the nicely nuanced discussion of this text in Dunn, *Romans 9–16,* 818–20, where he concludes: "To be noted is that Paul does not so much call for the abolition of the law of clean and unclean as for shifting the basis on which such a distinction may be regarded as relevant in the Christian community; that is, not as a boundary dividing one group from another and preventing communion, but as an issue affecting the expression of liberty *within* a community which embraces diverse viewpoints."

25. This thesis has been extensively argued by Dunn; see esp. *Romans 9–16,* 797–815. To be sure, while Dunn is emphatic and persuasive in making his case for Jewish dietary laws as the issue in debate in Romans 14, it is unclear to me whether he would agree with my contention that the context for the debate is the communal meal. See also Segal, *Paul the Convert,* 234–36, who argues that the "weak" in both Romans 14 and 1 Corinthians 10 are Jewish Christians.

26. Circumcision was being urged on the Galatians, whom Paul had originally converted, by a new group of Jewish Christian preachers who had recently arrived there. That is the primary controversy Paul is addressing in the letter (see esp. 5:2-6). Evidently, Jewish festival days were also at issue (4:10-11). Dietary laws were probably in the mix as well, since Paul makes the Antioch incident such a centerpiece of his argument. A possible reference to dietary laws is at 4:17, where a ritual act of "exclusion" is referred to; this makes most sense as a reference to exclusion from the community table, much like what Paul described as happening in Antioch.

27. See, e.g., Dunn, *Jesus, Paul and the Law*, 223: "It is because they have such a crucial role in defining 'Jewishness', membership of the covenant people, that circumcision and food laws feature so prominently in discussion of works of the law and righteousness." See also ibid., 243, 250–51, and numerous other references where Dunn discusses circumcision and food laws under the category of "the social function of the law," which he defines as its function to differentiate between Jew and Gentile. This is the aspect of the law that Paul opposed, according to Dunn, rather than the law per se.

28. Rudolf Bultmann, *Theology of the New Testament* (New York: Scribner's, 1970), 1.160–61. To be sure, Bultmann is primarily referring to the fact that the "gifts" of the spirit are experienced at worship. I would not deny this, but would argue that the presence of the spirit in the community should be understood in a broader sense.

29. See reference in chapter 3. The story of Epicurus setting up a meal in his memory is most probably also etiological.

30. Charles B. Cousar, *A Theology of the Cross: The Death of Jesus in the Pauline Letters* (Minneapolis: Fortress Press, 1990), 25–27.

31. See, e.g., the argument of Leander E. Keck in regard to the concept of the Christ "emptying" himself of divinity in taking on an earthly life. If Paul had written a Gospel according to this concept, Keck argues, it would be a Gospel without miracles, since the Jesus in Paul's Gospel would have had no claims to divine powers (*Paul and His Letters* [Philadelphia: Fortress Press, 1988], 47.

32. See, e.g., Theissen, "Social Integration," 164–67, 170 n. 12.

33. Thus Aelius Aristides, *Hymn to Sarapis* 54:13-15; see also Anton Höfler, *Der Sarapishymnus des Ailios Aristeides* (Tübingen Beiträge zur Altertumswissenschaft 27; Stuttgart–Berlin: W. Kohlhammer, 1935), 93–96.

34. Theissen, "Social Integration," 151–53.

35. Conzelmann has collected examples of this usage (*1 Corinthians*, 195 n. 27). See also BAGD, s.v.

36. Günther Bornkamm, "Lord's Supper and Church in Paul," in *Early Christian Experience* (New York: Harper & Row, 1969), 126; Conzelmann, *1 Corinthians*, 194–95, 202–3.

37. Pointed out by Theissen, "Social Integration," 149.

38. Plut. *Quaest. conv.* 643F–644A, 644D.

39. Theissen, "Social Integration," 151–53.

40. Ibid.

41. Ibid., 160.

42. See John G. Gager, review of Robert M. Grant, *Early Christianity and Society: Seven Studies;* Abraham J. Malherbe, *Social Aspects of Early Christianity;* and Gerd Theissen, *Sociology of Early Palestinian Christianity,* in *RelSRev* 5 (1979): 180; on class and status in Greco-Roman society in general, see Ramsay MacMullen, *Roman Social Relations 50 B.C. to A.D. 284* (New Haven, Conn.: Yale University Press, 1974), 88–120.

43. MacMullen, *Roman Social Relations,* 76–77.

44. Plut. *Quaest. conv.* 616F.

45. Plut. *Sept. sap. conv.* 150C.

46. Pliny the Younger *Ep.* 2.6.

47. On Paul's use of the diatribe, see Rudolf Bultmann, *Der Stil der paulinischen Predigt und die kynisch-stoische Diatribe* (FRLANT 13; Göttingen: Vandenhoeck and Ruprecht, 1910), and Stanley K. Stowers, *The Diatribe and Paul's Letter to the Romans* (Chico, Calif.: Scholars, 1981); see also Conzelmann, *1 Corinthians,* 5.

48. See, for example, the analysis of metaphor and hyperbole in the Pauline use of the diatribe in 1 Corinthians in Abraham J. Malherbe, "The Beasts of Ephesus," *JBL* 87 (1968): 71–80. Conzelmann refers to Paul's use of customary metaphors of the diatribe at 3:2; 9:11; and 13:11 (*1 Corinthians,* 5).

49. On Paul's view toward the sharing of wealth in the community, see 13:3: "If I give away all my possessions . . ." Note also that the list of spiritual gifts in Rom 12:6-8 includes "the giver, [who is to give] in generosity." Paul's reference to the collection for "the poor" (Gal 2:10) and "the saints" (2 Cor 8:4; 9:12) is most likely a reference to the collection for the church in Jerusalem (1 Cor 16:3; Rom 15:25-26), not for the poor in the Gentile churches. See further Dieter Georgi, *Remembering the Poor: The History of Paul's Collection for Jerusalem* (Nashville: Abingdon, 1991).

50. Theissen, "Social Integration," 153–59.

51. Plut. *Quaest. conv.* 666F.

52. Ibid., 147–51.

53. Xen. *Mem.* 3.5.20

54. Ibid., 2.2.13. Walter Grundmann, "Dokimos," *TDNT* 2 (1964): 255–60.

55. On this point, see especially Ernst Käsemann, "The Pauline Doctrine of the Lord's Supper," in *Essays on New Testament Themes* (SBT 41; Naperville, Ill.: Allenson, 1964), 119–27.

56. Plut. *Quaest. conv.* 616C.

57. See, e.g., 1 Cor 6:4; 9:27; 2 Cor 13:5-7; Gal 6:4.

58. See also Hans Freiherr von Soden, "Sakrament und Ethik bei Paulus," in *Marburger theologische Studien,* Rudolf Otto Festgruss, ed. H. Frick (Gotha: Klotz, 1931), 1.31–40: for Paul, the meal, or the sacrament, implied an ethical obligation; the two could not be separated.

59. Here I follow Bornkamm, "Lord's Supper and Church in Paul," with whom, on this point, I am in basic agreement.

60. See, e.g., Plut. *Quaest. conv.* 660B and the discussion in chapter 3.

61. Conzelmann (*1 Corinthians,* 211 nn. 7, 8) notes the widespread use of the metaphor of the body and its parts in popular and philosophical literature, especially as a metaphor for political relationships, and has collected pertinent evidence.

62. Gell. *NA* 7.13.1–4.

63. Lucian *Symp.* 17.

64. See, e.g., Conzelmann, *1 Corinthians,* 212 n. 17, whose English edition translates the phrase: "we were all imbued with one spirit"; he asks in the note, "Is

[this phrase] an allusion to the Lord's Supper?" He does not answer the question, so I will.

65. As, e.g., in Plut. *Quaest. conv.* 614E.

66. See discussions in chapter 5.

67. See discussions in chapter 5.

68. See also S. Stein on the Jewish Passover liturgy ("The Influence of Symposia Literature on the Literary Form of the Pesah Haggadah," in *Essays in Greco-Roman and Related Talmudic Literature*, ed. Henry A. Fischel [New York: KTAV, 1977], 13–44).

69. K. Weiss, "*Sympherō*," *TDNT* 9 (1973): 70–73.

70. Aristotle *Eth. Nic.* 5.1.13.

71. Diog. Laert. 10.150.

72. Ibid., 7.98–99.

73. See Conzelmann, *1 Corinthians*, 140–41; Otto Michel, "*Oikodomeō*," *TDNT* 5 (1968): 136–44; Philipp Vielhauer, *Oikodome, Das Bild vom Bau in der christlichen Literatur vom Neuen Testament bis Clemens Alexandrinus* (Karlsruhe-Durlach: Tron, 1940).

74. See, e.g., Xen. *Cyr.* 8.7.15; Epict. *Diatr.* 2.15.8. Paul's use is similar in Rom 15:20, where he describes his work as building on a foundation.

75. Thus Johannes Weiss, *Der erste Korintherbrief* (KEK 5; 10th ed.; Göttingen: Vandenhoek and Ruprecht, 1925), 215 n. 3.

76. For examples of ecstatic prophecy in paganism and Judaism of this period, see Helmut Krämer, Rolf Rendtorff, Rudolf Meyer, and Gerhard Friedrich, "*Prophētēs*," *TDNT* 6 (1968): 793, 813, 821.

77. Richard Reitzenstein, *Hellenistic Mystery Religions* (repr., Pittsburgh: Pickwick, 1978), 300; see also Conzelmann, *1 Corinthians*, 244 n. 35.

78. See Krämer et al., "*Prophētēs*," 829: "In Paul the word has a predominantly ethical and hortatory character."

79. Conzelmann, *1 Corinthians*, 205–6, 243 n. 25; Reitzenstein, *Hellenistic Mystery Religions*, 297–300.

80. See p. 130, "Statutes of the Iobakchoi," lines 63–65.

81. Thus Weiss, *Der erste Korintherbrief,* 341–42, versus Werner Foerster, "*Eirēnē*," *TDNT* 2 (1964): 412.

82. Plut. *Quaest. conv.* 615E–F.

83. Ibid., 614E, 615A.

84. See also Conzelmann, *1 Corinthians*, 245 n. 50.

85. Ibid., 246; Fee, *First Epistle to the Corinthians*, 699–708.

86. See, e.g., Elisabeth Schüssler Fiorenza, *In Memory of Her: A Feminist Theological Reconstruction of Christian Origins* (New York: Crossroad, 1983), 230–33, who argues that the text applies not to all women in the Corinthian community, but to wives only, and only in a specific situation: "the speaking and questioning of wives in the public worship assembly."

87. Petron. *Sat.* 67–69. Note, however, that the conversation at this meal is not presented as a philosophical discourse but rather as a disjointed conversation. On the seating chart for Trimalchio's banquet, see Martin S. Smith, ed., *Petronius: Cena Trimalchionis* (Oxford: Clarendon, 1975), 66, and figure 3 in this volume (p. 16).

88. See the discussion in chapter 2.

89. Lucian *Symp.* 8, 16, 44.

90. See chapter 5.

91. Thus John C. Hurd, *The Origin of I Corinthians* (New York: Seabury, 1965), 125.

92. It should be noted that the ethic of friendship in the context of a meal was expressed with a variety of terms, such as: *friend (philia), friendship (philophrosynē), pleasure (hēdonē),* and *festive joy (euphrosynē).* What these terms share in common is their function in the context of a meal to define social ethics among the participants. See also chapters 3 and 4.

93. Ezio Pellizer, "Outlines of a Morphology of Sympotic Entertainment," in *Sympotica: A Symposium on the Symposium,* ed. Oswyn Murray (Oxford: Clarendon, 1990), 180.

94. Plato *Symp.* 177a–212c.

95. Reitzenstein argued in a series of articles that the triad "faith, love, hope" *(pistis, agapē, elpis)* derived from various gnostic formulations in which *erōs* was the original term for "love," which Paul replaced with *agapē.* For a discussion of his position, with bibliography, see Conzelmann, *1 Corinthians,* 229; and Ceslaus Spicq, *Agapé dans le Nouveau Testament* (Études Bibliques; Paris: Gabalda, 1958–59), 2.365–78. For my purposes, the origin of the triad is not as important as is the use of *agapē* to refer to meal ethics.

96. Plato *Symp.* 197C–E; quoted in Conzelmann, *1 Corinthians,* 219. Translation adapted from that of the LCL by the author.

97. This text is also quoted in Conzelmann, *1 Corinthians,* 220; see also his discussion on p. 218.

98. Plut. *Sept. sap. conv.* 153A.

99. See further Conzelmann, *1 Corinthians,* 219 n. 16; Spicq, *Agapé dans le Nouveau Testament,* 2.62.

100. See, e.g., Conzelmann, *1 Corinthians,* 217–18, for a summary of arguments on this point.

101. The literal meaning of *kybernēsis* ("leadership") is "piloting," as in piloting or navigating a ship.

102. See further Conzelmann, *1 Corinthians,* 215.

103. See ibid., 216, on the background to the term *way (hodos).*

104. Spicq traces the interpretation back to Calvin that Paul values *agapē* because it "edifies" *(Agapé dans le Nouveau Testament,* 2.106–7).

105. See also Conzelmann, *1 Corinthians,* 220, who traces the background for Paul's ideas to Hellenistic Jewish wisdom tradition, as in 1 Esd 4:38 quoted above;

and Günther Bornkamm, "The More Excellent Way," in *Early Christian Experience* (New York: Harper & Row, 1969), 187–90.

106. Dunn, *Romans 9–16*, 799–802.

107. Stanley K. Stowers, *A Rereading of Romans: Justice, Jews, and Gentiles* (New Haven, Conn.: Yale University Press, 1994), 322. BAGD translates the term "to receive or accept into one's society, home, or circle of acquaintances."

108. See esp. Peter Lampe, "The Roman Christians of Romans 16," in *The Romans Debate*, ed. Karl P. Donfried (rev. and expanded ed.; Peabody, Mass.: Hendrickson, 1991), 216–30.

109. Compare 8:11, in which the relationship with "weak believers" is based on the fact that Christ died for them.

110. Note Theissen's argument that Paul proposes an ethic of "love-patriarchalism" in 1 Corinthians: "The Strong and the Weak in Corinth: A Sociological Analysis of a Theological Quarrel," in *The Social Setting of Pauline Christianity*, 139–40; "Social Integration," 163–68.

8. THE BANQUET IN THE GOSPELS

1. See also my article for the Georgi Festschrift, "Table Fellowship and the Historical Jesus," from which the arguments here are taken (in *Religious Propaganda and Missionary Competition in the New Testament World: Essays Honoring Dieter Georgi*, ed. Lukas Bormann, Kelly del Tredici, and Angela Standhartinger [Leiden: Brill, 1994], 135–62). For a critical review of historical Jesus research, see Dieter Georgi, "The Interest in Life of Jesus Theology as a Paradigm for the Social History of Biblical Criticism," *HTR* 85 (1992): 51–83.

2. Norman Perrin, *Rediscovering the Teaching of Jesus* (New York: Harper & Row, 1967), 102–8.

3. Ibid., 119–21, 161–64. Actually, his arguments are much more detailed than my cryptic summary suggests, but for the sake of brevity I would emphasize dissimilarity as the cornerstone of much of his argumentation.

4. Ibid., 103.

5. Ibid., 102–8.

6. James Breech, *The Silence of Jesus: The Authentic Voice of the Historical Man* (Philadelphia: Fortress Press, 1983), 22–64; E. P. Sanders, *Jesus and Judaism* (Philadelphia: Fortress Press, 1985), 174–211, 271–73; Richard Horsley, *Jesus and the Spiral of Violence: Popular Jewish Resistance in Roman Palestine* (New York: Harper & Row, 1987), 178–80; Marcus J. Borg, *Conflict, Holiness and Politics in the Teachings of Jesus* (Studies in the Bible and Early Christianity 5; Toronto: Edwin Mellen, 1984), 78–121; idem, *Jesus: A New Vision* (New York: Harper & Row, 1987), 101–2, 131–33; John Dominic Crossan, *The Historical Jesus: The Life of a Mediterranean Jewish Peasant* (San Francisco: HarperCollins, 1991), 260–64, 332–53; Bruce Chilton, *The Temple of Jesus: His Sacrificial Program within a Cultural History of Sacrifice* (University Park: Pennsylvania State University Press, 1992), 137–54; idem, *A*

Feast of Meanings: Eucharistic Theologies from Jesus through Johannine Circles (NovT-Sup 72; Leiden: Brill, 1994), 67–74; John P. Meier, *A Marginal Jew: Rethinking the Historical Jesus,* vol. 2: *Mentor, Message, and Miracles* (ABRL; New York: Doubleday, 1994), 2.302–9. To be sure, I have severely truncated the detailed and distinct arguments of these scholars by grouping them together in this way, but it is only to make the point that they all place significant emphasis on the table fellowship motif, though they may interpret it differently. Some of their distinct arguments will be referenced later in this chapter. Others who emphasize the table fellowship theme as part of the historical Jesus data are: Günther Bornkamm, *Jesus of Nazareth* (New York: Harper & Row, 1960), 80–81; Joachim Jeremias, *The Parables of Jesus,* trans. S. H. Hooke (rev. ed.; New York: Scribner's, 1963), 227; idem, *New Testament Theology: The Proclamation of Jesus,* trans. John Bowden (New York: Scribner's, 1971), 115–16; Geza Vermes, *Jesus the Jew: A Historian's Reading of the Gospels* (London: Collins, 1973), 224; Morton Smith, *Jesus the Magician* (San Francisco: Harper & Row, 1978), 122–23, 152; Martin Hengel, *The Charismatic Leader and His Followers* (Philadelphia: Fortress Press, 1974), 67; Elisabeth Schüssler Fiorenza, *In Memory of Her: A Feminist Theological Reconstruction of Christian Origins* (New York: Crossroad, 1983), 119–21, 126–30; Robert W. Funk and the Jesus Seminar, eds., *The Acts of Jesus: The Search for the Authentic Deeds of Jesus* (San Francisco: HarperCollins, 1998), 31. The list could go on. There are a few skeptics; see, e.g., William O. Walker, "Jesus and the Tax Collectors," *JBL* 97 (1978): 221–38; and Burton L. Mack, *A Myth of Innocence: Mark and Christian Origins* (Philadelphia: Fortress Press, 1988), 80–83.

7. Crossan, *The Historical Jesus,* 304.

8. In all of the meals of Jesus depicted in the Gospels, when a posture is mentioned, it is reclining, though the NRSV usually translates "sit at table" rather than the more accurate "recline." Jeremias argued that this overwhelming preference that the meals of Jesus be reclining banquets meant that the Gospels only referred to unusually festive meals (*The Eucharistic Words of Jesus,* 48–49). Rather, these references should be understood as presenting Jesus in a table setting corresponding to the conventions of the Greco-Roman banquet as it was practiced and represented in literature throughout the Greco-Roman world.

9. Luke 7:36-50; 11:37-54; 14:1-24; see below for a further discussion of these texts in their context in Luke.

10. See esp. Werner H. Kelber, "Conclusion: From Passion Narrative to Gospel," in *The Passion in Mark: Studies on Mark 14–16,* ed. Werner H. Kelber (Philadelphia: Fortress Press, 1976), 153–80, esp. 173.

11. Titles of texts and lists of parallels are taken from John Dominic Crossan, *Sayings Parallels: A Workbook for the Jesus Tradition* (Philadelphia: Fortress Press, 1986).

12. Jonathan Klawans, *Impurity and Sin in Ancient Judaism* (New York: Oxford University Press, 2000), 147.

13. The Jesus Seminar has concluded that while Jesus had his detractors, it is uncertain whether they were Pharisees (colored pink; see, e.g., Funk and the Jesus

Seminar, eds., *Acts of Jesus,* 31). What complicates the issue is the complex history of the Pharisees, which is still being debated among scholars.

14. Mack, *A Myth of Innocence,* 116–20; see also the discussion in chapter 7, esp. pp. 188–91.

15. Vernon K. Robbins, "Last Meal: Preparation, Betrayal, and Absence (Mark 14:12-25)," in Werner, ed., *The Passion in Mark,* 21–40; Robert M. Fowler, *Loaves and Fishes: The Function of the Feeding Stories in the Gospel of Mark* (SBLDS 54; Chico, Calif.: Scholars, 1981); Philip Sellew, "The Last Supper Discourse in Luke 22:21-38," *Forum* 3:3 (September 1987): 70–95; John L. White, "The Way of the Cross: Was There a Pre-Markan Passion Narrative?" *Forum* 3:2 (June 1987): 35–49; idem, "Beware of Leavened Bread: Markan Imagery in the Last Supper," *Forum* 3:4 (December 1987): 49–63.

16. Jeremias, *The Eucharistic Words of Jesus.*

17. See, e.g., Eduard Schweizer, *The Lord's Supper according to the New Testament* (FBBS 18; Philadelphia: Fortress Press, 1967), 29–32; Robbins, "Last Meal," 22–28.

18. See also the discussion in chapter 7, pp. 188–91.

19. This motif functions in all of the Gospels, from Mark's theme of the misunderstanding of the disciples to John's theological elaboration in which the disciples cannot understand everything until after Jesus' death (2:22; 16:12-13). Compare also the beginning of the story in Acts, in which the disciples misunderstand what comes next (1:6-7).

20. Burton Mack defines the transition from "Jesus movements," represented by Q and *Gospel of Thomas,* to "Christ cult," represented by pre-Pauline traditions, as a transition from the "Jesus movement" belief in Jesus as teacher (with no emphasis on his death) to the "Christ cult" belief in Jesus' death and resurrection as saving events; see Burton L. Mack, *Myth of Innocence,* 78–123, and idem, *Who Wrote the New Testament? The Making of the Christian Myth* (San Francisco: HarperSanFrancisco, 1995), 43–96.

21. The theme of Jesus' foreknowledge as a christological theme is basic to Markan interpretation; see, e.g., 8:31; 9:31; 10:33-34. Matthew and Luke develop this same theme. John's elaboration of this christological theme is so highly developed that in his story Jesus actually orchestrates his own death; see, e.g., 10:17-18; 18:4-12; 19:11; 19:17 ("carrying the cross *by himself*"); 19:28-30 ("When Jesus knew that all was now finished [fulfilled] . . . he bowed his head and gave up his spirit").

22. See, e.g., Chilton, *A Feast of Meanings,* 67–74, who argues that Jesus said the words, "this is my body/blood," but that he did not mean them self-referentially; he rather meant that the communal meal with wine and blood was to take the place of the temple sacrifice. Chilton also argues that there was not one but rather six early forms of the Eucharist, and the Last Supper account represented just one of them (*A Feast of Meanings,* 1–11). Consequently, it seems to me that he is arguing that Jesus had a last meal and said what the text says he said, but that it did not really matter.

23. Crossan, *The Historical Jesus,* 361. The Jesus Seminar, it should be noted, did go further. The seminar "readily conceded the possibility that Jesus may have performed some symbolic acts during table fellowship with his followers. And those symbolic acts may have involved bread and wine or perhaps fish." They did not judge the words of Jesus in the Last Supper text to be historical, however (Robert W. Funk, Roy W. Hoover, and the Jesus Seminar, *The Five Gospels: The Search for the Authentic Words of Jesus* [New York: Macmillan, 1993], 117–18). Scholarship on the Last Supper tends to vacillate between this position and its opposite, that the story is basically historical.

24. See esp. Ronald F. Hock and Edward N. O'Neil, *The Chreia in Ancient Rhetoric,* vol. 1: *The Progymnasmata* (SBLTT 27; Atlanta: Scholars, 1986). An excellent brief discussion of the *chreia* with an annotated bibliography is found in Vernon K. Robbins, "The Chreia," in *Greco-Roman Literature and the New Testament: Selected Forms and Genres,* ed. David E. Aune (SBLSBS 21; Atlanta: Scholars, 1988), 1–23. See also the helpful review of scholarship on this form in Mack, *A Myth of Innocence,* 172–78.

25. Robbins, "The Chreia," 2.

26. See especially Henry A. Fischel, "Studies in Cynicism and the Ancient Near East," in *Religions in Antiquity: Essays in Memory of Erwin Ramsdell Goodenough,* ed. Jacob Neusner (Studies in the History of Religions 14; Leiden: Brill, 1968), 372–411, esp. 374.

27. Ibid., 373. See also Mack, *A Myth of Innocence,* 179–82.

28. John S. Kloppenborg, *The Formation of Q: Trajectories in Ancient Wisdom Collections* (Studies in Antiquity and Christianity; Philadelphia: Fortress Press, 1987), 322–25; Mack, *A Myth of Innocence,* 182–92; see also idem, "The Kingdom That Didn't Come: A Social History of the Q Tradents," in *SBL 1988 Seminar Papers,* ed. David J. Lull (Atlanta: Scholars, 1988), 608–35; Ron Cameron, "'What Have You Come Out to See?' Characterizations of John and Jesus in the Gospels," *Semeia* 49 (1990): 35–69.

29. Mack, *A Myth of Innocence,* 183.

30. See esp. Diogenes *Epistles* 38.4: "I did not dine with everyone but only with those in need of therapy" (from Abraham J. Malherbe, ed., *The Cynic Epistles: A Study Edition* [SBLSBS 12; Missoula, Mont.: Scholars, 1977], 163; quoted in Leif E. Vaage, "Q: The Ethos and Ethics of an Itinerant Intelligence" [Ph.D. diss., Claremont Graduate School, 1987], 379). For other examples, see also Malherbe, "Self-Definition among Epicureans and Cynics," in *Jewish and Christian Self-Definition,* vol. 3: *Self-Definition in the Greco-Roman World,* ed. Ben F. Meyer and E. P. Sanders (Philadelphia: Fortress Press, 1982), 53; Mack, *A Myth of Innocence,* 183–84, esp. 184 n. 8.

31. Rudolf Bultmann confidently asserted about this text: "the artificiality of the composition is clear as day" (*The History of the Synoptic Tradition* [2nd ed.; New York: Harper & Row, 1968], 47–48). He noted especially how the story artificially involves the disciples. In this it is parallel to other stories in the tradition whose function is to

defend the conduct of the disciples. Thus it is ultimately the church rather than Jesus who is on trial; the text would therefore originate in the early church. For a more recent analysis that agrees with Bultmann's basic point, see Funk and the Jesus Seminar, eds., *Acts of Jesus*, 29–32; idem, *Honest to Jesus: Jesus for a New Millennium* (San Francisco: HarperSanFrancisco, 1996).

32. Bultmann, *History of the Synoptic Tradition*, 18 n. 3, 66; Walker, "Jesus and the Tax Collectors," 233.

33. See, e.g., Bultmann, *History of the Synoptic Tradition*, 163; K. L. Schmidt, "*kaleō*," *TDNT* 3 (1965): 488–89; examples of the use of this term in invitations can be found in chapters 2, 3, and 4 in this volume.

34. To be sure, the Greek of Mark 2:15 is a bit vague: "he reclined in his house" *(katakeisthai auton en tē oikia autou);* translators usually read the context to imply Levi's house. Matthew's version of Mark's story makes it even more vague, by omitting the personal pronoun and simply reading "the house" (9:10). Consequently, both Mark and Matthew could be read so that the house where the meal was held was Jesus' house.

35. According to Vernon K. Robbins (*Jesus the Teacher: A Socio-Rhetorical Interpretation of Mark* [Philadelphia: Fortress Press, 1984], esp. 109), the calling of the disciples in Mark is part of a larger theme in the Gospel as a whole in which the writer utilizes classic literary motifs of the day to present Jesus as a teacher who calls and instructs his disciples.

36. This story is also classified as a "typification" story by the Jesus Seminar (Funk and the Jesus Seminar, eds., *Acts of Jesus*, 31) and by Stephen J. Patterson (*The God of Jesus: The Historical Jesus and the Search for Meaning* [Harrisburg, Pa.: Trinity Press International, 1998], 81 n. 48).

37. Thus Mack, *A Myth of Innocence*, 183.

38. Sanders, *Jesus and Judaism*, 174–211.

39. Kloppenborg, *The Formation of Q*, 107–17.

40. Ibid., 317.

41. Ibid., 110–12; see also Arland Jacobson, "Wisdom Christology in Q" (Ph.D. diss., Claremont Graduate School, 1978), 84–91; Cameron, "'What Have You Come Out to See?'"

42. Kloppenborg, *The Formation of Q*, 111.

43. Also noted by Jacobson, "Wisdom Christology in Q," 86–87; and Wendy J. Cotter, "The Parable of the Children in the Market-Place, Q (Lk) 7:31-35: An Examination of the Parable's Image and Significance," *NovT* 29 (1987): 303 n. 58.

44. See, e.g., Plutarch's reference to "the friend-making character of the table" (*Quaest. conv.* 612D). This is a standard motif in banquet literature.

45. See, e.g., Jeremias, *New Testament Theology*, 109–13. Horsley proposes that the reference to tax collectors is strictly slanderous; thus while the accusation is historical, what it states, that Jesus dined with tax collectors, is not (*Jesus and the Spiral of Violence*, 212–17).

46. Jeremias, *New Testament Theology*, 110; John R. Donahue, "Tax Collectors and Sinners: An Attempt at Identification," *CBQ* 33 (1971): 39–61.

47. Quisling: Perrin, *Rediscovering the Teaching of Jesus*, 93–94. Dishonesty: Jeremias, *New Testament Theology*, 110–11; Donahue, "Tax Collectors and Sinners," 59.

48. As suggested in Jeremias, *New Testament Theology*, 109–13, esp. 112.

49. Sanders, *Jesus and Judaism*, 177.

50. Ibid., 203–8.

51. Ibid., 208; see also the similar interpretation of Perrin quoted above.

52. See, e.g., Joachim Jeremias (*Jerusalem in the Time of Jesus*, trans. F. H. Cave and C. H. Cave [rev. ed.; Philadelphia: Fortress Press, 1969], 303–12), who includes "tax collectors" in a list of "despised trades" culled from the Mishnah.

53. Thus J. D. G. Dunn, "Pharisees, Sinners, and Jesus," in *The Social World of Formative Christianity and Judaism: Essays in Tribute to Howard Clark Kee*, Jacob Neusner et al., eds. (Philadelphia: Fortress Press, 1988), 276–80, in opposition to Sanders.

54. Noted also by Sanders, *Jesus and Judaism*, 193, 202–3.

55. Note, however, that this would not be likely if he was an itinerant, as Crossan especially claims (*The Historical Jesus*, 345–48).

56. See my review of the evidence in regard to the messianic banquet in chapter 6, pp. 166–71.

57. The communal meal at Qumran is most often proposed as an example of such a banquet; see the discussion in chapter 6, pp. 156–58, 166–71.

58. Perrin, *Rediscovering the Teaching of Jesus*, 120.

59. The function of the orginal *chreia* to present a characterization of John and Jesus is nicely stated by Cameron, "'What Have You Come Out to See?'" 54, 60.

60. On the Cynic worldview and its relation to the early Jesus movement, see esp. Burton L. Mack, *The Lost Gospel: The Book of Q and Christian Origins* (San Francisco: HarperCollins, 1993), 111–30.

61. See esp. Cameron, "'What Have You Come Out to See?'"

62. Nevertheless, Crossan concludes: "The general background for the dress and equipment codes [of Jesus and his disciples] is the countercultural Cynic life-style" (*The Historical Jesus*, 338; see also 72–88); compare Mack, *The Lost Gospel*, 129.

63. Crossan, *The Historical Jesus*, 339. Compare Mack's interpretation of this same text: "Behavior is spelled out in terms of conventional rules of hospitality: Eat what they provide; do not offend the host by accepting another's hospitality and going on to another house" (*The Lost Gospel*, 129).

64. Crossan, *The Historical Jesus*, 341–44.

65. See especially ibid., 260–64.

66. Ibid., 304–10, 341.

67. Note that one of Crossan's key texts for the social egalitarian commensality of Jesus, that of the parable of the Great Feast, is one in which social stratification plays a key role, since the one who invites those of the streets to the feast is a person of

means who has a home and servants (Matt. 22:2-13 = Luke 14:16b-23 = *Gos. Thom.* 64:1). Crossan does not discuss this feature in his reconstruction, however. See ibid., 261–62.

68. Against Crossan, *The Historical Jesus,* 340: "Jesus, however, is establishing a rural rather than an urban mission."

69. Supporting the approach here is the definitive work by Kathleen E. Corley on the literary function of women in the meal stories in the synoptic Gospels and the implications for the theology of the evangelists regarding women (*Private Women, Public Meals: Social Conflict in the Synoptic Tradition* [Peabody, Mass.: Hendrickson, 1993]).

70. See, e.g., Robbins, *Jesus the Teacher,* 188.

71. On irony in Mark, see esp. Mack, *A Myth of Innocence,* 335–39.

72. Ibid., 325–31.

73. Examples: Fowler, *Loaves and Fishes*; Mack, *A Myth of Innocence,* passim.

74. Lee Edward Klosinski, "The Meals in Mark" (Ph.D. diss., Claremont Graduate School, 1988).

75. Mark's terminology follows a pattern in Greco-Roman literature—he uses more than one term for reclining, often in the context of the same story. His terms are as follows: *anakeisthai* (6:26, 14:18); *synanakeisthai* (2:15b, 6:22); *katakeisthai* (2:15a, 14:3); *anaklinein* (6:39); *anapiptein* (6:40, 8:6). See also *katakeisthai* for "sick in bed" at 1:30 and 2:4.

76. Robbins has provided a useful summary of Mark's literary heritage: "Mark's gospel intermingles sociocultural patterns whose heritage lies in both biblical and Greek traditions. . . . On the other hand, Mark exhibits explicit literary influence from biblical literature but not from Greek and Hellenistic literature written outside Jewish circles" (*Jesus the Teacher,* 76). The motif Robbins is tracing is that of the "disciple-gathering teacher-Messiah" (76). This characterization of the literary heritage of Mark correlates quite well with the form and scope of meal traditions that he utilizes. In contrast, Dennis MacDonald has recently proposed extensive use by Mark of motifs from Homer (*The Homeric Epics and the Gospel of Mark* [New Haven, Conn.: Yale University Press, 2000]).

77. See also the prayer before the *deipna* on the ground at 6:41 and 8:6-7.

78. See the analysis of this text in the historical Jesus section above, pp. 228–30.

79. Joanna Dewey has analyzed the literary connections in these stories in *Markan Public Debate: Literary Technique, Concentric Structure, and Theology in Mark 2:1—3:6* (SBLDS 48; Chico, Calif.: Scholars, 1980).

80. See also Fowler, *Loaves and Fishes,* 86, who notes that these two stories are meant to contrast with one another.

81. Note the connection with the messianic banquet themes of wedding feast and feast of joy.

82. On the motif of "following" Jesus in Mark, see also Robbins, *Jesus the Teacher.*

83. See also examples of typical Greek arguments against Jews that the dietary laws meant practicing inhospitality. Diodorus, for example, attributes their refusal to eat with Gentiles to their "hatred of humanity" (34.1.2). See further in chapter 6.

84. So argued by D. E. Nineham, *Saint Mark* (The Pelican New Testament Commentaries; Middlesex, Eng.: Penguin, 1963).

85. This is the reading that Luke gives this text, by the way, and so, to make this point clearer and give it a more consistent context, he moves this pericope from the context of the journey to Jerusalem to the context of an actual meal setting, that of the Last Supper (Luke 22:23-27). He also leaves out the reference to "ransom" in 10:45b, a reference that, as we will see, is not totally consistent with the table imagery.

86. Mack, *A Myth of Innocence,* esp. 315–31.

87. Ibid., 265; see also George W. E. Nickelsburg, "The Genre and Function of the Markan Passion Narrative," *HTR* 73 (1980): 153–84.

88. The Greek phrase *esthiein tous artous* ("to eat bread") is given the more general translation in the NRSV, "to eat," thus missing an important nuance of the Greek. Against this general translation is the fact that in the same context, Mark used the term *to eat* by itself (7:3-4), thus indicating that his reference to the specific idea that the disciples were eating *bread* (7:2) is deliberate and significant.

89. This standard outline of Mark 8–10 is derived from Norman Perrin and Dennis C. Duling, *The New Testament: An Introduction* (2nd ed.; New York: Harcourt Brace Jovanovich, 1982), 248–51.

90. On martyrdom as the overall model for the death of Jesus in Mark, see Mack, *A Myth of Innocence,* 261–68.

91. Mack, *Myth of Innocence.*

92. See, respectively, J. Delobel, "L'onction par la pécheresse: La composition littéraire de *Lc.* VII, 36-50," *ETL* 42 (1966): 415–75; E. Springs Steele, "Luke 11:37-54—A Modified Hellenistic Symposium?" *JBL* 103 (1984): 379–94; X. de Meeûs, "Composition de *Lc.,* XIV et genre symposiaque," *ETL* 37 (1961): 847–70; and more recently Willi Braun, *Feasting and Social Rhetoric in Luke 14* (Cambridge: Cambridge University Press, 1995). See also Steele, "Jesus' Table-Fellowship with Pharisees: An Editorial Analysis of Luke 7:36-50, 11:37-54, and 14:1-24" (Ph.D. diss., University of Notre Dame, 1981); Robert J. Karris, *Luke: Artist and Theologian: Luke's Passion Account as Literature* (New York: Paulist, 1985), 47–78; Jerome H. Neyrey, ed., *The Social World of Luke-Acts: Models for Interpretation* (Peabody, Mass.: Hendrickson, 1991); and Jonathan Brumberg-Kraus, "Symposium Scenes in Luke's Gospel with Special Attention to the Last Supper" (Ph.D. diss, Vanderbilt University, 1991). This section of chapter 8 is a revision of my article "Table Fellowship as a Literary Motif in the Gospel of Luke," JBL 106 (1987): 613–38.

93. Plut. *Sept. sap. conv.* 149B.

94. Ibid., 149F.

95. Plut. *Quaest. conv.* 1.3.

96. Ibid., 1.2.

97. The NRSV translates this as "sit down," thereby obscuring the clear reference in the Greek to the posture of reclining at the dining table.

98. Note that Luke uses three different terms for reclining in this one pericope.

99. Plut. *Quaest. conv.* 615F.

100. Plut. *Quaest. conv.* 616C–F.

101. See the discussion in chapter 3.

102. See Grundmann, "*Tapeinos,*" *TDNT* 8 (1972): 11–12.

103. On the relation of Plutarch to popular literature and morality of the early Christian period, see chapter 3 and Hans Dieter Betz, "Introduction," in idem, ed., *Plutarch's Ethical Writings and Early Christian Literature* (Leiden: Brill, 1978), 1–10.

104. See also William S. Kurz, "Luke 22:14-28 and Greco-Roman and Biblical Farewell Addresses," *JBL* 104 (1985): 251–68, who argues that Luke's redaction of this section is based on the model of the farewell address rather than the symposium, although he acknowledges the possible influence of the latter. Although our theories are not fundamentally opposed, I would argue that the anecdotal character of the text, as exemplified by 22:24, correlates especially well with the symposium setting rather than with the farewell address motif, although clearly Jesus' "table talk" on this occasion is also a farewell address.

105. Plato *Symp.* 176E.

106 Ath. 5.186a.

107. Josef Martin, *Symposion: Die Geschichte einer literarischen Form* (Paderborn: F. Schöningh, 1931), 167–84.

108. Plut. *Quaest. conv.* 697E.

109. Plut. *Quaest. conv.* 629C–D.

110. For topics related to meal etiquette, see chapter 3 and Plut. *Quaest. conv.* 1.2, 1.3, 1.4, 2.10, 3.1, 3.9, 4.3, 5.5, 5.6, 5.10, 7.4, 7.6–10, 8.6.

111. De Meeûs, "Composition de *Lc.*, XIV et genre symposiaque."

112. Ibid., 852.

113. Ibid., 852, 855–56.

114. Note that this conclusion of de Meeûs suggests a literary explanation for the function of the Pharisees in this text. Steele, utilizing the insights of de Meeûs, makes the same point in regard to the other two instances in which Jesus dines with Pharisees in Luke, a phenomenon that is found only in Luke's Gospel (see also 7:36-50; 11:37-54). He points out the anomaly that Jesus is invited to dine at the table of Pharisees without further explanation in the narrative, despite the fact that he is consistently portrayed as opposed to Pharisaic purity laws that apply to table fellowship. He concludes that both Luke and his audience were only minimally familiar with Pharisaic table customs and that the table settings with Pharisees are all modeled on the symposium genre and function as a literary vehicle for Luke's literary and theological interests ("Jesus' Table-Fellowship with Pharisees," 127–32, 178–82). Indeed,

here as well as throughout Luke the Pharisees tend to function primarily as a literary stereotype or as a foil for Jesus' proclamation of his message.

115. De Meeûs, "Composition de *Lc.*, XIV et genre symposiaque," 858–59.

116. So also David E. Aune, "Septem sapientium convivium," in Betz, ed., *Plutarch's Ethical Writings,* 70.

117. The term used here is *diakonia,* a term that regularly refers to table service; see further H. W. Beyer, "*Diakoneō,*" *TDNT* 2 (1964): 81–93.

118. So Steele, "Luke 11:37-54—A Modified Hellenistic Symposium?"; see also Delobel on 7:36-54 ("L'onction par la pécheresse," 458–64).

119. See Jean-Marie Dentzer, "Aux origines de l'iconographie du banquet couché," *Revue Archéologique* (1971): 215–58, and idem, *Le motif du banquet couché dans le proche-orient et le monde grec du VIIᵉ au IVᵉ siècle avant J.-C.* (Bibliothèque des écoles françaises d'Athènes et de Rome 246; Rome: École française de Rome, 1982).

120. Hor. *Sat.* 2.8. See also chapter 3 above; L. R. Shero, "The *Cena* in Roman Satire," 126-43; Martin, *Symposion,* 216-19.

121. Petron. *Sat.* 26–79; see also Shero, "The *Cena* in Roman Satire," *CP* 18 (1923): 134–39; Martin, *Symposion,* 216–19; Edwin S. Ramage, David L. Sigsbee, and Sigmund C. Fredericks, *Roman Satirists and Their Satire* (Park Ridge, N.J.: Noyes, 1974), 99–106.

122. The phrase "eat, drink, be merry" is a commonplace in Greek tradition and Jewish wisdom literature. See, e.g., the references collected in I. Howard Marshall, *The Gospel of Luke: A Commentary on the Greek Text* (NIGTC 3; Grand Rapids: Eerdmans, 1978), 524: Eccl 8:15; Tob 7:10; Sir 11:19; Euripides *Alcestis* 788f.; Lucian *Nav.* 25.

123. Notice how Luke correlates the rich man with the Pharisees by the addition of 16:14 as an introductory text to the parable and by the description of the rich man as one who reveres Moses and the prophets and believes in resurrection (16:29-31; see also Acts 23:6-9). Thus two literary stereotypes that normally function independently in the Gospel are connected here.

124. So also Marshall, *The Gospel of Luke,* 636; Jeremias, *The Parables of Jesus,* 184.

125. See the detailed discussion of this theme in chapter 6, pp. 166–71.

126. My translation; the NRSV translation reads: "will eat in the kingdom of God."

127. As noted earlier in this discussion, the identification of 22:14-38 as a farewell discourse, as in Kurz, "Luke 22:14-28 and Greco-Roman and Biblical Farewell Addresses," is not one I disagree with, but I think the table fellowship themes function here as well and explain many of the emphases much better.

128. With Arthur Vööbus, "A New Approach to the Problem of the Shorter and Longer Text in Luke," *NTS* 15 (1968–69): 457–63; Eric Franklin, *Christ the Lord: A Study in the Purpose and Theology of Luke–Acts* (Philadelphia: Westminster, 1975), 65; and B. P. Robinson, "The Place of the Emmaus Story in Luke–Acts," *NTS* 30

(1984): 488–89. These scholars have gone against the trend in recent scholarship in which the longer text is preferred, because, as Franklin notes, "the shorter text rather than the longer text is the true vehicle of Luke's theology" (199 n. 32). Note that recent commentators who have accepted the long text have nevertheless been forced to separate vv. 19-20 from vv. 15-18 because it clearly has a different emphasis (so Charles H. Talbert, *Reading Luke: A Literary and Theological Commentary on the Third Gospel* [New York: Crossroad, 1982], 207–8; Joseph A. Fitzmyer, *The Gospel according to Luke* [AB 28A; Garden City, N.Y.: Doubleday, 1985], 2.1389), one that does not tend to correlate with the predominant theological emphases in Luke (so Eduard Schweizer, *Luke: A Challenge to Present Theology* [Atlanta: John Knox, 1982], 45: Luke wrote vv. 19b-20 as a "mechanical repetition of a liturgy"). For detailed discussions of the basic text-critical data (with an emphasis, however, on arguments supporting the long text), see Jeremias, *The Eucharistic Words of Jesus,* 139–59; Bruce M. Metzger, *A Textual Commentary on the Greek New Testament* (London: United Bible Societies, 1971), 173–77, 191–93; Fitzmyer, *The Gospel according to Luke,* 1.130–32, 2.1386–89.

129. See especially Robinson, "The Place of the Emmaus Story in Luke–Acts." Note that Acts 1:4, where Jesus' last instructions are given "at table," correlates with this theme. On the table fellowship interpretation of Acts 1:4, see Ernst Haenchen, *The Acts of the Apostles: A Commentary* (Philadelphia: Westminster, 1971), 141 n. 3.

130. So Franklin, *Christ the Lord,* 65–66.

131. My translation; the NRSV translation reads: "the one who is at the table."

132. This is the sense of John 13:6-11 according to Raymond E. Brown, *The Gospel according to John* (AB 29A; Garden City, N.Y.: Doubleday, 1970), 2.558–68.

133. So John 13:12-20; see ibid., 2.569–72.

134. John's version is usually taken to be a development from Luke or the tradition utilized by Luke if, indeed, any relationship between the two is at all assumed; see, e.g., M. Sabbe, "The Footwashing in Jn 13 and Its Relation to the Synoptic Gospels," *ETL* 58 (1982): 279–308.

135. Note that the omission of Mark 10:45b correlates with the omission of Mark 14:24 in that both texts contain specific soteriological interpretations of the death of Jesus; without them Luke lacks such an interpretation in his Gospel. The issue of Luke's problematic soteriology that results from these omissions has been the subject of much discussion in scholarship on Luke. Most studies tend to find the explanation for these tendencies in Luke's theology. My study suggests that these omissions correlate with Luke's literary themes as well.

136. My translation; the NRSV translation reads: "have them sit down to eat."

137. See Corley, *Private Women, Public Meals,* for an extensive analysis of this text. She argues that Luke places Mary in a demeaning role, sitting at the feet of Jesus rather than reclining as a full participant in the banquet. I acknowledge the point, but would argue that, given the extensive literary tradition that women who reclined at a banquet were "loose" women, for which Corley has extensive documentation, Luke was

here not so much demeaning Mary as he was picturing her as a "respectable" woman according to the conventions of the literary tradition of the banquet.

138. At 4:38-39, the term for "serve" is *diakoneō;* at 10:38-42, the noun form, *diakonia,* is used. This term typically refers to service at table and derivatively to other types of service (see, e.g., Luke 12:37; 17:8; 22:26-27; Acts 1:17; 1:25; 6:1-4; 19:22; 10:24; 21:19; John 12:2). Beyer notes that the term retains the association with service at table throughout all periods and levels of Greek usage (*"Diakoneō,"* 81–93). In these contexts in Luke, when the term is used without further delineation of the type of service intended, and when the setting is the home, table service must be considered the primary meaning.

139. My translation; the NRSV translation reads: "take your place at the table."

140. See chapter 5.

141. See chapter 6.

142. Plato *Leg.* 2.671C–72A.

143. Plut. *Quaest. conv.* 612D.

144. Ibid., 660B.

145. Ibid., 1.1.

146. Ibid., 1.2

147. Ibid., 612D, 614E–15A, 616C, 616E.

148. Ibid., 616E–F.

149. This point is discussed by Gerd Theissen in his study of the Christian meal in 1 Corinthians ("Social Integration and Sacramental Activity: An Analysis of 1 Cor. 11:17-34," in *The Social Setting of Pauline Christianity: Essays on Corinth,* ed. and trans. John H. Schütz [Philadelphia: Fortress Press, 1982]). See further chapter 7.

150. See, e.g., Pliny the Younger (*Ep.* 2.6) and Martial (*Epig.* 3.60), who both describe situations in which those of lower status at the table are treated to a lesser quality food and wine than those of a higher status at the same table. Both of these moralists are highly critical of this custom.

151. On the "poor" as a literary motif in Luke, see esp. Luke Timothy Johnson, *The Literary Function of Possessions in Luke–Acts* (SBLDS 39; Missoula, Mont.: Scholars, 1977), 132–44; Fitzmyer, *The Gospel according to Luke,* 1.250–51.

152. See also David Tiede, *Prophecy and History in Luke–Acts* (Philadelphia: Fortress Press, 1980), chap. 2, esp. 52–53.

153. In this interpretation of Luke 14:12-14 and in the following interpretation of Luke 15:25-32, I am suggesting that the "Pharisees," who are clearly the referents in both texts, have become a literary stereotype to such an extent that these texts can be seen to function in more than one way. This interpretation is especially suggested by the hortatory nature of these passages. Here the "reader" is sometimes to see himself or herself as the "poor" or "prodigal" and sometimes as the "Pharisee/host" or "elder brother."

154. See especially Corley, *Private Women, Public Meals,* 147–86, for a detailed analysis of the literary motif of the meal in Matthew in relation to the portrayal of

women. Corley concludes that Matthew exhibits a more favorable view of women in these stories than either Mark or Luke.

155. Jack Dean Kingsbury, *Matthew as Story* (2nd ed.; Philadelphia: Fortress Press, 1988), 3.

156. Notice also the extended table talk during the meal (13:12—14:31; or possibly as far as 17:26).

157. The relation of John to Mark and Luke is still an unresolved issue, especially in the context of this story; see, e.g., Sabbe, "The Footwashing in Jn 13."

158. This dual interpretation of the scene is especially developed by Brown, *The Gospel according to John*, 2.558–62.

159. This story, with the walking on the water scene directly after, is one of the few stories in John, outside of the passion narrative, in which he parallels the synoptic tradition.

160. The classic study is by Peder Borgen, *Bread from Heaven: An Exegetical Study of the Concept of Manna in the Gospel of John* (Leiden: Brill, 1965).

161. The classic presentation of this position is by Rudolf Bultmann, *The Gospel of John: A Commentary* (Philadelphia: Westminster, 1971), 234–37.

162. The classic presentation of the context of John in which the Johannine community has experienced expulsion from the synagogue is found in J. Louis Martyn, *History and Theology in the Fourth Gospel* (Nashville: Abingdon, 1979).

9. THE BANQUET AND CHRISTIAN THEOLOGY

1. L. Michael White, "Regulating Fellowship in the Communal Meal: Early Jewish and Christian Evidence," in *Meals in a Social Context: Aspects of the Communal Meal in the Hellenistic and Roman World,* ed. Inge Nielsen and Hanna Sigismund Nielsen (Aarhus Studies in Mediterranean Antiquity I; Aarhus: Aarhus University Press, 1998), 180–81. See also idem, *The Social Origins of Christian Architecture,* vol. 1: *Building God's House in the Roman World* and vol. 2: *Texts and Monuments for the Christian Domus Ecclesiae in its Environment* (Harvard Theological Studies 42; Valley Forge, Pa.: Trinity Press International, 1997), 1.118–26, 2.16–18.

2. Clem. Al. *Paed.* 2.1.

3. See White, "Regulating Fellowship," 192–93, and idem, *The Social Origins of Christian Architecture*, esp. 1.102–23.

4. White, "Regulating Fellowship," 180.

5. Ibid.

6. As acknowledged also by Paul F. Bradshaw, *The Search for the Origins of Christian Worship: Sources and Methods for the Study of Early Liturgy* (New York: Oxford University Press, 1992).

BIBLIOGRAPHY

Alon, G. "The Levitical Uncleanness of Gentiles." In *Jews, Judaism and the Classical World,* 146–89. Jerusalem: Magnes, 1977.

Argetsinger, Kathryn. "Birthday Rituals: Friends and Patrons in Roman Poetry and Cult." *Classical Antiquity* 11 (1992): 175–93.

Armstrong, A. H., ed. *Cambridge History of Later Greek and Early Medieval Philosophy.* Cambridge: Cambridge University Press, 1970.

Aune, David E. "Septem sapientium convivium." In *Plutarch's Ethical Writings and Early Christian Literature,* ed. Hans Dieter Betz, 51–105.

Bahr, Gordon J. "The Seder of Passover and the Eucharistic Words." *NovT* 12 (1970): 181–202. Reprinted in *Essays in Greco-Roman and Related Talmudic Literature,* ed. Henry A. Fischel, 473–94.

Bailey, Cyril. *Epicurus: The Extant Remains.* Oxford: Clarendon, 1926.

Baldwin, Barry. "Lucian as Social Satirist." *CQ* 11 (1961): 199–208.

Balsdon, J. P. V. D. *Life and Leisure in Ancient Rome.* New York: McGraw-Hill, 1969.

Banks, Robert. *Paul's Idea of Community.* Rev. ed. Peabody, Mass.: Hendrickson, 1994.

Barclay, John M. G. *Jews in the Mediterranean Diaspora: From Alexander to Trajan (323 BCE–117 CE).* Berkeley: University of California Press, 1996.

Barrett, C. K. *A Commentary on the First Epistle to the Corinthians.* 2nd ed. London: Black, 1971.

Bauer, Walter. *Orthodoxy and Heresy in Earliest Christianity.* Philadelphia: Fortress Press, 1971.

Beall, Todd S. *Josephus' Description of the Essenes Illustrated by the Dead Sea Scrolls.* Cambridge: Cambridge University Press, 1988.

Becker, W. A. *Gallus.* Reprint of 1849 ed. 2nd ed. London: Longmans, Green, 1915.

Becker, W. A., and Hermann Göll. *Charikles.* 8th ed. London: Longmans, Green, 1889.

Bek, Lise. "*Questiones Convivales*: The Idea of the Triclinium and the Staging of Convivial Ceremony from Rome to Byzantium." *Analecta Romana Instituti Danici* 12 (1983): 81–107.

Berger, Klaus. "Hellenistische Gattungen im NT." *ANRW* 2.25.2 (1984): 1031–1432, 1831–1885.

Bergquist, Birgitta. *The Archaic Greek Temenos*. Acta Instituti Atheniensis Regni Sueciae 4.13. Lund: Gleerup, 1967.

———. "Sympotic Space: A Functional Aspect of Greek Dining-Rooms." In *Sympotica: A Symposium on the Symposium*, ed. Oswyn Murray, 37–65.

Bertram, Georg. "*Paideuō*." *TDNT* 5 (1968): 596–625.

Betz, Hans Dieter. "Introduction." In *Plutarch's Ethical Writings and Early Christian Literature*, ed. Hans Dieter Betz, 1–10.

———. *Galatians*. Hermeneia. Philadelphia: Fortress Press, 1979.

———, ed. *Plutarch's Ethical Writings and Early Christian Literature*. Leiden: Brill, 1978.

Beyer, H. W. "*Diakoneō*." *TDNT* 2 (1964): 81–93.

Bielohlawek, Karl. "Gastmahls- und Symposionslehren bei griechischen Dichtern. (Von Homer bis zur Theognissammlung und Kritias)." *Wiener Studien* 58 (1940): 11–30.

Blümner, Hugo. *The Home Life of the Ancient Greeks*. London: Cassell, 1893.

———. *Die römische Privataltertümer*. Handbuch der Klassischen Altertumswissenschaft 4.2.2. Munich: Beck, 1911.

Boak, A. E. R. "The Organization of Gilds in Greco-Roman Egypt." *TAPA* 68 (1937): 212–20.

Boardman, John. "*Symposion* Furniture." In *Sympotica: A Symposium on the Symposium*, ed. Oswyn Murray, 122–31.

Boèthius, Axel, and J. B. Ward-Perkins. *Etruscan and Roman Architecture*. Harmondsworth, Eng.: Penguin, 1970.

Bokser, Baruch. *The Origins of the Seder: The Passover Rite and Early Rabbinic Judaism*. Berkeley: University of California Press, 1984.

Bookidis, Nancy, and Ronald S. Stroud. *Corinth XVII, Part III: The Sanctuary of Demeter and Kore, Topography and Architecture*. Princeton, N.J.: The American School of Classical Studies at Athens, 1997.

Booth, Alan. "The Age for Reclining and Its Attendant Perils." In *Dining in a Classical Context*, ed. W. J. Slater, 105–20.

Borg, Marcus J. *Conflict, Holiness and Politics in the Teachings of Jesus*. Studies in the Bible and Early Christianity 5. Toronto: Edwin Mellen, 1984.

———. *Jesus: A New Vision*. New York: Harper & Row, 1987.

Borgen, Peder. *Bread from Heaven: An Exegetical Study of the Concept of Manna in the Gospel of John*. Leiden: Brill, 1965.

Borker, Christopher. *Festbankett und griechische Architektur*. Xenia 4. Konstanz: Universitätsverlag Konstanz GmbH, 1983.

Bornkamm, Günther. *Early Christian Experience*. New York: Harper & Row, 1969.

———. *Jesus of Nazareth*. New York: Harper & Row, 1960.

———. "Lord's Supper and Church in Paul." In *Early Christian Experience*, 123–60.

———. "The More Excellent Way." In *Early Christian Experience*, 180–93.

————. "On the Understanding of Worship." In *Early Christian Experience*, 161–79.

Boswell, John. *The Kindness of Strangers: The Abandonment of Children in Western Europe from Late Antiquity to the Renaissance*. New York: Pantheon, 1988.

Bradshaw, Paul F. *The Search for the Origins of Christian Worship: Sources and Methods for the Study of Early Liturgy*. New York: Oxford University Press, 1992.

Bradshaw, Paul F., and Lawrence A. Hoffman, eds. *The Making of Jewish and Christian Worship*. Notre Dame, Ind.: University of Notre Dame Press, 1991.

Branham, R. Bracht. *Unruly Eloquence: Lucian and the Comedy of Traditions*. Cambridge, Mass.: Harvard University Press, 1989.

Braun, Willi. *Feasting and Social Rhetoric in Luke 14*. Cambridge: Cambridge University Press, 1995.

Breech, James. *The Silence of Jesus: The Authentic Voice of the Historical Man*. Philadelphia: Fortress Press, 1983.

Bremmer, Jan N. "Adolescents, *Symposion,* and Pederasty." In *Sympotica: A Symposium on the Symposium*, ed. Oswyn Murray, 135–48.

Brothwell, Don R. "Foodstuffs, Cooking, and Drugs." In *Civilization of the Ancient Mediterranean: Greece and Rome,* ed. M. Grant and R. Kitzinger, 1.247–61.

Brothwell, Don R., and Patricia Brothwell. *Food in Antiquity: A Survey of the Diet of Early Peoples*. New York: Praeger, 1969.

Brown, Raymond E. *The Gospel according to John*. AB 29–29A. 2 vols. Garden City, N.Y.: Doubleday, 1966–70.

Bruit, Louise. "The Meal at the Hyakinthia: Ritual Consumption and Offering." In *Sympotica: A Symposium on the Symposium*, ed. Oswyn Murray, 162–74.

Brumberg-Kraus, Jonathan. "Symposium Scenes in Luke's Gospel with Special Attention to the Last Supper." Ph.D. diss., Vanderbilt University, 1991.

Bruneau, Phillippe. "Les cultes de l'établissement des Poseidoniastes de Bérytos à Délos." In *Hommages à Maarten J. Vermaseren,* ed. Margreet B. De Boer and T. A. Edridge, 1:160–90. EPRO 68. 3 vols. Leiden: Brill, 1978.

————. *Recherches sur les cultes de Délos à l'époque hellénistique et à l'époque impériale*. Bibliothèque des écoles françaises d'Athènes et de Rome, fasc. 217. Paris: De Boccard, 1970.

Bruns, Gerda. "Küchenwesen und Mahlzeiten." In *Archaeologia Homerica II,* ed. F. Matz and H. G. Buchholz, chapter Q. Göttingen: Vandenhoeck and Ruprecht, 1970.

Bultmann, Rudolf. "*Euphrainō.*" *TDNT* 2 (1964): 772–75.

————. *The Gospel of John: A Commentary*. Philadelphia: Westminster, 1971.

————. *The History of the Synoptic Tradition*. 2nd ed. New York: Harper & Row, 1968.

————. *Der Stil der paulinischen Predigt und die kynisch-stoische Diatribe*. FRLANT 13. Göttingen: Vandenhoeck and Ruprecht, 1910.

———. *Theology of the New Testament.* 2 vols. New York: Scribner's, 1970.

Burchard, C. "The Importance of Joseph and Aseneth for the Study of the New Testament: A General Survey and a Fresh Look at the Lord's Supper." *NTS* 33 (1987): 102–34.

———. "Joseph and Aseneth." *OTP* 2:177–247.

Burkert, Walter. *Greek Religion.* Cambridge, Mass.: Harvard University Press, 1985.

———. "Greek Tragedy and Sacrificial Ritual." *GRBS* 7 (1966): 87–121.

———. "Oriental Symposia: Contrasts and Parallels." In *Dining in a Classical Context,* ed. W. J. Slater, 7–24.

Burton, Joan B. "The Function of the Symposium Theme in Theocritus' *Idyll* 14." *GRBS* 33 (1992): 227–45.

———. "Women's Commensality in the Ancient Greek World." *Greece and Rome* 45:2 (October 1998): 143–65.

Cadbury, Henry J. *The Making of Luke–Acts.* New York: Macmillan, 1927.

Calza, G., G. Becatti, et al. *Scavi di Ostia, I: Topografia Generale.* Rome: La Libreria dello Stato, 1953.

Cameron, Ron. "'What Have You Come Out To See?' Characterizations of John and Jesus in the Gospels." *Semeia* 49 (1990): 35–69.

Carcopino, Jérôme. *Daily Life in Ancient Rome.* New Haven, Conn.: Yale University Press, 1940.

Casabona, Jean. *Recherches sur le vocabulaire des sacrifices en Grec, des origines à la fin de l'époque classique.* Paris: Ophrys, 1966.

Chilton, Bruce. *A Feast of Meanings: Eucharistic Theologies from Jesus through Johannine Circles.* NovTSup 72. Leiden: Brill, 1994.

———. *The Temple of Jesus: His Sacrificial Program within a Cultural History of Sacrifice.* University Park: Pennsylvania State University Press, 1992.

Chilton, C. W. *Diogenes of Oenoanda: The Fragments.* London: Oxford University Press, 1971.

———. *Diogenis Oenoandensis fragmenta.* Leipzig: Teubner, 1967.

Coffey, Michael. *Roman Satire.* New York: Barnes & Noble, 1976.

Cohen, Shaye J. D. *The Beginnings of Jewishness: Boundaries, Varieties, Uncertainties.* Berkeley: University of California Press, 1999.

———. *From the Maccabees to the Mishnah.* Library of Early Christianity. Philadelphia: Westminster, 1987.

———. "Patriarchs and Scholarchs." *Proceedings of the American Academy for Jewish Research* 48 (1981): 57–85.

Collins, Adela Yarbro. *The Combat Myth in the Book of Revelation.* HDR 9. Missoula, Mont.: Scholars, 1976.

Collins, John J. *Between Athens and Jerusalem: Jewish Identity in the Hellenistic Diaspora.* New York: Crossroad, 1983.

Conzelmann, Hans. *1 Corinthians*. Hermeneia. Philadelphia: Fortress Press, 1975.

Conzelmann, Hans, and Walther Zimmerli. "*Chairō*." *TDNT* 9 (1974): 359–415.

Cooper, Frederick, and Sarah Morris. "Dining in Round Buildings." In *Sympotica: A Symposium on the Symposium,* ed. Oswyn Murray, 66–85.

Corley, Kathleen E. *Private Women, Public Meals: Social Conflict in the Synoptic Tradition*. Peabody, Mass.: Hendrickson, 1993.

Cotter, Wendy J., C.S.J. "The Parable of the Children in the Market-Place, Q (Lk) 7:31-35: An Examination of the Parable's Image and Significance." *NovT* 29 (1987): 289–304.

Cousar, Charles B. *A Theology of the Cross: The Death of Jesus in the Pauline Letters*. Minneapolis: Fortress Press, 1990.

Cousin, G., and G. Deschamps. "Inscriptions du temple du Zeus Panamaros." *BCH* 15 (1891): 169–209.

Cross, Frank Moore, Jr. *The Ancient Library of Qumran and Modern Biblical Studies*. Garden City, N.Y.: Doubleday, 1961.

Crossan, John Dominic. *The Historical Jesus: The Life of a Mediterranean Jewish Peasant*. San Francisco: HarperCollins, 1991.

———, ed. *Sayings Parallels: A Workbook for the Jesus Tradition*. Philadelphia: Fortress Press, 1986.

Cumont, Franz. *After Life in Roman Paganism*. New Haven, Conn.: Yale University Press, 1922.

———. "La grande inscription bachique du Metropolitan Museum, II. Commentaire religieux de l'inscription." *AJA* 37 (1933): 232–63.

———. *Recherches sur le symbolisme funéraire des Romains*. Haut-Commissariat de l'État français en Syrie et au Liban, service des antiquités, bibliothèque archéologique et historique 35. Paris: Geuthner, 1942.

Danker, Frederick W. *Benefactor: Epigraphic Study of a Graeco-Roman and New Testament Semantic Field*. St. Louis: Clayton, 1982.

D'Arms, John H. "Control, Companionship, and *Clientela*: Some Social Functions of the Roman Communal Meal." *Classical Views* 28:3 (1984): 327–48.

———. "The Roman *Convivium* and the Idea of Equality." In *Sympotica: A Symposium on the Symposium,* ed. Oswyn Murray, 308–20.

———. "Slaves at Roman Convivia." In *Dining in a Classical Context,* ed. W. J. Slater, 171–83.

Daux, Georges. "La Grande Démarchie: Un nouveau calendrier sacrificiel d'Attique (Erchia)." *BCH* 87 (1963): 603–34.

Dayagi-Mendels, Michal. *Drink and Be Merry: Wine and Beer in Ancient Times*. Jerusalem: The Israel Museum, 1999.

Deissmann, Adolf. *Bible Studies*. Edinburgh: T. & T. Clark, 1901.

———. *Light from the Ancient East*. Reprint ed. Grand Rapids: Baker, 1965.

Delcor, M. "Repas cultuels esséniens et thérapeutes." *RevQ* 6 (1969): 401–25.

Delobel, J. "L'onction par la pécheresse: La composition littéraire de *Lc.*, VII, 36-50." *ETL* 42 (1966): 415–75.

de Meeûs, X. "Composition de *Lc.*, XIV et genre symposiaque." *ETL* 37 (1961): 847–70.

Dentzer, Jean-Marie. "Aux origines de l'iconographie du banquet couché." *Revue Archéologique* (1971): 215–58.

———. *Le motif du banquet couché dans le proche-orient et le monde grec du VIIe au IVe siècle avant J.-C.* Bibliothèque des écoles françaises d'Athènes et de Rome 246. Rome: École française de Rome, 1982.

Detienne, Marcel, and Jean-Pierre Vernant. *The Cuisine of Sacrifice among the Greeks.* Chicago: University of Chicago Press, 1989.

Deubner, Ludwig. *Attische Feste.* 2nd ed. Hildesheim: Georg Olms, 1969.

Dewey, Joanna. *Markan Public Debate: Literary Technique, Concentric Structure, and Theology in Mark 2:1—3:6.* SBLDS 48. Chico, Calif.: Scholars, 1980.

DeWitt, Norman W. *Epicurus and His Philosophy.* Minneapolis: University of Minnesota Press, 1954.

———. *St. Paul and Epicurus.* Minneapolis: University of Minnesota Press, 1954.

Diano, Carlo. "Epicure: La philosophie du plaisir et la société des amis." *Les études philosophiques* 22 (1967): 173–84.

Dihle, Albrecht. "Ethik." *RAC* 6 (1966): 646–796.

Di Lella, Alexander A. *The Wisdom of Ben Sira.* AB 39. New York: Doubleday, 1987.

Dill, Samuel. *Roman Society from Nero to Marcus Aurelius.* Reprint of 1904 ed. New York: World, 1956.

Disch, Robert, ed. *The Ecological Conscience.* Englewood Cliffs, N.J.: Prentice-Hall, 1970.

Dodds, E. R. *The Greeks and the Irrational.* Berkeley: University of California Press, 1951.

———, ed. *The Plays of Euripides: Bacchae.* 2nd ed. Oxford: Clarendon, 1960.

Dombrowski, B. W. "*Hyhd* in I QS and *to koinon*: An Instance of Early Greek and Jewish Synthesis." *HTR* 59 (1966): 293–307.

Donahue, John R. "Tax Collectors and Sinners: An Attempt at Identification." *CBQ* 33 (1971): 39–61.

Donceel, Robert, and Pauline Donceel-Voûte. "The Archaeology of Khirbet Qumran." In *Methods of Investigation of the Dead Sea Scrolls and the Khirbet Qumran Site: Present Realities and Future Prospects*, ed. Michael O. Wise et al., 1–31. Annals of the New York Academy of Sciences, vol. 722. New York: New York Academy of Sciences, 1994.

Donceel-Voûte, Pauline H. E. "'Coenaculum': La salle à l'étage du *locus* 30 à Khirbet Qumrân sur la mer morte." *Banquets d'Orient* (*Res Orientales* 4 [1992]): 61–84.

Dörpfeld, W. "Die Ausgrabungen am Westabhange der Akropolis." *AthMitt* 20 (1895): 161–206.

Douglas, Mary. "Critique and Commentary." Foreword to *The Idea of Purity* by Jacob Neusner, 137–42.

———. "Deciphering a Meal." *Daedalus* 101 (1972): 61–81.

———. *Food in the Social Order: Studies of Food and Festivities in Three American Communities.* New York: Russell Sage Foundation, 1984.

———. *In the Active Voice.* London: Routledge & Kegan Paul, 1982.

———. *Natural Symbols: Explorations in Cosmology.* 2nd ed. London: Barrie & Jenkins, 1973.

———. *Purity and Danger: An Analysis of Pollution and Taboo.* New York: Praeger, 1966.

Dover, K. J. *Greek Popular Morality in the Time of Plato and Aristotle.* Berkeley: University of California Press, 1974.

Dow, Sterling. "The Greater Demarkhia of Erkhia." *BCH* 89 (1965): 180–213.

Dow, Sterling, and David H. Gill. "The Greek Cult Table." *AJA* 69 (1965): 103–14.

Duff, J. Wight. *Roman Satire: Its Outlook on Social Life.* Berkeley: University of California Press, 1936.

Dugas, Laurent. *L'amitié antique d'après les moeurs populaires et les théories des philosophes.* Paris: F. Alcan, 1894.

Dunbabin, Katherine M. D. "Convivial Spaces: Dining and Entertainment in the Roman Villa." *Journal of Roman Archaeology* 9 (1996): 66–80.

———. "Triclinium and Stibadium." In *Dining in a Classical Context,* ed. W. J. Slater, 121–48.

———. "*Ut Graeco More Biberetur:* Greeks and Romans on the Dining Couch." In *Meals in a Social Context,* ed. I. Nielsen and H. S. Nielsen, 81–101.

Dunn, J. D. G. *Jesus, Paul and the Law: Studies in Mark and Galatians.* Louisville, Ky.: Westminster John Knox, 1990.

———. "Pharisees, Sinners, and Jesus." In *The Social World of Formative Christianity and Judaism: Essays in Tribute to Howard Clark Kee,* Jacob Neusner et al., eds., 276–80. Philadelphia: Fortress Press, 1988.

———. *Romans.* 2 vols. WBC 38A&B. Dallas: Word, 1988.

Durkheim, Émile. *The Elementary Forms of the Religious Life.* London: Allen and Unwin, 1976.

Easterling, P. E., and J. V. Muir, eds. *Greek Religion and Society.* Cambridge: Cambridge University Press, 1985.

Ehrenberg, Victor. *The People of Aristophanes.* 3rd ed. New York: Schocken, 1962.

Eliade, Mircea. *The Sacred and the Profane.* New York: Harcourt, 1959.

Elliott, John H. *A Home for the Homeless: A Sociological Exegesis of 1 Peter, Its Situation and Strategy.* Philadelphia: Fortress Press, 1981.

————. "Patronage and Clientism in Early Christian Society: A Short Reading Guide." *Forum* 3:4 (December 1987): 39–48.

————, ed. "Social Scientific Criticism of the New Testament and Its Social World." *Semeia* 35 (1986).

Engelmann, Helmut. *The Delian Aretalogy of Sarapis.* EPRO 44. Leiden: Brill, 1975.

Fee, Gordon D. *The First Epistle to the Corinthians.* NICNT. Grand Rapids: Eerdmans, 1987.

Feeley-Harnick, Gillian. *The Lord's Table: Eucharist and Passover in Early Christianity.* Philadelphia: University of Pennsylvania Press, 1981.

Fehr, Burkhard. "Entertainers at the *Symposion*: The *Akletoi* in the Archaic Period." In *Sympotica: A Symposium on the Symposium,* ed. Oswyn Murray, 185–95.

————. *Orientalische und griechische Gelage.* Bonn, 1971.

Feldman, Louis H. *Jew and Gentile in the Ancient World.* Princeton, N.J.: Princeton University Press, 1993.

Ferguson, W. S. "The Attic Orgeones." *HTR* 37 (1944): 61–140.

Festugière, A.-J. *Epicurus and His Gods.* Cambridge, Mass.: Harvard University Press, 1956.

————. "Les Mystères de Dionysos." *RB* 44 (1935): 192–211, 366–96.

Figueira, Thomas J., and Gregory Nagy, eds. *Theognis of Megara: Poetry and the Polis.* Baltimore: Johns Hopkins University Press, 1985.

Finley, Moses. "Foreword." In *Greek Religion and Society,* ed. P. E. Easterling and J. V. Muir, xiii–xx.

Fischel, Henry A. "Studies in Cynicism and the Ancient Near East." In *Religions in Antiquity,* ed. Jacob Neusner, 372–411.

————, ed. *Essays in Greco-Roman and Related Talmudic Literature.* New York: KTAV, 1977.

Fisher, N. R. E. "Drink, *Hybris,* and the Promotion of Harmony in Sparta." In *Classical Sparta: Techniques Behind Her Success,* ed. A. Powell, 26–50. Norman: University of Oklahoma Press, 1988.

Fitzgerald, John T., ed. *Greco-Roman Perspectives on Friendship.* SBLSBS 34. Atlanta: Scholars, 1997.

Fitzmyer, Joseph A. *The Gospel according to Luke.* 2 vols. AB 28 & 28A. Garden City, N.Y.: Doubleday, 1981, 1985.

Flacelière, Robert. *Daily Life in Greece at the Time of Pericles.* New York: Macmillan, 1966.

Flender, Helmut. *St. Luke: Theologian of Redemptive History.* London: SPCK, 1967.

Foerster, Werner. "*Eirēnē.*" *TDNT* 2 (1964): 400–20.

Foley, Helene P. *Ritual Irony: Poetry and Sacrifice in Euripides.* Ithaca, N.Y.: Cornell University Press, 1985.

Forbes, R. J. "Fermented Beverages 500 B.C.–1500 A.D." In *Studies in Ancient Technology,* 3.111–37. Leiden: Brill, 1965.

———. "Food in Classical Antiquity." In *Studies in Ancient Technology*, 3.86–110. Leiden: Brill, 1965.

Foucart, Paul. *Des associations religieuses chez les Grecs.* Paris: Klincksieck, 1873.

Fowler, Robert M. *Loaves and Fishes: The Function of the Feeding Stories in the Gospel of Mark.* SBLDS 54. Chico, Calif.: Scholars, 1981.

Fraisse, Jean-Claude. *Philia: La notion d'amitié dans la philosophie antique.* Paris: Vrin, 1974.

Frank, Tenney. *Aspects of Social Behavior in Ancient Rome.* Cambridge, Mass.: Harvard University Press, 1932.

Franklin, Eric. *Christ the Lord: A Study in the Purpose and Theology of Luke–Acts.* Philadelphia: Westminster, 1975.

Frazer, James George. *The Golden Bough: A Study in Magic and Religion.* 12 vols. 3rd ed. New York: Macmillan, 1935.

Frickenhaus, August. "Griechische Banketthäuser." *Jahrbuch des deutschen archäologischen Instituts* 32 (1917): 114–33.

———. "Das Herakleion von Melite." *AthMitt* 36 (1911): 113–44.

Friedländer, Ludwig. *Roman Life and Manners under the Early Empire.* 4 vols. New York: Barnes & Noble, 1968.

Funk, Robert W. *The Acts of Jesus.* San Francisco: HarperCollins, 1998.

———. *Honest to Jesus: Jesus for a New Millennium.* San Francisco: HarperSanFrancisco, 1996.

Funk, Robert W., Roy W. Hoover, and the Jesus Seminar. *The Five Gospels: The Search for the Authentic Words of Jesus.* New York: Macmillan, 1993.

Gager, John G. *Kingdom and Community: The Social World of Early Christianity.* Englewood Cliffs, N.J.: Prentice-Hall, 1975.

———. *The Origins of Anti-Semitism: Attitudes toward Judaism in Pagan and Christian Antiquity.* New York: Oxford University Press, 1983.

———. Review of Robert M. Grant, *Early Christianity and Society: Seven Studies*; Abraham J. Malherbe, *Social Aspects of Early Christianity*; and Gerd Theissen, *Sociology of Early Palestinian Christianity. RelSRev* 5 (1979): 174–80.

Gammie, John G. *Holiness in Israel.* Overtures to Biblical Theology. Minneapolis: Fortress Press, 1989.

Gardner, E. A. "Food and Drink: Meals, Cooking, and Entertainments." In *A Companion to Greek Studies,* ed. Leonard Whibley, 639–43. 4th ed. Cambridge: Cambridge University Press, 1931.

Garland, Robert. *The Greek Way of Death.* Ithaca, N.Y.: Cornell University Press, 1985.

Garrett, Susan R. Review of *Christian Origins and Cultural Anthropology,* by Bruce J. Malina. *JBL* 107 (1988): 532–34.

———. "Sociology of Early Christianity." *ABD,* 6:89–99.

Gaster, T. H. *Myth, Legend, and Custom in the Old Testament.* New York: Harper, 1969.

———. *Thespis: Ritual, Myth, and Drama in the Ancient Near East.* Garden City, N.Y.: Doubleday, 1961.

Geertz, Clifford. *The Interpretation of Cultures.* New York: Basic, 1973.

———. "Religion as a Cultural System." In *The Interpretation of Cultures,* 87–125.

———. "Thick Description: Toward an Interpretive Theory of Culture." In *The Interpretation of Cultures,* 3–30.

Georgi, Dieter. "The Interest in Life of Jesus Theology as a Paradigm for the Social History of Biblical Criticism." *HTR* 85 (1992): 51–83.

———. *Remembering the Poor: The History of Paul's Collection for Jerusalem.* Nashville: Abingdon, 1991.

Giangrande, Giuseppe. "Sympotic Literature and Epigram." In *L'épigramme grecque,* 93–177. Fondation Hardt pour l'étude de l'antiquité classique, entretiens 14. Geneva: Fondation Hardt, 1967.

Giannini, Olga. "Nuovi papiri fiorentini, 7. Invito ad una festa." *Annali della scuola normale superiore di Pisa* 2.35 (1966): 18–19.

Gill, David. "*Trapezomata:* A Neglected Aspect of Greek Sacrifice." *HTR* 67 (1974): 117–37.

Gilliam, J. R. "Invitations to the *Kline* of Sarapis." In *Collectanea Papyrologica: Texts Published in Honor of H. C. Youtie,* ed. Ann Ellis Hanson, 1.315–24. Papyrologische Texte und Abhandlungen 19. 2 vols. Bonn: Rudolf Habelt, 1976.

Ginzburg, Louis. *The Legends of the Jews.* 7 vols. Philadelphia: Jewish Publication Society of America, 1909–38.

Goldstein, M. S. "The Setting of the Ritual Meal in Greek Sanctuaries: 600–300 B.C." Ph.D. diss., University of California, Berkeley, 1979.

Goodenough, E. R. *Jewish Symbols in the Greco-Roman Period.* 13 vols. New York: Pantheon, 1953–68.

Goody, Jack. *Cooking, Cuisine and Class: A Study in Comparative Sociology.* Cambridge: Cambridge University Press, 1982.

Gould, John. "On Making Sense of Greek Religion." In *Greek Religion and Society,* ed. P. E. Easterling and J. V. Muir, 1–33.

Gowers, Emily. *The Loaded Table: Representations of Food in Roman Literature.* Oxford: Clarendon, 1993.

Grant, Michael, and Rachel Kitzinger. *Civilization of the Ancient Mediterranean: Greece and Rome.* 3 vols. New York: Scribner's, 1988.

Griffin, Jasper. *Latin Poets and Roman Life.* Chapel Hill: University of North Carolina Press, 1986.

Grundmann, Walter. "*Dokimos.*" *TDNT* 2 (1964): 255–60.

———. "*Tapeinos.*" *TDNT* 8 (1972): 1–26.

Gulick, Charles Burton. *The Life of the Ancient Greeks.* New York: D. Appleton, 1902.

Hadas, Moses. *Aristeas to Philocrates.* Jewish Apocryphal Literature. New York: KTAV, 1973.

Haenchen, Ernst. *The Acts of the Apostles: A Commentary.* Philadelphia: Westminster, 1971.

Hands, A. R. *Charities and Social Aid in Greece and Rome.* Aspects of Greek and Roman Life. Ithaca, N.Y.: Cornell University Press, 1968.

Hanson, Paul D. *The Dawn of Apocalyptic.* Philadelphia: Fortress Press, 1975.

———. "Zechariah 9 and the Recapitulation of an Ancient Ritual Pattern." *JBL* 92 (1973): 37–59.

Harrington, Hannah K. *The Impurity Systems of Qumran and the Rabbis: Biblical Foundations.* SBLDS 143. Atlanta: Scholars, 1993.

Harrison, Jane E. *Prolegomena to the Study of Greek Religion.* 3rd ed. Cleveland: World, 1922.

———. *Themis: A Study of the Social Origins of Greek Religion.* 2nd ed. Reprint of 1927 ed. Cleveland: World, 1962.

Hatzfeld, J. "Inscriptions de Panamara." *BCH* 51 (1927): 57–122.

Hengel, Martin. *The Charismatic Leader and His Followers.* Philadelphia: Fortress Press, 1974.

———. *Judaism and Hellenism.* 2 vols. Philadelphia: Fortress Press, 1974.

Henrichs, Albert. "Changing Dionysiac Identities." In *Jewish and Christian Self-Definition,* vol. 3: *Self-Definition in the Greco-Roman World,* ed. B. F. Meyer and E. P. Sanders, 137–60.

———. "Human Sacrifice in Greek Religion: Three Case Studies." In *Le sacrifice dans l'antiquité,* 195–235. Fondation Hardt pour l'étude de l'antiquité classique, entretiens tome 27. Geneva: Fondation Hardt, 1980.

Henry, Alan S. "Entertainment in the Prytaneion." In idem, *Honours and Privileges in Athenian Decrees,* 262–90. Hildesheim: Georg Olms, 1983.

Hock, Ronald F., and Edward N. O'Neil. *The Chreia in Ancient Rhetoric,* vol. 1: *The Progymnasmata.* SBLTT 27. Atlanta: Scholars, 1986.

Höfler, Anton. *Der Sarapishymnus des Ailios Aristeides.* Tübingen Beiträge zur Altertumswissenschaft 27. Stuttgart–Berlin: W. Kohlhammer, 1935.

Horsley, G. H. R., ed. *New Documents Illustrating Early Christianity.* 2 vols. Sydney, Aus.: The Ancient History Documentary Research Centre, Macquarie University, 1981.

Horsley, Richard. *Jesus and the Spiral of Violence: Popular Jewish Resistance in Roman Palestine.* New York: Harper & Row, 1987.

Humphreys, S. C. *The Family, Women and Death: Comparative Studies.* 2nd ed. Ann Arbor: University of Michigan Press, 1993.

———. "*Oikos* and *Polis.*" In *The Family, Women and Death: Comparative Studies,* 1–21.

———. "Women in Antiquity." *The Family, Women and Death: Comparative Studies,* 33–57.

Hurd, John C. *The Origin of I Corinthians.* New York: Seabury, 1965.

Isenberg, M. "The Sale of Sacrificial Meat." *CP* 70 (1975): 271–73.

Jacobson, Arland. "Wisdom Christology in Q." Ph.D. diss., Claremont Graduate School, 1978.

Jaeger, Werner. *Paideia: The Ideals of Greek Culture.* 3 vols. New York: Oxford University Press, 1943.

Jameson, Michael. "Domestic Space in the Greek City-State." In *Domestic Architecture and the Use of Space,* ed. Susan Kent, 92–113. Cambridge: Cambridge University Press, 1990.

———. "Private Space and the Greek City." In *The Greek City from Homer to Alexander,* ed. Oswyn Murray and Simon Price, 171–95.

———. "Sacrifice and Ritual: Greece." In *Civilization of the Ancient Mediterranean,* ed. Michael Grant and Rachel Kitzinger, 2.959–79.

———. "Theoxenia." In *Ancient Greek Cult Practice from the Archaeological Evidence,* ed. Robin Hägg. Proceedings of the Fourth International Seminar on Ancient Greek Cult, organized by the Swedish Institute at Athens, October 22–24, 1993. Stockholm: Svenska Institutet i Athen; P. Åströms, 1998. 35–57.

Jeremias, Joachim. *The Eucharistic Words of Jesus.* Translated by Norman Perrin. 3rd ed. New York: Scribner's, 1966.

———. *Jerusalem in the Time of Jesus.* Translated by F. H. Cave and C. H. Cave. Rev. ed. Philadelphia: Fortress Press, 1969.

———. *New Testament Theology: The Proclamation of Jesus.* Translated by John Bowden. New York: Scribner's, 1971.

———. *The Parables of Jesus.* Translated by S. H. Hooke. Rev. ed. New York: Scribner's, 1963.

Johnson, Luke Timothy. *The Literary Function of Possessions in Luke–Acts.* SBLDS 39. Missoula, Mont.: Scholars, 1977.

Jones, Christopher P. "Dinner Theater." In *Dining in a Classical Context,* ed. W. J. Slater, 185–98.

———. *Plutarch and Rome.* Oxford: Clarendon, 1971.

Jones, Richard. "Burial Customs of Rome and the Provinces." In *The Roman World,* ed. John Wacher, vol. 2, 812ff. London: Routledge & Kegan Paul, 1987.

Judge, E. A. *The Social Pattern of Christian Groups in the First Century.* London: Tyndale, 1960.

Kane, J. P. "The Mithraic Cult Meal in Its Greek and Roman Environment." In *Mithraic Studies.* Proceedings of the First International Congress of Mithraic Studies, ed. John R. Hinnells, 2.313–51. 2 vols. Manchester: Manchester University, 1975.

Karris, Robert J. *Luke: Artist and Theologian. Luke's Passion Account as Literature.* New York: Paulist, 1985.

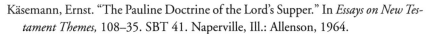

Käsemann, Ernst. "The Pauline Doctrine of the Lord's Supper." In *Essays on New Testament Themes,* 108–35. SBT 41. Naperville, Ill.: Allenson, 1964.

Keck, Leander E. *Paul and his Letters.* Philadelphia: Fortress Press, 1988.

Kee, Howard Clark. *Christian Origins in Sociological Perspective.* Philadelphia: Westminster, 1980.

———. *Knowing the Truth: A Sociological Approach to New Testament Interpretation.* Minneapolis: Fortress Press, 1989.

———. "Sociology of The New Testament." *HBD,* 961–68.

Kelber, Werner H., ed. "Conclusion: From Passion Narrative to Gospel." In *The Passion in Mark,* ed. Werner H. Kelber, 153–80.

———. *The Passion in Mark: Studies on Mark 14–16.* Philadelphia: Fortress Press, 1976.

Kerenyi, C. *Dionysus.* Princeton, N.J.: Princeton University Press, 1976.

Kern, O. "Mysterien." PW 16 (1935): 1293–97.

Kim, Chan-Hie. "The Papyrus Invitation." *JBL* 94 (1975): 391–402.

Kingsbury, Jack Dean. *Matthew as Story.* 2nd ed. Philadelphia: Fortress Press, 1988.

Kircher, Karl. *Die sacrale Bedeutung des Weines.* RVV 9.2. Giessen: A. Töpelmann, 1910.

Klauck, Hans-Josef. *Hausgemeinde und Hauskirche im frühen Christentum.* Stuttgarter Bibelstudien 103. Stuttgart: Katholisches Bibelwerk, 1981.

———. *Herrenmahl und hellenistischer Kult: Eine religionsgeschichtliche Untersuchung zum ersten Korintherbrief.* Neutestamentliche Abhandlungen, N. F., 15. Münster: Aschendorff, 1982.

Klawans, Jonathan. *Impurity and Sin in Ancient Judaism.* New York: Oxford University Press, 2000.

———. "Notions of Gentile Impurity in Ancient Judaism." *AJSR* 20:2 (1995): 285–312.

Kleberg, Tönnes. *Hôtels, restaurants et cabarets dans l'antiquité romaine.* Uppsala, Swe.: Almqvist and Wiksells, 1957.

Klinghardt, Matthias. *Gemeinschaftsmahl und Mahlgemeinschaft: Soziologie und Liturgie frühchristlicher Mahlfeiern.* Texte und Arbeiten zum neutestamentlichen Zeitalter 13. Tübingen: Francke Verlag, 1996.

Kloppenborg, John S. "Collegia and *Thiasoi*: Issues in Function, Taxonomy and Membership." In *Voluntary Associations in the Graeco-Roman World,* ed. John S. Kloppenborg and Stephen G. Wilson, 16–30.

———. *The Formation of Q: Trajectories in Ancient Wisdom Collections.* Studies in Antiquity and Christianity. Philadelphia: Fortress Press, 1987.

Kloppenborg, John S., and Stephen G. Wilson, eds. *Voluntary Associations in the Graeco-Roman World.* New York: Routledge, 1996.

Klosinski, Lee Edward. "The Meals in Mark." Ph.D. diss., Claremont Graduate School, 1988.

Knoche, Ulrich. *Roman Satire*. Bloomington: Indiana University Press, 1975.

Koenen, Ludwig. "Eine Einladung zur *Kline* des Sarapis." *ZPE* 1 (1967): 121–26.

Koenig, John. *New Testament Hospitality: Partnership with Strangers as Promise and Mission*. Overtures to Biblical Theology. Philadelphia: Fortress Press, 1985.

Kollmann, Bernd. *Ursprung und Gestalten der frühchristlichen Mahlfeier*. Göttinger Theologische Arbeiten 43. Göttingen: Vandenhoeck and Ruprecht, 1990.

Kornemann, E. "Collegium." PW 4.1 (1900): 380–480.

Kraemer, Ross S. *Her Share of the Blessings: Women's Religions Among Pagans, Jews, and Christians in the Greco-Roman World*. New York: Oxford University Press, 1992.

Krämer, Helmut, Rolf Rendtorff, Rudolf Meyer, and Gerhard Friedrich. "*Prophētēs*." *TDNT* 6 (1968): 781–861.

Krauss, Samuel. *Talmudische Archaeologie*. 3 vols. Leipzig: Gustav Fock, 1910–12.

Kroll, W. "Iobakchoi." PW 9 (1916): 1829–30.

Kuhn, K. G. "The Lord's Supper and the Communal Meal at Qumran." In *The Scrolls and the New Testament*, ed. Krister Stendahl, 63–93. London: SCM, 1958.

Kurtz, Donna C., and John Boardman. *Greek Burial Customs*. Aspects of Greek and Roman Life. London: Thames and Hudson, 1971.

Kurz, William S. "Luke 22:14-28 and Greco-Roman and Biblical Farewell Addresses." *JBL* 104 (1985): 251–68.

Lampe, Peter. "The Corinthian Eucharistic Dinner Party: Exegesis of a Cultural Context (1 Cor. 11:17-34)." *Affirmation* 4:2 (1991): 1–15.

———. "Das korinthische Herrenmahl im Schnittpunkt hellenistisch-römischer Mahlpraxis und paulinischer Theologia Crucis (1 Kor 11,17-34)." *ZNW* 82 (1991): 183–213.

———. "The Roman Christians of Romans 16." In *The Romans Debate*, ed. Karl P. Donfried, 216–30. Rev. and expanded ed. Peabody, Mass.: Hendrickson, 1991.

Lattimore, Richmond. *Themes in Greek and Latin Epitaphs*. Urbana: University of Illinois Press, 1962.

Laumonier, Alfred. *Les cultes indigènes en Carie*. Paris: De Boccard, 1958.

Levenson, Jon D. *Sinai and Zion: An Entry into the Jewish Bible*. New York: Harper & Row, 1987.

Lévi-Strauss, Claude. *The Raw and the Cooked*. New York: Harper & Row, 1969.

Levine, Daniel B. "Symposium and the Polis." In *Theognis of Megara*, ed. Thomas J. Figueira and Gregory Nagy, 176–96.

Lewis, Naphtali, and Meyer Reinhold. *Roman Civilization*. 2 vols. New York: Harper, 1966.

Liebenam, Wilhelm. *Zur Geschichte und Organisation des römischen Vereinswesens: Drei Untersuchungen*. Leipzig: Teubner, 1890.

Lietzmann, Hans. *Mass and Lord's Supper*. Leiden: Brill, 1953–55.

Lissarrague, François. "Around the *Krater:* An Aspect of Banquet Imagery." In *Sympotica: A Symposium on the Symposium,* ed. Oswyn Murray, 196–209.

Lohse, Ernst. "*Sabbaton.*" *TDNT* 7 (1971): 1–35.

Maass, Ernst. *Orpheus.* Munich: Beck, 1895.

MacDonald, Dennis R. *The Homeric Epics and the Gospel of Mark.* New Haven, Conn.: Yale University Press, 2000.

———. *There Is No Male and Female: The Fate of a Dominical Saying in Paul and Gnosticism.* HDR 20. Philadelphia: Fortress Press, 1987.

Mack, Burton L. *The Christian Myth: Origins, Logic, and Legacy.* New York: Continuum, 2001.

———. "The Kingdom That Didn't Come: A Social History of the Q Tradents." In *SBL 1988 Seminar Papers,* ed. David J. Lull, 608–35. Atlanta: Scholars, 1988.

———. *The Lost Gospel: The Book of Q and Christian Origins.* San Francisco: HarperCollins, 1993.

———. *A Myth of Innocence: Mark and Christian Origins.* Philadelphia: Fortress Press, 1988.

———. *Who Wrote the New Testament? The Making of the Christian Myth.* San Francisco: HarperSanFrancisco, 1995.

MacMullen, Ramsay. *Enemies of the Roman Order.* Cambridge, Mass.: Harvard University Press, 1966.

———. *Roman Social Relations 50 B.C. to A.D. 284.* New Haven, Conn.: Yale University Press, 1974.

Malherbe, Abraham J. "The Beasts of Ephesus." *JBL* 87 (1968): 71–80.

———. "Hellenistic Moralists and the New Testament." *ANRW* 2.26.1 (1992): 267–333.

———. "Self-Definition among Epicureans and Cynics." In *Jewish and Christian Self-Definition,* vol. 3: *Self-Definition in the Greco-Roman World,* ed. Ben F. Meyer and E. P. Sanders, 46–59, 192–97.

———. *Social Aspects of Early Christianity.* 2nd ed., enl. Philadelphia: Fortress Press, 1983.

———, ed. *The Cynic Epistles: A Study Edition.* SBLSBS 12. Missoula, Mont.: Scholars, 1977.

———. "The Inhospitality of Diotrephes." In *God's Christ and His People: Studies in Honour of Nils Alstrup Dahl,* ed. Jacob Jervell and Wayne A. Meeks, 222–32. Oslo: Universitetsforlaget, 1977; enlarged and reprinted in *Social Aspects of Early Christianity,* chap. 4, 92–112.

Malina, Bruce J. *Christian Origins and Cultural Anthropology: Practical Models for Biblical Interpretation.* Atlanta: John Knox, 1986.

———. *The New Testament World: Insights from Cultural Anthropology.* Atlanta: John Knox, 1981.

——. Review of *The First Urban Christians,* by Wayne A. Meeks. *JBL* 104 (1985): 346–49.

Marquardt, Joachim. *Das Privatleben der Römer.* 2 vols. Handbuch der römischen Alterthümer 7. 2nd ed. Leipzig: Hirzel, 1886.

Marshall, I. Howard. *The Gospel of Luke: A Commentary on the Greek Text.* NIGTC 3. Grand Rapids: Eerdmans, 1978.

——. *Last Supper and Lord's Supper.* Grand Rapids: Eerdmans, 1980.

——. *Luke: Historian and Theologian.* Exeter: Paternoster, 1970.

Marshall, Peter. *Enmity in Corinth: Social Conventions in Paul's Relations with the Corinthians.* Wissenschaftliche Untersuchungen zum Neuen Testament, 2. Reihe 23. Tübingen: Mohr (Siebeck), 1987.

Martin, Josef. *Symposion: Die Geschichte einer literarischen Form.* Paderborn: F. Schöningh, 1931.

Martyn, J. Louis. "Events in Galatia: Modified Covenantal Nomism versus God's Invasion of the Cosmos in the Singular Gospel: A Response to J. D. G. Dunn and B. R. Gaventa." In *Pauline Theology,* vol. 1: *Thessalonians, Philippians, Galatians, Philemon,* ed. Jouette M. Bassler, 160–79. Minneapolis: Fortress Press, 1991.

——. *History and Theology in the Fourth Gospel.* Nashville: Abingdon, 1979.

Mau, A. "Convivium." PW 4 (1900): 1201–8.

McGowan, Andrew. *Ascetic Eucharists: Food and Drink in Early Christian Ritual Meals.* Oxford Early Christian Studies. Oxford: Clarendon, 1999.

McKay, A. G. *Houses, Villas, and Palaces in the Roman World: Aspects of Greek and Roman Life.* Ithaca, N.Y.: Cornell University Press, 1975.

Meeks, Wayne A. *The First Urban Christians: The Social World of the Apostle Paul.* New Haven, Conn.: Yale University Press, 1983.

Meier, John P. *A Marginal Jew: Rethinking the Historical Jesus,* vol. 2: *Mentor, Message, and Miracles.* ABRL. New York: Doubleday, 1994.

Meiggs, Russell. *Roman Ostia.* 2nd ed. Oxford: Clarendon, 1973.

Mellink, Machteld J. "Archaeology in Asia Minor." *AJA* 83 (1979): 340–41.

Mendell, C. W. "Satire as Popular Philosophy." *CP* 15 (1920): 138–57.

Meritt, Benjamin D. "A Decree of Orgeones." *Hesperia* 11 (1942): 282–87.

Merlan, Philip. "Greek Philosophy from Plato to Plotinus." In *The Cambridge History of Later Greek and Early Medieval Philosophy,* ed. A. H. Armstrong, 14–132. Cambridge: Cambridge University Press, 1970.

Metzger, Bruce M. *A Textual Commentary on the Greek New Testament.* London: United Bible Societies, 1971.

Meyer, Ben F., and E. P. Sanders, eds. *Jewish and Christian Self-Definition,* vol. 3: *Self-Definition in the Greco-Roman World.* Philadelphia: Fortress Press, 1982.

Meyers, Carol L. *The Tabernacle Menorah: A Synthetic Study of a Symbol from the Biblical Cult.* Missoula, Mont.: Scholars, 1976.

Michel, Otto. "*Oikos.*" *TDNT* 5 (1968): 119–59.

Middendorp, Th. *Die Stellung Jesu Ben Siras zwischen Judentum und Hellenismus.* Leiden: Brill, 1973.

Milgrom, Jacob. *Leviticus 1–16.* AB 3. New York: Doubleday, 1991.

Milik, J. T. *Recherches d'épigraphie proche-orientale, I: Dédicaces faites par des dieux (Palmyre, Hatra, Tyr) et des thiases sémitiques à l'époque romaine.* Institut français d'archéologie de Beyrouth, bibliothèque archéologique et historique, 92. Paris: Librairie orientaliste Paul Geuthner, 1972.

Miller, Margaret. "Foreigners at the Greek Symposium?" In *Dining in a Classical Context,* ed. W. J. Slater, 59–81.

Miller, Stephen G. *The Prytaneion: Its Function and Architectural Form.* Berkeley: University of California Press, 1978.

Milne, J. Grafton. "The *Kline* of Sarapis." *JEA* 11 (1925): 6–9.

Mommsen, Theodor. *De collegiis et sodaliciis Romanorum.* Kiliae: Libraria Schwersiana, 1843.

Moore, George Foote. *Judaism.* 3 vols. Cambridge, Mass.: Harvard University Press, 1927.

Morel, Ch., and E. Saglio. "Coena." DarSag 1.2 (1877): 1269–82.

Moretti, Luigi. "Il regolamento degli Iobacchi ateniesi." In *L'association dionysiaque dans les sociétés anciennes,* 247–59. Actes de la table ronde organisée par l'École française de Rome, 24–25 Mai 1984. Collection de l'École française de Rome 89. Paris: De Boccard, 1986.

Morris, Ian. *Death-Ritual and Social Structure in Classical Antiquity.* Key Themes in Ancient History. Cambridge: Cambridge University Press, 1992.

Müller, Iwan von. *Die griechischen Privataltertümer.* Handbuch der klassischen Altertumswissenschaft 4.1.2. 2nd ed. Munich: Beck, 1893.

Mumford, Lewis. "Closing Statement." In *The Ecological Conscience,* ed. Robert Disch. Englewood Cliffs, N.J.: Prentice-Hall, 1970.

Murphy-O'Connor, Jerome, O.P. *St. Paul's Corinth: Texts and Archaeology.* Good News Studies 6. Wilmington, Del.: Glazier, 1983.

Murray, Oswyn. "The Affair of the Mysteries: Democracy and the Drinking Group." In *Sympotica: A Symposium on the Symposium,* ed. Oswyn Murray, 149–61.

———. "Death and the Symposion." *AION* 10 (1988): 239–57.

———. "The Greek Symposion in History." In *Tria Corda: Seritti in onore de A. Momigliano,* ed. E. Gabba, 255–72. Como, Italy: Edizioni New Press, 1983.

———. "The Symposion as Social Organisation." In *The Greek Renaissance of the Eighth Century B.C.: Tradition and Innovation.* Proceedings of the Second International Symposium at the Swedish Institute in Athens, 1–5 June, 1981, ed. Robin Hägg, 195–99. Acta Inst. Atheniensis Regni Sueciae Ser. 4, 30. Stockholm: Aström, 1983.

———. "Symposium and Genre in the Poetry of Horace." *JRS* 75 (1985): 39–50.

———. "Sympotic History." In *Sympotica: A Symposium on the Symposium,* ed. Oswyn Murray, 3–13.

———. "War and the Symposium." In *Dining in a Classical Context,* ed. W. J. Slater, 83–103.

———, ed. *Sympotica: A Symposium on the Symposium.* Oxford: Clarendon, 1990.

Murray, Oswyn, and Simon Price, eds. *The Greek City from Homer to Alexander.* Oxford: Clarendon, 1990.

Nagy, Gregory. *The Best of the Achaeans: Concepts of the Hero in Archaic Greek Poetry.* Baltimore: Johns Hopkins University Press, 1979.

Neuenzeit, Paul. *Das Herrenmahl.* Munich: Kösel-Verlag, 1960.

Neusner, Jacob. *From Politics to Piety: The Emergence of Pharisaic Judaism.* Englewood Cliffs, N.J.: Prentice-Hall, 1973.

———. *The Idea of Purity in Ancient Judaism.* SJLA 1. Leiden: Brill, 1973.

———. "Two Pictures of the Pharisees: Philosophical Circle or Eating Club." *ATR* 64 (1982): 525–38.

Neyrey, Jerome H., ed. *The Social World of Luke–Acts: Models for Interpretation.* Peabody, Mass.: Hendrickson, 1991.

Nickelsburg, George W. E. "The Genre and Function of the Markan Passion Narrative." *HTR* 73 (1980): 153–84.

———. *Jewish Literature between the Bible and the Mishnah.* Philadelphia: Fortress Press, 1981.

Nielsen, Inge, and Hanna Sigismund Nielsen, eds. *Meals in a Social Context: Aspects of the Communal Meal in the Hellenistic and Roman World.* Aarhus Studies in Mediterranean Antiquity I. Aarhus: Aarhus University Press, 1998.

Nilsson, Martin P. *The Dionysiac Mysteries of the Hellenistic and Roman Age.* Lund: Gleerup, 1957.

———. "Die Götter des Symposions." In *Opuscula selecta,* 1.428–42. 3 vols. Lund: Gleerup, 1951–60.

Nineham, D. E. *Saint Mark.* The Pelican New Testament Commentaries. Middlesex, Eng.: Penguin, 1963.

Nock, A. D. "The Cult of Heroes," *HTR* 37 (1944): 141–74. Reprinted in A. D. Nock, *Essays on Religion and the Ancient World,* ed. Zeph Stewart, 2.575–602.

———. *Early Gentile Christianity and its Hellenistic Background.* New York: Harper, 1964.

———. *Essays on Religion and the Ancient World.* Ed. Zeph Stewart. 2 vols. Cambridge, Mass.: Harvard University Press, 1972.

———. "The Gild of Zeus Hypsistos." *HTR* 29 (1936): 41–44 and 55–88.

———. "The Historical Importance of Cult-Associations." *CR* 38 (1924): 105–9.

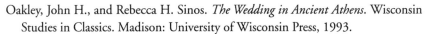

Oakley, John H., and Rebecca H. Sinos. *The Wedding in Ancient Athens.* Wisconsin Studies in Classics. Madison: University of Wisconsin Press, 1993.

Oppermann, Hans. *Zeus Panamaros.* Giessen: A. Töpelmann, 1924.

Osborne, Michael J. "Entertainment in the Prytaneion at Athens." *ZPE* 41 (1981): 153–70.

Osiek, Carolyn A. *What Are They Saying about the Social Setting of the New Testament?* 2nd ed. Mahwah, N.J.: Paulist, 1992.

Packer, James E. *The Insulae of Imperial Ostia.* MAAR 31. Rome: American Academy in Rome, 1971.

Patterson, Stephen J. *The God of Jesus: The Historical Jesus and the Search for Meaning.* Harrisburg, Pa.: Trinity Press International, 1998.

Paul, George. "Symposia and Deipna in Plutarch's Lives and in Other Historical Writings." In *Dining in a Classical Context,* ed. W. J. Slater, 157–69.

Paul, Shalom. *Amos.* Hermeneia. Minneapolis: Fortress Press, 1991.

Pearson, Lionel I. C. *Popular Ethics in Ancient Greece.* Stanford: Stanford University Press, 1962.

Pellizer, Ezio. "Outlines of a Morphology of Sympotic Entertainment." In *Sympotica: A Symposium on the Symposium,* ed. Oswyn Murray, 177–84.

Perrin, Norman. *Rediscovering the Teaching of Jesus.* New York: Harper & Row, 1967.

Perrin, Norman, and Dennis C. Duling. *The New Testament: An Introduction.* 2nd ed. New York: Harcourt Brace Jovanovich, 1982.

Pervo, Richard I. "Wisdom and Power: Petronius' Satyricon and the Social World of Early Christianity." *ATR* 67 (1985): 307–25.

Petersen, Norman. *Rediscovering Paul: Philemon and the Sociology of Paul's Narrative World.* Philadelphia: Fortress Press, 1985.

Pickard-Cambridge, Arthur. *The Dramatic Festivals of Athens.* 2nd ed. Oxford: Clarendon, 1968.

Plümacher, Eckhardt. *Lukas als hellenistischer Schriftsteller: Studien zur Apostelgeschichte.* SUNT 9. Göttingen: Vandenhoeck and Ruprecht, 1972.

Poland, Franz. *Geschichte des griechischen Vereinswesens.* Leipzig: Teubner, 1909.

———. *"Stibadeion."* PW 3A (1929): 2481.

———. *"Stibas."* PW 3A (1929): 2482–84.

Pope, Marvin H. *Song of Songs.* AB 7C. Garden City, N.Y.: Doubleday, 1977.

Porten, Bezalel. *Archives from Elephantine: The Life of an Ancient Jewish Military Colony.* Berkeley: University of California Press, 1968.

Ramage, Edwin S., David L. Sigsbee, and Sigmund C. Fredericks. *Roman Satirists and Their Satire.* Park Ridge, N.J.: Noyes, 1974.

Rathje, Annette. "The Adoption of the Homeric Banquet in Central Italy in the Orientalizing Period." In *Sympotica,* ed. Oswyn Murray, 279–88.

Raubitschek, A. E. "A New Attic Club (ERANOS)." *The J. Paul Getty Museum Journal* 9 (1981): 93–98.

Reicke, Bo. *Diakonie, Festfreude und Zelos in Verbindung mit der altchristlichen Agapenfeier.* Uppsala Universitets Årsskrift 1951:5. Uppsala: A.-B. Lundequistska, 1951.

Reitzenstein, Richard. *Hellenistic Mystery Religions.* Reprint ed. Pittsburgh: Pickwick, 1978.

Richlin, Amy, ed. *Pornography and Representation in Greece and Rome.* Oxford: Oxford University Press, 1992.

Richter, Gisela M. A. *The Furniture of the Greeks, Etruscans, and Romans.* London: Phaidon, 1966.

Rist, J. M. *Epicurus: An Introduction.* Cambridge: Cambridge University Press, 1972.

Rivkin, Ellis. *A Hidden Revolution: The Pharisees' Search for the Kingdom Within.* Nashville: Abingdon, 1978.

Robbins, Vernon K. "The Chreia." In *Greco-Roman Literature and the New Testament: Selected Forms and Genres,* ed. David E. Aune, 1–23. SBLSBS 21. Atlanta: Scholars, 1988.

———. *Jesus the Teacher: A Socio-Rhetorical Interpretation of Mark.* Philadelphia: Fortress Press, 1984.

———. "Last Meal: Preparation, Betrayal, and Absence (Mark 14:12-25)." In *The Passion in Mark,* ed. Werner H. Kelber, 21–40.

Robert, Louis. "Deux décrets d'une association à Athènes." *ArchEph* (1969): 7–14.

———. "Epigramme de Thasos." *Hellenica* 2 (1946): 114–118.

———. "Sur un papyrus de Paris glossaire latin-grec." *Hellenica* 11–12 (1960): 5–15.

———. "Villes et monnaies de Lycia." *Hellenica* 10 (1955): 188–222.

Robert, Louis, and Jeanne Robert. "Bulletin épigraphique." *REG* 71 (1958).

Robertis, Francesco Maria de. *Il fenomeno associative nel mondo romano.* Naples: Libreria scientifica editrace, 1955.

Roberts, Colin, T. C. Skeat, and A. D. Nock. "The Gild of Zeus Hypsistos." *HTR* 29 (1936): 39–88.

Robertson, Noel. "The Betrothal Symposium in Early Greece." In *Dining in a Classical Context,* ed. W. J. Slater, 25–57.

Robinson, B. P. "The Place of the Emmaus Story in Luke–Acts." *NTS* 30 (1984): 488–89.

Robinson, D. M., and J. W. Graham, *Excavations at Olynthus, Part VIII: The Hellenic House.* Baltimore: Johns Hopkins University Press, 1938.

Robinson, J. A. T. *The Body: A Study in Pauline Theology.* SBT 5. London: SCM, 1952.

Robinson, James M., and Helmut Koester, eds. *Trajectories through Early Christianity.* Philadelphia: Fortress Press, 1971.

Robinson, Thomas L. "Dionysos in Athens." Unpublished seminar paper, Harvard Divinity School, December 11, 1972.

Roebuck, Carl. *Corinth XIV: The Asklepieion and Lerna.* Princeton, N.J.: American School of Classical Studies at Athens, 1951.

Ross, J. F. "Meals." *IDB* 3 (1962): 315–18.

Roussel, Pierre. *Les cultes égyptiens à Délos.* Nancy: Berger-Levrault, 1916.

———. "Le miracle de Zeus Panamaros." *BCH* 55 (1931): 70–116.

———. "Les mystères de Panamara." *BCH* 51 (1927): 123–37.

Rudd, Niall. *The Satires of Horace.* 2nd ed. Berkeley: University of California Press, 1982.

———. *Themes in Roman Satire.* Norman: University of Oklahoma Press, 1986.

Sabbe, M. "The Footwashing in Jn 13 and its Relation to the Synoptic Gospels." *ETL* 58 (1982): 279–308.

Safrai, S., and M. Stern, eds. *Compendia Rerum Iudaicarum ad Novum Testamentum, Section One: The Jewish People in the First Century.* 2 vols. Philadelphia: Fortress Press, 1976.

———. "Home and Family" and "Religion in Everyday Life." In *Compendia Rerum Iudaicarum ad Novum Testamentum,* ed. S. Safrai and M. Stern, 728–833.

Sanders, E. P. "Jewish Association with Gentiles and Galatians 2:11-14." In *The Conversation Continues: Studies in Paul and John in Honor of J. Louis Martyn,* ed. Robert T. Fortna and Beverly R. Gaventa, 170–88. Nashville: Abingdon, 1990.

———. *Jewish Law from Jesus to the Mishnah: Five Studies.* Philadelphia: Trinity Press International, 1990.

———. *Jesus and Judaism.* Philadelphia: Fortress Press, 1985.

———. *Judaism: Jewish Practice and Belief 63 BCE–66 CE.* London and Philadelphia: SCM and Trinity Press International, 1992.

———. *Paul and Palestinian Judaism: A Comparison of Patterns of Religion.* Philadelphia: Fortress Press, 1977.

Sanders, Jack T. *Ben Sira and Demotic Wisdom.* SBLMS 28. Chico, Calif.: Scholars, 1983.

Sandmel, Samuel. *Judaism and Christian Beginnings.* New York: Oxford University Press, 1978.

San Nicolo, Mariano. *Aegyptisches Vereinswesen zur Zeit der Ptolemäer und Römer.* 2nd ed. 2 vols. Münchener Beiträge zur Papyrusforschung und antiken Rechtsgeschichte 2.1. Munich: Beck, 1972.

———. "Zur Vereinsgerichtsbarkeit im hellenistischen Ägypten." In *Eritymbion: Heinrich Swoboda dargebracht,* 255–300. Reichenberg: Gebrüder Stiepel, 1927.

Schaefer, Peter. *Judeophobia: Attitudes Toward the Jews in the Ancient World.* Cambridge, Mass.: Harvard University Press, 1997.

Scaife, Ross. "From *Kottabos* to War in Aristophanes' *Acharnians*." *GRBS* 33 (1992): 25–35.

Schiffman, Lawrence H. *Reclaiming the Dead Sea Scrolls*. Philadelphia: Jewish Publication Society, 1994.

Schiffman, Lawrence H., and James C. VanderKam, eds. *Encyclopedia of the Dead Sea Scrolls*. Oxford: Oxford University Press, 2000.

Schillebeeckx, Edward. *Jesus: An Experiment in Christology*. New York: Seabury, 1979.

Schlier, Heinrich. "*Aireomai*." *TDNT* 1 (1964): 180–85.

Schmid, Wolfgang. "Epicur." *RAC* 5 (1961): 719–26.

Schmidt, K. L. "*Kaleō*." *TDNT* 3 (1965): 487–536.

Schmidt, Wilhelm. *Geburtstag im Altertum*. RVV 7.1. Giessen: A. Töpelmann, 1908.

Schmithals, Walter. *Gnosticism in Corinth*. Nashville: Abingdon, 1971.

Schmitt-Pantel, Pauline. *La cité au banquet: histoire des repas publics dans les cités grecques*. Collection de l'École française de Rome 157. Rome: École française de Rome, 1992.

———. "Collective Activities and the Political in the Greek City." In *The Greek City from Homer to Alexander*, ed. Oswyn Murray and Simon Price, 199–213.

———. "Sacrificial Meal and *Symposion:* Two Models of Civic Institutions in the Archaic City?" In *Sympotica: A Symposium on the Symposium*, ed. Oswyn Murray, 14–33.

Schürer, Emil. *The History of the Jewish People in the Age of Jesus Christ*. Rev. ed. by Geza Vermes, Fergus Millar, and Matthew Black. 3 vols. Edinburgh: T. & T. Clark, 1973–87.

Schüssler Fiorenza, Elisabeth. *In Memory of Her: A Feminist Theological Reconstruction of Christian Origins*. New York: Crossroad, 1983.

Schweizer, Eduard. *The Lord's Supper according to the New Testament*. FBBS 18. Philadelphia: Fortress Press, 1967.

———. *Luke: A Challenge to Present Theology*. Atlanta: John Knox, 1982.

Segal, Alan F. "Acts 15 as Jewish and Christian History." *Forum* 4:1. Forthcoming.

———. *The Other Judaisms of Late Antiquity*. Brown Judaic Studies 127. Atlanta: Scholars, 1987.

———. *Paul the Convert: The Apostolate and Apostasy of Saul the Pharisee*. New Haven, Conn.: Yale University Press, 1990.

———. *Rebecca's Children: Judaism and Christianity in the Roman World*. Cambridge, Mass.: Harvard University Press, 1986.

———. "Romans 7 and Jewish Dietary Laws." In *The Other Judaisms of Late Antiquity*, 167–94.

Sellew, Philip. "The Last Supper Discourse in Luke 22:21-38." *Forum* 3:3 (September 1987): 70–95.

Seyrig, Henri. "Quatre cultes de Thasos." *BCH* 51 (1927): 178–223.

Shapiro, H. A. "Eros in Love: Pederasty and Pornography in Greece." In *Pornography and Representation*, ed. Amy Richlin, 53–72.

Shero, L. R. "The *Cena* in Roman Satire." *CP* 18 (1923): 126–43.

Sherwin-White, A. N. *The Letters of Pliny*. Oxford: Clarendon, 1966.

Slater, William J., ed. *Dining in a Classical Context*. Ann Arbor: University of Michigan Press, 1991.

Smend, Rudolf. *Die Weisheit des Jesus Sirach Erklärt*. Berlin: Georg Reimer, 1906.

Smith, Dennis E. "Meal Customs (Greco-Roman)." *ABD*, 4.650–53.

———. "Meal Customs (Sacred Meals)." *ABD*, 4.653–55.

———. "Meals." In *EncyDSS*, 530–32.

———. "Messianic Banquet." *ABD*, 4.788–91.

———. "The Messianic Banquet Reconsidered." In *The Future of Early Christianity: Essays in Honor of Helmut Koester*, ed. Birger A. Pearson, 64–73. Minneapolis: Fortress Press, 1991.

———. "Table Fellowship." *ABD*, 6.302–304.

———. "Table Fellowship and the Historical Jesus." In *Religious Propaganda and Missionary Competition in the New Testament World: Essays Honoring Dieter Georgi*, ed. Lukas Bormann, Kelly del Tredici, and Angela Standhartinger, 135–62. Leiden: Brill, 1994.

———. "Table Fellowship as a Literary Motif in the Gospel of Luke." *JBL* 106 (1987): 613–38.

Smith, Dennis E., and Hal E. Taussig. *Many Tables: The Eucharist in the New Testament and Liturgy Today*. Philadelphia: Trinity Press International, 1990.

Smith, Martin S., ed. *Petronius: Cena Trimalchionis*. Oxford: Clarendon, 1975.

Smith, Morton. "Goodenough's *Jewish Symbols* in Retrospect." *JBL* 86 (1967): 53–68.

———. *Jesus the Magician*. San Francisco: Harper & Row, 1978.

———. "On the Wine God in Palestine." In *Salo Wittmayer Baron Jubilee Volume*, 815–29. Jerusalem: Central Press for the American Academy for Jewish Research, 1974.

———. "Palestinian Judaism in the First Century." In *Essays in Greco-Roman and Related Talmudic Literature*, ed. Henry A. Fischel, 183–97.

Smith, S. "The Practice of Kingship in Early Semitic Kingdoms." In *Myth, Ritual and Kingship*, ed. S. H. Hooke, 22–73. Oxford: Oxford University Press, 1958.

Smith, William Robertson. *Lectures on the Religion of the Semites: The Fundamental Institutions*. 3rd ed. Reprint. New York: KTAV, 1969.

Snaith, John G. *Ecclesiasticus, or the Wisdom of Jesus Son of Sirach*. London: Cambridge University Press, 1974.

Snyder, Graydon F. *Ante Pacem: Archaeological Evidence of Church Life before Constantine*. Macon, Ga.: Mercer University Press, 1985.

Sokolowski, Franciszek. *Lois sacrées de l'Asie Mineure*. EFATM 9. Paris: De Boccard, 1955.

Sparkes, Brian A. "Kottabos: An Athenian After-Dinner Game." *Archaeology* 13 (1960): 202–7.

Spicq, Ceslaus. *Agapé dans le Nouveau Testament.* 3 vols. Études Bibliques. Paris: Gabalda, 1958–59.

Stählin, Gustav. "*Phileō.*" *TDNT* 9 (1974): 113–71.

Stambaugh, John E. "The Functions of Roman Temples." *ANRW* 2.16.1 (1978): 554–608.

Starcky, J. "Autour d'une dédicace palmyrénienne à Sadrafa et à du Anat, 6: Salles de banquets rituels dans les sanctuaires orientaux." *Syria* 26 (1949): 62–67.

Starr, Chester G. "An Evening with the Flute-Girls." *La parola del passato* 33 (1978): 401–10.

Steele, E. Springs. "Jesus' Table-Fellowship with Pharisees: An Editorial Analysis of Luke 7:36-50, 11:37-54, and 14:1-24." Ph.D. diss., University of Notre Dame, 1981.

———. "Luke 11:37-54: A Modified Hellenistic Symposium?" *JBL* 103 (1984): 379–94.

Stein, S. "The Influence of Symposia Literature on the Literary Form of the Pesah Haggadah." *JJS* 8 (1957): 13–44. Reprinted in *Essays in Greco-Roman and Related Talmudic Literature,* ed. Henry A. Fischel, 13–44.

Stern, Menahem, ed. *Greek and Latin Authors on Jews and Judaism.* Fontes ad res Judaicus spectantes. 3 vols. Jerusalem: Israel Academy of Sciences and Humanities, 1974–84.

Stowers, Stanley K. *The Diatribe and Paul's Letter to the Romans.* Chico, Calif.: Scholars, 1981.

———. "Greeks Who Sacrifice and Those Who Don't: Toward an Anthropology of Greek Religion." In *The Social World of the First Christians: Essays in Honor of Wayne A. Meeks,* ed. L. Michael White and O. Larry Yarbrough, 293–333.

———. *A Rereading of Romans: Justice, Jews, and Gentiles.* New Haven, Conn.: Yale University Press, 1994.

———. "The Social Sciences and the Study of Early Christianity." In *Approaches to Ancient Judaism,* vol. 5, ed. W. S. Green, 149–81. Brown Judaic Studies 32. Atlanta: Scholars, 1985.

Strack, Hermann L. and Paul Billerbeck. *Kommentar zum Neuen Testament aus Talmud und Midrasch.* 6 vols. Munich: Beck, 1922–61.

Ström, Åke V. "Abendmahl I. Das sakrale Mahl in den Religionen der Welt." *TRE* 1 (1977): 43–47.

Sutton, Robert F., Jr. "Pornography and Persuasion on Attic Pottery." In *Pornography and Representation,* ed. Amy Richlin, 3–35.

Talbert, Charles H. *Literary Patterns, Theological Themes, and the Genre of Luke–Acts.* SBLMS 20. Missoula, Mont.: Scholars, 1975.

———. *Reading Luke: A Literary and Theological Commentary on the Third Gospel.* New York: Crossroad, 1982.

Tannahill, Reay. *Food in History.* Rev. ed. New York: Crown, 1988.

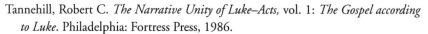

Tannehill, Robert C. *The Narrative Unity of Luke–Acts,* vol. 1: *The Gospel according to Luke.* Philadelphia: Fortress Press, 1986.

Tarn, W. W. "The Hellenistic Ruler-Cult and the Daemon." *JHS* 48 (1928): 206–19.

Tcherikover, Victor. *Hellenistic Civilization and the Jews.* Philadelphia: Jewish Publication Society of America, 1966.

Temporini, Hildegarde, and Wolfgang Haase, eds. *Aufstieg und Niedergang der römischen Welt.* Berlin: de Gruyter, 1972–.

Theissen, Gerd. *The Social Setting of Pauline Christianity: Essays on Corinth.* Edited and translated by John H. Schütz. Philadelphia: Fortress Press, 1982.

———. "Social Integration and Sacramental Activity: An Analysis of 1 Cor. 11:17-34." In *The Social Setting of Pauline Christianity,* 145–74.

———. "Social Stratification in the Corinthian Community: A Contribution to the Sociology of Early Hellenistic Christianity." In *The Social Setting of Pauline Christianity,* 69–119.

———. "The Strong and the Weak in Corinth: A Sociological Analysis of a Theological Quarrel." In *The Social Setting of Pauline Christianity,* 121–43.

Tiede, David. *Prophecy and History in Luke–Acts.* Philadelphia: Fortress Press, 1980.

Tod, M. N. *Sidelights on Greek History.* Reprint ed. Chicago: Ares, 1974.

Tolbert, Mary Ann. *Sowing the Gospel: Mark's World in Literary-Historical Perspective.* Minneapolis: Fortress Press, 1989.

Tomlinson, R. A. "Perachora: The Remains outside the Two Sanctuaries." *BSA* 64 (1969): 164–72.

———. "Two Buildings in Sanctuaries of Asklepios." *JHS* 89 (1969): 106–9.

Toynbee, J. M. C. *Death and Burial in the Roman World.* Aspects of Greek and Roman Life. London: Thames and Hudson, 1971.

Travlos, John. *Pictorial Dictionary of Ancient Athens.* New York: Praeger, 1971.

Treu, K. "Freundschaft." *RAC* 8 (1969): 418–34.

Treves, P., and C. Bailey. "Collegium." *OCD* 2, 264.

Usener, Hermann, ed. *Epicurea.* Leipzig: Teubner, 1887.

Vaage, Leif E. "Q: The Ethos and Ethics of an Itinerant Intelligence." Ph.D. diss., Claremont Graduate School, 1987.

van Unnik, W. C. "Eléments artistiques dans l'Évangile de Luc." *ETL* 46 (1970): 401–12.

VanderKam, James C. *The Dead Sea Scrolls Today.* Grand Rapids: Eerdmans, 1994.

Vandoni, Mariangela. *Feste pubbliche e private nei documenti greci.* Testi e documenti per lo studio dell'antichita, serie papirologica 8. Milan: Instituto Editoriale Cisalpino, 1964.

Vaux, Roland de. *Archaeology and the Dead Sea Scrolls.* London: Oxford University Press for the British Academy, 1973.

Vielhauer, Philipp. *Oikodome: Das Bild vom Bau in der christlichen Literatur vom Neuen Testament bis Clemens Alexandrinus.* Karlsruhe-Durlach: Tron, 1940.

Vermes, Geza. *The Dead Sea Scrolls in English.* Harmondsworth, Eng.: Penguin, 1970.

———. *The Dead Sea Scrolls: Qumran in Perspective.* Cleveland: Collins/World, 1978.

———. *Jesus the Jew: A Historian's Reading of the Gospels.* London: Collins, 1973.

Veyne, Paul, ed. *A History of Private Life,* vol. 1: *From Pagan Rome to Byzantium.* Cambridge, Mass.: Belknap Press of Harvard University Press, 1987.

———. "The Roman Empire." In *A History of Private Life,* vol. 1: *From Pagan Rome to Byzantium,* ed. Paul Veyne, 5–233.

Vickers, Michael. *Greek Symposia.* London: Joint Association of Classical Teachers, 1978.

Vogliano, Achille, ed. *Epicuri et Epicureorum scripta in Herculanensibus papyris servata.* Berlin: Weidmann, 1928.

———. "La grande inscrizione bacchica del metropolitan museum." *AJA* 37 (1933): 215–31.

von der Mühll, Peter. "Das griechische Symposion." In *Ausgewählte Kleine Schriften von Peter von der Mühll,* ed. Bernhard Wyss, 483–505. Schweizerische Beiträge zur Altertumswissenschaft 12. Basel: Friedrich Reinhardt, 1976.

von Soden, Hans Freiherr. "Sakrament und Ethik bei Paulus." In *Marburger theologische Studien.* Rudolf Otto Festgruss, ed. H. Frick, 1.1–40. Gotha: Klotz, 1931.

Vööbus, Arthur. "A New Approach to the Problem of the Shorter and Longer Text in Luke." *NTS* 15 (1968–69): 457–63.

Walker, Susan. "Women and Housing in Classical Greek: The Archaeological Evidence." In *Images of Women in Antiquity,* ed. Averil Cameron and Amélie Kuhrt, 81–91. Detroit: Wayne State University Press, 1983.

Walker, William O. "Jesus and the Tax Collectors." *JBL* 97 (1978): 221–38.

Wallace-Hadrill, Andrew. *Houses and Society in Pompeii and Herculaneum.* Princeton, N.J.: Princeton University Press, 1994.

Waltzing, Jean-Pierre. *Étude historique sur les corporations professionnelles chez les Romains.* 4 vols. Louvain: Peeters, 1895–1900.

Weinfeld, Moshe. *The Organizational Pattern and the Penal Code of the Qumran Sect: A Comparison with Guilds and Religious Associations of the Hellenistic-Roman Period.* Novum Testamentum et Orbis Antiquus 2. Göttingen: Vandenhoeck and Ruprecht, 1986.

Weiss, Johannes. *Der erste Korintherbrief.* KEK 5. 10th ed. Göttingen: Vandenhoek and Ruprecht, 1925.

Weiss, Konrad. "*Pherō.*" *TDNT* 9 (1973): 56–87.

Welter, Gabriel. *Troizen und Kalaureia.* Berlin: Gebr. Mann, 1941.

White, John L. "Beware of Leavened Bread: Markan Imagery in the Last Supper." *Forum* 3:4 (December 1987): 49–63.

———. "The Way of the Cross: Was There a Pre-Markan Passion Narrative?" *Forum* 3:2 (June 1987): 35–49.

White, L. Michael. "Regulating Fellowship in the Communal Meal: Early Jewish and Christian Evidence." In *Meals in a Social Context,* ed. Inge Nielsen and Hanna Sigismund Nielsen, 177–205.

———. *The Social Origins of Christian Architecture,* vol. 1: *Building God's House in the Roman World;* vol. 2: *Texts and Monuments for the Christian Domus Ecclesiae in its Environment.* Harvard Theological Studies 42. Valley Forge, Pa.: Trinity Press International, 1997.

White, L. Michael, and O. Larry Yarbrough, eds. *The Social World of the First Christians: Essays in Honor of Wayne A. Meeks.* Minneapolis: Fortress Press, 1995.

Wide, Sam. "Inschrift der Iobakchen." *AthMitt* 19 (1894): 248–82.

Wilken, Robert L. "Collegia, Philosophical Schools, and Theology." In *The Catacombs and the Colosseum,* ed. Stephen Benko and John J. O'Rourke, 268–91. Valley Forge, Pa.: Judson, 1971.

Williams, Margaret H. *The Jews among the Greeks and Romans: A Diasporan Sourcebook.* Baltimore: Johns Hopkins University Press, 1998.

Williams, Sam K. *Jesus' Death as Saving Event: The Background and Origin of a Concept.* HDR 2. Missoula, Mont.: Scholars, 1975.

Willis, Wendell Lee. *Idol Meat in Corinth: The Pauline Argument in 1 Corinthians 8 and 10.* SBLDS 68. Chico, Calif.: Scholars, 1985.

Wilson, Stephen G. "Voluntary Associations: An Overview." In *Voluntary Associations in the Graeco-Roman World,* ed. John S. Kloppenborg and Stephen G. Wilson, 1–15.

Witke, Charles. *Latin Satire: The Structure of Persuasion.* Leiden: Brill, 1970.

Wolff, Hans Walter. *Joel and Amos.* Hermeneia. Hermeneia. Philadelphia: Fortress Press, 1977.

Yerkes, Royden Keith. *Sacrifice in Greek and Roman Religions and Early Judaism.* New York: Scribner's, 1952.

Youtie, Herbert C. "The *Kline* of Sarapis." *HTR* 41 (1948): 9–29.

Zeller, Eduard. *The Stoics, Epicureans and Sceptics.* New York: Russell & Russell, 1879.

Ziebarth, Erich. *Das griechische Vereinswesen.* Fürstlich Jablonowski'schen Gesellschaft zu Leipzig, Priesschriften 34. Leipzig: S. Hirzel, 1896.

Ziegler, Konrat. "Plutarchos von Chaironeia." PW 21 (1951): 636–962.

Ziehen, Ludwig. "Opfer." PW 18 (1939): 579–627.

INDEX OF ANCIENT SOURCES

INDEX OF SUBJECTS